MUSE *of* FIRE

# MUSE
## of
# FIRE

*World War I as Seen
Through the Lives of
the Soldier Poets*

# Michael
# Korda

**Liveright Publishing Corporation**

*A Division of W. W. Norton & Company
Independent Publishers Since 1923*

Excerpt from "The Death of the Ball Turret Gunner" from *The Complete Poems* by Randall Jarrell. Copyright © 1969, renewed 1997 by Mary von S. Jarrell. Reprinted by permission of Farrar, Straus and Giroux and Faber and Faber Ltd. All rights reserved.

For information about permission to reproduce selections from this book, write to Permissions, Liveright Publishing Corporation, a division of W. W. Norton & Company, Inc., 500 Fifth Avenue, New York, NY 10110

For information about special discounts for bulk purchases, please contact W. W. Norton Special Sales at specialsales@wwnorton.com or 800-233-4830

Manufacturing by Lakeside Book Company
Book design by Lovedog Studio
Production manager: Anna Oler

ISBN 978-1-63149-688-2

Liveright Publishing Corporation
500 Fifth Avenue, New York, N.Y. 10110
www.wwnorton.com

W. W. Norton & Company Ltd.
15 Carlisle Street, London W1D 3BS

1 2 3 4 5 6 7 8 9 0

*For Maggie*

*With love,*
*Now and always*

O for a muse of fire, that would ascend
The brightest heaven of invention,
A kingdom for a stage, princes to act
And monarchs to behold the swelling scene!

  —William Shakespeare, *Henry V*, prologue


My subject is War, and the pity of war.
The Poetry is in the pity.

  —Wilfred Owen, May 1918

# CONTENTS

# INTRODUCTION
## *The Breaking Point*

I WAS BORN BEFORE THE SECOND WORLD WAR—I was six when it began in September 1939—but I have lived all my life in the shadow of the First.

All my family fought in that war, but on opposite sides. On my mother's side—English back to the days when Britons stripped naked and dyed themselves blue with woad to fight the Romans—my grandfather Octavius fought in the British Army. On my paternal side, assimilated Hungarian Jews, my father served in the Austro-Hungarian infantry and my uncle Zoltan as a cavalry officer—unusual for a Jew in that army. Zoli was wounded, gassed, and captured by the Russians. After the 1917 revolution, he fought his way back to Hungary by joining the Red Army. My uncle Alex was exempted from military service because of his poor eyesight, but his first film, which he made in 1916 when he was twenty-one years old, was a patriotic picture called *The Officer's Swordknot* (*A tiszti karbojt*). He wrote the script while sitting in the New York Café in Budapest. His notes read: "a captain of Hussars is cashiered for gambling debts, re-enlists as a private when war breaks out, regains his commission by gallantry in the field, is wounded and falls in love with his nurse, a happy ending."

None of my relatives who lived through that war ever talked about it. Like millions of other men on both sides who survived it, they had no desire to revisit it—the horrors were beyond description. If the war ever came up in conversation, the "Great War," as it was called until 1939, my grandfather Ockie would carefully change the subject, a glazed and distant look flickering briefly in his eyes as if he were repressing his memory of life in the trenches.

You could not live in Great Britain without being reminded of the war, the two minutes of silence on Armistice Day, the omnipresent lists of the war dead, their names painted or carved in stone in every school, institution, and public building. Monuments to the dead were in every city, town, and village, large and small. When I was a child, a small poppy was pinned to my coat or pullover every November 11. My nanny explained its meaning to me so carefully and with such seriousness that I still wear one on that day some eighty-three years later.

Of course, she saw the First World War through the prism of the Western Front, where over three-quarters of a million Britons were killed in four years of trench warfare, most of them in Flanders and northeastern France amid the mud and barbed wire that in our mind's eye form the landscape of the war. In fact, the war was too big for anyone to see as whole—the fighting in the Carpathians, where my father and Uncle Zoltan saw combat, was equally bloody, but different, as it was in the Middle East, where T. E. Lawrence fought. In Poland and the Ukraine, Russia was bled to death, losing nearly two million men, while in northern Italy, half a million Italians died against the glittering background of the Alps. Looking at a whale close up, we can see only a bit of it at a time. What English speakers remember, when we look back at the war, are the trenches and no-man's-land, a bleak landscape of misery seldom surpassed in history.

Perhaps ironically, the First World War is to a remarkable extent defined in our minds by its poetry. This is not unique, of course—most of what we know about the Trojan War we get from reading the *Iliad* and the *Odyssey*. But in modern times, this has seldom been the case. We live in an age when poetry no longer commands a wide readership, or even much respect, and when poets are seldom celebrities.* The soldier poets of the First World War lived at the tail end of the Victorian and Edwardian age, when there was still a sub-

---

* Sylvia Plath is an exception, but it is as much her failed marriage, depression, and suicide that make her famous as her poetry, except perhaps for "Daddy."

stantial readership for poetry. Tennyson and Kipling were national figures, and poetry mattered to people in a way it no longer does to us. It had a place in popular culture, it could still capture the attention, portray current or recent events and touch people's emotions, as did Tennyson's "The Charge of the Light Brigade" and Sir Henry Newbolt's "Vitaï Lampada." The rising rate of literacy had *increased* the number of people who read poetry, rather than smothering it, as some had feared it would, bestowing on Rupert Brooke, for instance, the equivalent of rock stardom today.

Perhaps never before was a war more tightly censored than the First World War. From the very first, as the casualty lists climbed swiftly to previously unimaginable numbers—250,000 French and British casualties and over 250,000 Germans in the first *month*— every effort was made to protect the general public from the brutal reality of the fighting. At the time, still cameras were bulky and unwieldy—the first Leica would not go on sale until 1925—and motion picture cameras were even more so; photographs from the front line, when they appeared at all, were generally staged to produce a heroic image, free from corpses and the wounded. Newspaper communiqués were pitched at a high level of optimism. Mail from the front was even more strictly censored, which, when combined with the natural tendency of the British to play down the horror of war and "keep smiling through," in the words of a popular song, effectively prevented the public from getting any sense that the war was descending into a bloody nightmare unparalleled in history.

Curiously, the one thing that was *not* censored or repressed was poetry. Book and magazine publishers to a certain degree censored themselves, for fear of being prosecuted under the Defence of the Realm Act (DORA), or of having their supply of paper cut off. The meteoric rise to fame of Rupert Brooke—one of whose war poems was read aloud from the pulpit by the dean of St. Paul's in 1915, then was published in *The Times* and the *Times Literary Supplement*— showed that poetry could reach a much larger readership than had hitherto been thought possible, and that a poet might become a national hero. It helped that Brooke was not only talented but glamorous and that his war poems favored the war—nobody considered that celebrated soldier poets might one day turn *against* the war.

In any case, by 1917 poetry had become a chink through which civilians might glimpse the sheer horror of the Western Front. The men who wrote it were writing out of their own experience. They were soldiers *and* poets. Indeed some of them composed their poems in the trenches, under fire, and not a few of them were decorated heroes. Many were wounded or killed in battle. What gave their poems their enormous impact was their authenticity and in some cases their brutal realism. The official war artists, who were organized as a group by the Ministry of Information and were given officer status, watched and painted the war from a distance, but the soldier poets fought, killed, and sometimes died in battle. They made no attempt to prettify the war for home consumption: on the contrary, they wrote with anger and disgust and sometimes with a savage contempt for their generals and politicians.

Looking at their often-intertwined lives is one way to understand how the initial enthusiasm for the war gradually gave way to embittered resignation, as it came to resemble some vast natural disaster, a tsunami beyond anybody's control, sweeping away a whole generation.

I AM NOT A LITERARY CRITIC; nor is this a book about poetry as such. It is about the lives of some of the major soldier poets and how, for a brief period, they came to symbolize the progress of what Woodrow Wilson optimistically called "the war to end all wars." The First World War left behind itself a legacy of hatred and a thirst for revenge and a map of Europe and the Middle East so poorly drawn that it is still being fought over today. The war began over 110 years ago, yet we still live amid its ruins, its errors of judgment, and its fatal consequences.

Unlike the Second World War, which was preceded by a series of mounting diplomatic crises as Germany tested its ability to break or rescind the limitations imposed on it by the victorious Allies at the Versailles Peace Conference in 1919, the First World War erupted suddenly, like a summer storm out of a clear blue sky, catching perhaps its most famous poet, and most of his friends and companions, as well as the great powers of Europe, by surprise.

MUSE OF FIRE

# CHAPTER 1

# HALCYON DAYS

## Rupert Brooke and
## the Long Peace

THE HOT, CLOUDLESS SUMMER OF 1911 MAY HAVE been the last time that Rupert Brooke—celebrated by his fellow poet William Butler Yeats as "the handsomest young man in England" and already its most admired younger poet—was able to enjoy one of the strenuous outdoor camping holidays, with nude bathing and thirty-mile hikes, that had till then played a large part in his life.

His companions at the tented camp on Dartmoor included a smattering of the young intellectual elite of post-Edwardian England, among them Lytton Strachey, the author-to-be of *Eminent Victorians*; Lytton's brother James, future translator and proselytizer of Freud; Virginia Stephen, the future novelist, who would marry Leonard Woolf the next year; and Maynard Keynes, the future guru of world economics. Also present were three of the young women whom Brooke had pursued relentlessly for several years, so far without success: the motherly Katherine Cox, known to everybody as "Ka," and two of four famously beautiful sisters, Noel Olivier (eighteen) and Brynhild (twenty-four), whom everybody called "Bryn." The women mostly dressed in shapeless homemade garments, while the men favored heavy tweeds and open-necked shirts. All went barefoot or wore hiking boots, depending on the weather. Except for the absence of drugs or anything involving electricity, they resembled a more sedate and less colorful version of a hippie commune of the 1960s. But unlike their counterparts fifty years later, they were uniformly upper middle class and good-mannered, a part of the Establishment more than rebels against it.

Rupert Brooke.

Certainly they rejected the legacy of Victorian prudery. Some of them were products of "progressive" coeducational schools like Bedales, where healthy outdoor work, sports, and carefully supervised nude bathing of boys and girls together, as well as the absence of physical punishment, were intended to break down furtive shame and ignorance between the sexes. Which is not to say that much sexual activity, if any, was taking place in the camp. James Strachey, who was unapologetically homosexual, lusted after Brooke, while Brooke in his tortured way lusted after Ka, Bryn, or Noel Olivier—he was not yet sure which. There was much serious discussion about sex and a certain amount of intrigue, preceded by incredible amounts of impassioned letter writing, but in the age before the widespread availability of reliable contraception, even young women with a progressive education approached the act cautiously, none more so than the beautiful but extremely sensible Olivier sisters. Noel was willing to dive naked from a bridge while being stared at by gaping yokels, but not to surrender her virginity to Rupert Brooke; nor was her watchful sister Bryn about to let that happen.*

---

* Their much younger first cousin was the actor Laurence Olivier.

Although the eighteen-day camp may have been sexually disappointing for Brooke, there was plenty of talk on every imaginable subject from theater to music. The one subject that does *not* seem to have been discussed, however, was the possibility of a major European war in the near future. This was not a result of ignorance or of looking at the world through rose-colored glasses. All these young people were serious, well educated, and well informed. The father of the Olivier girls, Sir Sydney Olivier, was a colonial governor who would rise to become a cabinet minister and peer. Many of the campers had family or friends who moved in high political circles— indeed, Rupert Brooke's greatest admirer, Edward Marsh, was private secretary to Winston Churchill, cabinet member and first lord of the Admiralty, the civilian minister responsible for the Royal Navy. Europe was at peace. There had been no major European war since that between Prussia and France in 1870, and that one had not drawn in any of the other great powers. While hostility between Germany and France still simmered, Great Britain was under no obligation to come to the aid of France in the event that war broke out again between the two countries. The only way Great Britain could be drawn into a European war would be by an infringement of the neutrality of Belgium, which all the major European powers, chief among them Great Britain, had guaranteed since 1839.

Such a possibility seemed far-fetched to almost everybody; hence the huge international success in 1909 of *The Great Illusion*, Norman Angell's best-selling book demonstrating that a general European war was no longer possible due to the "economic interdependence" of the great powers. In the unlikely event that such a war were to break out, it would be short, since international capitalism and trade were now more important than great armies and navies, Angell declared, and had more power to shape events than kings, cabinets, or generals.* Converts to this idea included Lord Esher, who had been largely responsible for reforming the British Army in the years after the Boer War, and Admiral Lord Fisher, the first sea

---

* Angell lived to great old age and would see his thesis proved wrong twice, by the First and then the Second World War, yet he was awarded a knighthood and the Nobel Prize for Peace.

lord. But *The Great Illusion* failed to produce any adherents in the German Great General Staff, where the secret war plan since 1892 had called for the immediate invasion of Belgium as "an unfortunate necessity."

Germans were—or thought they were—surrounded by enemies. Their only continental ally was the increasingly ramshackle Austro-Hungarian Empire, ruled by Emperor Franz Josef, who was eighty years old in 1910 and had been on the throne since 1848. The Dual Empire (Franz Josef was also the Apostolic King of Hungary) was bewilderingly multilingual and multiethnic and was mired in the problems of its unruly Balkan possessions. Further, it feared the historic enmity of the giant Russian Empire to the east: whatever their failings, the czars had always thought of themselves as the protectors of *all* Slavs, including those in the Austro-Hungarian Empire.

The unlikely alliance between republican France and czarist Russia in 1892 reinforced German fear of "encirclement" and determined German military strategy. The presiding genius of the general staff, General Count Alfred von Schlieffen, facing the fact that the German Army would be outnumbered by the combined armies of France and Russia, boldly decided to strike first at France, on the outbreak of war, counting on the slower mobilization of the Russian Army due to Russia's huge distances, inadequate railway system, and Slav inefficiency. Leaving only a thin screen in the east to defend Prussia, a significant portion of the German Army of over four million men would wheel through Belgium, then turn southwest from the English Channel to the *west* of Paris, cutting the capital off from the rest of France and threatening the bulk of the French Army from the rear.

Once it defeated France, the German Army, thanks to the excellent German railway system, would be able to move rapidly to the east to fight the Russian Army before it was even fully deployed. Thus German victory would depend on delivering a swift knockout blow to France, the first of a one-two punch. Over the next two decades, the Schlieffen Plan, as it came to be called, was perfected and expanded with methodical Teutonic attention to detail. Every bridge, every railway carriage and boxcar, every road was studied to ensure a swift and orderly advance on an exact timetable. Nothing was to be left to chance, Schlieffen's dying words in 1913 were said to have been, "Remember to keep the right wing strong." He urged his successor to make sure that the right sleeve of the soldier on far right of the German advance should "brush the English Channel." That the Belgians, with a population of only 7.5 million, might actually fight, or that the British might send their small, but well trained regular army—so small by continental standards that the kaiser referred to it as "contemptible"—and thereby fatally delay and deflect the attack of the German First Army, had not been considered.

Looking back from the distance of over one hundred years, today's historians are inclined to describe Europe in the years before the war as a powder keg, requiring only the smallest of sparks to produce an explosion. (Bismarck had correctly predicted that if a general European war came, it would be caused by "some damned fool thing in the Balkans."). But people did not think so at the time. We can now see that the system of alliances between the major European powers was like a house of cards, that even the slightest disruption might bring it down with catastrophic results, but at the time people saw every treaty and alliance as a form of insurance, as creating stability rather than threatening it. Diplomats saw their job as tending the complex web of agreements and negotiating modifications over time as necessary, while generals were to provide a credible threat to ensure that the treaties would be enforced—the mailed fist behind the velvet glove. For over forty years, that system had provided peace in Europe, so it cannot be easily dismissed. Indeed a diplomat of genius, a Metternich, a Bismarck, or a Disraeli, might have found a way to paper over the Austro-Hungarian attack on Serbia after the assassination of Archduke Franz Ferdinand and his wife in Sarajevo on June 28, 1914. But no such genius emerged, so events took their fatal course, with consequences that we still live with.

One by one, each step led inexorably to the next. The mobilization of the Austro-Hungarian Army against Serbia caused Russia to begin a partial mobilization, which made it necessary for Germany to mobilize, which led to the French mobilization. Since the German war plan called for the immediate invasion of Belgium, the

British government, horrified and reluctant, had to fulfill its historic obligation to defend Belgian neutrality. Six weeks from the assassination of Archduke Franz Ferdinand and his wife, the major powers of Europe were at war. It would last four years and cost the lives of over 25 million people.*

After the war, a certain class of people looked back on the years before the war, from 1910 to 1914, as having been idyllic, like the overture from Strauss's 1912 *Rosenkavalier*, the calm before the storm. For them, no doubt they were. But those years were also marked, in Great Britain, by a rising tide of social and political problems—major strikes, violence in Ireland, and growing suffragette protests that culminated in the death of Emily Davison, who famously threw herself in front of the king's horse in the Derby at Epsom. The Britain of grimy industrialization, vast wealth inequality, rigid class distinction, labor unrest, and social strife was being radically challenged as the Liberal government, prodded by David Lloyd George, introduced old age pensions, national insurance against unemployment, the disenfranchisement of the Church of England in Wales, the reform of the House of Lords, and an unprecedented mass of radical legislation that became the foundation of a modern national welfare state.

One would not have guessed any of this from the poetry of the day. Rupert Brooke wrote about his own decidedly complex emotions or about an idealized upper-middle-class vision of rural England, with thatched cottages, clear streams, and gently rolling downs. Wales, Scotland, and Ireland (even then racked by armed violence, terrorism, and apparently unbridgeable ethnic and religious strife) scarcely figure in his poetry at all, still less the clamorous industrial cities of the north belching smoke, or the coal mines, or the great ports from which Britain's products were being shipped all over the world. William Blake's anger that the "dark Satanic mills" had been drawing a shadow over "England's pleasant pastures" since the eighteenth-century was stilled. Brooke's England was a land of sentimental picture postcards of a countryside that

---

* If we include the deaths from the Spanish influenza that followed the war and the Russian Civil War, the total is more like 45 million.

was disappearing fast except where wealthy landowners were keeping it alive, and that did not include a rural tenantry living in substandard housing with antiquated plumbing if any, and little access to education or health care.

This helps to explain Brooke's success at such an early age and the popularity of his poems throughout his short life and afterward. He was writing about an England that a certain class of readers yearned for, an imagined eighteenth-century rural land shorn of cruelty, poverty, injustice, and a ferocious legal system that could punish even the most minor theft by hanging or transportation to Australia. The new "Georgians," as Brooke and the poets around him would come to be known, looked back to an England before the Industrial Revolution. They were modern only in the sense that they rejected the grand subjects and religious enthusiasm of the Victorian Age, and they would themselves shortly come to seem old-fashioned with the postwar rise of the modernist poets T. S. Eliot and Ezra Pound.

That Brooke should be remembered as a "war poet" is ironic and tragic. Until 1914 his best-remembered line of poetry, rooted firmly but fondly in his view of England as an earthly paradise, and in his remarkable gift for grabbing the reader's attention by dropping a line of ordinary conversation into his poetry, was from "The Old Vicarage, Grantchester": "And is there honey still for tea?" evoked a world of tea served outdoors on a lawn under trees that would soon vanish. But instead, after his death in 1915, Brooke would be remembered for the first three lines of "The Soldier":

> If I should die, think only this of me:
>     That there's some corner of a foreign field
> That is for ever England.

It is fitting that Rupert Brooke came to symbolize the spirit in which Britain entered the Great War: optimistic, willing and even eager to sacrifice, patriotic. At the outbreak of war, Brooke himself joined up without doubts, as did so many young men, and he died too soon to develop them. His image is forever fixed in the epigrammatical lines that the poet Frances Cornford had written on meeting him nearly a decade earlier:

> A young Apollo, golden-haired,
> Stands dreaming on the verge of strife,
> Magnificently unprepared
> For the long littleness of life.

Like so many others in August 1914, Brooke embraced the war with a mixture of excitement and relief, believing that it would sweep away all the inequities and problems of the Victorian and Edwardian past, as well as all his own personal failings, regrets, and mistakes, and provide a bold new start. His was the first and perhaps the best remembered of those poetic voices who would soon be stilled by the war he greeted with such enthusiasm.

Englishmen of a certain class used to be divided into two distinct groups: those who were brutalized in school and grow up to hate their years there, and those who looked back on their schooldays as the happiest time of their life. Brooke was firmly in the second group. "I had been happier at Rugby," he wrote when he was at Cambridge, "than I can find words to say. As I looked back at five years, I seemed to see almost every hour as golden and radiant. . . . I could not (and cannot) hope for or even quite imagine such happiness elsewhere." Rugby School is the subject of perhaps the most famous novel in English literature about life in a great English public school, Thomas Hughes's *Tom Brown's School Days*. Despite its adulatory tone, it does not play down the physical discomforts, the beatings, the bullying, the cruelty, misogyny, snobbery and rote learning of the schools to which the English upper class and the prosperous who aspired to the upper middle class sent their sons. Rugby's most famous headmaster, Thomas Arnold, defined the school's particular ethos in the first half of the nineteenth century as "muscular Christianity," in which games (like the eponymous rugby football), physical strength, and high-mindedness combined to produce an English gentleman. Arnold aimed unapologetically to produce an elite, in an age when elitism was applauded rather than disapproved. Although Sir Henry Newbolt was not, as it happened, himself an old Rugbeian, he expressed its ethos perfectly in the last stanza of "Vitaï Lampada":

This is the word that year by year,
While in her place the school is set,
Every one of her sons must hear,
And none that hear it dare forget.
This they all with a joyful mind
Bear through life like a torch in flame,
And falling fling to the host behind—
Play up! Play up! And play the game!

Although Brooke's poetry, even those few poems he wrote as a soldier, is devoid of this kind of simple-minded patriotism and exhortation, the message of "Vitaï Lampada" was not one with which he would have disagreed. Rugby *was* where he had been happiest: he not only went to school there, he had been *born* there. He was a fiercely competent and competitive athlete as well as a scholar and poet. His patriotism and sense of duty were everything Professor Arnold could have desired. On the moral and sexual level, however, he oscillated between puritanism (combined with a deep misogynistic streak) and ceaseless sexual pursuit that, when successful, produced in him alternating waves of guilt and revulsion. "My subconsciousness is angry with every dreary young woman I meet, if she doesn't fall in love with me: and my consciousness is furious with her if she does," Brooke confessed, accurately enough. He was romantic in the best and worst sense of the word, and although the word was not then in much use, he was already a celebrity as a Cambridge undergraduate, at once weaving a myth about himself and trapped by it.

In the years since Brooke's death in 1915, demolishing his myth has been something like a literary cottage industry. With his astonishing good looks, easy charm, and apparently effortless ability to spout graceful poetry on demand (this was deceptive, in fact he worked hard at it), he was an easy target. When people think about the poets of the First World War, it is the *anti*-war poets they usually have in mind, not Rupert Brooke, who appeared to greet the war's outbreak with joy and who died before its image became one of mass slaughter in the trenches and in the mud and barbed wire of no-man's-land. He went to war with enthusiasm, died before disgust set in, and feared growing old more than death. In a way, he was lucky—certainly nobody could have been more suitable to lead the way for other poets to join up, or to serve as a symbol of service and self-sacrifice.

RUPERT BROOKE DID NOT COME FROM a military family; his background was one of academics and clergymen. His father, William Parker Brooke—diminutive, self-effacing, and overshadowed by his domineering wife—could trace his ancestry back to Anne Boleyn's private chaplain, who somehow managed to survive her fall and beheading to end as archbishop of Canterbury under her daughter, Queen Elizabeth I. That argues for a certain degree of flexibility and political skill. To rise to the highest rank of the new Church of England and then die in your own bed at the age of seventy in Tudor England, when religious differences were often settled by the headsman's ax or the bonfire, was no small achievement.

Rupert Brooke's mother, Ruth, was an altogether more formidable personality. Tall and slim, with features attractive in a somewhat hawklike way, she was opinionated, inquisitive, and determined to have her own way in all things great and small. She traced her ancestry back to one of the parliamentarians who signed the death warrant of King Charles I, and she retained something of that fierce Puritan spirit. Rupert Brooke often referred to his mother (although never to her face) as "the Ranee," a Hindi word signifying the wife of a maharajah, or a female ruler in her own right. He spent much of his short life in complicated schemes intended to conceal his private life from her. His features were very much like hers, only sharper, the eyes much the same shape, except that hers have the unmistakable steeliness of H. Rider Haggard's "She-Who-Must-Be-Obeyed" in his novel *She*.

As the wife of a housemaster at Rugby School, Mrs. Brooke wielded unchallenged power over around fifty boys ranging in age from ten to seventeen, one of them her middle son Rupert. Sons of housemasters at English public schools have often suffered from divided loyalty: for just that reason, the future English novelist Graham Greene, while at school, attempted suicide, first by playing Russian roulette with a revolver and then by taking an overdose of aspirin. But in the case of Rupert Brooke, it was both his father *and* his mother who presided over the house. Brooke, unlike so many other young Englishmen of his class, seems to have had no difficulty fitting in. He was a natural athlete and although he worked hard, he made it look easy. As he grew older, his face ceased to be that of an exceptionally pretty child and became one of pure beauty, without the slightest suggestion of effeminacy. He excelled at cricket and, perhaps more important, at rugby football, a much more bruising and dangerous game, and he rose to the rank of captain in the Rugby Officer Training Corps.

Alone among the great European powers, Britain had no military conscription. France required all men to perform three years of military service once they reached the age of twenty and to remain at various levels of the reserve until forty-eight. This meant the government could produce an army of nearly three million men in less than two weeks. Military service was a respected French national institution, in part because it bound together for a time men of different regions, dialects, classes, and political and religious beliefs or lack thereof. In Germany, with its larger population, similar measures would produce an army of four million, and in Russia, of over six million (more men, it would soon transpire, than could be armed). Britain, however, still relied on volunteers rather than conscription, despite an elaborate system of reforms instituted after the Boer War. The Officer Training Corps at the major "public schools" (which in England are essentially private) and universities were intended to provide some degree of military training for the children of the upper-middle and upper classes and to produce a pool of potential junior officers.

Despite affecting a becoming English modesty later on about his cadet training at Rugby, Brooke excelled at that as he did at everything else; indeed, photographs of him in his cadet officer uniform could have served as the poster boy for the whole recruitment scheme. His long hair—already slightly too long for a Rugbeian or for his mother's taste—is tucked up under an officer's peaked cap, and his expression is firm but wary, more poet than soldier. His uniform and shiny Sam Browne belt are well looked after, almost certainly by a maid: a housemaster at Rugby and his family lived comfortably, with a cook and an Edwardian abundance of servant girls. Throughout his life, Rupert Brooke would be looked after. There is no record of his ever preparing a meal or washing the dishes. Even when he "lived rough" on camping trips, adoring young women—or young women he wanted to be adored by—took care of him. By the time the war broke out, he had never gone through any kind of basic training that involved polishing his own boots and Sam Browne belt. Yet he was commissioned as an officer by a stroke of Winston Churchill's pen, in the belief that a Rugbeian and Cantabrigian would naturally know how to lead men in battle.

In all Brooke's voluminous and often tortuous correspondence, the subject of his own beauty does not come up. Like many beautiful people, it may not have been as obvious to him as it was to others. He was not vain—he may simply have taken it for granted. He was aware of the effect he had on men and women, but it was not something he enjoyed or took pride in. Admiration he simply took as his due, receiving it from people as different as Henry James and Winston Churchill. Brooke's good looks meant that he was always the center of attention, at school, at Cambridge, even during his brief experience as a junior officer, all the more so because it was accompanied by charm, intelligence, and a genuine interest in people. Behind the handsome mask, however, lay hidden depths, without which his poetry would merely have been pretty. All his life he struggled between the fierce Puritanism inherited from his formidable mother (and her efforts to impose it on him) and his own deeply sensual yearnings, which he found difficult to resolve until the last year of his short life. He spent a lot of his time putting as much distance as he could between himself and his mother. Finally, inspired by Paul Gauguin, he escaped to Tahiti and Fiji, as far as he could get from his home in Rugby and from his mother's ideas about how his life should be lived.

In a photograph of the adult Rupert Brooke with his mother, he towers above her. She is smiling affectionately, but he is standing a couple of feet away, as if to avoid physical contact, his eyes on the far horizon. He was then about four weeks from death, the ultimate escape. Mrs. Brooke is dressed entirely in black, as if anticipating the event, but in the Victorian tradition she had probably remained in mourning since the death of her husband in 1910. She had already lost a daughter and a son to illness, and she would lose her two remaining sons to the war in 1915.

PHOTOGRAPHS REVEAL THE MAN, and the boy, but Brooke's poetry stands for itself, slightly old-fashioned, often pretty rather than deep, but always felicitously phrased. His letters, from his schooldays on, reveal the many-layered complexity of his character, as well as his remarkable gift for friendship, but we must take his charm, on which everybody who ever met him agreed, on faith. "Charm," as Evelyn Waugh wrote in *Brideshead Revisited*, "is the great English blight, it does not exist outside these damp islands." Clearly Brooke had charm in spades. His good looks opened doors for him, and teachers and Cambridge dons fawned over him at first sight. But there was more to it than that. Just before his makeshift division was to embark for the Middle East, he was suffering from a bad cold in the damp and draughty naval barracks. To recover, he was invited to spend nine days at 10 Downing Street, fussed over by Prime Minister Henry Asquith's daughter Violet and visited at his sickbed by Henry James.

That would not have been possible if he had merely been a pretty face or an accomplished poet. He was able to mold himself into what others wanted him to be: he could be outrageously "campy" with "gay"\* friends, yet switch in an instant to serious conversation with the prime minister. He was a handsome chameleon in any company, the center of attention even when he was trying not to be. In four years, he rose from Cambridge undergraduate and well-regarded minor poet to become a fellow of King's College, Cambridge, a superstar as a poet, a social celebrity who hobnobbed with the great and famous, and he was about to achieve, although he could not have imagined it, undying fame and glamour as a national hero.

Within days of Brooke's death, his friends, his admirers (including Winston Churchill), and the national press were uniting to turn him into the poet-hero that the nation needed, erasing anything in his life that might smudge that portrait. From early adulthood on, Brooke's friends had speculated about what he would become when he grew older, as if his good looks commandeered a great future. One of them predicted he would become prime minister, for he was deeply, even passionately devoted to what we might now describe as a left-wing political agenda. His mother was politically active for a woman of the nineteenth century—she would become both a guardian of the poor and a justice of the peace, unusual roles for a woman then, and she was a deeply committed Liberal in the days when the Liberal Party represented a progressive, even radical agenda of political reform and social welfare. Without telling her, Rupert in his first year at Cambridge took a large step to the left when he became an associate member of the left-wing Fabian Society and very soon an admirer of Beatrice and Sidney Webb, George Bernard Shaw, and H. G. Wells, fiery stuff for a boy of nineteen.

---

\* Neither of these words was then in use in its contemporary meaning.

He never lost his interest in politics or his political idealism, but friendships were more important to him, and he had no stomach for the committees and electioneering that are the starting points of a serious political career. Other friends predicted a brilliant academic career for him, but it is hard to see Brooke as a middle-aged Cambridge don, striding from the lecture hall to the senior common room and the High Table in his flowing gown, balding (his father lost most of his hair at an early age) and absorbed in the poetry and drama of the late sixteenth century. Indeed, nobody found that harder to imagine than Brooke himself, which no doubt explains why he was so slow to take up whatever duties his fellowship of King's College might entail.

Not surprisingly, he admired J. M. Barrie's 1904 play *Peter Pan*, which he saw many times with undisguised enthusiasm. Few ever wrote more brutally about the process of aging than Rupert Brooke.

> And you, that loved young life and clean, must tend
> A foul sick fumbling dribbling body and old,
> When his rare lips hang flabby and can't hold
> Slobber.

None of Peter Pan's "pixie dust" here—this is nasty stuff, not relieved even by the slight oedipal undercurrent.

Again and again in his poetry, Brooke rhapsodized about early death, long before he wrote the three lines of "The Soldier" that may be among the most famous in English literature. It's as if the line from Peter Pan was etched in his mind: "To die would be an awfully big adventure." Indeed, he would write to a friend when war broke out, "Come and die. It will be great fun."

This kind of thing occurs quite often in Brooke's poetry, despite his reputation as a champion of the English landscape and the Edwardian upper-middle-class twilight. One of his biographers wrote of Brooke's mother, rather gently, that "throughout her life she found it difficult to give or take the affection she felt," and Brooke sometimes referred her to as "the Granite Lady," but his own emotions and affections were enormous, turbulent, violent, and often contradictory. Behind that sleek surface, a volcano rumbled, leading to a year-long "nervous breakdown" in 1912, during which he felt himself lost in a "ferocious tempestuous ocean of lust."

Brooke was better at stirring up passions in women than at satisfying them. He craved sex with Ka, but when she finally gave in to him, he despised her for it. The war between his innate puritanism and his lust would go on until 1913, when he managed to call a truce to the struggle, and in the lush, sensual warmth of Polynesia, he finally found himself, at the age of twenty-six, able at last to give and receive sexual love on equal terms.

During the brief four months between Brooke's return to England and the outbreak of war, his enormous correspondence is noticeably less heated, with less of the old obsession of equating sex with "filth." Indeed, some of his letters to Cathleen Nesbitt are positively elegiac: "It's the one thing I've got, to love you and to feel love growing, and the strength and peace growing, and to learn to worship you, and to want to protect you, to desire both to possess every atom of your body and soul, and to lose myself in your kindliness like a child." This is a far cry from Brooke's confused and almost hysterical letters to Ka in 1912: "I feel better for being beastly to you. . . . Oh, my God, I want you tonight. Your nakedness and beauty—your mouth and breasts and cunt, I'd burn you like a fire if I could get hold of you." His letters, from schooldays on, teem with attempts to explain his behavior, perhaps as much to himself as to anyone else, of which "I feel better for being beastly to you" is a typical example.

Despite the efforts of friends—and his mother—to imagine careers for him, Brooke never seems to have considered becoming anything but a poet. By the age of twelve, he was already composing poems with surprising technical skill, and at nineteen his sonnet "The Sea" won a contest and was published in the *Westminster Gazette*, for which he received half a guinea (10s. 6d.), his first literary earnings. At school he fell under the literary influence of Oscar Wilde and Charles Baudelaire, which produced a long period of purple, decadent prose and even more purple, decadent poems. He modeled himself after Aubrey Beardsley and affected—out of sight of his mother—a languid, pale listlessness that sharply contrasted with the robust captain of the Rugby cricket eleven. He read Wilde's

*De Profundis* twice (it was published in 1905) and was bowled over by it. A product of a public school education, he grew up in an all-male environment, and inevitably his early "pashes" were directed, however discreetly, at attractive young men. After all, except for two cousins, two maiden aunts, and his mother, he hardly even *knew* any women. His love poems, at least until his second year at Cambridge, must be read in this light, that the object of his affection was a boy, not a girl.

Brooke did not make the transition from Rugby to King's College, Cambridge, easily or without stress. At Rugby he had been a star, perhaps the most gifted and certainly the most glamorous boy in the school, but as a first-year undergraduate at King's College, he was a nobody.

At Rugby, Brooke had lived at home rather than boarding like the rest of the students; at King's, he had, in those days, a sitting room and a bedroom; a "gyp," the Cambridge equivalent of an Oxford "scout," a manservant whose services he shared with several undergraduates and a don on the same staircase; and a "bedder" or "bedmaker," an elderly woman who served as a maid. Brooke was, at last, free from the constant supervision of the Ranee. At home, his mother was only too likely to sweep into his bedroom unbidden, but at Cambridge all he had to do was "sport his oak"—close the outer door of his rooms—to prevent anyone from entering or even knocking. It would take him some time to find his feet.

It can't have helped that he had won a classical scholarship to King's, Latin and Greek being two subjects in which he took very little interest. A photograph of him taken just before he went up to Cambridge shows him resting his chin on his right fist, looking uncommonly handsome, but glowering and sulky, perhaps at the thought of all the Latin and Greek that lay ahead of him when what really interested him was poetry, theater, and politics.

Like most first-year undergraduates, he found the dons very different from his schoolmasters. They were permitted, even encouraged to be eccentric. It was not their task to enforce a set of rules on the undergraduates or to discipline them. The don whose rooms faced Brooke's, for instance, was Oscar Browning, a controversial celebrity, radical education reformer, prolific historian and biographer, friend of Oscar Wilde, and avid social climber. Although he was an old Etonian, he had been dismissed as a master at Eton for having "inappropriate" friendships with his pupils. Browning quickly invited his handsome young neighbor across the hall to tea, but did not make a good first impression on Brooke, who described him cautiously to his mother as "quaint." Browning may have come on a little bit too strong for Brooke. To use a more modern, and more accurate description of him, he was flamboyantly gay, while Brooke was still in many respects his mother's son and easily shocked.

On the other hand, Brooke's tutor Walter Headlam impressed him by declaiming "in Greek the speeches of Agamemnon with dramatic zest—nervously pulling at his pipe, now going into a small room adjoining for more tobacco, now striding to the bottle of ale on the piano to fill his glass. . . . He lived in a world of pure scholarship, cricket, and music, oblivious to anything else." Headlam steered Brooke away from the classics toward the Elizabethan playwrights, particularly the plays of John Webster, and he encouraged Brooke to read the poetry of John Donne, which he had previously denigrated.

Cambridge almost at once performed its first task: it opened up Brooke's mind. He soon acquired friends there, many of whom would play a major role in his life, among them Justin Brooke (no relation). A graduate of Bedales, the notoriously progressive coeducational boarding school, Justin encouraged him to look in on a rehearsal of the Cambridge Amateur Dramatic Club at its theater on Jesus Street. There Rupert Brooke's appearance in the stalls set off a chain of events that opened up a whole new world for him and made him a much bigger student celebrity than he had been at Rugby. To say that he was noticed would be to put it mildly. On the spot, he was offered a nonspeaking part in the play, the *Eumenides* of Aeschylus, in which he would have to pretend to blow a trumpet and appear in a skimpy and revealing costume. Neither seemed like a challenge, but Brooke's appearance on stage nevertheless created a sensation.

Neither then nor later did Brooke show any talent for the theater. He did not suffer from stage fright, but however dramatic his appearance, he tended to mumble his lines and shift his weight nervously from foot to foot. The Amateur Dramatic Club would become one of his major interests at Cambridge: he acted, he stage managed, he produced, and eventually he would even *write* a play. Still, as much as he loved the theater and was an avid playgoer, it was not a career path for him. It did, however, put him on the map in Cambridge, and many of his closest friendships would come out of his involvement with the club. It was there that he met his lifelong friend Jacques Reverat, a Bedalian, the bilingual son of a wealthy Frenchman; Ka Cox; the beautiful Noel Olivier, herself a Bedalian (living proof that mixed nude bathing and sex education would not necessarily encourage girls to immoral behavior); and Edward Marsh, who would do more than anyone else to tend the flame of Brooke's reputation and career.

Brooke's first year at Cambridge was not an academic success, and it was marred by tragedy as well: his elder brother Richard died of pneumonia, plunging the boys' father into grief from which he would never completely recover. Rupert and his mother had both been ill at the time, possibly with the flu. Despite his robust appearance, Rupert, like his brother Dick, was often ill. In the age before antibiotics, the only cure was prolonged bed rest, strictly enforced under the watchful eye of Mrs. Brooke at home. Throughout his life, it took a long time for Brooke to recover from even minor injuries and illnesses, suggesting that he may have had what we would now call a weak immune system.

The results of Brooke's exam at the end of his first year were disappointing—as a scholar of King's, he was expected to do much better. It was not enough to look glamorous and have a magnetic personality. His poor exam result might have reflected his lack of interest in the classics, but it was probably also a consequence of his widening interests and growing friendships. He was spreading himself thin. He was not only active in the theater, he began to write for *The Cambridge Review*, which published one of his poems. Even more important, his fellow Kingsman Hugh Dalton, an Etonian who would rise to become chancellor of the exchequer in Britain's 1945 Labour government, stoked Brooke's involvement in politics, encouraging him to move further left, from Liberalism to Socialism. He introduced him to the nascent Fabian movement at Cambridge, which had recently begun with a modest grand total of six members.

Dalton introduced Brooke to Ben Keeling, the moving spirit of the Cambridge Fabians, in Keeling's rooms at Trinity College, under a framed poster of "the workers of the world surging forward with clenched fists." That image would inspire Brooke to write "his only Socialist poem," which was still being quoted in election speeches forty years later:

Yet, behind the night, Waits for the great unborn, somewhere afar, Some white tremendous daybreak.

All these extracurricular interests took their toll on Brooke's studies, but it was Fabian socialism that had the greatest effect on Brooke's life. The young women who attended Cambridge were strictly segregated and discriminated against, and they did not receive a degree even if they scored higher on their final exam than men. They could work at the ADC but could not perform on stage—female roles had to be played by male undergraduates. Worse yet, women could participate in social events only under the supervision of a chaperone. Even their freedom to read books in the libraries was strictly curtailed. It was therefore a provocative act that the Cambridge Fabian leadership chose a young woman as their treasurer, first Amber Reeves, then Katherine Cox, who would play a major role in Brooke's life. Margery Olivier, of the four beautiful sisters, was also a member. The Fabian Society was one of the few places at Cambridge where young women and men could meet on an equal footing.

Justin Brooke, who had introduced Rupert to the ADC, also made him an instant convert to the co-ed long-distance hikes, ski trips, and camping excursions that would become such an important part of his life. He seems also to have been responsible for getting Rupert to join a mixed party of students for a Christmas skiing holiday in Andermatt, Switzerland, which included Ka Cox and two Olivier sisters, Margery and Brynhild. This was surely Brooke's first experience of living in the company of young women, and although it was decorous and well supervised, it made a big impact on him. It was all very proper, photographs show the young women skiing in long skirts, but when they put on a performance of Oscar Wilde's *The Importance of Being Earnest* in the hotel ballroom, the female parts were played by the girls, which was still forbidden at Cambridge. Brooke came away partly—and temporarily—in love with Bryn, and his interest in the traditional masculine team sports, rugby football and cricket, was soon noticeably replaced by interest in the few outdoor events in which young women took part on equal terms.

Amid all this, Brooke was still writing poems. "The Beginning" was written in this period, in which his amazing verbal skill is by now almost perfected, and which—although it is passionately romantic, even erotic in tone—may have been triggered by the death of his brother. The grace of the language and the contempt for old age that are the hallmarks of Brooke's mature work are already here; it is very far from what one thinks of as schoolboy or undergraduate verse.

Some day I shall rise and leave my friends
And seek you again through the world's far ends,
You whom I found so fair
(Touch of your hands and smell of your hair!),
My only God in the days that were.
My eager feet shall find you again,
Though the sullen years and the mark of pain
Have changed you wholly; for I shall know
(How could I forget having loved you so?) . . .
And seeing your age and ashen hair
I'll curse the thing that once you were,
Because it is changed and pale and old
(Lips that were scarlet, hair that was gold!),
And I loved you before you were old and wise
When the flame of youth was strong in your eyes,
—And my heart is sick with memories.

Who the "you" is remains unclear. It is far too early to have been Ka Cox or any of the Olivier sisters. Brooke had a single fiercely consummated sexual relationship with a young man in 1909, and wrote about it in exquisite detail to his friend James Strachey in 1912, but that would mean that he was still technically a virgin when he wrote "The Beginning." Still, none of that matters: the essential Brooke is here, passionate, consumed by powerful emotions with which he did not know how to cope, already raging against the prospect of growing old. "The flame of youth" is a powerful phrase and a good description of what made Brooke attractive to so many people. His own youth would burn like a flame to the very end.

As his first year at Cambridge drew to an end, Brooke seemed to have found his way. He was making plans for an elaborate production of Milton's *Comus*, which would be a major theatrical and intellectual event. *Comus* had been first performed in 1643 but seldom since—it was a masque, not a play, written for a nobleman whose three children all played leading roles in it. It was a pantomime, in which the lavishly costumed performers mixed with the audience. Putting on *Comus* was Brooke's idea, and a brilliant one, since it involved a combination of amateur show business and literary scholarship that was bound to attract approval at the highest level of the university as well as in London.

Brooke also joined the board of *The Cambridge Review* and, as a young Fabian, entertained H. G. Wells in his rooms and breakfasted with Sidney Webb. He had formed a nucleus of friends, both male and female, and become a glamorous and much-admired celebrity in the Cambridge world. With his long, flowing hair, his habit of tossing his head to shake it out if his eyes, his *vie de Bohème* clothing, and his startling good looks, he seemed poised for great success in any number of ways, poetic, academic, cultural, and political.

Without having shown any particular interest in the group, Brooke was even invited to join the quasi-secret, elite Cambridge Apostles, who met on Saturday nights at midnight over coffee and sardines on toast to discuss intellectual and literary topics. Founded in 1820 or 1830 (it is not clear which), the Apostles had originally consisted of twelve undergraduates. Membership was by invitation only and for life. Former Apostles who had graduated, called Angels, included Samuel Taylor Coleridge and Alfred, Lord Tennyson. Current members at the time of Brooke's selection included

Maynard Keynes, Lytton and James Strachey, and Bertrand Russell, the future mathematician, philosopher, and Nobel Prize winner, all brilliant intellectuals with radical ideas. A certain degree of homosexuality (or at least of tolerance for it) ran through the Apostles in the late nineteenth and early twentieth centuries, but the members were by no means exclusively homosexual, and like Edward Marsh, they networked at the very highest level of the government and the serious press. For someone ending his first year at Cambridge, Rupert Brooke could hardly have made more of a splash.

# CHAPTER 2

# "THIS SIDE OF PARADISE!"

P OETS ARE SOMETIMES DISMISSED AS HEAD-IN-the-clouds dreamers, but Rupert Brooke was emphatically nothing of the kind. In 1907, as he approached his second year at Cambridge, he was fiercely engaged in the politics and social issues of the day. Vast social change was under way in Britain: the Labour Party, just eight years old and already splintered between the intellectuals of the Fabian Society and working-class labor organizers, was nonetheless emerging as a powerful political force. Brooke found himself moving down two separate but interconnected paths. The first was political. He had committed himself completely to Fabian socialism, signing "The Basis," which formally pledged him to the abolition of classes and private property, and to "equal citizenship for women." Fabian socialism, the brainchild of H. G. Wells, Sidney and Beatrice Webb, and George Bernard Shaw, represented, in purified form, what would come to be called democratic socialism in Europe. The Fabians represented a typically English middle ground between Karl Marx's doctrine of class warfare and the social utopianism of William Morris, which turned its back on industrialism in favor of pastoralism, arts and crafts, and simple living.

The Fabians embraced industrialism and science but wanted them nationalized. It was the profit motive they intended to eliminate, replacing it with rationalism, idealism, and "fact-based decision making." Whereas Marx had demanded the "dictatorship of the proletariat" and welcomed whatever violence was needed to impose it or might follow from it, the Fabians wanted a society ruled

Essays by G. Bernard Shaw, Sydney Olivier, Wm. Clarke, Hubert Bland, Sidney Webb, Annie Besant, G. Wallas.

benevolently by people like themselves. They did not envisage a repetition of the storming of the Bastille or the Terror, and they repudiated class warfare. The future was to be attained incrementally, by peaceful means. The only clause in "The Basis" that Brooke would have opposed was the equality of women, about which he was, and would remain, deeply ambivalent.

Brooke's second path was embodied by his membership in the Apostles, with its unwritten creed of intellectual superiority and belief in a male intellectual elite. A list of the people who attended an Apostles meeting reads like an intellectual who's who of early twentieth-century England. At meetings, the distinguished philosopher G. E. Moore played and sang Schubert to an audience that included Brooke, Lytton Strachey, the economist Maynard Keynes, the historian R. C. Trevelyan, the novelist E. M. Forster, and the critic Desmond MacCarthy.

Some of these people, together with a number of more or less emancipated young women, would form the circle that came to be known as Bloomsbury, which was at once literary and social and included both Stracheys, Keynes, Virginia Woolf, Vanessa Bell, and for a time Rupert Brooke. It intersected with a group known as the Neo-Pagans, who pursued hiking, camping, nude bathing, and "reading parties." The Neo-Pagans included Ka Cox, the Olivier sisters, Justin Brooke, Jacques Reverat, and Frances Cornford. Rupert Brooke was one of their acknowledged leaders. Both groups were motivated by the determination to overturn Victorianism, with its puritanism, hypocrisy, rigid rules of behavior, and high-minded moralism. Still, they did not repudiate class distinction or disdain receiving an allowance from their parents. Physically, the Neo-Pagans looked healthier and more robust than the Bloomsberries, in part because the latter lived in London while the former lived in, or yearned for, the country. The sexes intermingled, wearing casual clothing that was shocking during Queen Victoria's lifetime, but the sexual barrier between them remained as high as ever.

Brooke was the center of attention in *all* these circles, remarkable for what Lytton Strachey described as his "pink cheeks and bright yellow hair" but also for his wit and exuberance. He was "good company," although in his private relationships he was difficult, unpredictable, and moody. So it is hardly surprising that he was the life and soul of a dinner party given in 1908 for Sir Sydney Olivier, one of the eminent co-founders of Fabianism, who was now governor of Jamaica. Sir Sydney was an imposing figure, tall, rugged, and dramatically handsome, living proof that socialist ideals could be combined with a successful career as a member of the ruling class. He would go on to become secretary of state for India and a privy councilor, raised to the peerage as Baron Olivier. He was the father of the four Olivier sisters, the youngest of whom, Noel, he brought to the dinner which, in keeping with Fabian principles of the simple life, consisted of only one course, followed by fruit.

Noel, at fifteen, had just entered Bedales and was wearing what passed for the Bedalian school uniform; given the school's progressive nature, it is surprising that it even *had* a uniform. Noel was by far the most beautiful of the four sisters. Photographs of her—she was photographed almost as often as Rupert Brooke—show almost perfect features, with startling pale blue eyes that caused Virginia Woolf to wonder unkindly whether there was anything going on behind them. Since Noel would go on to become both a doctor and a surgeon (the two professions are separate in England), and to marry and have five children, this may be one time when Woolf's ability to read character failed her. In any case, for Rupert Brooke it was a *coup de foudre*, love at first sight. Noel dropped and broke a valuable coffee cup, he kneeled down to pick up the pieces, and Cupid's arrow struck him. She was young, nervous, tongue-tied, and mortified at her own clumsiness, while he tried to put her at ease. For the next seven years, she would be the woman he loved most, yet would staunchly remain the one he could not have. His voluminous correspondence with her is a tidal wave of recriminations, pleas, and unrequited passion. The last is perhaps unfair: Noel Olivier *did* love Rupert Brooke, but hers was always the voice of reason, caution, and common sense. However deeply she was attracted to him, she was intelligent enough to realize that he was not marriageable material and that sleeping with him would be the mistake of a lifetime.

Picking up the broken pieces of the green and gold demitasse cup Noel had dropped was a turning point in Brooke's emotional life. Being smitten by a beautiful fifteen-year-old schoolgirl is not uncommon, but Noel was not a flirtatious one. On the contrary, she was thoughtful and serious: her hobby was dissecting dead animals found in the woods—excellent preparation for her later career as a surgeon. Although she could not have known it, Brooke's understanding of women at the age of twenty-one was near zero. His only, very limited sexual experiences had been with young men his own age at Rugby. The fact that he was admired by both sexes served only to exacerbate his sexual frustration. He could hardly have chosen a less appropriate or less likely erotic target than Noel Olivier, and it is difficult to suppress the suspicion that even at fifteen, she was more realistic about sex than Rupert Brooke.

After all, she had grown up in a very progressive family; her father was a Fabian with radical ideas about everything under the sun, and her mother a member of the Fellowship of the New Life, a group that was in part inspired by Thoreau's writings, of which Havelock Ellis, the groundbreaking English sexologist, was a founding member. The Olivier daughters would have received as much practical and down-to-earth advice about sex as any girls in England, perhaps more, not to speak of all that mixed bathing in the nude. But Brooke had grown up under the stifling Victorian prudery of his overbearing mother, and at Rugby, one of the masters summed up the state of sex education in the school by warning his pupils, "If you touch it, it will fall off." In short, Brooke had no experience as a seducer, and Noel Olivier had no intention of being seduced.

As the year went by, he became more and more involved with the production of Milton's masque *Comus*. He became the director and the stage manager and played one of the leading roles. *Comus* should not be thought of as a run-of-the-mill amateur student production. It coincided with the tercentenary of John Milton's birth and received the support of Christ's College, from which the great poet had been graduated in 1632. Indeed, the master of Christ's was instrumental in arranging for the masque to be produced at the New Theatre in Cambridge, a lavishly decorated full-size theater that could seat an audience of fourteen hundred. Rupert poured himself into the production heart and soul, revealing only bit by bit to his mother how much time he was spending on it—she would have worried, with good reason, that he was spreading himself too thin, and in danger of becoming exhausted, finally admitting to her that "they wanted me to take a part and made such a fuss that I've had to give in." This did not calm Mrs. Brooke's anxiety and had the undesired side effect of making her determined to attend the opening night herself—something else for Brooke to worry about.

He got the distinguished artist William Rothenstein up from London to design the scenery. (Rothenstein brought with him "the Incomparable" Max Beerbohm, another feather in Brooke's cap). He succeeded in persuading Noel Olivier to help paint the backdrops. He took over the choreography and enlisted George Mallory as one of the Morris dancers. In addition to all this, he learned his lines as the Attending Spirit, the longest part in the masque. Many of the people who would be his close companions for life were involved in the project, including Dorothy Lamb, whose brother Henry would become Brooke's rival for the heart of Ka Cox; Frances Cornford, who played the part of Comus; and Frances Darwin, whom he would soon marry and who wrote the short poem comparing Rupert Brooke to the young Apollo.

Brooke's acting and his stage voice were disappointing, but as usual his appearance more than made up for all that, particularly since "his short, spangled, sky-blue tunic" was in fact "so short and tight he couldn't sit down." In every other respect, the production was a success. The master of Christ's College gave a formal banquet to precede the opening night, which was attended by a number of heavyweight cultural figures including the poet laureate and the aged poet and novelist Thomas Hardy, author of *Far from the Madding*

*Crowd* and *Tess of the d'Urbervilles*, with whom Brooke had breakfast the next day. This was serious company for an undergraduate at Cambridge. Even the London papers were respectful, one of them commenting that Brooke was "the best of the performers and a better reciter of blank verse than we have heard anywhere," while the Cambridge papers waxed lyrical.

The performance was followed by a dance, with the players still in costume. Rupert stood by his mother, in his glittery, revealing costume, introducing his friends to her. The Ranee was gracious, but her steely eyes missed nothing. She came to the conclusion that the Olivier girls, on whom her son set such store, were "fast," and that Rupert's friend Justin Brooke was too informal. Of course, hardly anybody could meet Mrs. Brooke's standards for behavior— the Olivier girls were in fact quite the reverse of fast, but this was largely the clash of Victorian standards of good manners and those of the younger generation. True to form, she spirited him away back to Rugby, rather than leave him to hang about Cambridge relishing his triumph.

EVERY DON QUIXOTE NEEDS HIS SANCHO PANZA. Rupert Brooke was no exception; his was Dudley Ward, of St. John's College, Cambridge, an economist and devoted Fabian. One of Brooke's biographers would dismiss him as "dour and studious," but he must have had a lighter side to him since he was Brooke's companion on most of Brooke's camping excursions and hikes, and he tirelessly helped to plot Brooke's attempts to achieve a tête-à-tête with Noel Olivier. He would later arrange to get Brooke and Ka Cox to the same place at the same time, like a latter-day Figaro busy managing Brooke's *affaires*. He appears in almost all the snapshots of Brooke's circle of friends, bespectacled, beginning to lose his hair at an early age, clearly devoted to Brooke, who relied on him unconditionally to the end of his life.

Ward shared this role with an altogether different personality, Edward Marsh (later Sir Edward Marsh). Marsh was older, an "Angel," and a closeted homosexual. Unlike Ward, Marsh had no desire to go on hikes, live in a tent, or pursue the simple life. Nor was he a Fabian. Wealthy, educated at Westminster School and Trinity College, Cambridge, he was a respected civil servant who would spend a lifetime as Winston Churchill's private secretary and carefully revise and copyedit the great man's prose. Marsh was part of "the Establishment," as the governing classes came to be called, rather than in revolt against it. His prestige and literary taste were such that when it became necessary to name a new poet laureate, it was he who advised the prime minister on whom to choose. He was also a social butterfly, a sought-after dinner guest, a devoted theatergoer with an interest in all the arts, and a shrewd and influential judge of poetry as well as painting.

Very early on Marsh was attracted both to Brooke's person and to his poetry, and he would go on not only to oversee, and when necessary pay for, the publication of Brooke's poems, but even to edit them meticulously and respectfully. Marsh also acted as what we might call a supremely discreet public relations man for Brooke too, deftly influencing reviewers and editors. Brooke eventually took to using the spare bedroom in Marsh's elegant, comfortable two-floor flat at 5 Raymond Buildings, Gray's Inn, in central London, overlooking its private gardens, as his London residence. Brooke was looked after there by Mrs. Elgy, Marsh's housekeeper, who in the last year of Brooke's life, when he was having an affair with Phyllis Gardner, would be shocked to find a woman's hairpins in his bed when she made it up in the morning. Marsh had a superb collection of modern English painting, a matchless library, and a rare gift for putting people together: he would introduce Brooke to Siegfried Sassoon, for example, as well as Churchill and Asquith.

Some people have a genius for friendship, while others do not. Brooke's friendships were perhaps the most important part of his life. He won people over instantly, with his jaunty good humor and genuine interest in others. Only a very few were allowed to glimpse his inner turmoil and sexual frustration, or his inability to settle down to grown-up life. In some ways, he would remain to the end a schoolboy or a university student. He never owned a home of his own; he lived on an allowance from his mother, to which he added the relatively small income from his poems and his fellowship at King's. It was not just the complexity of his emotions and the ambivalence of his sexuality that hampered his pursuit of Noel Olivier or his relationship with Ka Cox. Brooke had no domestic base to offer any woman. He lived out of a suitcase in rented rooms, or in London at the Liberal Club, or at Edward Marsh's flat. He was the least marriageable of men—indeed, his poetry is marked by savage denunciations of the very *idea* of marriage. He wrote of Menelaus and Helen, imagining their life after she has returned home from Troy to resume the marriage, addressing his lines to his fellow poet Homer, who had left out this part of the story:

> How should he behold
> That journey home, the long connubial years?
> He does not tell how while Helen bears
> Child on legitimate child, becomes a scold,
> Haggard with virtue. Menelaus bold
> Waxed garrulous, and sacked a hundred Troys
> 'Twixt noon and supper. And her golden voice
> Got shrill as he grew deafer. And both were old.

Brooke rejects not just marriage but *age*. "And both were old" is his ultimate, disgusted condemnation. Although she was still a schoolgirl, Noel Olivier was smart enough to see that Brooke offered her no future—a brief, blazing present, perhaps, had she wanted it, but nothing more. Even Ka Cox eventually realized that however much she loved Brooke, the relationship was a dead end. There would be no marriage, no home, no children.

Brooke himself was buoyantly aware of this; he sailed on, a ship without a destination. His only fixed abode was just where he least wanted to be, at home in Rugby with his mother.

✣ ✣ ✣ ✣

As SOON AS BROOKE WAS ABLE TO, he got clear of his mother and attended a Fabian summer school in Wales. There he at first impressed Beatrice Webb as being cocksure and conceited. When he came back up to Cambridge for the Michaelmas term, he continued to let his social and political interests dominate his time, to the detriment of his studies. He had the misfortune of having rooms on the ground floor, against which Charles Ryder's dreadful cousin Jasper warns him in Evelyn Waugh's *Brideshead Revisited.* "One last point. Change your rooms. . . . I've seen many a man ruined through having ground-floor rooms in the front quad. . . . People start dropping in. They leave their gowns here and come and collect them before hall; you start giving them sherry. Before you know where you are, you've opened a free bar for all the undesirables of the college." This was exactly the case with Rupert Brooke, so much so that his senior tutor suggested that he should live out of college, indeed out of town altogether, and switch from the classics to English literature. Brooke agreed to both and also to the suggestion that he should "submit an essay for the Charles Oldham Shakespeare Scholarship that year." This was intended to give Brooke a good head start in his new chosen subject, the playwrights of the late sixteenth- and early seventeenth-century English theater, as well as a chance for a bit of academic fame and money.

Brooke was happy to give up the classics for a subject that interested him, and he yearned to live somewhere on his own, in the country. He even managed to persuade his mother to let him spend eleven days in Klosters, Switzerland, over Christmas, artfully concealing from her the fact that Noel Olivier would be there, with her sister Margery as her alert and tireless chaperone. As it turned out, Noel might not even have needed a chaperone—she took good care to display a polite indifference and to carefully avoid any chance for a tête-à-tête with Brooke. She remained infuriatingly calm and unruffled, the beautiful blue-gray eyes and gentle smile signifying—nothing.

Brooke's feelings for Noel, apart from inspiring him to write a rash of letters that she found disconcerting, spurred him to produce his finest poem to date:

Oh! Death will find me, long before I tire
    Of watching you; and swing me suddenly
Into the shade and loneliness and mire
    Of the last land! There, waiting patiently,

One day, I think, I'll feel a cool wind blowing,
    See a slow light across the Stygian tide,
And hear the Dead about me stir, unknowing,
    And tremble. And *I* shall know that you have died,

And watch you, a broad-browed and smiling dream,
    Pass, light as ever, through the lightless host,
Quietly ponder, start, and sway, and gleam—
    Most individual and bewildering ghost!—

And turn, and toss your brown delightful head
Amusedly, among the ancient Dead.

The line "and toss your brown delightful head" is as good as any-
thing Rupert Brooke ever wrote, even in the war poems he is most
famous for. His calm contemplation of his own death is here too,
even at the age of twenty-two. It is a constant theme of his verse to
the very end: "If I should die, think only this of me." Then again, as
to its effect, how many sixteen-year-old girls want to read a poem in
which the poet writes not only about *his* death but about *hers*?

Brooke's life at King's continued to be as hectic as ever. He per-
formed in one play (a minor role), and his involvement in Fabian
affairs remained intense. He gave a dinner party in his rooms for his
fellow Apostles, with Hilaire Belloc as the guest of honor, a major
and prolific literary figure of the period now chiefly remembered
for his verses for children and his *Father Brown* stories. Brooke was
an admirer of Belloc's work and sympathetic to Belloc's rejection of
capitalism, industrialism, and the modern state in favor of a some-
what sentimentalized "Merrie Olde England" view of the past. In
person, Belloc was physically intimidating, truculent, argumenta-
tive, a heavy drinker, a combative Catholic—he was once described
as more Catholic than the pope—and an anti-Semite; but like
Brooke he had a great love of the outdoors and a profound, almost
mystical belief in the English countryside.

His admiration for Belloc may have inspired Brooke to write a
long, satiric poem—not his usual style at all—making savage fun of
the pretentions of the English middle class, as personified by "John

Rump." The name, apart from its obvious reference to hindquarters, may also be an attempt to show how far England had fallen by replacing John Bull, the stout, hearty, truculent, beer-swilling, countryman symbol of the old England with the pompous urban Rump of the new, pure Belloc territory. On Rump's arrival in Heaven he announces:

> I am John Rump, this is my hat, and this
> My umbrella. I stand here for sense,
> Invincible, inviolable, eternal.

"John Rump" was written to be read at a meeting of the Carbonari, a radical political discussion group that Brooke and Hugh Dalton had created during their first term at King's, membership of which seems to have overlapped with membership in the Cambridge Fabians or the Labour Party. By Brooke's second year at Cambridge, his preference for shirts with attached collars (instead of a separate starched collar secured by collar studs, as most men of the tie-wearing class sported in those days), his flowing ties, almost like a knotted scarf, and his long hair had already made him a recognizable figure. He was beginning to look like what he was, a poet.

For all his strong left-wing opinions, Brooke remained his mother's son. He was a chauvinist, intolerant of foreigners, mildly anti-Semitic, contemptuous of people who didn't share his physical hardiness or his willingness to hike many miles in the rain and live under canvas, and he was patriotic to a fault.

As Brooke plodded through the year, he was sustained by the knowledge that he could soon give up the classics and by his plans to see Noel Olivier again. At Eastertime, her parents would be in Jamaica, and she would be under the supervision of her sister Margery. He learned this because he had been writing regularly to Margery ever since the Christmas holiday in Klosters, giving poor Margery the impression that he was pursuing *her*. Actually his purpose was to find out more about Noel's whereabouts. He drafted his friend Dudley Ward to be his go-between, then bombarded him with lengthy, detailed instructions and warnings. "But oh! Be tactful, be gentle, be gently tactful! . . . Do not intrude! apologize! apologize!"

Brooke was supposed to spend Easter with his parents in Sidmouth, a bland seaside resort, under the direct eye of the Ranee. So he had to invent a whole different trip to Cornwall and a series of false addresses to allay her suspicions and delay his arrival. Moreover, he needed to find a way to convince Margery that he and Ward had been on a hiking trip in the New Forest and stumbled across her and Noel by happy accident. Brooke drew up charts of what would happen on each day and arranged for letters and cards to be posted to his mother to hide his whereabouts. Twenty-one years of living with her had given him the skills of a good spy. He even toyed with the idea of wearing a disguise.

Once he and Ward arrived in Bank, an ancient, tiny village in a clearing of the New Forest where the two Olivier sisters were staying, Brooke pretended that he and Ward had come there by accident, then managed to carve out some time alone with Noel— despite the fact that Margery still thought that it was she in whom Brooke was interested. There is no doubt that it was the pursuit that excited Brooke—neither sister was about to sleep with him, especially under the watchful eyes of the aptly named Mr. and Mrs. Primmer, who owned the forest boarding house and about whose cooking Brooke waxed enthusiastic.

Brooke's account of the time he spent with Noel begins, naturally enough, with his triumph at evading his mother. "I was lost for four days. . . . I was, for the first time in my life, a free man, and my own master! Oh! The joy of it!"

Considering that he was only trying to spend a couple of hours alone with Noel, and was twenty-one years old, this is a remarkable tribute to the fear Mrs. Brooke inspired in him. In a letter to his friend Jacques Reverat in Cannes, Brooke's description of his time alone with Noel (not counting mealtimes shared with Margery and Ward, and served by Mr. Primmer, a retired butler to the gentry), is wildly poetic. But it ends with a disappointing thump of reality, another tribute to Brooke's astonishing gift of dropping from the sublime to the everyday in his verse: "And so I walked and laughed and met many people and made a thousand songs—all very good—

and, in the end of the days, came to a Woman who was more glorious than the sun and stronger than the sea, and kinder than the earth, who is a flower made out of fire, a star that laughs all day, whose brain is clean and clear like a man's and her heart is full of courage and kindness; and whom I love. I told her that the Earth was crowned with wind-flowers and dancing down the violent ways of Spring: that her mouth was like the sunlight on a gull's wings. As a matter of fact I believe I said 'Hello! Isn't it rippin' weather!'"

The last line probably represents something more like the truth about his hasty meeting alone with Noel, the calm, cautious schoolgirl of sixteen in her Bedales tunic, who surely did not see herself as "a flower made out of fire" or as more glorious than the sun, and who would have fled in embarrassment if Brooke had actually said any of this to her. Whatever Noel's feelings about this brief encounter might have been (or Margery's dawning discovery that she was not the object of Brooke's desire despite all those letters), Brooke was head over heels enraptured by it. "From being sad I have travelled far, to the same goal as you, that of laughing, at times—often—for the joy of life. . . . Splendour is everywhere. I have come out of the Night; and out of the past."

He came out of the night and the past to join his parents at a boarding house in Sidmouth, to face the reality that he was going to have to lie about where he had been over the past four days. He would also have to disappoint his mother about how he would do at his coming Tripos examination in May, at which he had already guessed he was unlikely to receive the First she and his father expected.

WHEN BROOKE SAT FOR THE TRIPOS IN MAY, he does not seem to have given it his undivided attention. Clad formally in a dark subfusc suit, a stiff white wingtip collar, white bow tie, and gown, he wrote a letter to a friend from the examination room at the Guildhall, in a break from his labors. "Your tidings make even this grey place, in which I sit, bright. For I am a prisoner beneath the picture of the late Queen Victoria, in a room where a hundred and eight damned fools are writing Greek verses for the classical Trip. And I am writing an ode to Spring and a letter to you. Also there is a bald invigilating don, asleep." This was not the spirit in which to gain a First, so he cannot have been surprised when he received a not particularly good Second.

He cheered up, however, at the thought of spending a few days with friends in Surrey, since that would place him near Bedales, Noel's school. More important, Brooke arranged for rooms for the next term, a sitting room on the ground floor and a bedroom above, looking out over the garden at the orchard in Grantchester, on the Cam River, about two miles south of Cambridge. It would be in Grantchester that Brooke would write much of his poetry, including perhaps his most famous poem, "The Old Vicarage, Grantchester," and here too that he would begin at last, with small and faltering steps, to live an independent life.

# CHAPTER 3

# "UNDER AN ENGLISH HEAVEN"

O NE OF THE BENEFITS OF AN EDUCATION AT Oxford or Cambridge University is the length of the "long vac," from early June through the first week of October. It gave Brooke the time to apply himself to his tutor's suggestion that he submit an essay for the Charles Oldham Shakespeare Scholarship. In view of his disappointing Second, he hoped to make up for it with this essay.

THE

# TRAGEDY

*OF THE DVTCHESSE*
*Of* Malfy.

*As it was* Presented priuatly, at the Black-
Friers; and publiquely at the Globe, By the
Kings Maiesties Seruants.

The perfect and exact Coppy, with diuerse
things Printed, that the length of the Play would
not beare in the Presentment.

VVritten by *John Webster.*

Hora. ——— *Si quid----*
——— *Candidus Impertis si non his vtere mecum.*

LONDON

Printed by NICHOLAS OKES, for IOHN
WATERSON, and are to be sold at the
signe of the Crowne, in *Paules*
Church-yard, 1623.

His choice of subject was unusual but inspired: John Webster, the Jacobean playwright whose most famous play is perhaps the bloodiest, most violent, sexually frank, and over-the-top melodramatic work of the English theater. Not surprisingly, *The Duchess of Malfi* had virtually vanished from the stage in Victorian times, and its author had sunk into obscurity. The play's themes include incest and lycanthropy: one of the duchess's two murderous brothers is a werewolf, while the other is a cardinal who murders his mistress by making her kiss a poisoned Bible. The duchess herself is garroted on stage after being presented with the severed hand of her lover with the ring she had given him still on it. Considering all that, it might seem an odd choice.

Brooke's interest in Webster had been sparked by his classics tutor Walter Headlam, so it was likely that Headlam, at least, would look on the choice of subject favorably. Also Brooke's involvement with the Marlowe Society had included a production of Christopher Marlowe's *Doctor Faustus*, in which he had played the role of Mephistopheles, which may have given him a taste for melodrama. Since Webster had been prolific, Brooke had his work cut out for him: much of his summer would be spent reading into the obscurities of early seventeenth-century drama.

Unlike many undergraduates, Brooke enjoyed living out of college; formal meals in hall and all the rituals of college life had never interested him much, still less chapel. He was a confirmed agnostic, with an ingrained loathing of the Church of England. He loved the countryside, the garden, and the river. He took to going barefoot (to the shock of his landlady) and living the kind of life he had always wanted, with simple meals, plenty of places to bathe, and no schedule to keep. Since Grantchester lay at no great distance from Cambridge, he walked in for dinner with Henry James—author of, among much else, *The Turn of the Screw* and *The Wings of the Dove*—and made such an impression on the master that Brooke took him out in a punt on the Cam the next day. He received the useful advice from James that he should not be afraid of being happy.

Brooke was by no means isolated at Grantchester. He spent time with the painter Augustus John, who had camped nearby in a horse-drawn Gypsy caravan with his wife, his mistress, and five of his children. (John is reputed to have fathered over a hundred children by many different women over his long lifetime.) Brooke's social schedule seemed as crowded as ever. His interest in politics remained unabated, he attended the annual Fabian Summer School in Wales, and with the help of Dudley Ward, he even managed to engineer a visit to Bedales School, where he got a brief glimpse of Noel but was not permitted to take her out to tea.

However, his ever-resourceful friend Ward later succeeded in discovering that three of the four Olivier sisters, excluding Margery, were in a Bedales-style tented camp in Kent, south of London. That information enabled himself and Brooke to turn up as if by accident, once again. Brooke was able to take a walk along the banks of the aptly named Eden River with Noel, and after supper the three Olivier girls, along with a few of Brooke's friends, went bathing by the light of a bicycle lamp, which may have given him his first, and only dim sight of Noel nude. Given her upbringing, she would not necessarily have attributed anything particularly intimate to that, but its effect on Brooke may be imagined.

In August 1909, his parents rented a large house in Somerset for the month, and Mrs. Brooke incautiously suggested he invite his friends to stay. She must have been dismayed by the arrival of almost a dozen young people, including two of the Olivier sisters (but not Noel). She did not hide her displeasure at their breezy manners, their lateness at mealtimes, their casual clothing, or the fact that her son played tennis barefoot.

If Mrs. Brooke expected that her son's friends would sit around after dinner making conversation in the drawing room, she must have been disappointed. She made no secret of the fact: Brooke had to call them together and ask them to be kinder to his mother. An injury received when roughhousing with his friends in what seems to have been an English version of touch football laid him up in bed for a time under his mother's ever-watchful eye. That forced him to give up his plan to pay a visit to the Oliviers and led to a terrific row with his mother, which she won, as usual—she had a gift for the last word. With Brooke, even comparatively small injuries became medical dramas. The local doctor worried that the wound on his patient's ankle would lead to an abscess that would penetrate to the bone. Despite his robust appearance, Brooke's immune system seems to have been impaired, with what would eventually be fatal consequences.

Of more concern than Brooke's row with his mother was a seven-page letter from Margery Olivier, the oldest of the four sisters, warning him off Noel. Margery was of the opinion that no woman should marry before twenty-six or -seven, and that bringing love into Noel's life now would hinder her intellectual development. Whether Noel knew about Margery's letter is unclear, but it put Brooke into a simmering rage. To keep all this in perspective, however, it is worth bearing in mind that Noel was still a sixteen-year-old schoolgirl, and that Brooke at twenty-one had no means of support except an allowance from his parents, plus whatever small sums his poems brought in from magazines. He was hardly in a position to sweep Noel off her feet, even if she had wanted to be swept.

On the brighter side, Brooke had the pleasure of seeing four of his poems published and winning the occasional literary competition. He eventually got down to work on his essay. Even so, despite a phenomenal level of energy, he still seems to have been easily distracted from his work. He was as involved as ever in Fabian politics and also invested an enormous amount of time trying to recruit his friends into a scheme intended to prevent the onset of age, still his great fear. He outlined it in a letter over a thousand words long to Jacques Reverat, planning his "escape back into youth" and inveighing against "the pale serene Anglican windless harmonium-buzzing Eternity of the Christians." Brooke even suggested that he and a carefully selected few of his chosen friends—including Ka, Ward, and Margery and Bryn Olivier (but oddly not Noel)—should meet and compare notes on May 1, 1933, at breakfast time in, of all places, the Basel railway station in Switzerland. It is an oddly hysterical and irrational document but perhaps not so surprising for a man who had seen *Peter Pan* more times than he could count. Ironically, neither its author nor Jacques Reverat, to whom it had been addressed, would live to see 1933.

In December 1909, Brooke received the welcome news that his essay on John Webster for the Oldham Shakespearian Scholarship had won. It earned him a prize of seventy pounds, not an inconsiderable amount, given that his allowance from his parents was 150 pounds a year. His social life continued as busy as ever, and he once again went to Switzerland to ski after Christmas, although in the absence of Ka and Noel, he had nobody to pine over or lust after. On the way home, he ate some bad honey and arrived in Rugby so ill that it was feared he might die.

This time, however, Brooke's recovery ushered in a family tragedy at School Field House. His father was showing alarming signs of illness—his eyesight was failing, and he had lapses of memory and periods of severe depression. Today these would be signs pointing toward the possibility of a brain tumor, but in the early years of the twentieth century, the only suggestion the doctors could make was that Parker Brooke should rest and let Rupert take over as many of his father's duties as housemaster as he could. A visit to a specialist in London produced merely a tentative diagnosis of neuralgia, possibly the result of a blood clot in the brain. No treatment was suggested or indeed possible, and after a bedside vigil, Parker Brooke died less than two weeks later, at the age of fifty-nine. Almost needless to add, Rupert caught the flu at his father's funeral and had to be put to bed himself under the care of his mother.

Brooke was obliged to take a term off from Cambridge, but the bigger problem was that the house in which he had been born and grown up did not belong to the Brookes—it went with the job of being house master. Mrs. Brooke would have to be out of it before Easter. So Rupert found himself plunged into the unwelcome job of being a schoolmaster—exactly the future he least wanted for himself—and finding his mother another house. Domesticity in any form was abhorrent to Brooke, and all of a sudden he was plunged into the most extreme and demanding form of it. He was even given the task of putting down Tibby, the family cat, with poison in her milk.

Astonishingly, none of this prevented Brooke from writing poems, including one of his more controversial works, "A Channel Passage." H. W. Nevinson, the editor of *The Nation*,* described it as

---

* A British magazine in no way related to the American one with the same name.

a "disgusting sonnet," written because Brooke was afraid of being dismissed as "one more beautiful poet of beautiful themes."

> The damned ship lurched and shivered. Quiet and quick
>> My cold gorge rose; the long sea rolled; I knew
> I must think hard of something, or be sick;
>> And could think hard of only one thing—*you*!
> You, you alone could hold my fancy ever!
>> And with you memories come, sharp pain, and dole.
> Now there's a choice—heartache or tortured liver!
>> A sea-sick body, or a you-sick soul!
> Do I forget you? Retchings twist and tie me,
>> Old meat, good meals, brown goblets, up I throw.
> Do I remember? Acrid return and slimy,
>> The sole and slobber of a last year's woe.

Certainly this is not Brooke at his best, but it is doubtful that he wrote it in a deliberate attempt to shock the reader, still less Nevinson. It is, rather, another example of Brooke's remarkable felicity, his ability to turn anything, even seasickness, into verse.

Brooke was relieved when his mother was installed in her new home and he could return to Cambridge, having done his duty. In a perfect expression of innate class prejudice, he noted that for the first time in his life, his home had a number, 24 Bilton Road, Rugby, as opposed to a name, the School Field House. It was a small but distinct drop down the English social scale. A poet Brooke might be, and bohemian in his dress and appearance, but he never forgot that he was Rugbeian, a Cantabrigian, and a member of the upper class.

Despite Nevinson's dislike of "A Channel Passage," he would publish several of Brooke's poems in *The Nation*, and he was, predictably, swept off his feet when the poet himself eventually paid a surprise visit to the office. "Suddenly he came—an astonishing apparition. . . . Loose hair of deep-browny gold; smooth, ruddy face; eyes not grey bluish-white, but of living blue, really like the sky. . . . The whole effect was almost ludicrously beautiful." Nevinson was no impressionable girl—he was an experienced war correspondent who would be wounded in the same Gallipoli campaign that ended Brooke's life.

The notion that *how* you spend your time at Oxford or Cambridge is more important than what you learn there was seldom more true than it was of Brooke. He and Dudley Ward rented a horse and caravan to tour southwestern England campaigning for reform of the Poor Law: they favored replacing the workhouse with unemployment insurance, a core Fabian demand. He helped to put on a repeat performance of *Doctor Faustus*, with Ka Cox (a little unfairly given her weight) playing Gluttony, one of the Seven Deadly Sins. He managed to bring off a spectacular emotional coup by paying a surprise visit to a tented camp near Buckler's Hard, a picturesque village on the Beaulieu River in Hampshire, where Noel was living under canvas with her sister Bryn and a whole host of Brooke's friends.

He got her alone long enough to tell her how much he loved her and that he wanted to marry her. Noel cannot have been surprised by this, considering the torrential—and emotionally hysterical—flow of his letters, but she either failed to say no clearly enough or said she might do so when she was older. One guesses that she was more anxious to calm him down and end the conversation than flattered. Either way she and her sisters cannot have been pleased with the result, which was that although sworn to secrecy, Brooke told everyone that he and Noel were engaged. Since he did not tell his mother, nor Noel her parents (and there was of course no announcement in the newspapers), it was merely one more emotional dead end in his pursuit of her.

Academically, Brooke kept his head above water, winning another essay prize (yet again a welcome seventy pounds), demonstrating that he was still in the running for a fellowship, even though he wasn't sure he wanted one. On the other hand, what else was he to do? It was that or become a schoolmaster—he could hardly expect to make a living as a poet. His tutors advised him that he should probably write two dissertations, one in 1911, the other in 1912—"they think two shots is much the best thing," he wrote. The dissertations should involve original research and literary criticism, they said, and he should learn German, since much of the scholarship was in that language. This was a formidable task to accomplish in two years and would involve spending a term in Germany. In the meantime, his stays at 24 Bilton Place in Rugby grew shorter and less frequent, although he returned in haste at one point when his mother was knocked down in the street by a horse and briefly bedridden, a reminder that the automobile was not yet the chief danger to pedestrians.

Indeed, the only troubling thing in Brooke's life was a growing attraction to Ka Cox, who though not a stunning beauty like the Olivier sisters, was a stupendously good listener, warm, sympathetic, practical, and—it may have seemed to Brooke—far more likely to go to bed with him than Noel was in the foreseeable future.

The bohemian ways of Brooke and his friends, as mild as they might seem to us, had led to problems with his landlady. He arranged to move next door to the Old Vicarage when he returned from Germany, where the owners, Mr. and Mrs. Neeve, seemed more easygoing. The house was dilapidated and the garden untended, but Brooke was not a man who cared much about comfort, and despite the presence of wood lice in the summer, which dropped from the ceiling onto his bed, it would be as near as he ever came to a home of his own. He would make it into one of the most famous houses in England and the enduring symbol of the peace and tranquility in the last days of Edwardian England before the catastrophe that was coming.

BROOKE'S CHRISTMAS 1910 was full of self-imposed emotional stress. Ka had taken him to a bookshop to buy him a belated Christmas present, offering him any book in the shop he wanted, but instead of looking, he had waved at the shopkeepers as if to suggest that any book would do, he didn't care which. Afterward he blamed himself bitterly and wrote her a hysterical letter of apology for what seems to have been a minor incident. "I hate myself because I wickedly and unnecessarily hurt you several times. . . . I hurt you, Ka, for a bit, unforgivably and filthily and infamously; and I can't bear it." Ka wrote back calmly to say that it was all right. Calmness was Ka's strong suit, and her specialty was what she called "H to H," or heart-to-heart, intimate fireside talk. Brooke replied with yet another emotionally charged letter, then told her all about his love for the unreachable Noel.

Then he paid a visit to Noel to describe the whole incident to *her.* One can imagine the calm expression in those beautiful, placid blue-gray eyes as Brooke opened up to her this raging, turbulent mess of conflicting emotions and violent self-criticism in which he had assigned her, to her dismay, the starring role. Some measure of how matters stood between Brooke and Noel can be gleaned by comparing the letters they wrote to each other: Brooke's were long and bullying, while hers were short and apologetic. "Noel, Noel, Noel, I'll not let you go. I'll hold you by the shoulders, tight, tight, tight," he wrote. She replied that he should not think of her as a lover: "I'm not, Rupert, I'm affectionate, reverent, anything you like but not that. . . . I never feel jealous; only afraid of your loving me too much."

This is a pretty accurate description of Noel's position. It is unlikely that Brooke had ever held her tight. The most he may have gotten out of her was a gentle kiss on his forehead, which she referred to in one of her letters and which was likely an expression of sympathy or an attempt to calm him down. He wrote about all this in detail to Ka, looking for her approval or at least her sympathy. He had told Ka that he was in love with Noel, although she had surely already guessed, and he told Noel about his growing feelings for Ka, which was pretty much a guarantee that both women would feel hurt, confused, and even abused.

Under the circumstances, his going to Germany for a few months may have seemed like a blessing to all three of them.

THE FACT THAT HE WAS IN MUNICH did not prevent him from writing long, impassioned letters to both of them. He suffered from a certain degree of homesickness—he spent a lot of time in cafés drinking hot milk or coffee and reading *The Times* of the day before. His social life was almost as busy as it had been at home, and between his remarkable good looks, his charm, and his growing reputation as a poet, he was never short of invitations and saw almost as much theater as he did in England.

Judging by the length of his letters home, he must have spent many hours in the Munich cafés, scribbling away to his friends and his mother, and at least some time on his bed in his *Pension* studying German.

He stepped out of character momentarily in November to join in Munich's famous *Fasching*,* or Carnival, an event rather like a European version of New Orleans Mardi Gras. Munich was full of university students and artists. Not for many years would it establish a reputation as the birthplace of Nazism and as the white-hot center of German anti-Semitism and of what historian Hugh Trevor-Roper would later so aptly call "bestial Nordic nonsense."

Brooke wrote a Bowdlerized account of *Fasching* to his friend Jacques Reverat: "The young lay around in couples, huggin' and kissin', I roamed round, wondering if I couldn't, once, be even as they, as the animals. I found a round damp young sculptress. . . . We curled passionate limbs around each other in a perfunctory manner and lay in a corner, sipping each other and beer in polite alternation."

Perhaps because Reverat was close to Ka Cox, indeed had at one time been a rival for her affection, Brooke spared him the details. The "damp young sculptress" was in fact Élisabeth van Rysselberghe, the daughter of a distinguished Belgian neo-impressionist painter who had, among other things, befriended Vincent van Gogh, and whose wife Marie was a writer and close friend of the French Nobel Prize–winning novelist and essayist André Gide. Élisabeth is best described as "a free spirit." Indeed the phrase might have been coined for her— she would eventually fall in love with Gide, like her mother, although he was a homosexual, a former lover of Oscar Wilde, and an unapologetic pederast. Gide would eventually arrange what fellow French novelist Roger Martin du Gard called a rather cold-blooded "laboratory experiment" for Élisabeth and Gide's lover Marc Allégret to have an affair in the hopes of producing a son. That did not succeed, but Élisabeth, Gide, and Marc lived and traveled together for some time. She eventually produced a daughter, of whom Gide was the father (he would later adopt the girl, making it official), and she was rejected by her father for having a child out of wedlock.

---

* By a strange coincidence, *Fasching* begins at 11:00 a.m on November 11, exactly when the Great War ended, "on the 11th hour, of the 11th day, of the 11th month."

Much of this lay in the future, but Brooke must soon have become aware that Élisabeth van Rysselberghe was dramatically less easily shocked than Noel Olivier or Ka Cox. Brooke was, in fact, although he may not have realized it at first, severely upstaged by a young woman who had more sexual experience and far fewer inhibitions than he had. He mentioned her in passing, in letters to a few of his friends, although misspelling her name. But it was James Strachey, the future Freudian psychoanalyst, to whom he appealed for help, asking for advice about contraceptives.

Strachey was happy, or at any rate amused, to do his best in exploring "the whole sordid business," and replied with a long, detailed letter, including drawings, on the comparative merits of condoms, pessaries, and syringes. He was strongly against condoms; perhaps they were thicker then and more likely to tear than they are today. One would have thought they were more reliable and less trouble than the alternatives, about which Strachey hardly bothered to conceal his distaste. "Oh, but isn't it all too incredibly filthy?" he asked at the end of the letter. "Won't it perhaps make you sick of it?— Come quietly to bed with me instead."

Brooke seems to have complicated matters with Élisabeth by suggesting they go to Venice, certainly a more romantic setting than Munich, but at the last moment she decided against going, perhaps because Brooke overdid things in describing the various forms of contraceptives to her. It seems to have been his old fault of explaining and arranging things in detail, including the trip to Venice, when it is fairly clear that had he made an effort, Élisabeth might well have slept with him the morning after they had snuggled together sipping "each other and beer," at *Fasching*. The adage "strike while the iron is hot" seems not yet to have occurred to Brooke when dealing with women. Some of his biographers simply leave all this out. Nigel Jones, on the other hand, has suggested that Brooke may have suffered from premature ejaculation. Brooke wrote—once again to James Strachey, of all people—that his leave-taking of Élisabeth was "most painful." She had been lying on a sofa with her hair down, threatening to kill herself (she was apparently more than Brooke's equal in staging dramatic scenes), and adding that "it's not honest to want to be raped." That would seem to suggest that she offered herself to Brooke then and there, on the sofa, and that for reasons unknown he failed to take advantage of the moment. It was not the end of the story, for Élisabeth would continue to pursue him, and the jury is still out on whether their relationship was eventually consummated.

By this time, he had had enough of Munich and moved on to Vienna, which he did not like much better. He put up there with E. P. Goldschmidt, an acquaintance from Cambridge, whom he described to his mother as "a very rich and clever Jew who used to be at Trinity." He hoped that Ka might join him, but in the event he had to go to Florence to meet his brother Alfred, who was conducting Rupert's newly widowed aged godfather from Rugby on a tour as a kind of antidote to his grief. He trod through the museums and the sights of Florence dutifully but without enthusiasm, and wrote to Gwen Darwin a heartfelt cri de coeur, "Oh, my God! Do I long for England!" By the middle of May, he was back and installed in his rooms at the Old Vicarage, no doubt with a sigh of relief.

THE FACT THAT HE WAS AT HOME did not slow down the rate of Brooke's letters to Ka or for that matter to Noel. He was working hard on his Elizabethan playwrights—it must gradually have been dawning on him that if he wanted any kind of independent future, he would have to gain a fellowship at King's—and luxuriating in the picturesque garden of the Old Vicarage. He bathed daily in the cold water of the river, often more than once a day, and took up canoeing. His poems reflect his love of the English countryside, and to some degree his preference for plain, simple food. By choice he went barefoot and boasted that he didn't spend more than three pounds a year on clothes. He had reached the age when he was conscious of doing what he ridiculed as his "fresh, boyish stunt," which had so impressed Henry James, but by now it was second nature to him.

Frances Cornford, who had compared him to a young Apollo, had known him long enough to be inoculated against his boyish charm, but still rhapsodized about him: "It was a continual pleasure to look at him fresh every day—his radiant fairness, beauty of build, his broad head with its flung-back hair." She also shrewdly remarked that "he was both puritanical and romantic at once," not an easy combination. He sought endlessly to persuade Ka Cox to come and stay at the Old Vicarage, although she was stuck with looking after an elderly aunt. "Come. We'll be wholly frank!" he writes, "If you don't understand quite—nor, you know (don't tell anyone) do I. We'll explain and discuss, discover and guess, everything. . . . Come!"

But when she finally *did* come after weeks of passionate pleading, she stayed in Mrs. Neeve's side of the house, not his, no doubt partly not to shock Mrs. Neeve, but also because the puritan in Rupert Brooke constantly collided with his romantic impulses. Ka was all the things that Noel was not: she was big and heavy, had weak eyes, and wore a pince-nez. She was serious and devoted to Fabian politics. It is hard not to see her as having a much more maternal personality than the sharp-tongued and sharp-eyed Mrs. Brooke. Virginia Woolf, in *The Years*, compared her to a bear and nicknamed her "Bruin." Even Brooke, who was in the process of deciding that he loved her, compared her to a vegetable, and although he seems to have meant that as a compliment, it is hard to see why. She was intelligent, calm, and kindly, a good listener, and she offered—or seemed to Brooke to offer—a kind of pillowy comfort, unlike the spectacular beauty and sharp commonsense of Noel. He still considered himself engaged to Noel, however. Had he been an accomplished womanizer, he could hardly have created a more stressful situation—and that is without counting Élisabeth van Rysselberghe, who would soon arrive in hot pursuit.

Even leaving to one side the demands of Brooke's love life, he kept an amazing schedule. He was struggling to complete the dissertation on which his future depended. He was working with a young Swedish girl who visited him daily to edit two plays she had translated into English and from whom he hoped to learn enough Swedish to read the plays of Strindberg in the original. And he was also writing poems and negotiating for their publication, for which his mother had agreed to pay. Ironically, after Brooke's death, his books of poetry would sell hundreds of thousands of copies and earn the three fellow poets to whom he left the income from his works a substantial amount.

Brooke would get along well enough with his publisher, Frank

Sidgwick, a co-founder of Sidgwick & Jackson, himself a prolific writer of verse and prose who lived near Mrs. Brooke in Rugby. Sidgwick had a discerning eye for poetry, and although the author's mother was paying for the printing of the book, he did not hesitate to lock horns with Brooke over which poems should be excluded or revised so as not to shock the reader. Brooke was torn between the understandable desire to see his work published between hard covers at last and his dislike of being censored or told what to do by his publisher. Sidgwick disliked what he called "the seasick lover," "A Channel Passage," which he thought (correctly) reviewers would "pounce upon," and he finally persuaded Brooke to hide it at the very end of the book, where it might not be noticed. But he drew the line at "Lust," which he thought was neither good poetry nor "decent." Brooke thought eliminating it might move the book in the direction of "unimportant prettiness," in which he was perfectly correct, and finally persuaded Sidgwick to include it by changing the title to "Libido." But Sidgwick was not wrong in thinking that it, and "A Channel Passage," would be attacked.

## Libido

How should I know? The enormous wheels of will
    Drove me cold-eyed on tired and sleepless feet.
Night was void arms and you a phantom still
    And day your far light swaying down the street.
As never fool for love, I starved for you;
    My throat was dry and my eyes hot to see,
Your mouth so lying was most heaven in view,
    And your remembered smell most agony.

Love wakens love! I felt your hot wrist shiver
    And suddenly the mad victory I planned
Flashed real, in your burning bending head. . . .
My conqueror's blood was cool as a deep river
    In shadow; and my heart beneath your hand
        Quieter than a dead man on the bed.

Sidgwick particularly disliked "your remembered smell," but Brooke was adamant about what he referred to as "a woman's smell." It is clear enough that the poem describes the night he spent with Élisabeth in Munich that ended in her threat of suicide, but Brooke was not about to explain all that to Sidgwick. Brooke reluctantly agreed to a compromise: he would change the title, and Sidgwick would move the poem back in the book so that it wasn't among the first things the reader would see on opening it. As is so often the case with Brooke's poems, the sting is in the brutal last line, when he moves from verse to a simple familiar line of prose: "a dead man on a bed."

In Nigel Jones's *Rupert Brooke: The Life, Death and Myth,* Jones interprets this as the consequence of "a secret fear of sexual failure with women," which may or may not be true. Parsing Rupert Brooke's verse as straight autobiography, however, is dangerous territory. Brooke often gives the reader a glimpse of himself, but the poetry itself always seems more important to him than any hint of the confessional. The poem *could* equally well be read as a paean to sexual conquest. "The mad victory I planned / Flashed real, in your burning bending head," might be a reference to oral sex, while "your remembered smell" does not necessarily imply disgust, whatever Sidgwick may have thought; rather, the contrary. "Love wakens love" is not only the phrase of a great poet but suggests mutual sexual fulfillment rather than the reverse. Whatever had happened between them, it did not dampen Élisabeth van Rysselberghe's determination to see Brooke again.

TOWARD THE END OF THE SUMMER OF 1911, Brooke took a break, making plans to join his friends in a tented camp. He invited Virginia Stephen (soon to become Virginia Woolf) to visit him at the Old Vicarage and took her for a naked swim in the moonlight. Ironically, since she would eventually end her life by drowning herself, she enjoyed the bathing and was suitably impressed when Brooke performed his trademark trick of emerging from the water with an instant erection. She was correcting the proofs of her first novel, *The Voyage Out,* while he worked on his dissertation, but despite the nude bathing she stayed primly in Mrs. Neeve's half of the house.

In August, Brooke and his friends took over a tented camp near Dartmoor, in Devon, that a group of Old Bedalians (graduates of Noel's school) had put up. He had persuaded Ka and Virginia to join, as well as three of the Olivier sisters, including most important from his point of view Noel, and a mixed bag of male friends, which included Justin Brooke, a reluctant James Strachey, and Geoffrey and Maynard Keynes. To the amusement of everyone else, Strachey gave it up after one night and went to stay in a nearby inn.

The back-to-nature side of Brooke's personality was strong and very much of the time—it was a movement that the English and the Germans shared, although it took a different form in each of the two countries. In Germany, the *Wandervögel* hiked and communed with nature in the woods, with hearty organized marching and singing—this German passion for the outdoors would eventually be highjacked by the Nazis. In England, it took the form of tented camps and outdoor life, with simple (mostly vegetarian) food cooked over an open fire, long hikes, nude bathing, and reading aloud around the campfire at night. The fact that young men and women participated equally was shocking to their elders but a great attraction to the young.

Photographs of Brooke and his friends in camp show the women in long, loose skirts, their hair covered in Gypsy scarves, the men barefoot and in rough clothes. Life was not, and was not *meant* to be, easy. Ka, who apparently took to the camping life naturally, was up before dawn to cook the porridge, with the help of Virginia. Among the Neo-Pagans, women still seem to have been doing most of the cooking and washing up. Brooke set a pace for hiking that was vigorous and demanding, the more so because Dartmoor contains some of the wildest country in England, with hills of huge mossy rocks, wind-stunted trees, and bogs that could reputedly swallow a man or a horse. It is no accident that Arthur Conan Doyle's *The Hound of the Baskervilles* takes place on the moor. The 1911 camp was tinged for Brooke with a certain melancholy, as one by one his friends were getting engaged or married and beginning careers, and it may have crossed his mind that this might be one of the last of these occasions.

After the camp, Brooke was obliged to leave his semirural paradise in Grantchester for London so as to use the library of the British Museum for his dissertation. Although he did not have a good ear for music, he decided to add to his workload by taking singing lessons, apparently with mixed results. Unsurprisingly, he was often so tired that "he could barely lift his head," although that did not prevent him taking long walks on Hampstead Heath.

The pressure he felt over his dissertation, the fact that he loved both Ka and Noel, and the sudden presence of Élisabeth van Rysselberghe in London, "ostensibly to improve her English," all took a toll on Brooke, who reacted with a barrage of emotionally supercharged letters in which he accused Noel of coldness and indifference, and Ka of arousing in him sexual feelings she had no intention of satisfying. The completion of his dissertation did not lift his spirits; nor the publication of his book of poems—almost all the reviewers disliked "Libido" and "A Channel Passage," just as Sidgwick had predicted, and despite Brooke having set Ka to work correcting the proofs, there were still misprints, which aggravated him. He carefully changed "Libido" back to "Lust" in the copies he gave to friends, though not in his mother's.

He saw Nijinsky dance in *L'après-midi d'un faune* when the Ballets Russes came to London almost as many times as he had seen *Peter Pan*—he estimated fifteen. Although he met Élisabeth several times in London, they appear to have had no dramatic encounter or attempt to renew their sexual encounter in Munich, however it had concluded. Even to Brooke, whose indifference to comfort was notorious, his "sordid" rented room in London did not seem like an appropriate love nest. He suggested that *she* should find some place where they could meet, while she apparently thought that if Brooke wanted to sleep with her, he should be the one to make the arrangements. The result was that it all fizzled out, which may have been Brooke's intention all along, since he already had enough on his hands with Ka and Noel.

Seldom in the long history of male-female relationships has anybody ever produced a bigger storm of neurotic angst, jealousy, self-pity, and complaints than Brooke did in the autumn and winter of 1911, with so little to show for it in terms of sex. As for Élisabeth van Rysselberghe, although almost everybody describes her as "Rupert

Brooke's lover," this is an exaggeration. She retained strong feel-
ings for Brooke, but she put a more romantic spin on their relation-
ship than it merited. Apart from the scene in Munich that inspired
Brooke's "Libido," they do not seem to have had sex again.

In any case, he was caught up in a new romantic drama, or
rather *two* dramas. Noel, while still in constant correspondence
with Brooke, had met a fellow Bedalian, Ferenc Békássy, a young
Hungarian who was now an undergraduate at King's College, Cam-
bridge. Békássy was wealthy, handsome, and mildly exotic. A poet,
he was instantly attracted to Noel. Ka, in her slow and submissive
way, was attracted to Henry Lamb, a doctor who had given up med-
icine for painting and become a student and acolyte of Augustus
John. Lamb would go on to become a major figure in British art; a
frontline doctor in World War I, awarded the Military Cross; and a
respected war artist in the Second World War. He was good-looking
in a rugged way, but also everything that Brooke was not, sexu-
ally confident and a successful womanizer, without a romantic bone
in his body. There was no puritan undertow in Lamb's libido—he
followed it where it led, without guilt, which of course made him
attractive to many women. Certainly it affected Ka, who as much
as she loved Brooke was surely tired of dealing with the Sturm und
Drang that accompanied his feelings.

For years Brooke had been in the habit of joining a "reading
party" of his friends, at Lulworth, Dorset, after the inevitable stress
of Christmas with his mother in Rugby. Lulworth Cove is now a
popular tourist attraction, with over half a million visitors every July
and August, but it was then a quiet and secluded fishing village with
a single inn. In front of it was the cove, a perfect half circle cut by
the waves into the rolling, grassy hills behind it. It would be hard to
find a more picturesque spot in England. Brooke had accepted the
presence of "Signor Bekashy (as it's pronounced)," as he described
him, before the discovery that Békássy was writing letters to Noel.
Worse yet, he had not realized that Henry Lamb would be joining
the party while Ka was there. It was an emotional one-two punch,
and his nerves, already stretched to the breaking point by Christmas
with his mother, shortly gave way and produced a major crisis—
perhaps *the* major crisis—in his life.

*

The reading party consisted of two groups that have since seemed to be almost separate, the Neo-Pagans and the Bloomsbury group. The Neo-Pagans centered around Brooke and were outdoorsy, keen on tented camps and hikes, while the Bloomsberries were London-based, their central figures James and Lytton Strachey. Ka, the Olivier sisters, Gwen and Jacques Reverat, and Justin Brooke were in the first group; Henry Lamb, the Stracheys, Virginia Stephen (Woolf), Maynard Keynes, and the painter Duncan Grant were in the second. At the time, the two groups were not sharply divided. It was Brooke who later drew the line that separated them.

He arrived in Lulworth in a state of pitiable exhaustion and misery, despite a letter of high praise for his book from Edward Marsh. Ka, on the contrary, was observed to be in high spirits and was absent for most of the first day, taking a long walk with Henry Lamb, who was staying nearby with Augustus John and his sprawling family group. At least one biographer has speculated that Ka and Lamb may have had sex on their walk, but given what we know of Ka, that does not seem likely. Besides, it was the end of December. To those who have experienced the English wintertime seaside climate, outdoor sex on the windy cliffs around Lulworth sounds like a dubious proposition.

Whatever took place, Ka's emotions were inflamed, and the next day she decided to have it out with Brooke. She told him that she was in love with Lamb. The result was a stormy scene in which Brooke offered to marry her, while she, for once, stuck to her guns. She intended to marry Lamb. (He was already married, but nobody seemed to have paid any attention to that, least of all Lamb.) Ka did not point out that Brooke had been telling her about his feelings for Noel Olivier for three years, or that he had even shared with her a somewhat sanitized account of his relationship with Élisabeth van Rysselberghe. Who, she might have asked, was *he* to talk about fidelity? He was in such a state that Ka promised she would join him in Munich, where he intended to continue his study of German, since otherwise he threatened to go mad.

None of this was hidden from the other members of the reading party. Almost before it was over, Lytton Strachey was writing long descriptions of what had happened, coupled with advice to Henry

Lamb, who had wisely fled back to Augustus John's family group. The notion that he might be expected to *marry* Ka, not just sleep with her, had apparently not occurred to him.

The presence of the unfortunate Békássy, who had been pursuing Noel, was perhaps the final blow to Brooke's fragile ego—fragile anyway when it came to women—and he was reduced to such an anguished state of mind that the Reverats thought it necessary to get him down to London and put him in the hands of a professional. Dr. Maurice Craig, a Harley Street psychiatrist (referred to as a "nerve specialist," to avoid any suggestion that his patients were mentally ill), was a doctor of some substance, whose patients would include Virginia Woolf and HRH the Prince of Wales. In those pre-Freudian days, though, Craig could diagnose Brooke's problem only as "a severe nervous breakdown."*

Brooke's ongoing seesaw between homosexual and heterosexual impulses, his love-hate relationship with his dominating mother, the war between his puritan instincts and his own desires, his disgust at female eroticism once he had aroused it, his heightened sensitivity as a poet, none of these touchy issues were explored. Craig's judgment was simply that Brooke was overworked and too introspective for his own good. He needed complete rest, food (Brooke had lost a stone, fourteen pounds), and the removal of any form of intellectual stimulus. Bedrest and a rich diet, including milk and stout, were prescribed, and since Brooke's mother was paying a visit to Cannes, Brooke should be sent there at once to be put under her care. It is hard to imagine a more destructive scenario for Brooke than that, but by that time he was in no position to resist.

Brooke's stay in Cannes with his mother overseeing his recovery would have been a comic nightmare, except that it was real. He put on weight—the recovery of mental patients was then measured by how much weight they gained—but depriving Brooke of outdoor

---

* In 1917–18, Dr. Craig, not surprisingly, became one of the doctors who treated officers for "neurasthenia," or "shell shock," like Siegfried Sassoon and Wilfred Owen, so that they were stable enough to be sent back to the lines to resume their duties and be killed. Other Ranks (i.e., common soldiers) with the same symptoms were more likely to be court-martialed and in some extreme cases executed by a firing squad for "cowardice in the face of the enemy."

exercise and intellectual stimulation could only make him worse. It was here, tucked up on a chaise longue, covered by a blanket under the Mediterranean sun, sipping Bovril and watched over by his mother, that Brooke began to develop many of the explanations for what had happened to him, which came increasingly to shape his personality beneath the surface charm and good looks. He blamed James Strachey for pushing Ka toward Henry Lamb, totally overlooking the possibility that Ka, as a grown woman, might have a mind of her own about the man she wanted to go to bed with. This would lead Brooke to a growing dislike of homosexuals and a mistrust of all the Bloomsberries, as people who were too clever for their own good and had conspired against him, having been misled by Strachey, to whom he assigned the role of the serpent in Eden.

This was not an instant moment of insight; it would take some time to develop fully in Brooke's mind, but it would end by separating him from many of those who were his friends and strengthening some of his core prejudices. He was against feminism, and his nascent anti-Semitism was sharpened by the fact that Virginia Stephen would shortly marry Leonard Woolf, a Jew. It was as if an embryo Colonel Blimp were growing beneath the good looks, the charm, and the poetic genius.

Evidently Mrs. Brooke did not read the letters her son was writing. Those to Ka Cox are long, and full of ideas that would have dismayed Dr. Craig. Brooke complained very reasonably about being stuffed like "an overfed puppy" and pointed out that his mother was one of those formidable Englishwomen who supposed that every foreigner would understand what she said so long as she spoke English loudly and firmly enough. Then he shifted gears to a supercharged emotional level that no doubt made Ka wish she had not promised to meet him in Munich. "I'm concentrating on getting well. . . . I can't help feeling such amazing energy and life in all my limbs and mind, that I'm racked to be up and off to meet you at the Hauptbahnhof. You go burning through every vein and inch of me, till I'm all Ka; and my brain's suddenly bursting with ideas and lines and flames, and my body's all for you." His letters to Ka are a strange mixture of everyday concerns—he worried that she wouldn't know how to get to Munich on her own by train, on his usual assumption that women couldn't do anything by themselves—and sudden returns to hysteria, melodrama, and self-abasement: "I'm so hampered and spoilt because there are things I dare not face, and depths I dare not look into."

Again and again he reminded her of her promise to join him in Munich, and that his survival depended on it. "But you, and only you in the world, understand my horrible nature. It's so importantly my humiliation and my—safety, joy, what is it called? I may be, and shall be, perhaps, sane and everything else one day. But, the dirty abyss I am now—I've let you see. Don't pretend you don't know me, fool."

It seems unlikely that any of this was reassuring to Ka, but one of her virtues was that she was totally dependable: once she had given her word, she would keep it. It was Brooke's mother who was keeping him in Cannes, perhaps with good reason, since on his first day out of bed, he was so weak that he had to be supported by his brother Alfred. "I can see the Ranee thinks she's going to keep a hand on me for a month or six weeks," he wrote Ka. "But I give her ten days at the outside. I shall have to be beastly to her, I suppose."

One has to bear in mind that Brooke was twenty-four. There is no plausible reason to suppose that he couldn't have gotten out of bed and taken a train to Munich if he wanted to, but part of his problem was that he still accepted his mother's authority and feared confronting her. That he *was* getting better is certain—he even managed to write a heartfelt letter to James Strachey, mentioning how his mother mixed his Ovaltine and admitting, "I thought I was mad for two days," without specifying which two days he was thinking about. If Brooke was referring to Lulworth, then the letter may be read as a kind of apology.

Whatever Dr. Craig might have thought of this tsunami of letters from Brooke's hotel in Cannes, most of us today would recognize them as emotional blackmail, an attempt to place the blame for Brooke's "breakdown" on the submissive Ka and to convince her that his sanity depended on her doing exactly what he wanted her to do. For days this barrage of letters continued—Ka was already in Munich while Rupert, still under his mother's thumb, was sipping Ovaltine and Bovril in Cannes.

Inadvertently, the tone of Brooke's entire correspondence with Ka was about to descend from tragedy to farce. Brooke had sent her a long letter written while he was in "a slough of despond." He delayed sending one that said he was feeling well enough for tea with Balfour, alarming Ka so badly that she sent *him* a telegram to say that she was coming to Cannes at once. This put the fat in the fire. Mrs. Brooke had no idea that Ka was the person to whom Rupert was writing, still less that Rupert was planning to meet her as soon as possible. The sudden appearance of Ka in Cannes was out of the question, so he had to persuade her that she must stay in Munich, that it was a much more difficult journey than she had supposed. He managed to escape from his mother long enough to send Ka a telegram begging her not to come, but she did not reply at once, so he spent the next two days in fear that she might arrive in the hotel lobby at any moment.

Brooke was put out of his misery at last by a telegram from Ka to say that she was staying put, but over the next few days he sent her a wild fury of long letters, half erotic ("I kiss every inch, every inch of you, and every thought of your heart"), half reading like a railway schedule or a travel itinerary from Thomas Cook & Son, an office of which was just around the corner from his hotel. Brooke was now planning to meet Ka in Verona, perhaps because of its romantic *Romeo and Juliet* associations.

Eventually, since he could not put it off any longer, Brooke finally had it out with his mother, causing a scene in which she gave way and agreed to pay his travel expenses. He warned Ka against making too many friends in Munich, since they might interfere with the time they had together. He was still going to absurd lengths to hide the truth from his mother. Ka must find a way to post a card from him to the Ranee from Munich so she would not know that he was in Verona. His letter is full of complicated plans for outwitting the Ranee. "Your duty's so very simple," he wrote Ka, "You get into the 10.40 p.m on Monday night. . . . Then we commence rushing towards each other." Upset that Ka had gone to a dance against his wishes, he left the bother of choosing a hotel in Verona to her, and as usual he added a word of advice, in the form of a command: "You're to travel with a RUG, because the Brenner's *cold.*"

He was not wrong—the Brenner Pass *is* cold—but Ka could hardly have enjoyed being treated like a child, and she surely must have felt uncomfortable at the unspoken reality that however much she felt sorry for Brooke, she was in love with another man.

IF KA THOUGHT VERONA would be the passionate lovefest Brooke had promised her in his letters, she would have been sharply disappointed. He arrived in such a state of exhaustion and mental turmoil that she rushed to a pharmacy to buy tonics and pills and effectively took over from his mother the job of nursing him. Her patience and calm succeeded rather better than his mother's strictness, but he was still in a miserable state. The romantic interlude Brooke had planned in Venice had to be abandoned. A pause in Salzburg was transformed into an all-night crisis in which Brooke bared his soul. From there they made their way on to Munich, a very subdued couple, rather more like an invalid and his nurse than Romeo and Juliet.

He had resumed correspondence with James Strachey, describing himself as "a broken blossom," a bad sign because Strachey was not only gay and manipulative but also seems to have had a wide streak of Schadenfreude in him—he enjoyed the emotional suffering of his friends. It is hard not to imagine a snide, malicious smile on his face when he informed Brooke that the Hungarian Ferenc Békássy, his rival for the affection of Noel Olivier, had been invited to become an Apostle. What exactly was ailing Brooke is hard to guess; it may have been hysteria brought on by the approaching need to make critical life decisions and assume the role of an independent adult. Should he reach for an academic career? The result of his dissertation would influence that, of course, but was it what he wanted? Should he marry Ka, if she would have him? Should he continue to pursue Noel, who was almost old enough by now to get married but showed no signs of wanting to? Could he make a clean break with his mother, at the risk of her cutting off his 150-pound annual allowance? How long could he go on living an undergraduate life in lodgings in Grantchester, writing poems and book reviews, while his friends got married or pursued real careers? Was his libido homosexual or heterosexual? That it might combine both does not seem to have occurred to him, although James Strachey was forever slyly hinting at the possibility in his letters.

That Brooke felt boxed in is understandable. He was trying to decide not only what to do with his life but who he really was. He was surely not helped by Dr. Craig's attempt to treat all this as a physical illness, with force-feeding and bedrest, rather than as an existential one. Today he would be treated with some form of psychotherapy, to get at the underlying cause of his emotional distress. He would be given prescriptions to calm his anxiety, from Abilify to Xanax, none of which were available in the early twentieth century, for Ka to pick up at the *farmacia* in Verona. He was adrift in a sea of Freudian symptoms in the pre-Freudian age, all of it intensified by the fact that he was off-the-chart handsome and an immensely gifted poet. He had everything, in fact, but the happiness and independence he craved, and it is hard to see how marrying Ka would have changed that except by making him dependent on Ka's money instead of his mother's.

Ka got him reinstalled in his old rooms in Munich and took care of him in her practical, self-sacrificing way, while Brooke communicated all this in letters to his friends in England. He was now feeling almost as resentful of Ka as he had been of his mother. He still believed that getting Ka away to some secluded, romantic place and having sex with her would solve his problems.

Brooke had intended to take both Élisabeth and Ka to Venice and failed, so this time he took Ka to a *Pension* on the Starnberg-ersee, nineteen miles from Munich, a famous beauty spot with snow-covered mountains visible from the lake, in which Mad King Ludwig had died. As if to underscore the purpose of the trip, he registered them as *Herr und Frau* Brooke, probably also necessary because most places then would not have allowed an unmarried couple to share a room. Still, it must have let Ka know what was going to be expected of her.

The results of this night together were traumatic for them both. It is impossible to know whether Ka was a virgin (and Brooke was the person least likely to guess), but she cannot help but have felt that she was being pressured into having sex with him while she loved Henry Lamb. In addition, she had to cope with the unpleasant realities of turn-of-the-century contraception. The irrigator method, recommended by the ever-resourceful James Strachey, involved rushing down the corridor to the shared toilet immediately after sex to rinse out the vagina with a syringe. That procedure was neither reliable nor, one would think, likely to produce warm postcoital afterplay. Things cannot have been made easier by Ka's decision—she was always one for complete honesty, even when it was inappropriate—to tell Brooke that just before leaving for Germany, she had spent a weekend at a country house where Henry Lamb was also a guest. This was surely not the ideal moment for this confession. It is possible, even likely, that it was also Brooke's first experience of heterosexual intercourse (assuming that the attempt with Élisabeth van Rysselberghe was a humiliating washout). His rage at being told that Ka had been under the same roof as Henry Lamb cannot have made things easier.

In the aftermath, he alternated between bouts of anger at Ka's "betrayal" and passionate declarations of love. His sexual experience with Ka, apparently repeated the next night, seems to have aroused in him a certain clinical curiosity, which for once James Strachey could not supply the answer. Only a couple of weeks after their first night together on the Starnbergersee, he wrote Ka a rather incoherent letter addressing the subject of female orgasm: "The important thing, I want to be quite clear about, is, about women 'coming off.' What it means, objectively—What happens. And also what you feel when it happens."

It is hard to imagine that Ka can have enjoyed this line of questioning, but it was surely better than Brooke in a dominating vein: "Ka, you've once given yourself to me: and that means more than you think. It means very importantly that you're not your own mistress. And that far more truly and dangerously than if I had you under lock and key—and with my 'physical superiority.' It means that you're not as free to do anything as you were. It means you mayn't hurt yourself, because it hurts me." This is probably a warning against Ka's seeing Henry Lamb again: Lamb would hurt Ka, and Ka's being hurt would hurt Brooke, but the subtext is clear: once she had "given herself" to him, Ka belonged to Brooke.

Not surprisingly, Ka was overwhelmed by the alternating storms of passion and recrimination, coupled with the need to keep nursing Brooke and to deal with his determination to keep the whole affair secret from his mother. Four days later, she ended the idyll and took him home to England like a patient being sent from one sickbed to the next. Brooke's collapse did not prevent him from planning for the future. His friend from King's, Dudley Ward, engaged now to Annemarie von der Planitz, was moving to Berlin in April as the correspondent of *The Economist*. Once Dudley and Annemarie were settled, Brooke planned to come to Berlin as their guest and seek out a place where he and Ka could live together secretly, on the pretext that he was improving his German. Ka gave in to this, one suspects because that seemed easier than arguing about it.

NATURALLY, SHE DID NOT DELIVER HIM personally to his mother. In fact, no sooner was he home than Brooke was frantically urging his friends not to mention that Ka had been with him in Munich. It is remarkable the degree that Brooke still had to tiptoe around his mother and how cleverly he succeeded, despite her determination to protect him—from what, one wonders? It is hard to see why she would have objected to Ka, whom she preferred to the Olivier girls. Ka had perfect manners, she was well educated but far from being a bluestocking, she was of the same class as the Brookes, and her Fabianism was not that much farther left than Mrs. Brooke's own Liberal sympathies. Not only did she own her own small cottage in Woking, and a flat in Westminster shared with her sister, but she had had a modest private income left to her by late father.

Of course, the Ranee might have objected to *anyone* Rupert wanted to marry. In the days when a maid was likely to place the post on a gleaming silver tray twice a day, one would have thought that Mrs. Brooke's eagle eye would have noticed the number of letters from Woking in Ka's firm handwriting, but apparently not.

Brooke was determined to have Ka to stay, but he was unsure how best to approach it with his mother. He endlessly wrote Ka long letters proposing different ways he might bring the subject up with the Ranee. It was a doubly delicate task since he wasn't sure that Ka wanted to come to Rugby in the first place. The letters are jocular in tone, but only on the surface—after all, this is a twenty-four-year-old man strategizing about how to ask his mother if he could ask a friend to visit for a weekend! The notion of having Mrs. Brooke as a mother-in-law might have been enough to discourage Ka from marrying Rupert Brooke, even had she wanted to.

It was his idea to ask Ka and James Strachey together, perhaps in the unlikely hope that the Ranee might think the two were fond of each other. His account of the conversation with his mother is harrowing, although meant to be light-hearted. "I think she suspects you a bit," he adds. "But she always does. You, I, she, James: what a tangle of cross-motives and dissimulations it'll be! We'll want our clear heads. But it'll be fun."

But it was not fun. Ka came, and in a rare moment when Mrs. Brooke left them alone for a moment, Brooke had a fit of temper, and Ka, who had hardly even unpacked, left after one night with a "garbled" excuse that must have made the Ranee even more suspicions. It cannot have helped matters to see the man who wanted to marry her sitting like a well-behaved, albeit resentful teenager making small talk with his mother.

Ka's departure from Bilton Road was followed, for Brooke, by two pieces of destabilizing bad news. First, his dissertation had not done the trick: the fellowship at King's College had gone to a professor of physiology by thirteen votes to one. Brooke claimed that he was not surprised, and that he didn't really want the fellowship, but it would have given him a substantial degree of independence from his mother and a center to his life. This blow was softened by hints from fellow Angels that if he was patient, he would get the next fellowship, but his letters reflect an angry, acrimonious, and self-pitying pessimism. He made the sensible decision to get out of the house and visit people, including the Oliviers, where he resumed his pursuit of Noel.

When he arrived at Ka's cottage, he was startled by a second piece of bad news. She told him she had missed her period and was pregnant. This set Brooke off on another storm of anguished correspondence. He toyed with the idea of suicide; he thought Ka should—*must*—marry him at once, before he left for Berlin; he agonized over the dates when he and Ka had made love and over whose fault it was that the irrigator (syringe) recommended by James Strachey had apparently not worked. He then went off to the New Forest with James to brood upon his fate and write letters to Noel. He may, or may not, have shopped for a pistol with which to kill himself, but in the end he borrowed from James for the trip to Berlin and went there to wait for Ka.

Aside from the availability of Dudley Ward and his bride-to-be, there does not appear to be a good reason for Brooke's having chosen Berlin as the place in which to reconcile with Ka. One might have thought that a big, noisy, foreign city would be the last place that would appeal to Brooke, but perhaps the main thing it had to recommend it was that it was a long way from Rugby and his mother. Dudley Ward's apartment was crowded and busy with the preparations for his wedding to Annemarie, including both mothers-in-law.

Brooke spent his time hunting for a place for himself and Ka to stay, settling on Neustrelitz, a pretty little town about an hour from Berlin. Perhaps to avoid the mothers-in-law, he took to sitting several hours a day over a cup of coffee or hot milk at the Café des Westens on the Kurfürstendamm in Charlottenburg, the equivalent of the Café de Flore in Paris, but without the outdoor tables.* Here he wrote what is surely his best-known poem, a curious blend of homesickness and satire in which he unveiled his innermost prejudices, while at the same time making fun of them. "The Old Vicarage, Grantchester" is a triumphant work of art, ranging from lyricism to robust comedy, all of it very English. It ends with the lines that not only sealed Brooke's reputation as a major English poet but described for all time the quiet, upper-middle-class Edwardian world that was about to be destroyed.

Just now the lilac is in bloom,
All before my little room;
And in my flower-beds, I think,

---

* My uncle, Sir Alexander Korda, used to go there often in the 1920s when he was making films in Berlin. He said if you sat there long enough, you would meet everyone you knew—and a lot of people you didn't want to know. It received a direct hit during a Royal Air Force bombing raid in 1945 and was completely destroyed.

Smile the carnation and the pink;
And down the borders, well I know,
The poppy and the pansy blow. . . .
Oh! there the chestnuts, summer through,
Beside the river make for you
A tunnel of green gloom, and sleep
Deeply above; and green and deep
The stream mysterious glides beneath,
Green as a dream and deep as death.
Oh! damn! I know it! and I know
How the May fields all golden show,
And when the day is young and sweet,
Gild gloriously the bare feet
That run to bathe. . . .

                              *Du Lieber Gott!*
Here am I, sweating sick, and hot,
And there the shadowed waters fresh
Lean up to embrace the naked flesh.
*Temperamentvoll* German Jews
Drink beer around; and *there* the dews
Are soft beneath a morn of gold.
Here tulips bloom as they are told; . . .


                    #
God! I will pack, and take a train,
And get me to England once again!
For England's the one land, I know,
Where men with Splendid Hearts may go;
And Cambridgeshire, of all England,
The shire for Men who Understand;
And of *that* district I prefer
The lovely hamlet Grantchester. . . .

Oh, is the water sweet and cool,
Gentle and brown, above the pool?
And laughs the immortal river still

Under the mill, under the mill?
Say, is there Beauty yet to find?
And Certainty? and Quiet kind?
Deep meadows yet, for to forget
The lies, and truths, and pain? . . . oh! yet
Stands the Church clock at ten to three?
And is there honey still for tea?

Brooke liked to pretend that he didn't take his own poetry seriously, but his real feelings can be measured by the cable he sent the editor of *Basileon*, the King's College magazine, who was holding up the printing for Brooke's contribution: A MASTERPIECE IS ON ITS WAY. He made two copies, one for *Basileon*, and the other, interestingly enough, for Bryn Olivier, to whom he described it with typical Brookean understatement as "a silly quickly written thing." He was reaching out toward Bryn now with long letters about marriage, mostly pessimistic. "Everybody's a pretty lonely figure, drifting in the gloom," sums up his view of the institution, despite which he was clearly still suggesting marriage to Bryn, even though he was waiting for Ka, presumably pregnant, to arrive. Noel's evasive replies to Brooke's suggestions of marriage to *her* seem to have cooled him off on that subject, although nothing she could do would ever break the emotional tie that had bound Brooke to her since the evening her father had brought her at the age of fifteen to the one-course Fabian dinner at King's College, where his eyes had met hers over the shards of the broken coffee cup.

It was Brooke's fate to love and be loved by women who did not want to marry him, perhaps because they recognized that part of his appeal was that he was *not* marriageable, that the everyday responsibilities and commitments of marriage were beyond him. He had reacted in fury the last time Bryn turned him down—he described her rebuffing letter cattily to James Strachey as giving "the impression of a thoroughly superior housemaid." But despite this new "absolute smack in the face for me," he was still proposing marriage to her, and sent a copy of his poem to her instead of to Ka, or to Noel, who might calmly have picked it apart.

The poem almost immediately became Brooke's most popular

and anthologized piece of work, making him famous far beyond the relatively small numbers of people who had read his poetry before. It represents in its own sly way Brooke's view of an idealized, preindustrial, rural England, still rooted in local pride.

Brooke might have steered a conventional poetic course through rural rhapsodies with just enough patriotism thrown in to give him a chance at being named poet laureate when he was old, but he constantly set challenges for himself that most poets would have avoided. Who else would write not one but *two* poems from the point of view of a fish, "Heaven" and "The Fish," both of them brilliant? "The Old Vicarage, Grantchester," with its odd blend of knockabout music-hall comedy and lyricism soaring toward perhaps one of the most famous last lines of any English poem is Brooke at his best.

THE PLANNED-FOR IDYLL with Ka did not go well. They stayed only two days in Neustrelitz, then moved on twice from there. Quite apart from Brooke's muddled feelings, Ka was sick, possibly the result of a miscarriage, and rather to the relief of both of them, she was summoned home to help her sister, leaving Brooke to stay on with Dudley Ward and his new bride. "I remain dead," he told Dudley, "I care practically nothing for any person in the world. I've anxiety, and a sort of affection for Ka—but I don't really care." He had reached perhaps the lowest point of the nervous breakdown that had engulfed him during the past year. Writing "The Old Vicarage, Grantchester" may have been, in that sense, cathartic. He visited the Van Gogh exhibition in Cologne, where James Strachey joined him, and they returned together to England. Brooke hastened to Rugby to mend things with the Ranee—he had not kept in touch with her except for brief messages and could not tell her that the purpose of his stay in Germany had been to be with Ka Cox, still less that it had been a failure.

He returned to Grantchester with some relief in July. On his first afternoon home, his landlady Mrs. Neeve brought in his tea tray and brightly remarked, "You see? There *is* honey still for tea!" a sign that his poem had already begun to enter into the English consciousness.

Brooke's correspondence over the next couple of months, as well as his restless travel, reveals that he had not yet found peace in Grantchester. He saw Ka once more, a meeting that seems to have stressed even the normally calm Ka. He began to elaborate a complicated explanation for his continuing unhappiness that centered on Lytton Strachey for having intrigued and gossiped against him and that eventually came to include all the members of the Bloomsbury Group. He was still, for the moment, unable to choose—in his own mind—between Bryn, Noel, and Ka, or to finally accept that his own behavior toward Ka had for all practical purposes ended their relationship. Like Noel, she would always love him, but realistically, without any supposition that they would ever share a life.

Edward Marsh, although mildly miffed by the fact that Brooke had neglected to send him a copy of his new poem, lavished praise on it, ever so slightly diluted by astute criticism. He rearranged his flat at Gray's Inn to give Brooke a pied-à-terre in London. But Brooke had already taken the first steps toward the decision that would change his life: to cut loose from everyone and everything for a new beginning.

In the meantime, he was in the unusual position of being pursued by an attractive young woman, rather than pursuing her. Of all days, on November 11, 1911 (the First World War would end on November 11, 1918), Phyllis Gardner, a striking, red-haired twenty-one-year-old art student at the Slade School of Fine Art in London, was having tea with her mother at Kings Cross railway station. While waiting to board a train to Cambridge, her mother pointed Brooke out to her across the room.

Phyllis would later remark that she fell in love with Brooke the moment she saw him, which is certainly possible—he had that effect even on far less impressionable people. She was drawn to his "mop of silky golden hair," his profile, and his expression of fierce intelligence. Even over tea in a railway station buffet, he seemed to glimmer like a vision. On the train, to her surprise, he took a seat in the compartment where she was sitting. Her mother, who was seeing her off, would play a remarkable role in the affair between her daughter and Rupert Brooke, rather like that of the nurse in *Romeo and Juliet*, albeit with less tragic results. Mrs. Gardner, from the platform, leaned in through the open window and mentioned all of Phyllis's friends in Cambridge, in the hope that Brooke might say he knew one and strike up a conversation with her daughter. But he turned his attention to a sheaf of manuscripts instead, so Phyllis took a sketch pad from her purse and proceeded to draw him. They did not exchange words, but that night at Newnham College, where her aunt was a don, she was tempted to put the sketch pad under her pillow, then decided to prop it up on a chair instead, opened to the sketch so she could look at it.

Phyllis was not easily ignored. The next day she showed the sketch to as many people as she could, asking for the man's name. She thought that "a dark, tragic-looking creature with great wistful eyes" showed some recognition. This was in fact Margery, the oldest of the Olivier sisters, who cannot have been pleased that this young woman was trying to track down the man who claimed to love her sister Noel. The next day Phyllis was taken to tea by her aunt, and on the way, to her astonishment—Cambridge is a small town—the young man passed her riding a bicycle and gave her "a wild smile" and a look of recognition. She was astute enough to notice he was not wearing an undergraduate's gown. When she showed the sketch at tea, her hostess instantly put a name to it: Rupert Brooke.

Phyllis's attraction to Brooke was instant and magnetic—it was literally love at first sight. Her mother's interest in pushing Phyllis toward Brooke came about because she herself was a poet and was eager to have her work read and, if possible, published. Unknown to either of them, it was not the best moment to attract Brooke's attention. He was, to put it gently, distracted: dealing with the emotional fallout of his affair with Ka, revising his poems for inclusion in Edward Marsh's *Georgian Poetry*, still trying to thaw the impregnable Noel, and working on the thesis about John Webster and the Elizabethan theater that would determine whether he would finally be offered a fellowship by King's College. He was overworked, under severe mental pressure, and was developing a hard kernel of fear, so far largely repressed, that he was being persecuted by James and Lytton Strachey and that they had turned the whole Bloomsbury group against him.

Phyllis set out to track Brooke down—at one point she actually cornered Noel, who, however little she wanted to sleep with Brooke herself, was understandably unwilling to share him with this redheaded art student. She merely told Phyllis that he was hard to "catch." Brooke himself soon heard of Phyllis's pursuit of him and at first was amused rather than interested. Suffering from his usual delusion that the women in his life wanted to hear all about their rivals, he wrote to Ka about it, referring to Phyllis jocularly as "the Romance of my Life."

He managed to avoid Phyllis for a considerable time, but her mother proved every bit as overbearing and formidable as his own. Eventually he was trapped into a lunch with both of them at a party of people interested in poetry and the arts. It was hardly Brooke's milieu, one would think—he was very conscious of being a professional poet, as opposed to Mrs. Gardner, who was an amateur one. Nor could Mrs. Gardner easily ask him to read her poems there, or Phyllis have an intimate conversation with him. He arrived late, but his effect on Phyllis is best described by herself: "the door opened and it was as though the sun had suddenly risen. Whether or not he was really about a head taller than most of us there I am not in a position to say: but it seemed so to me. Also I do not know if other people found his presence as radiant and full of sunshine as I did; it was extremely easy to see him in one's mind's eye with a halo of gold."

Rarely has any young woman gone into a love affair with more untrammeled illusions than Phyllis Gardner, or had more help from her own mother. Soon Brooke was staying with the Gardners for a weekend. His bedroom was close to Phyllis's, so that when she looked out her window, she caught a glimpse of his profile in the moonlight as he leaned on his windowsill. Before long, she accepted his invitation to drop in on him when she was in London, and she happened to do so while he and Eddie Marsh were having a late breakfast. She was struck by the contrast between Brooke "with his wild golden hair and keen blue eyes" and the smooth, man-of-the-world, buttoned-up demeanor of Marsh. She had already worked out that carrying her paint box, with the implication that she was going to paint Brooke's portrait, would serve as an explanation for her visit.

When Phyllis and her mother spent a weekend with friends in Cambridge, she was allowed to bicycle to tea at Grantchester unchaperoned, unusual for the day. Brooke wore a blue, open-necked shirt and white flannels, as Phyllis carefully noted with a painter's eye, and after tea he took her for a walk along the river, when they came to a place where they couldn't cross. He suggested they swim across it. Although this was early October in England, the weather hardly likely to have been warm, they both stripped naked and swam across the river holding their clothes above their heads. She dropped his boots. Naked bathing by moonlight seems to have been Brooke's standard operating procedure, as he had done with Virginia Woolf during her visit to the Old Vicarage. When they emerged from the river, he did not surprise her with an instant erection, as he had James Strachey and Virginia Woolf. "He looked like a beautiful statue, and I could keep away from him no longer," Phyllis would later recall. They ran across a large meadow. He tried to catch her but tripped her up, perhaps accidentally. Then they sat down by their clothes, and she attempted to dry him with her hair. (Although perhaps not practical, this is plausible, as in a self-portrait her red hair is waist length.) "You've rather a beautiful body," he told her, then leaned over and kissed her.

They walked back to the Old Vicarage in the rain, Brooke took her up to his bedroom and lent her his hairbrush. His landlady served them supper, after which Phyllis cycled home alone in the rain, despite Brooke's offer to accompany her. She does not mention what her mother thought about her returning late at night, soaking wet, from an invitation to tea—Mrs. Gardner's desire to have Rupert Brooke read her poetry might have been stronger than any concerns about her daughter's behavior. As for Phyllis, she summed up the day with a wild burst of romantic enthusiasm. "If he should ever come to love me, I should be more happily placed than can well be imagined; if not, I had a little already of a wild joy that nothing could take from me."

Given the superheated nature of Phyllis's prose it is hard to tell when or even if the relationship was consummated. It may have been she who shocked Mrs. Elgy by shouting out to Brooke from the hallway, "Oh, you gorgeous piece of flesh!" She certainly spent some afternoons with him in his room at Marsh's flat, causing Mrs. Elgy further concern on discovering hairpins when she made Brooke's bed. Once when she was late meeting her mother for tea, Mrs. Gardner noticed that her daughter's face was flushed and asked if she had been in an accident. When Phyllis said she hadn't, her mother asked, "Has Rupert been making love to you, then?" to which Phyllis replied, "Yes."

His letters to her are almost as passionate as hers to him. "Well, you are strange, Phyllis, what I wanted to say was this: you are incredibly beautiful when you're naked, and your wonderful hair is blowing about you, fire runs through me to think of it." He complimented her on her fine legs and slim ankles.*

From time to time, there is a jarring note in Brooke's conversation and correspondence with Phyllis, as if something is going wrong beneath the surface. What to make, for example, of, "You're a fine creature. It's funny that you and I should be blown together by the winds, to be like that. One day you'll die." After taking her for the naked swim at Grantchester and admiring her body in the moonlight, Brooke speculated on how long it would take to strangle her, and he put his hands around her throat, which made her, understandably, nervous.

He may of course merely have been trying to shock Phyllis, or perhaps to conjure up the flickering shade of a Byronic image ("Mad, bad and dangerous to know," as Lady Caroline Lamb wrote famously of her lover Byron) to make himself more interesting to her. After all, they had been swimming in the same body of water where Byron had once swum, and Brooke shared the earlier poet's magnetic beauty and presence. Women had been known to swoon at the mere sight of the young Byron, and if they did not faint at the sight of Brooke, at least they gushed. Certainly he had that effect on

---

* Judging from photographs of Ka, including one in which she posed frontally nude for the camera with that slightly embarrassed but defiant display of nakedness that was so popular among the Neo-Pagans, her legs and ankles were as sturdy, solid, and well padded as the rest of her.

Phyllis, who began one letter to him with "O thou most beautiful." She never married after his death, indeed she became one of his chief mourners, behaving as if she were his widow, and gave up a promising career as an artist to devote the rest of her life to become Britain's leading authority on breeding Irish wolfhounds.

It is possible, even likely, that Brooke stirred up in Phyllis Gardner more passion than he knew what to do with, or at least more than he was comfortable with. Although Phyllis's letters certainly *sound* as if it were consummated, it strangely foundered after five months over the question of birth control. When Brooke suggested to Phyllis that she find some way to spend the night with him, she said that "would hardly do," and he replied "There are ways."

That turns out to have been, as the modern phrase goes, a deal-breaker. Phyllis was "repelled" at the thought of any kind of birth control, and the affair degenerated into a series of long letters in which she objected to his "hedonism," while he explained at great length his reluctance to have children. She expressed her feelings firmly: "But if going on seeing you means that: intercourse without result—I do definitely refuse it." These strong words make it seem improbable that they had been having intercourse "without result" over the last five months. It probably did not help that Brooke told her "All women are beasts!" and that he hoped they would never get the vote. He must have known how deeply that would hurt, as Phyllis was in favor of woman suffrage and was, for the day, an active and determined feminist.

When Phyllis admitted to her mother that Rupert had been making love to her, she might have been trying to shock her (although Mrs. Gardner sounds virtually unshockable). But it seems unlikely that she meant actual sexual intercourse. Possibly she meant what later generations would call heavy petting, although taking all their clothes off for that would seem to be either unnecessary or tempting fate. By that time, Brooke was putting the finishing touches to the dissertation on which so much of his future rested—and he had acquired a new love interest. He and Phyllis remained friends; they were in correspondence with each other until very shortly before his death. Two of her best woodcuts were one of her mourning for Brooke, and another of his grave. The sexual tension between them,

Woodcut by Phyllis Gardner.

whether it had ever been resolved or not, was broken. She believed that his spirit visited her, and ten years before she died in 1939 of metastatic breast cancer, she wrote about him:

I strove with Fate that you should be my friend;
Though you face forth into Earth's uttermost end,
And though in Time we may not meet again,
Eternally we two fight side by side.

EDDIE MARSH WAS A DEDICATED THEATERGOER and not surprisingly had many friends in the theater world. Indeed, the love of his life was the glamorous composer and actor Ivor Novello (whose other lovers included the youngest brother of King George VI, HRH the Duke of Kent, and Lord Louis Mountbatten, uncle of the late Prince Philip). Marsh almost certainly knew nothing of Phyllis Gardner when he introduced Brooke to one of his theatrical friends, Cathleen Nesbitt.

They met at a lunch given by Marsh, and it was a case of like attracts like—they were both breathtakingly beautiful. Cathleen was a very different kind of woman from those who had so far played a role in Brooke's life. She was almost the same age as he, and she was already a successful actress, who had made her debut on the London stage in 1910 in Arthur Wing Pinero's *The Cabinet Minister,* which catapulted her to stardom, and had performed with the Irish Players on Broadway in John Millington Synge's *The Playboy of the Western World.* She had a sharp, dramatic profile and a slender, delicate figure. She was witty, smart, and self-supporting, more than a match for Brooke. She would go on to an eighty-year-long, successful stage, film, and television career, appearing in such films as *Three Coins in the Fountain* and *Promise Her Anything,* on stage as Rex Harrison's mother in *My Fair Lady,* and on television in *Upstairs, Downstairs.* She died at the age of ninety-three in 1982, having been made a Companion of the Order of the British Empire.

Brooke referred to her as "incredibly, devastatingly, immortally, calamitously, hearteningly, adorably beautiful." Photographs bear this out, but with his infallible instinct for choosing women with firm principles against premarital sex, Brooke was paying court to one who did not share the theater world's comparatively tolerant view of sex. Their romance grew, but when they went to country inns to spend time together, they not only booked separate rooms but actually *slept* in separate rooms. Cathleen would later say that Brooke sometimes visited her to sit on the bed and talk with her until dawn. She denied that they had ever been "lovers," but claimed for nearly seventy years that they had been "engaged," which is unlikely since Brooke was already engaged (at any rate in his own mind) to Noel. Cathleen may have *felt* she was engaged. They were obviously soulmates, and Brooke may have been more comfortable having her as an intimate friend than trying to sleep with her. In any case, he did not subject her to torrents of abuse on the subject, as he had done with Ka, Noel, and Phyllis—he was still corresponding with all of them. He also told Cathleen his version of the affair with Ka, as if it were in the past.

He even managed to see Élisabeth van Rysselberghe again and gave her helpful instructions on how to make one of her rings look like a wedding ring, so they could check into a hotel as a married couple. In the meantime, Eddie Marsh was carefully elevating his protégé's social status with elegant dinner parties—his guests included W. B. Yeats, Mrs. Winston Churchill, and Violet Asquith, the daughter of the prime minister, with whom Brooke would shortly have another romantic fling. Brooke sent to Grantchester for his white waistcoat and boasted facetiously to Noel that he had been introduced both to Queen Alexandra, the widow of King Edward VII, and to Mrs. George Keppel, the late king's mistress. Brooke would also soon be dining, along with Eddie Marsh, at 10 Downing Street as a guest of the prime minister. His social life was now that of a celebrity, while his reputation as a poet continued to grow. As if all this were not enough, Brooke's dissertation *John Webster and the Elizabethan Drama* finally won him a fellowship at King's, and he dined at last at the High Table, in white tie and academic gown among his fellow dons, in a blaze of candlelight and ancient silver. A fellowship, an affair (platonic, but who was to know) with a beautiful actress, and a glamorous social life—all the fragments of his life seemed to have at last fallen neatly into place.

It was at just this moment that he decided to leave England, travel across the United States and Canada, and continue on from there to Tahiti, to follow in the footsteps of Paul Gauguin.

CHAPTER 4

# "SOME CORNER OF A FOREIGN FIELD THAT IS FOR EVER ENGLAND"

W HEN BYRON "SHOOK THE DUST OF ENGLAND from his shoes" in 1816, he left with the determination to lead, or at least to be part of, the liberation of Greece from the Ottomans. Rupert Brooke had no similar motive. He had been thinking rather vaguely for some time of going to California, which seen from England was still a remote and exotic destination. Eddie Marsh had once again been helpful to Brooke, urging *The Westminster Gazette* to commission some travel pieces from him. Starting with the United States and Canada, Brooke would gradually expand the voyage to include Polynesia.

He was under no great pressure to go—his mother, not surprisingly, was strongly against it, which may have been a deciding factor for him. But he may also have simply placed himself in too many emotionally fraught situations, such that the only way out was to leave for a time, if possible to a place where letters could not reach him. Mrs. Gardner had written him a pretty tough letter, accusing him of what amounts to caddish behavior toward Phyllis, who had fallen ill from the emotional shock of breaking with Brooke, but that does not seem to have been enough to induce him go to Tahiti, and Phyllis and her mother soon forgave him. Like many artists, he may simply have felt the need for new vistas and yearned for landscapes more exotic than that of Cambridgeshire. It is as if his muse needed to be jump-started. It is surely no accident that this long voyage would produce some of his best poems, as well as bring him at last happiness of a kind that that he had never before found.

Brooke had no great curiosity about the United States, but in an unexpected benefit of his voyage, he turned out to be a very good travel writer. *The Westminster Gazette* got more than its money's worth. Collected in book form after his death—with an admiring preface by Henry James, supposedly the last thing the master wrote before *his* death in 1916—they are almost something of a period piece, unexpectedly funny, sometimes reading unintentionally like an English mirror-image of Mark Twain's *A Connecticut Yankee in King Arthur's Court.*

Brooke's voyage across the Atlantic in 1913 took nine days, good speed for the time. A friend had given him a tablet of writing paper as a going-away present, and he used it to write long letters to the usual suspects. He wrote to Cathleen, promising her future happiness. He had been overjoyed to find that she had left a letter, a telegram, and "a silver boot," possibly a key fob, waiting for him in the purser's office of RMS *Cedric*. He wrote Ka rather more bleakly, urging her to get on with her life. He also wrote to Noel and to Élisabeth. He ordered clam chowder on board *Cedric*, without knowing what it was, and sent Cathleen a poem about it, significantly without mentioning that the poem was a parody of Algernon Swinburne's "If you were Queen of Pleasure, And I were King of Pain," a poem that, given Swinburne's lifestyle, had raised eyebrows in his day.

If you were like Clam Chowder,
    And I were like the spoon,
And the band were playing louder
    And a little more in tune,

I'd stir you till I spilled you,
    Or I'd kiss you till I killed you.
If you were like Clam Chowder
    And I were like the spoon.

He constantly addresses Cathleen as "child" in his letters, a male chauvinist habit he had when writing to all of the women in his life.

Rather touchingly, he also mentions that since nobody had seen him off from the pier at Liverpool, he had hired a grubby urchin for six-pence to wave goodbye to him with his handkerchief.

Brooke had carelessly left behind the sixty-seven letters of introduction that he and Marsh had gathered to important or interesting people, so his first few days in New York City were lonely and sad. He hated his hotel, he hated the June heat, and he hated the food. "I want to die," he wrote Cathleen. Then his letters of introduction arrived, and he cheered up, although he wrote to an old friend from Rugby, "America is no place for a gentleman, to begin with, the lower classes (many of whom are BLACKS) insult one." He wrote to Eddie Marsh, reminding him of a promise to introduce him to a rich widow in Canada, a promise that would have unexpected consequences. He wrote to Cathleen that an American lawyer had taken him canoeing on the Delaware River, seventy miles from New York City. "Once, we came round a wild turn of the river, and there was a voice singing wonderfully, and when we got round, we saw a little house, high on the bank, with an orchard, and a verandah, and wooden steps down to the great river, and at the top of them was a tall girl, very beautiful, standing like a goddess, with wonderful red hair, her head thrown back, singing, singing."

As always, his spirits revived swiftly in the open air. Cities weighed him down, but three hours of vigorous paddling and shooting the rapids, followed by a night of sleeping under the stars, restored him enough to undertake a journey to Boston. There he called on the American poet Amy Lowell, to pay his respects. Brooke surely did not know that after she heard him read his poems in London, she had thought she would throw up. She was an admirer of Ezra Pound and found Brooke's poetry old-fashioned. He called on the editor of *The Atlantic Monthly*, who reacted to Brooke's appearance in his office with a typical burst of admiration. "A young man more beautiful than he I had never seen. Tall beyond the common, his loose tweeds accentuated his height and the athletic grace of his walk. . . . His auburn hair rippled back from the central parting, careless but perfect. . . . I went home under the spell of it and at the foot of the stairs cried aloud to my wife, 'I have seen Shelley plain!'"

The reaction to Rupert Brooke in the new world was very much the same as it had been in the old; his looks and his charm opened every door. His appetite for travel was inexhaustible. He returned to New York from Boston, then took the Montreal Express to Canada and toured the city. He visited Québec and did a tour of that city, then left that evening to go down the St. Lawrence on a boat and bathe in the freezing water of the Saguenay River. He traveled on to Ottawa, where he was invited to lunch by the Canadian prime minister—the two of them discussed Winston Churchill's plans to expand the Royal Navy rather than poetry. Brooke's letters of introduction never failed him; nor did he seem ever to tire of being shown the next tourist site. The Canadians loved him, but he was occasionally homesick; he wrote from Ottawa to Eddie Marsh:

> Would to God I were eating plovers' eggs
>     And drinking dry champagne,
> With the Bernard Shaws, Mr. & Mrs. Masefield,
> Lady Horner, Noel Primrose, Ralegh, the Right
> Honourable Augustine Birrell, Eddie, six or
> Seven Asquiths, and Felicity Tree,*
>     In Downing Street again.

The neat and unexpected rhyme at the tail of the poem is a typical Brooke touch. His poems nearly always carry a surprise for the reader, even when he is just dashing off a joke.

Brooke met and became a friend of Canada's leading poet Duncan Campbell Scott, with whom he stayed, taking his lunch every day at the Royal Ottawa Golf Club. Scott was deputy director of Indian affairs and an enthusiast of the wilderness. In his company, Brooke changed his somewhat fluid plans. Whatever he was searching for, it was not going to be found in eastern Canada, with its

---

* This was a grander guest list than it may sound. John Masefield was a future poet laureate. Lady Horner was Frances Jane Horner, a society hostess and a discriminating patron of the arts, with one of the most beautiful houses in England. Noel Primrose was the fifth Earl Primrose, a former prime minister. Augustine Birrell KC was the Chief Secretary for Ireland. And Felicity Tree was the daughter of the great Edwardian actor-manager Sir Herbert Beerbohm Tree and half-sister of the English film director Carol Reed.

European roots. Brooke's itinerary had never been firmly fixed. The idea of going to Polynesia had been in the back of his mind, but he had made no plans to go there, nor did he now. He simply traveled farther and farther west and let chance, and the advice of the last person he talked to, carry him from one place to the next. He was free in a way he had never been before.

He took a boat up the St. Lawrence and across Lake Ontario to Toronto, where, as usual, he was described as "the veritable picture of a Greek God—of Apollo himself," and journeyed from there to Niagara Falls. From there he crossed Lake Huron and Lake Superior, then went on to Winnipeg by train. Within a day of arriving there, he made his way through the woods to a log cabin on a lake, where he helped a local trapper butcher a gigantic deer by firelight. (Judging from the size, which Brooke estimated at five hundred pounds, it may have been an elk.)

This put the tenting and hiking of the Neo-Pagans to shame. He kept up a constant stream of long, passionate letters to Cathleen Nesbitt but showed no sign of coming back to England to see her. Instead, he moved on to Edmonton and from there to Calgary, where, for mysterious reasons, he was interviewed as a political writer rather than a poet.

From Calgary, Brooke traveled to the Rockies, overwhelmed by the scenery. Lake Louise he described to Cathleen as "the most beautiful place in the world, just sheer beauty." He stayed there for ten days in unaccustomed grand luxury at the Château Lake Louise, which is still a beautiful, luxurious, and expensive destination over a hundred years later. What he did *not* tell Cathleen is that this was where the "rich widow" whom Eddie Marsh had promised him was staying.

Marchesa Capponi was, in fact, *twice* widowed. Born Agnes Smith, "daughter of a midwestern physician," she was a graduate of Stanford University—unusual then for a woman—and lived now in Minneapolis. Her late second husband had been a member of a distinguished Tuscan banking and political family; there is a bold statue of the heroic fifteenth-century statesman Piero Capponi in the Uffizi Gallery in Florence. In portraits, she has a certain severe beauty. Brooke stayed with her for a week and a half and wrote to her often after that. Her feelings for him were strong enough that she paid a visit to his mother in Rugby on her next trip to England.

The marchesa was very different from the other women in Brooke's life. She was wealthy, sophisticated, twice married, a mother, and nearly fifteen years older than he was, although she generally shaved ten years off her age when she was obliged to give it. This did not prevent Brooke from addressing her as "my little girl" in Greek, in his first letter to her after Lake Louise. In his letters he throws in a few phrases in German—her late first husband was a German—and ends it: "At Field an Eastward train came in, labelled—Minneapolis and St. Paul. . . . When no-one was looking I stole behind and fixed a tiny kiss to the rear buffer. Did you get it? I feared it might fall off."

Brooke was unfailingly good at the charming touch when he wanted to be. He not only wrote to Agnes often, he even mentioned her to his mother, describing her as "a woman who could speak five languages, and knew Galsworthy." The breezy intimacy in his letters to Agnes makes it clear they were lovers, and their easygoing familiarity suggests they had told each other a lot about their lives. It must have mattered that Agnes was almost old enough to be his mother, was a mother herself, and was sexually experienced—she not only married twice, but there were other men in her busy life—and that pregnancy (and the complications of birth control) was no longer an issue for her.

Unlike Ka, Noel, Élisabeth, Phyllis, and Cathleen, she surely did not approach sex with fear or moral scruples. Nor does she appear to have harbored any desire to be married again. She simply accepted Brooke for what he was, an unexpected and happy experience in her life, which she was willing to renew when he passed through Washington, D.C. (where she also had a house), on his way home. Not even the Ranee seems to have expressed any objections to her, although England being England, it cannot have hurt that Agnes had a title, even if it was a foreign one. Rupert's letters to her are free from his usual rants about women. They read in fact like normal letters from one adult to another, surely a big step forward. He continued to write to Agnes until just before his death, with affection, humor, and a certain degree of gratitude.

After they parted, he went on to Vancouver, where it was erro-

neously reported that he was there to write about the question of
Japanese immigration; then to Victoria, British Columbia, which is
about as English a place as exists in North America; and from there
to San Francisco. He had so far not revealed to anybody what his
further plans were, and he may not as yet have made the final deci-
sion to go to Polynesia. To a friend, he wrote from the comfort of the
Southern Pacific's Shasta Limited: "In the immediate future I'll be
in San Francisco, after that I don't know." He must have mentioned
his intention to Agnes Capponi, however, because he remarks off-
handedly in a letter to her, "I guess I shall be off to the South Seas."
About a week later he broke the news to Cathleen and to Marsh
that he was leaving for Honolulu, Samoa, Fiji, and Tahiti, and (small
world) he let Marsh know that before he left, he was meeting Mr.
and Mrs. Winston Churchill for dinner in San Francisco.

LIVING AS WE DO IN A WORLD where communication is instant and
travel so swift that it takes longer to recover from a plane flight than
the flight itself lasts, it is hard for us to appreciate the immense dis-
tance Brooke was putting between himself and home. Cathleen had
given him her blessing for the long journey, with a cable that read
GOD BLESS YOU DEAR HEART CATHLEEN, and he replied with a long
letter saying that he would not finish until he was on the beach in
Hawaii. On the way there, he worked on six sonnets that he would
complete shipboard, which are among his finest. He describes the
long process of writing one of them in his letter to Cathleen, chid-
ing himself as "Clumsy! Clumsy."

## Clouds

Down the blue night the unending columns press
　In noiseless tumult, break and wave and flow,
　Now tread the far South, or lift rounds of snow
Up to the white moon's hidden loveliness. . . .

They say that the Dead die not, but remain
　Near to the rich heirs of their grief and mirth.

I think they ride the calm mid-heaven, as these,
In wise majestic melancholy train,
    And watch the moon, and the still-raging seas,
And men, coming and going on the earth.

He wrote too "how much more tenderly in his poetry than in his letters" of the long, sad disaster of his affair with Ka:

An empty tale, of idleness and pain,
    Of two who loved—or did not love—and one
Whose perplexed heart did evil foolishly,
A long while since, and by some other sea.

He wrote also of his feelings for Cathleen:

### One Day

Today, I have been happy. All this day
    I held the memory of you, and wove
Its laughter with the dancing light o' the spray,
    And sowed the sky with tiny clouds of love.

Poetry doesn't get much better than sowing "tiny clouds of love." These poems, grouped as he intended them to be in a series he thought of as *Modern Love*, deftly combine autobiography, confession, and a superb lyrical gift for the vast seascape before him, as if his muse had been liberated at last from the confining fields, streams, and woods of England, freed to fly in the vast emptiness of the Pacific.

From Honolulu he mailed his poems back to London and finally completed his letter to Cathleen, commenting that he was writing "just a few feet away from a wonderful blue and green sea," in which Hawaiian women waded and swam gathering seaweed, clad "in sadly diaphanous garments," while Japanese women "walked past in neat kimonos." But Brooke was not one for sitting still on a beach, however beautiful. He visited another island and trekked on horseback to bathe under a waterfall, got badly sunburned, and learned to like ukulele music.

He then took passage on a ship bound for Samoa to pay his respects at the grave of Robert Louis Stevenson. There was no direct approach to where he wanted to go, nor any reliable schedule. He watched a native dance in Samoa, "thrilling and tropical and savage," boarded a schooner to visit several of the other islands, sleeping on deck, then found a steamer bound for Fiji. "But there it is: there it wonderfully is," he wrote to Marsh from on board, "heaven on earth, the ideal life, little work, dancing, singing and eating, naked people of incredible loveliness, perfect manners, and intense kindliness, a divine tropic climate, and intoxicating beauty of scenery."

He was free from much that had aggravated his life, although even in paradise he was still nursing a grudge against Lytton Strachey, whom he blamed for his problems with Ka and Noel. The closeted world of the Bloomsbury intellectuals was one of the things he was fleeing. It was manly adventure he sought, not gossip whispered about in drawing rooms. He stayed in a thatched hut with a Samoan family, all gravely courteous, with nine children, including a bare-breasted proud eighteen year old beauty, as well as hens and "a gaudy scarlet and gold parrot" that shat on his clothes from the rafters. He spent his days on the ship "drinking Australian champagne from breakfast to lunch" with white men straight out of the pages of Kipling or Conrad.

To Jacques Reverat, he wrote about what life would be like when he got home: "Ho, but we shall have fun. Now we have so painfully achieved middle-age, shall we not reap the fruits of that achievement, my dyspeptic friend?" Brooke was truly coming into focus in his own eyes, so far away and alone in the South Seas. He was at the height of his powers as a poet, and he was in love with Cathleen, but his brief and for once nontraumatic affair with Agnes had given him confidence. He was making quite sensible plans for how he might live as a fellow of King's and enjoy the company of both his old and his more glamorous new friends. If nothing else, he regained a joie de vivre among the islands and washed away much bitterness. He seemed at last at peace. "Won't 1914 be fun!" he exclaimed to Jacques.

The war that would end his life was just eight months away.

✦ ✦ ✦ ✦

HE SET OFF FROM FIJI TO TAHITI but had to go the long way around, via Auckland, New Zealand, where he missed his connection. By Christmas Day, he was suffering from a septic foot after a long and arduous trek through the jungle in Fiji, nursing a cold, and waiting for a loan to finance the next stage of his trip. New Zealand he found "very English, in accent clothes mind and everything" without much enthusiasm, and he stayed not very happily on a sheep farm until he was finally able to depart.

Brooke did not intend to stay long in Tahiti. He wanted to visit it—Paul Gauguin had made it an obligatory stop for anybody of culture traveling in the South Seas. Brooke was planning on making a brief stop, then sailing directly to San Francisco. He was ready to resume his life at home on a happier basis than before. By an odd twist of fate, however, not all of his loan arrived, so for a time he was stranded in Tahiti without enough money to buy a ticket to San Francisco. This was fortunate, however, as it was to lead to one of his happiest love affairs and to perhaps his greatest poems.

He did not like Papeete any more than Gauguin had. It was too big a town, too hot, and marred by French officialdom (Tahiti was then a French colony) and by attempts to duplicate French life in the tropics. But he soon moved about thirty miles away to Mataia, where it was cooler, into a kind of *pension* run by "a ¾ white man" and his Australian girlfriend. Brooke was no doubt attracted by its cheapness and by the fact that Gauguin had once lived there.

He described his life, with some restraint, in a letter to his mother: "We bathe four times a day. The water is cool in day time and warm at night, and never very rough, because it's inside a reef (and sharks don't come!). The average day is this (they combine Tahitian and French customs here). Up at 6 and bathe. *Petit déjeuner* of coffee and fruit at 6.45. Work until 10.30. Bathe. *Déjeuner* (=lunch) 11. Sleep 12–1 or 1.30. 1.30 to 6.30 work or some expedition. 6.30 dinner. Bed about 10 or 10.30, unless we go night fishing. So you see I do plenty of work. . . . It's an ideal life."

He repeated much of this in rather higher spirits to Cathleen (who had graduated from "child" to "my sweet one"), adding, "The boat's ready to start. The brown lovely people in their bright clothes are gathered on the old wharf to wave her away. Everyone has a white flower behind their ear—Tuatamata had given me one. Do you know the significance of a white flower worn over the ear?"

A white flower of the *right* ear means
    I am looking for a sweetheart
A white flower over the *left* ear means
    I have found a sweetheart
And a white flower of each ear means
    I have one sweetheart and am looking for another.

He did not mention where he was wearing *his* flower, but later that evening the natives twined red blooms in his hair and sang "slumberous South Sea songs to the concertina drank red French wine and danced obscure native dances." Then he bathed in a soft lagoon by moonlight and ate "great squelchy tropical fruits— custard apples, papaia, pomegranate, mango, guava, and the rest." He did not, however, explain who Tuatamata was.

A visiting English writer described him in the usual extravagant terms: "The water was four or five fathoms deep, dazzling in the vibrance of the Southern sun, and Brooke, a brilliant blond, gleamed in the violet radiancy like a dream figure of ivory." A Kodak snapshot taken of him at the time does indeed show that his hair has turned surfer blond, he is wearing a flowered sarong, and he looks Apollo-like and happy. His letters, poems, and last pieces about Canada for *The Westminster Gazette* do indeed show that he was telling his mother the truth about that part of his life at least—he was working hard.

About his affair with Tuatamata, not much is known (including the correct spelling of her name; I am using Brooke's spelling of it). He took a snapshot of her with his Kodak, but unfortunately he had no great skill as a photographer. She is wearing a wide-brimmed straw hat and a dress or robe drawn up around her neck. The face is striking in semiprofile, and the nose a touch more European than what one thinks of as Polynesian, but she is beautiful and intelligent, with an enigmatic smile. Her pose is graceful and relaxed, suggesting a trim figure and a certain physical strength. Whether Brooke was wearing a flower over his right ear when they first met we do not know, but he and Tuatamata became lovers very shortly after he arrived at Mataia. Brooke's biographers differ on who she was. Some suggest that she was the village chief's daughter, but since the chief and his wife took in more than a score of children and treated them as their own, that could mean anything. Another suggests she was little more than a prostitute "vaguely attached" to the *pension* where he was living, but that too remains unproven, and both Brooke's poems about her and the one letter from her to him suggest an altogether noncommercial relationship.

In any case, Tuatamata lived by a wholly different set of behavioral standards than that of Europeans. No Judeo-Christian shame or guilt was attached to sex, the notion of family was elastic, and illegitimacy was nothing to be ashamed about. Ever since Captain Cook's crew first encountered the Polynesian culture in 1768, Westerners had struggled to square Christian principles with a society in which it was acceptable for the woman to make the first move, in which nakedness was normal, and in which the Western definition of virtue, however little respected in fact, had no place. Brooke was not the first to have been seduced by a culture so different from his own. He worked at writing poems every day, but he was drawn into a life of sensuality and guiltless pleasure that erased, at any rate for the time being, his numerous inhibitions and his resentment of women.

Tuatamata may or may not have had four children before Brooke met her. That would not have been seen as a problem in her culture, but that she loved him is indisputable. Her letter to him, written in early May 1914, after he had left to return home, did not arrive until January 1915, just four months before his death. The ship carrying it had sunk in the St. Lawrence River, not so far from where Brooke had swum only a few months earlier, but divers eventually managed to rescue the mailbags more or less undamaged. Written in a mixture of pidgin French and English, it nevertheless conveys her feelings about Brooke very clearly:

*I wish you were here that night I get fat all time Sweetheart you*
*know I always thinking about you*
*that time when you left me I been sorry for a long time. whe have good*
*time when you was here I always remember about you forget me all*
*ready oh!* Mon cher bien aimé je t'aimerai toujours . . .
Je me rappeler votre petite etroite figure et la petite bouche
qui me baise bien tu m'as percee mon coeur et j'aime
toujours . . . *I send my kiss to you darling xxxxxxxxxxxxxx*
mille *kiss Tuatamata*

It is possible but by no means certain that "fat" refers to her being pregnant. Brooke thought not, with some regret, but there is no hint of accusation in her letter and no request for help or money. The part in French reads: "My beloved, I will always love you. . . . I remember your slim little face and the little mouth that kissed me so well, you have pierced my heart and I will always love you."

It has been pointed out rather snarkily that only a month after Tuatamata wrote her letter to Brooke, she was out dancing with the cadets from an Argentinian naval training ship in Papeete. But the fact that she missed him need not have prevented her from going out and having a good time. She had nursed him through weeks of suffering after he cut his leg on a piece of coral, the wounds became infected, he ran a high temperature, and he had to be transported to Papeete to consult a doctor, perhaps another example of a compromised immune system that turned every mishap into a medical crisis. He wrote to Marsh from his sickbed: "I have been nursed and waited on by a girl with wonderful eyes, the walk of a goddess, and the heart of an angel, who is, luckily, devoted to me."

Like his fleeting relationship with Marchesa Capponi in Lake Louise, the one with Tuatamata seems to have calmed his misogyny. "I think life's FAR more romantic than any books," he wrote his old friend Dudley Ward after deciphering Tuatamata's water-smudged letter.

Among the poems he wrote in Tahiti is one to her, "Tiare Tahiti," which one hopes he had read aloud to her:

Mamua, when our laughter ends,
And hearts and bodies, brown as white,
Are dust about the doors of friends,
Or scent blowing down the night,
Then, oh! then, the wise agree,
Comes our immortality.
Mamua, there waits a land
Hard for us to understand.
Out of time, beyond the sun,
All are one in Paradise . . .
     And my laughter, and my pain,
Shall home to the Eternal Brain.
And all lovely things, they say,
Meet in Loveliness again; . . .


     *Taü here*, Mamua,
Crown the hair, and come away!
Hear the calling of the moon,
And the whispering scents that stray
About the idle warm lagoon.
Hasten, hand in human hand,
Down the dark, the flowered way,
Along the whiteness of the sand,
And in the water's soft caress,
Wash the mind of foolishness,
Mamua, until the day.
Spend the glittering moonlight there
Pursuing down the soundless deep
Limbs that gleam and shadowy hair,
Or floating lazy, half-asleep.
Dive and double and follow after,
Snare in flowers, and kiss, and call,
With lips that fade, and human laughter
And faces individual,
Well this side of Paradise! . . .
There's little comfort in the wise.

✝ ✝ ✝ ✝

HE HAD BEEN THIS SIDE OF PARADISE, and now he was going home. "The Game is Up, Eddie," he wrote Marsh. "If I've gained facts by knocking about with Conrad characters in a Gauguin entourage— I've lost a dream or two. I tried to be a poet. And because I'm a clever writer, & because I was forty times as sensitive as anybody else—I succeeded a little." In fact he had succeeded beyond his wildest dreams: the manuscripts that he posted to Marsh contain some of his finest poems. He was no longer the poet of the peaceful green English countryside, however much he yearned to see it again. It was as if Tahiti had released in him an altogether more unorthodox and playful muse, as when he described, in "Heaven," religion as it might be imagined in the mind of a fish, at once gentle satire and a fierce attack on Christianity:

Fish (fly-replete, in depth of June,
Dawdling away their wat'ry noon)
Ponder deep wisdom, dark or clear,
Each secret fishy hope or fear.
Fish say, they have their Stream and Pond;
But is there anything Beyond? . . .
But somewhere, beyond Space and Time
Is wetter water, slimier slime!
And there (they trust) there swimmeth One
Who swam ere rivers were begun.
Immense, of fishy form and mind,
Squamous, omnipotent, and kind;
And under that Almighty Fin,
The littlest fish may enter in . . .
And in that Heaven of all their wish,
There shall be no more land, say fish.

This is not the Brooke of the broken church clock and the honey for tea at Grantchester. He was returning from Tahiti in 1914 a more interesting and original poet, on the cusp of greatness. His letters strike a calmer tone, not quite live-and-let-live yet but almost. From the mid-Pacific he wrote to Cathleen, addressing her as "Sweetheart" for the first time: *"Mia cara,* or rather *tau here,* I greatly desire to see you. Your image in my heart breaks like a flower.... I'll write from America. While I have written this page, the boat has ploughed five miles nearer to you. And while I sleep tonight, it will go a hundred more. I wonder if you feel it."

*Mia cara,* one guesses, is a phrase he picked up from Marchesa Capponi, and *tau here* from Tuatamata. But even if Brooke was not yet a sailor with a girl in every port, his love letters had become works of art. His feelings for the moment were no longer interrupted by angry diatribes about feminism or any of the other bees in his bonnet. He had not given up on them: the closer he got to England, the more they would reemerge, buzzing and stinging, but he sounds like a happy man, going from one he loved to another he loved with neither guilt nor shame.

FROM SAN FRANCISCO, at once a seaport and a metropolis, he wrote Marsh, "Oh, God! oh, God! How I hate civilization & houses & trains & collars.... One must remember one has trousers on again." He toyed with the idea of going to Mexico, where fighting was breaking out with the forces of Pancho Villa in 1914—the idea of becoming a war correspondent was one that occurred to him often. In the end, he kept going on the California Limited through Arizona to Santa Fe, marveling to Cathleen at the colors of the desert, and then on to the Grand Canyon, from where he sent a telegram and a letter to Agnes Capponi.

> *Well, I'm going on to Chicago tomorrow. I reach there Tuesday (?). I stay there perhaps six days. Then one day at Pittsburgh— then Washington.... I am tired of doing things for myself. I've done it for eleven months. I shall require you to tell me what to buy and where to buy it, and how much to eat, and when to go to bed, and where to stay, and what to see, and what to say, and when to brush my hair and wash my hands. Will you? ... I want to lie on a sofa and talk. There's lots of things I want. Aufwiedersehn, RUPERT.*

Whatever took place between himself and Agnes, when he arrived in Washington, he stayed at the Willard Hotel rather than at her house and had dinner one night with the British ambassador, where he drank too much champagne. Their affection for each other cannot have diminished, for they were still corresponding until shortly before his death. He went on from there to Boston, to Yale, and possibly to Princeton, where he may have read some of his poems to a group of undergraduates that *might* have included the young F. Scott Fitzgerald.*

He wrote to Cathleen, with growing excitement,

> *I sail from New York on May 29; and reach Plymouth (o blessed name o loveliness! . . . Drake's Plymouth! English, western Plymouth! city where men speak softly and things are sold for shillings, not for dollars, and there is love and beauty and old houses . . . ) on Friday, June 5. Cathleen, keep that day in your heart. Do not tell it: but do not forget it. Keep, if you are in London, that evening empty. No, do not. Haven't we all time before us? . . Carissima, I have dreamt of you. I want to see your face. . . . Your loving, RUPERT*

He spent the voyage reading the huge pile of mail that had been waiting for him in New York City, as well as D. H. Lawrence's *Sons and Lovers*, just published, a copy of which Marsh had sent to him from England. After staying one night in London, he went straight to Rugby to see his mother and to decide what to do next. The notion of going back to King's College as a fellow was no more appealing than it had been before he left on his voyages, yet something like it loomed inexorably before him. A week later he was back in the swing of things, staying at Eddie Marsh's flat and enjoying a dizzyingly busy social schedule, including a reunion of the Apos-

---

* Whether they met actually is uncertain—indeed, the whole story may be folklore, Fitzgerald sometimes alluded to it, but he was always one to glamorize his life. Brooke never mentions meeting Fitzgerald. In any event, Fitzgerald's marrying Zelda depended on the success of his first novel, the title of which he wisely changed from *The Romantic Egotist* to *This Side of Paradise*.

tles in London, dinner at 10 Downing Street, and lunch with D. H. Lawrence and his wife Frieda. He even managed to fit in tea with Ka Cox. He did not leap at her invitation, worried that it would upset her, but in the end it went off well enough, and both seemed relieved.

ALTHOUGH BROOKE COULD NOT have imagined it at the time, perhaps his most significant meeting was with the poet Siegfried Sassoon, over breakfast in Marsh's rooms. Sassoon, a year younger than Brooke, was a member of a wealthy Jewish Baghdadi family that had been thoroughly assimilated in England since the mid-nineteenth century, and author of a mildly successful privately printed parody of John Masefield's ghastly bathetic narrative poem *The Everlasting Mercy*. Marsh had a keen eye for spotting talent early on, so it is hardly surprising that he had invited Sassoon, then left the two poets alone for half an hour to talk. Brooke would write the definitive poem in praise of the war, and Sassoon would not only repudiate the war but write some of the fiercest poems condemning it. Brooke was then famous and lionized, Sassoon still comparatively unknown. Sassoon would have been anxious not to seem like a fan, Brooke anxious not to behave like a star.

At first they did not hit off. Sassoon made a disparaging remark about Rudyard Kipling, and Brooke, surprisingly, came to Kipling's defense. Their conversation, as Sassoon later remembered it, seems to have been somewhat strained, perhaps a reflection of Brooke's anti-Semitism, which burned at a steady blue flame but occasionally erupted into higher heat. Except for that, he and Sassoon should have gotten along well enough. Sassoon was a passionate lifelong cricketer and a dedicated breakneck fox-hunter. He had attended Marlborough College (almost as prestigious a public school as Rugby) and Clare College, Cambridge.

He would go on to become a decorated war hero poet, his fame rivaling Brooke's, but none of that was predictable at the time. Sassoon may have sensed Brooke's anti-Semitism—his description of Brooke is less than enthusiastic, he remarked on Brooke's "radiant good looks," as everybody did, but thought that it was as if Brooke were "a being singled out for some . . . enshrined achievement." There is just the slightest suggestion that Brooke is carrying on "a transplendent performance," in other words that he was putting on, very successfully, a show to impress Sassoon, which he would drop the moment the door closed behind Sassoon. Sassoon was a man of great sensitivity, who noted "the almost meditative deliberation of [Brooke's] voice," but he was wrong about Brooke's putting on a show. The one thing that almost everybody who knew Brooke remarked was that his manner was always the same. He was who he was—the boyish charm was real, not an act, although he could certainly turn it up a notch or two for, say, Henry James or Gide.

Although neither Brooke nor Sassoon mentions it, their brief breakfast meeting took place exactly eleven days after an event that would dramatically change both their lives: the assassination of the Archduke Franz Ferdinand, heir to the Austro-Hungarian throne, and his wife Sophie, Duchess of Hohenberg, in Sarajevo, on June 28. Although brutal, this event did not seem to most people to endanger Britain. In Vienna, the draft of an Austrian ultimatum to the Royal Serbian Government was already being prepared, the first, fatal step toward the major European war that Bismarck had predicted would be ignited by "some damn fool thing in the Balkans." Neither in Britain nor in Europe was the assassination seen as the prelude to Armageddon.

Brooke had every reason to be pleased. His South Seas poems were already creating a stir and would soon be published in the second edition of *Georgian Poetry*, while his social life swiftly ascended: he dined at 10 Downing Street, and a few days later he and Marsh dined with the Duchess of Leeds, where he was seated next to Lady Eileen Wellesley, a daughter of the fourth Duke of Wellington. After dinner they went on to General Sir Ian Hamilton's house for a dance performance. (Sir Ian would be Brooke's commander in chief in the Middle East.) Then he took Lady Eileen home to Apsley House in the early hours of the morning.

Brooke and Lady Eileen hit it off at once, and he immediately started corresponding with her. He had been contemplating marriage, now that he was home again, but couldn't decide whom he wanted to marry. "It seems such an important step," he complained to Jacques Reverat—he wasn't sure whether it was worse to be married or unmarried. Ka and Noel were out of the running. Cathleen was a possibility, but she seemed unlikely to give up her stage career. Eileen may have struck him as a potential contender—she was attractive, intelligent, well read, and superbly well connected. Not even the Ranee could have found fault with a daughter of the Duke of Wellington. Not that the practical side of life ever bothered Brooke much—he was contemplating marriage without owning a home of his own. Tahiti had been admirably better suited for that approach to life than England, and from time to time that occurred to him.

An early letter to Eileen conveys his view of himself. It is hard to date exactly, but it seems to have been written about July 23, the date when the Austro-Hungarian Ministry of Foreign Affairs finally finished dotting the i's and crossing the t's of the Austrian ultimatum to Serbia and ordered the Austro-Hungarian ambassador in Belgrade to deliver it by hand to the acting Serbian foreign minister. The Serbian government was given forty-eight hours to give a satisfactory reply.

Considerable thought had gone into the document that would take the lives of as many as 45 million people. It was intended to make demands on the Serbians so severe that they could never accept it, thus giving the Austrians an excuse to mobilize their army, invade Serbia, take Belgrade, and impose peace on their own terms in the Balkans. The Austrians already had the full backing of their ally Germany, the famous "blank check" that Germany would support Austria whatever happened. Serbia, the kaiser wrote, was not so much a nation as "a band of robbers." "Europe is trembling on the verge of a general war," wrote Winston Churchill, first lord of the Admiralty, calling the Austrian ultimatum "the most insolent document of its kind ever devised."

At this point the general public in Britain had no idea how serious the situation was, still less that Britain might be drawn into what seemed like a distant and remote crisis in South-Central Europe.

Brooke had read the newspapers, he told her, "& then thought about it & then thought about other things. . . . I'm a Warwickshire man," he wrote. "Don't talk to me of Dartmoor or Snowden or the

Thames or the Lakes. I know the *heart* of England. It has a hedgy, warm bountiful dimpled air. Baby fields run up & down the little hills, & all the roads wiggle with pleasure. . . . Eileen, there's something solid & real & wonderful about you, in a world of shadows. Do you know how real you are? The time with you is the only waking hours in a life of dreams. All that's another way of saying I adore you."

It is oddly ironic, this tribute to a peaceful, bucolic England that was just about to be plunged into four years of war. Hardly anybody but Brooke could have written about baby fields running up and down the little hills; it's an England that seems no less a creation of the imagination than the peaceful Shire of Frodo Baggins in *The Lord of the Rings*. It was apparently written to contradict Eileen's conviction that Hampshire, where her father's great mansion and seventeen-thousand-acre estate were located, was the most beautiful part of England.

To the consternation of the Austrians, Serbia backed down and accepted the humiliating terms of the ultimatum except for a few minor points. But the Austrians, with German backing, refused a British offer to mediate and proceeded to mobilize their army, despite warnings that Russia might take that as a signal to start partial mobilization of the Russian Army to support Serbia. By July 28 Austria had completed full mobilization and withdrawn her ambassador from Belgrade. Partial Russian mobilization triggered German mobilization, followed by that of France. At that point the iron schedule of the Schlieffen Plan took effect, compelling the German Army to invade neutral Belgium for the knockout blow against France—an event, the *only* event, that could bring Britain into the war.

By the end of July, it was clear to all but the most stubborn optimists that Britain would be drawn in, however unwillingly or poorly prepared. Brooke had been planning on a holiday with Jacques Reverat, but at the end of a letter to the artist Stanley Spencer on July 31, he wrote, "But this damn war business . . . If fighting starts, I shall have to enlist, or go as a correspondent. . . . At present I'm so depressed about the war, that I can't talk, think, or write coherently."

"Everything's just the wrong way round," he later wrote to Jacques, the holiday postponed. "*I* want Germany to smash Russia

BRAVO, BELGIUM.

*Punch*, 1914.

to fragments, and then France to break Germany. Instead of which I'm afraid Germany will badly smash France, and then be wiped out by Russia." This represented a widespread British feeling, extending up to the king, that Russia represented reaction and backwardness, as well as the age-old British suspicion that the French were not to be trusted. These feelings were reciprocated. The czar managed to combine two prejudices in one sentence when he remarked, "All Englishmen are yids," and many people in France remembered that England had been the traditional enemy of French greatness for over a thousand years. That France, Russia, and Great Britain had ended up on the same side in a war seemed to many the ultimate irony.

On August 2, one day before his twenty-seventh birthday and two days before the British declaration of war, Brooke wrote to

Eddie Marsh, asking him to find him a job, either fighting or as a war correspondent.

He was in a curious state of limbo. Those who had been Territorials or reservists were being called up for service, but Britain, unlike the continental powers, had no conscription, and nobody was looking for twenty-seven-year-old civilian volunteers, however much they wanted to fight. He wrote to Eileen that he was spending his time assailing "Territorial Bodies, O.T.C. corps [Officer Training Courses], etc.," putting his name on innumerable lists, in the expectation that "when one is accepted, one will be taken away & trained for months: & then—perhaps—put to guard a footbridge in Glamorgan," rather than being sent to the front.

He got in a few days of drilling with the OTC of the Inns at Court (mostly lawyers) but then learned that his old friend Andrew Gow was taking applications from Cantabrigians for commissions in the armed forces. Brooke filled out the forms punctiliously, as did his brother Alfred, but with a sinking feeling that they would produce nothing. Then Eddie Marsh told him that Winston Churchill was forming an infantry division out of Royal Marines and reserve sailors who had not yet been allocated to ships. It would need junior officers. With one stroke of his pen, Churchill had Brooke commissioned as a sublieutenant in the Royal Navy—there was no question of physical fitness, military experience, or anything else. The Royal Naval Division was a hasty improvisation of Churchill's, giving him his own small card to play in land warfare, beyond the reach of that august and severe potentate, the new secretary of state for war, Field Marshal the Earl Kitchener.

Armed with obsolete rifles and dazed by their sudden transformation into infantry, the sailors who made up the bulk of the Royal Naval Division were divided into five battalions with junior officers who were as untrained as themselves. It is typical of Churchill's swashbuckling approach that he gave Rupert Brooke and Arthur ("Oc") Asquith, third son of the prime minister, not only instant commissions but command of one of the battalions to his own ex-stepfather.

As he did at most of the big moments in his life, Brooke fell ill, with what he diagnosed as "a neuralgic earache," although that

didn't prevent him from going to lunch with Henry James. He was staying, of all places, at 10 Downing Street, the prime minister's residence, and occupying himself with letters to Cathleen Nesbitt and Lady Eileen. He wrote reassuringly to Marchesa Capponi but added—it was to become a theme—"Death doesn't matter." He declined an invitation from Ka Cox, for fear of reopening old wounds, and urged her to marry and have children—which she did. He had been measured for his uniform, but the tailor had not finished it, so he was still in civilian clothes when he had lunch with Winston Churchill, about which he wrote (with a notable disregard for security) to Cathleen Nesbitt: "But my uniform really will be done tomorrow. Dear love, Winston was very cheerful at lunch, and said one thing which was exciting, but a *dead* secret. You mustn't *breathe* it. That is, that it's his game to hold the Northern ports— Dunkirk to Havre—at all costs. So if there's a raid on any of them, at *any* moment, we shall be flung across to help the French reservists. So we may go to Camp on Saturday, and be under fire in France on Monday!" Much as he desired it, Brooke was rightly skeptical that this would happen. Despite what was now a bad cold, he was busy acquiring his kit and sorting out equipment for the division in the Crystal Palace. From the beginning, Churchill treated the Royal Naval Division as a kind of private army, in the service of his own strategy.

Brooke's younger brother Alfred had managed to get a commission in the Post Office Rifles (Active Service Battalion) and was already in uniform. Rupert chafed at being left behind, but by the end of September, he was fully kitted out, complete with a sleeping bag that was a gift from the Cornfords and a pair of field glasses from E. M. Forster. His transformation into a soldier had widened the gulf between himself and the Bloomsberries, many of whom, like the Stracheys, E. M. Forster, and Bertrand Russell, were pacifists or conscientious objectors. By the beginning of October, Brooke was a platoon commander in the Anson Battalion, Second Brigade, RND, "drilling like Hell. . . . This afternoon I had to inspect two hundred rifles," he wrote Cathleen. "Now I'm lying on my camp bed snatching a rest, before dressing for a 'night-attack.' We start out at 4.30, and have to 'fight' and march through the night, returning at dawn. There'll be a full moon, and it'll be damned cold." Then two days later he added, "We leave here at 9 for Dover. Leave Dover at 2. Tonight I sleep in France."

It is about this time that he wrote the first of the war sonnets that would make him famous, "Peace":

"Now, God be thanked Who has matched us with His hour,
    And caught our youth, and wakened us from sleeping,
With hand made sure, clear eye, and sharpened power,
    To turn, as swimmers into cleanness leaping,
Glad from a world grown old and cold and weary,
    Leave the sick hearts that honour could not move,
And half-men, and their dirty songs and dreary,
    And all the little emptiness of love!

Brooke was not alone in greeting the war with exultation. All over Europe, crowds had reacted to the outbreak of war jubilantly: in Berlin "people cheered wildly," in Paris the crowds "wept and cried, '*Vive l'Alsace!*'" and in St. Petersburg vast crowds gathered to sing the national anthem and cheer the czar. Only in Brussels was there silence, the residents knowing that the full force of the German Army was about to descend on them. Even the most level-headed of men had responded to the mobilization orders with a sense of enthusiasm. It was not just a question of patriotism; every country had its own long-standing national grievance that was at last going to be addressed by force. For France, it was the return of Alsace and Lorraine. Russia would defend the Slavs against the Austrians and Germans. Germany welcomed the moment to achieve her "place in the sun" as *the* world power, and Britain would use the largest navy in the world to secure the unchallenged continuance of her imperial role. For men of the right age, war offered an adventure, a break from the humdrum responsibilities of everyday life, a chance to escape emotional entanglements, like "swimmers into cleanness leaping," as Brooke wrote, echoing the national mood. The huge success of his war sonnets came from the fact that he expressed what other people were feeling. He embodied the national spirit perfectly, in poetry that gave dignity and grace to the sacrifice and suffering of war.

PUNCH, OR THE LONDON CHARIVARI.—August 12, 1914.

FOR FRIENDSHIP AND HONOUR.

Brooke's poems had often rhapsodized about early death. It was the logical extension of his fear of aging. If you can't, or rather *won't* accept old age, the only alternative is death, and this theme runs through much of Brooke's poetry. His preoccupation with death as a deliverance was not a poetic theme—it was a deeply felt reality. Perhaps it was a reflection of his beauty, although he does not appear to have been particularly vain. Still, he may have feared the encroaching realties of age. Perhaps he really *had* taken *Peter Pan* seriously all those times he had seen it, though he seems to have been too smart for that. In any event, he had written often enough about death as a blessed release; now that he was being called upon to face it, it dominated what we have come think of as his war poetry.

The later war poets, like Siegfried Sassoon, knew everything there was to know about death in war; they had seen it all and done it all and hated it. But Brooke *hailed* death, as the Nationalist soldiers later would in the Spanish Civil War—their rallying cry would be "*Viva la Muerte!*" (Long live death!) Once again, Brooke expressed the national mood, as Britain suddenly awoke to the realization that death in unimaginable quantity was going to be needed to win the war. Brooke's war poems, as few as they were, sounded the right note for a country facing this stark reality:

> Blow out, you bugles, over the rich Dead!
>> There's none of these so lonely and poor of old,
>> But, dying, has made us rarer gifts than gold.
> These laid the world away; poured out the red
> Sweet wine of youth: gave up the years to be
>> Of work and joy, and that unhoped serene,
>> That men call age; and those who would have been,
> Their sons, they gave, their immortality.

Brooke's war poems could have served as recruiting posters, in praise of death. Just as he had imagined death only a year ago in "Tiare Tahiti" as "the eternal Brain," he now saw it as a place where "Time [may] hold some golden space / Where I'll unpack that scented store / Of song and flower and sky and face." Death had "come back, as a king, to earth," death is safety, "though all safety's lost; safe where men fall; / And if these poor limbs die, safest of all."

These are not just poetic images. They are deeply felt and help to explain in part Brooke's sudden popularity in 1915—he caught the national mood. The notion of death at an early age was patriotic, even popular, praised from the pulpit, encouraged in the newspapers, and drummed into boys at school. It wanted only a poet with a death wish to express it. To paraphrase Voltaire, if Brooke had not existed, one would have needed to invent him.* Yet Brooke did not see himself as writing what we might now call propaganda. He wrote out of his own feelings, in which patriotism and an exalted spirit of self-sacrifice combined effortlessly with his own tendency to think of death as a welcome release from the obligations of ordinary life and the grim realities of aging.

For the moment, he champed at the bit, learning his craft as an infantry subaltern on the job and trying to shape his fifty-odd sailors into a recognizable platoon. His vestigial training in the Rugby Cadet Corps gave him a leg up—he knew the basics. So did all the years of hiking, living under canvas or in the open, cooking over a fire, and bathing naked in freezing cold water. The Neo-Pagans may not have been warlike, nor even imagined themselves going to war, but living rough came naturally to them, indeed was a source of pride. As beautiful as she was, Noel Olivier could have given lessons in fieldcraft to Brooke's sailors.

Brooke was about to get the experience he craved. Eager to use his own small army, ill prepared as it was, Churchill decided to employ the RND to save the all-important port of Antwerp, which the Germans had all but surrounded. The northern ports in France and Belgium—Antwerp, Dunkirk, Boulogne, and Calais—were of vital strategic importance in 1914 as they would be in May 1940, but the notion that Antwerp could be held by remnants of the retreating Belgian Army and the RND was an illusion. The Belgian Army was already fought out. The French Army, wrongfooted in its own plan to attack Germany, was about to stumble into the decisive battle of

---

* *"Si Dieu n'existait pas, il fallait l'inventer."*

the war on the Marne, which would pit over a million men against 900,000 Germans to save Paris.*

The Royal Naval Division was transported from Dover to Dunkirk, then by train to Antwerp. "After dark," Brooke wrote to Cathleen (with his usual disregard for security) "the senior officers rushed around and informed us that we were going to Antwerp, and that our train was sure to be attacked, and that if we got through we'd have to sit in trenches till we were wiped out. . . . So we got out at Antwerp, and marched through the streets, and everyone cheered and flung themselves on us and gave us apples and chocolate and flags and kisses, and cried *Vivent les Anglais.* . . . As it grew dark the thunders increased, and the sky was lit up by extraordinary glares. . . . We were all issued entrenching tools. Everybody looked worried." With good reason.

By dawn, the RND had dug trenches and were manning them, and German shells were raining down on them. Brooke was relieved to discover that he was "incredibly brave," despite "incessant thunder, shaking buildings and ground," and the wailing of shells. By the second evening, the forts on the division's left had been destroyed, and the Belgians on the left had run away, so the division had to retreat, through sodden fields and roads jammed by refugees with their carts. The night sky was lit by burning houses and farms, then by the blaze of gas tanks, from which "rivers and seas of flames [leaped] up hundreds of feet, crowned by black smoke that covered the entire heavens," lighting up "houses wrecked by shells, dead horses, demolished railway stations, engines that had been taken up with their lines and signals, and all twisted round and pulled out, as a bad child spoils a toy."

The division crossed a makeshift pontoon bridge that two Germans spies had just been caught trying to blow up; they were executed on the spot. "After a thousand years," the RND boarded red London buses that had been shipped over and still bore signs for Fleet Street and Hammersmith, then went back to Dunkirk and home. The RND, without artillery, had endured fire from some of

---

* Sixty-four French divisions and six British against fifty-one German divisions, with over a quarter of a million casualties on both sides.

the German Army's heaviest siege guns and returned after less than a week having accomplished nothing and taken about 2,650 casualties.* Brooke had certainly had his baptism of fire.

✣ ✣ ✣ ✣

As usual in a crisis, Brooke was ill, this time with conjunctivitis. His sleeping bag had been destroyed, he had lost his field glasses, and much of his kit was gone. He wrote to Ka, always the dependable one among his lady friends, a list of things he needed at once: "(1) A little mirror, to stand or hang. (2) A tin mug with a handle. (3) A collapsible aluminum cup. (4) Toilet paper. (5) A bit of sweet-scented soap." The Anson Battalion was quartered now at the Royal Naval Barracks in Chatham, which did not have, for Brooke, the charm of tented living. The RND was being transformed from sailors with rifles and boots into khaki-clad soldiers, with all the delays, confusion, and kit inspections that this entailed. He managed to get away to Rugby to see his mother, and to London, where he saw both Noel and her sister Bryn, and he surprised everybody with his short military haircut.

For weeks on end, he was posted from battalion to battalion, until Eddie Marsh, at the epicenter of command and always the supreme fixer, managed to get him transferred to the Hood Battalion (each battalion of the RND was named after a British naval hero) along with his friend Oc Asquith. Brooke was assigned as a platoon commander to A Company, which was commanded by a New Zealander, Bernard Freyberg, whom Brooke instantly liked. Freyberg was a legendary adventurer, a champion swimmer who had fought with Pancho Villa's army in Mexico. He had raised the money for his passage to Britain to join the war by prizefighting in New York, and he would go on to become one of the most highly decorated officers in the British Army.†

Freyberg was a supremely competent professional soldier, so A Com-

---

* This number includes dead, seriously wounded, and captured.
† Freyberg would win the Victoria Cross and *four* Distinguished Service Orders. The youngest general in the British Army in World War I, he would serve as a general in World War II and eventually as governor-general of New Zealand.

pany was soon installed in huts, in Blandford, Dorset, with such com-
forts as the navy and Brooke's mother could supply. Brooke was still
pondering marriage, on the grounds that he ought to leave a son behind
if he was killed. If the war hadn't come, he wrote his old friend Dudley
Ward, imagining his life as a fellow of King's, he might have "relapsed
into a friendly celibate middle-age, the amiable bachelor . . . or a less
distinguished Eddie, with my rooms and bedder and hosts of young
friends. . . . Now, if I *knew* I'd be shot, I'd marry in a flash."

He wrote to Cathleen that he was in a state of extreme depression,
brought on by the second round of the dreaded inoculation against
typhoid,* but added, cheerfully enough, about his new battalion:
"Oc [Asquith] is about; and I'm in a company with a rather good lot
of officers." My mind's gone stupid with drill and arranging about
the men's food," he wrote. "It's all good fun. . . . I'm rather happy,
I've a restful feeling that all's going well, and I'm not harming any-
one, and probably even doing good." Apart from sheer unadulter-
ated courage under fire, if there was one thing Freyberg believed,
it was that an officer should take care of his men. Hence no doubt
a telegram from Brooke to Ka just before Christmas: SEND MINCE
PIES FOR SIXTY MEN AND A FEW CAKES TO ME BLANDFORD STATION
IMMEDIATELY GET SOMEONE TO HELP YOU RUPERT.

He himself was felled—laryngitis had replaced conjunctivitis.
There was rarely a moment when Brooke was not suffering from
*something*, and life in a cramped, drafty hut in midwinter while drill-
ing all day long in pouring rain and freezing mud was unlikely to
produce a cure. His throat had collapsed and left him voiceless, he
wrote to Violet Asquith, the prime minister's daughter, who had
added herself to the list of women who adored Rupert Brooke. He
had recovered by the new year and was able to come up to Lon-
don for dinner with "Clemmie & Winston [Churchill]" and Eddie
Marsh. He may have heard a hint there of what Churchill had in
mind for the next use of the RND: his latest and most inventive plan
to end the futile strategy and staggering losses of trench warfare was
to attack Germany's recent and weakest ally, the Ottoman Empire.

---

* The inoculation was still dreaded in 1951, when the author joined the Royal Air
Force.

The heart of Churchill's plan was to use some of the French and the Royal Navy's superannuated battleships to break through the narrow straits of the Dardanelles, which the ancient Greek hero Leander and Lord Byron had swum, into the Sea of Marmara. There they would threaten Constantinople, thereby forcing the Ottomans out of the war. As unlikely as it may seem for so ambitious a plan to have germinated even in the fertile mind of the first lord of the Admiralty, it was in fact a reflection of a much larger concern: the possible collapse of Russia.

By 1915 the fabled "Russian steamroller," the slow-moving but vast Russian Army that was supposed to overwhelm the Germans from the east by sheer numbers, had run out of steam. Its catastrophic defeat at the Battle of Tannenberg in August 1914, in which the Russians lost 170,000 killed against fewer than 14,000 German dead, had been followed by disaster after disaster: a million men captured, 900,000 killed, and retreat after retreat. It became increasingly apparent that the fecklessness of the czar, the incompetence of his generals, the corruption of his administration, the shortage of ammunition of every kind and even of rifles, and the czar's apparent indifference to the suffering of his soldiers had brought Russia close to defeat or revolution.

The physically imposing Grand Duke Nicholas (he was over six feet six inches tall), the czar's uncle, the most sensible and admired member of the imperial family, recognized what the czar and the czarina (who were getting their advice from the debauched religious prophet Rasputin) were unwilling or unable see: that Russia was teetering on the brink of defeat. Grand Duke Nicholas believed that if Russia had a year-round warm water passage through the Dardanelles to the open sea, the Allies could ship weapons and munitions to Odessa, and Russia could send vast quantities of wheat out to pay for them.* Looked at on a map, Churchill's plan seemed like a bold move that might at once drive the Ottomans out of the war

---

* Tactfully overlooked was the fact that capturing Constantinople from the Turks had been the first aim of Russian foreign policy for centuries, as well as a Russian Orthodox theological imperative: Russians regarded Constantinople as "the Second Rome" and Moscow as "the Third Rome."

and save Russia, without withdrawing significant numbers of troops from the Western Front.

Churchill's passionate, energetic proselytizing carried away more timid souls—after all, Russia's fall would allow Germany to move over a million soldiers to the Western Front, where they could overwhelm the French and the British. The facts that the Dardanelles is only three-quarters of a mile wide at its narrowest point, that the Turks had surely mined it, and that Turkish guns had been installed on the northern bank of Gallipoli overlooking the strait were conveniently overlooked in the rush of Churchill's eloquence. It was anticipated that the battleships would do the job, blasting away the Turkish artillery with their big guns. If necessary, Britain could land a small number of troops on the Gallipoli peninsula to neutralize the Turkish guns, including the Royal Naval Division, Churchill's private army, for which a role had been found at last.

Brooke suffered through January at Blandford with endless drills and training in the rain and mud. He wrote encouragingly to his friend the poet and playwright John Drinkwater, "Come and die. It will be great fun." He knew he had only about four more weeks in England. He had another bad cold, he wrote Violet Asquith, and was feeling "irritable, depressed and uncomfortable." He and Oc Asquith managed to get away in mid-February, to stay at 10 Downing Street and have dinner with Churchill. He wrote at once to Dudley Ward, with his usual disregard for security: "It's wonderful. We're going in four days. And the best expedition of the war. Figure me celebrating the first Holy Mass in St Sophia since 1453.*. . . Reviewed by the King on Wednesday. . . . Anyhow I'll send you some instructions etc. It should be a mildish affair. But one *might* get shot. . . . What bloody fun!"

He had already written the poem that would make him famous throughout the English-speaking world, the next-to-last of his war sonnets, "The Soldier."

---

* The greatest monument of Byzantine culture, Hagia Sophia was converted into a mosque in 1453 when the Ottoman Turks conquered Constantinople.

If I should die, think only this of me:
 That there's some corner of a foreign field
That is for ever England. There shall be
 In that rich earth a richer dust concealed;
A dust whom England bore, shaped, made aware,
  Gave, once, her flowers to love, her ways to roam,
A body of England's, breathing English air,
 Washed by the rivers, blest by suns of home.

And think, this heart, all evil shed away,
  A pulse in the eternal mind, no less
   Gives somewhere back the thoughts by England given;
Her sights and sounds; dreams happy as her day;
  And laughter, learned of friends; and gentleness,
   In hearts at peace, under an English heaven.

HE WROTE TO HIS MOTHER: "What follows is a dead secret (as is our day of starting). We are going to be part of a landing force to help the fleet break through the Hellespont and the Bosphorus and take Constantinople, and open up the Black Sea. It's going to be one of the most important things of the war, if it comes off. We take 14–16 days to get there. We shall be fighting for anything from 2 to 6 weeks. And back (they reckon) in May. . . . Don't tell Alfred where we're going." (Rupert's brother Alfred was an infantry subaltern, who would be killed in France in June 1915.) In his letter to his mother, Brooke is clearly repeating what Churchill had told him at dinner. It even *reads* like Churchill. Brooke's enthusiasm was unbridled. He wrote to Violet Asquith, the prime minister's daughter, who was also in on the secret, since her father was a heavy drinker and held nothing back about his plans over the dinner table. "Oh, Violet, it's too wonderful for belief. . . . Do you think perhaps the fort on the Asiatic corner will want quelling, and we'll land and come at it from behind and they'll make a sortie and meet us on the plains of Troy? . . . Will Hero's Tower

HOOD BATTALION,
2nd NAVAL BRIGADE,
BLANDFORD,
DORSET.

crumble under the 15 in. guns? Will the sea be polyphloisbic* and wine-dark?"

Overlying the daring plan, not just for Brooke but for every educated Briton of a certain class, was the shadow of greater events. Troy had once stood here. This was where Paris had taken Helen after her abduction, setting in motion the ten-year siege of Troy. Where Brooke imagined landing, Helen had looked out as the Greek fleet landed, she of whom Christopher Marlowe wrote, "Was this the face that launched a thousand ships, and burnt the topless towers of Illium?" Here on the plains of Troy, Achilles slew Hector, Cassandra predicted disaster, wily Odysseus planned the Trojan Horse, and gods and heroes fought to preserve or destroy the great city whose story is perhaps more central to our culture than any other.

Here was Homer's "wine-dark sea," the site of the *Iliad* and the *Odyssey*. From here, Aeneas carried his father Priam from the burning ruins of Troy to found Rome, and from here, Agamemnon had sailed for home, to be murdered by his wife Clytemnestra. All this

* Roaring, thundering.

was familiar territory: events that had taken place here more than eight hundred years before the birth of Christ were as real to Churchill, Brooke, and the prime minister as the present. The geography of the Siege of Troy was as familiar as that of their home, and perhaps more disconcerting, the unpredictability of war was never so starkly pointed out.

Churchill came down to inspect the RND before it embarked, in weather that reminded Brooke of Lear in the storm scene. Brooke dashed a quick note to Ka: "Briefly, we're the best job of the war, we're to take Constantinople. Isn't it luck? I've never been so happy." The next letter he wrote was from the sea, north of Tunis, to Eddie Marsh: "We've had rather a nice voyage: a bit unsteady the first day (when I was sick), & today: otherwise very smooth and delicious."

By March 8, Brooke's ship, *Grantully Castle*, was approaching Malta. He had seen nothing of Spain on the voyage but had paused in Malta long enough to see *Tosca* at the opera house in Valetta. He wrote breezily to Ka, "I suppose you're the best I can do in the way of a widow," then, growing more serious, "You were the best thing I found in life." By March 11, the *Grantully Castle* was anchored in Mudros Bay, on the island of Lemnos, surrounded by other liners that had been converted into troop ships and by most of the warships that were intended to break through the Dardanelles. There Brooke had a chance to see Mount Olympus faintly with his new field glasses, though he could not, he wrote Cathleen, see the gods.

UNFORTUNATELY, a few days after Brooke's first sight of Mount Olympus, the primary mission of the expedition had already failed. The attempt to force the strait with eighteen British and French battleships, accompanied by cruisers and destroyers, ended the day it had begun with the loss of one French battleship, three British, and two more French badly damaged. The minesweepers, manned by civilian crews, had been reluctant to clear a safe passage through the minefields under heavy and accurate fire from the shore. The loss of so many capital ships, however elderly, shook the nerve of the naval commander, Admiral Sir Sackville Carden—nothing shakes the nerve of an admiral like losing a battleship, never mind four. He

ordered the "general recall" of the naval forces, then promptly fell ill
from "stress" and had to be replaced by Admiral Sir John de Robeck.

The "Nelson Touch" seems to have been missing at the Darda-
nelles, and attempts by Churchill to inspire it from London failed.
The civilian crews of the minesweepers would have to be replaced
by sailors, which would take time, and the guns overlooking the
Dardanelles would have to be eliminated by landing troops. In the
original plan the troops had been thought of as playing a secondary
role, perhaps as only an occupying force to secure Constantinople
once the navy had arrived in the Sea of Marmara to threaten the city
with its big guns. It was neither equipped nor trained to fight against
an entrenched enemy in the difficult terrain of Gallipoli. Both the
British and the French severely underestimated the Ottoman Army,
based on a combination of racial prejudice and the poor perfor-
mance of Turkish troops in Libya and the Balkan wars. They had
ignored the fact that the Turks would fight when defending their
own capital, as well as the substantial effect of German advisers and
modern German weapons.

The Royal Naval Division played a small part in the disaster of
March 18. Brooke described it in a letter to Ka Cox:

> *The other day we—some of us—were told that we sailed next
> day to make a landing. A few thousand of us. Off we stole that
> night through the phosphorescent Aegean, scribbling farewell
> letters, and snatching periods of dream-broken, excited sleep. At
> four we rose, buckled on our panoply, hung ourselves with glasses
> compasses periscopes revolvers food and the rest. . . . Slowly the
> day became wan and green and opal. Everyone's face looked
> drawn and ghastly. If we landed, my company was to be the first
> to land. . . . The light grew. The shore looked to be crammed
> with Fate, and most ominously silent. . . . About seven someone
> said "We're going home."*

To Brooke's disappointment, the landing had been a feint,
intended only to distract the Turks. The RND sailed for Port Said,
Egypt, for more training, for the decision had been made that the

main attack would be on land rather than by sea, a much more ambitious plan that would end in tragedy.

No sooner was Brooke encamped in the desert than he was felled by sunstroke. "It began with a racking headache," he wrote his mother, "sickness and diarrhea." He was not alone—a good part of the RND was suffering from the same thing. He was lying on a canvas folding cot under a tent flap in the desert, his head bound with wet towels. Being Brooke, he was visited on his sickbed by no less a personage than the General Officer Commanding-in-Chief General Sir Ian Hamilton. Slender, courteous, and handsome, Sir Ian was at once sensitive and courageous, with the fingers of a concert pianist, a combination rare in generals even in the British Army. He was himself a published poet, a prolific writer, and a great admirer of Brooke's poetry. He offered Brooke a post as an aide-de-camp on his staff, which would have kept him out of the fighting, but Brooke said he preferred to remain with his men, which Sir Ian perfectly understood. "We are encamped on . . . sand; loose, hot, bloody sand," Brooke wrote Cathleen. "We ate sand and drank it, and breathed and thought and dreamed it. And above all a fierce torrid sun." Sir Ian had Brooke moved to Shepheard's Hotel in Cairo, until he was well enough to shop for antiquities as presents in the bazaar.

In the meantime, news of a different sort was taking place in England. On Easter Sunday, the dean of St. Paul's gave his sermon at the cathedral, taking as his text Isaiah 26:19, "The dead shall live, my dead bodies shall arise, Awake and sing, ye that dwell in the dust." Then Dean William Inge went on to say that he had just read a poem on this subject by a young man who would, "he ventured to think, take rank with our great poets," and he read aloud Rupert Brooke's "The Soldier." Inge went on to praise "the enthusiasm of a pure and elevated patriotism," complaining only that Brooke had fallen somewhat short of Isaiah's vision of "Christian hope." *The Times* went on the next day to publish the sermon and Dean Inge's comment.

Within days the issue of *New Numbers* in which the poem appeared was sold out. Editorials and letters to the editor sang Brooke's praises. Henry James praised the author. He had been reading the war poems over and over to himself aloud "as if to reach the far-off author, in whatever unimaginable conditions, by some miraculous telepathic intimation that I am in quavering communion with him." It is not too much to say that a large number of the British public was also in "quavering communication" with the sunstroke victim in Egypt, who had expressed the national mood so perfectly.

Brooke was still unsteady on his feet, emaciated, and suffering from a variety of ailments, including what appeared to be an infected mosquito bite on the left side of his upper lip. But he was determined not to report sick and risk being left behind just as his battalion was about to go into action at last.

The delay in Egypt had been inevitable, now that the land component of the operation had become as important as the naval one. The initial landing force was to consist of five divisions, one of them Brooke's RND, close to seventy-five thousand men, including two ANZAC (Australian and New Zealand) divisions. The amphibious operation would be immense for the time. The kind of landing craft that were in common use on the Allied side in World War II did not exist, so the converted liners that served as troop ships would be towing lighters and barges of various sizes to ferry the troops on shore.

Further delay was caused when it was discovered that back in England, the fighting equipment and ammunition had been loaded *first* instead of last, so it was necessary to unload everything in Egypt and reload the ships the right way. That laborious and time-consuming task gave the German general, Otto Liman von Sanders, and his Ottoman counterpart, General Mustafa Kemal (the future Kemal Atatürk, founder and first president of the Republic of Turkey), time to dig six Ottoman divisions in on the high ground overlooking the beaches where the British landings were anticipated. That set the stage for a long, bloody debacle that would cost the British Empire over 300,000 casualties before ending in a humiliating evacuation.

On April 10 the invasion fleet, including the *Grantully Castle*, sailed for the island of Lemnos, where it would assemble before the assault on Gallipoli. The ships were slowed down by the need to tow the lighters, cumbersome craft, some of which sheared their towline and had to be recovered. Brooke, still not feeling well, stayed in his cabin, resting, until midday. News of his sudden fame at home had reached him, and he remarked with fine irony that that the dean of St. Paul's appeared to prefer Isaiah to his poem. The port at Lemnos was too crowded when they reached it, so the *Grantully Castle* was ordered to proceed to Trebuki Bay, on Skyros, where the ships carrying the RND were to assemble. Here Brooke received his mail, including the news that *The Voyage Out*, the novel that Virginia Woolf had been working on when she went skinny-dipping with him at Grantchester, had just been published to complimentary reviews. Brooke wrote to Marsh that he was working on a long poem and gave him a teasing taste of it with the line, "In Avons of the heart her rivers run," the last line of poetry he would write. The swelling on the left side of his lip had gone away, but now there was a swelling on the right side, to which nobody attributed much importance.

April 20 was a divisional field day, with an exhausting and interminable exercise in full kit in the hot sun. At some point during the exercise, Brooke and his fellow officers paused in a small grove of olive trees by a dry river bed to consult their maps. Brooke remarked how much he liked it. At the end of the day, Freyberg and the other officers decided to swim back to the ship, but Brooke said he was too tired—normally he could never resist a swim—and he was rowed back with their clothes.

That evening at dinner he was very subdued, and the next day he felt "seedy" and not up to much. The following day he was worse, complaining that he felt "damnably ill." He was running a temperature of 101 degrees, and poultices were being applied to his upper lip to bring down the swelling. The next day his temperature rose to 103, and he complained of pain in his back and chest. At this point, a trio of doctors gathered at his bedside. It became evident that he was suffering from septicemia, or blood poisoning.

The next day his temperature rose to 106, and he was comatose. Since there was no suitable medical facility on board the *Grantully Castle*, it was decided to take Brooke to a French hospital ship that was anchored nearby. After an attempt to drain the infection, the chief medical officer declared that he was in an *"état désespéré"*—a hopeless state. The day afterward W. Denis Browne, a composer, music critic, and organist of considerable distinction who had been Brooke's friend since their days together at Rugby and at Cambridge,* witnessed his death. "I sat with Rupert. At 4 o'clock he became weaker, and at 4:46 he died, with the sun shining all around his cabin, and the cool sea-breeze blowing through the door and the shaded windows. No one could have wished for a quieter or calmer end than in that lovely bay, shielded by the mountains and fragrant with sage and thyme."

Since the fleet was under orders to sail for Gallipoli at six the next morning, Oc Asquith, Browne, and his other friends decided to bury Brooke that evening. Browne described it in a letter to Eddie Marsh:

> *We buried him the same evening in the olive grove I mentioned*
> *before—one of the loveliest places on this earth, with grey-green*
> *olives round him, one weeping above his head: the ground covered*
> *with flowering sage, bluish grey & smelling more delicious than*
> *any other flower I know. . . . First came one of his men carrying*
> *a great white wooden cross with his name painted on it in black:*
> *then the firing party, commanded by Patrick; and then the coffin*
> *followed by our officers. . . . We lined his grave with all the flow-*
> *ers we could find & Quilter set a wreath of olive on the coffin.*

Once the grave had been filled in, Freyberg and the other officers covered it with pieces of pink and white marble, and the Greek interpreter set up a second cross at the foot of the grave. On the back of the bigger one, he had written, in Greek, "Here lies the servant of God, Sub-lieutenant in the English Navy, who died for the deliverance of Constantinople from the Turks."

Winston Churchill cabled his younger brother John Churchill to attend the funeral if possible. (It was too late.) Marsh was told of the news and sent a telegram to Mrs. Brooke. General Sir Ian Hamilton

---

* He would be fatally wounded in an attack on the Turkish trenches two months later. Before dying he wrote to Edward Marsh, "I've gone too; not too badly, I hope. I'm luckier than Rupert, because I've fought. But there's no one to bury me as I buried him, so perhaps he's best off in the long run."

was informed and confided to his diary a most unmilitary but prophetic reaction: "War will smash, pulverize, sweep into the dustbin of eternity the whole fabric of the old world; therefore, the firstborn of intellect must die. Is *that* the meaning of the riddle?"

BROOKE'S OFFICIAL BIOGRAPHER Christopher Hassall points out that he was the first fellow of a Cambridge college to die in the war, but already sixty-six Cambridge men had been killed, and forty-two gravely wounded, the beginning of a holocaust that would sweep away a whole generation. Of the five young officers who attended his funeral, only two would survive Gallipoli, Freyberg and Oc Asquith, who would later lose a leg.

Rupert Brooke's obituary in *The Times* was written by Winston Churchill (although probably drafted and edited by Edward Marsh). It praised Brooke's "valiant spirit" and his willingness to die, and it ended with a blast of splendid Churchillian prose: "Joyous, fearless, versatile, deeply instructed, with classic symmetry of mind and body, he was all that one would wish England's noblest sons to be in days when no sacrifice but the most precious is acceptable, and the most precious is that which is most freely proffered."

This was the first step in the transformation of Rupert Brooke into a recruiting symbol, for the only major country participating in the war that did not as yet have conscription, as in the ubiquitous poster of Field Marshal Kitchener pointing his finger above the caption "Your Country Needs YOU." Brooke was conscripted as a means of encouraging more men to enlist, with the result that not only was he a victim of the war, but so was his poetry: for many years only the war sonnets were remembered, as if the rest did not exist.

Churchill's obituary was written just as the troops were landing at Gallipoli, where they discovered that the terrain was impossibly difficult and that the Turks were dug into carefully prepared positions. In the British military disaster that followed, Brooke would almost certainly have been killed. Within eight months, the Battle of Verdun would begin, in which the French would take over 355,000 casualties and the Germans over 400,000, and in which another poet, almost the same age, would be killed.

# CHAPTER 5

# ALAN SEEGER'S "RENDEZVOUS WITH DEATH"

O N OCTOBER 30, 1953, EDWARD R. MURROW aired an interview with the recently elected junior senator from Massachusetts, John F. Kennedy, and his wife Jacqueline. Mrs. Kennedy was attractive, gracious, and a little stiff, perhaps because she was obliged to play second fiddle ever so slightly to her husband, who was rail-thin and completely self-assured. At one point, Murrow asked Senator Kennedy if he had a favorite poem. Unhesitatingly, he answered that he often read Alan Seeger's poems, and recited the first two lines of Seeger's most famous:

I have a rendezvous with Death
At some disputed barricade.

Leaving to one side the unintended irony of that moment, those two lines from Seeger's poem are perhaps the best known and most quoted of any written in the English language during the First World War. Seeger was a New Yorker, born on East 73rd Street in June 1888 to middle-class parents. Unlike Rupert Brooke, he seems to have had a comparatively normal relationship with his parents and his siblings: the Sturm und Drang and emotional intensity that marked Brooke's life and all his relationships was completely absent from Seeger's, as was Brooke's unstoppable torrent of letters. Unlike Brooke, whose "star power," burned bright even while he was a schoolboy, Seeger was something of a loner who remained a mystery even to his friends. His poems did not receive the kind of attention Brooke's did; indeed, the bulk of them were not published until after his death, which, with supreme irony, took place on July 4, 1916.

Seeger's parents are often described as "prosperous," but there is some hint of a seesaw-like trend in their finances. Their address changed throughout his childhood, first on Manhattan's East Side; then they moved to "a spacious Victorian style home" with a view of New York Harbor on four acres in Tompkinsville, Staten Island; next, to a brownstone on Manhattan's West Side; and finally, after Seeger's father's import-export business collapsed, to Mexico City. There he took on a job "selling farm machinery to sugar plantations." The Seegers were musical rather than literary. Alan's father played the piano, and the family gathered together to sing on Sunday evenings. Alan's older brother Charles would go on to become a renowned musicologist (and unlike Alan a dedicated pacifist). Charles in turn would father the folk singers Pete Seeger and Margaret (Peggy) Seeger.

Alan's schooling reflected the family's changes of fortune and residence. He went to the Staten Island Academy, a private school the alumni of which included many members of the Vanderbilt family, the polar explorer Admiral Matthew Perry, and Horace Mann. Once the family moved to Mexico City, Alan and his brother were sent to Hackley School, a preparatory boarding school in Tarrytown, New York, which was intended as a Unitarian rival to such Episcopalian prep schools as Choate, St. Paul's, and Phillips Exeter. According to Alan Seeger's nephew Pete Seeger, "The family was enormously Christian, in the Puritan, Calvinist, New England tradition," but if so, that doesn't seem to have imprinted itself much on Alan.

Mexico, on the other hand, gave his early poems a most un-Puritan splash of color and imagery. It was the high point of his childhood, a world in which he and his brother roamed free, liberated from the restraints of school. They learned to ride and were educated at home by a tutor. The impracticability of that as a system of education eventually led the elder Seeger to send his two sons to boarding school in Tarrytown. The two boys were separated from their parents and the exotic life in Mexico for long periods of time, with long journeys home by sea and rail for the summer vacations, from New York to Havana, by boat, then on by boat to Vera Cruz.

In Alan's case, this pattern was interrupted by a long stay in New England and California with family friends to recuperate from a recurrence of scarlet fever, which set him back by almost two school years. For a boy who was already something of an introvert, it cannot have been easy to be separated from his family—particularly such a close-knit and loving one—for so long.

Early in his short life, Alan Seeger managed to combine two opposing character traits: he was at once a shy dreamer and a young man who thirsted for danger and glory. The room he shared with his brother Charles at Hackley was decorated with bullfight posters, and he dreamed of being a hero. Tall, lanky, and awkward, he was no good at the team sports that matter so much to schoolboys. A contemporary at Hackley remarked that Alan always seemed "wrapped up in his own thoughts," and Seeger himself would later write that he felt "no need for companionship." The amount of time Alan had been out of school meant that his brother Charles went to Harvard* before he did, leaving Alan alone at Hackley. His nickname there was "Little Nemo," the central figure of a then-popular comic strip in the *New York Herald* about a child who dreams fantastic adventures in which he is the hero, then wakes up at the end of every episode. The fact that Alan's head was in the clouds did not prevent him from editing the school paper or playing tennis, at which his height was an advantage.

Alan went to Harvard in 1906, causing Charles considerable surprise at the change in his appearance—he had not seen his brother for two years. Alan was alarmingly thin and seemed to have taken on the withdrawn personality of a medieval monk or scholar. He took himself seriously and expected others to—perhaps not the best way to approach Harvard. He gradually morphed into the appearance of a poet, like Rodolfo in Puccini's recent *La Bohème*, but without a Mimi. For the next seven years, he would cultivate that image, to the concern of his family, until August 25, 1914, when he joined the Foreign Legion to fight for France.

Alan might have felt lonely after his brother graduated from Har-

* Alan and Charles's father had been offered a scholarship to Harvard but turned it down to pursue his business career.

vard in 1908, but fortunately he had made a few friends by then. Most of his Harvard contemporaries were buttoned up and ambitious, like T. S. Eliot, who at Harvard wore the same neat three-piece suits that he would wear for the rest of his life, and Walter Lippmann, who was taking his first steps from what Ronald Steel called the "gilded Jewish ghetto" to his role as mainstream adviser to presidents and syndicated pundit. Alan's friends were more bohemian, "long-haired, often sloppily dressed," and in their company he began to shed his ascetic ways and his shyness in favor of a new, more gregarious way of being, and he spent his nights "at some noisy, smoke-filled student haunt, drinking beer and hotly arguing on any subject that cropped up," which did not necessarily conflict with the more romantic role of poet. That beneath all this he still daydreamed of being a hero was not unusual: he was born only twenty-three years after the end of the Civil War, and there had been no major war for Americans since then. He was not the only young American to yearn for the test of courage and the baptism of fire in a country now imbued with the spirit of fellow Harvard man Horatio Alger.

Alan's best friend was the exuberant, left-leaning extrovert John Reed, who would witness the Bolshevik revolution and write *Ten Days That Shook the World*, his eyewitness account of the revolution. He would be buried in the Kremlin. Reed's circle was unorthodox, radical and determined to shake the world, not to graduate supinely into it. Alan Seeger fit at once into Reed's group at Harvard, and his friendship for Reed would survive to the end of his life. He was a rebel and a poet looking for a cause, which he would find only four years after he graduated from Harvard. It would lead him to a hero's death, memorialized by a life-size bronze statue on the Place des États-Unis in Paris, and which his own robust poetry, shorn of the color and romanticism of his youthful work, would describe.

Be they remembered here with each reviving spring,
Not only that in May, when life is loveliest,
Around Neuville-Saint-Vaast and the disputed crest
Of Vimy, they, superb, unfaltering,
In that fine onslaught that no fire could halt,
Parted impetuous to their first assault.

✛  ✛  ✛  ✛

"I HAVE A RENDEZVOUS WITH DEATH at some disputed barricade,"
"they came for honor not for gain," "that rare privilege of dying
well": in his own way, Seeger was as romantic about war and as
*eager* for death as Rupert Brooke. Yet unlike Brooke, he experienced
the war at its ghastly worst—the misery, the filth, and the constant
casual death. He experienced the adrenaline rush of advancing,
bayonet fixed, through muddy shell holes and rusty barbed wire
on which corpses rotted toward the enemy trenches in the face of
machine gun and artillery fire. At the Battle of Vimy in April 1917,
the Hecatomb of the Canadian Army, the Canadians took almost
eleven thousand casualties in one day. (The hundred-acre Cana-
dian war cemetery at Vimy is overlooked by the statue of a grieving
woman named "Canada Bereft."). The attack on the disputed ridge
of Vimy that Seeger mentions in his poem is not this battle but
an earlier French attempt to prevent the Germans from taking the
ridge in 1916 that was almost equally bloody.

By 1916, Seeger's war had taken on the quality of an unstoppa-
ble nightmare, very different from the kind of glory Rupert Brooke
had sought in 1915. The line of warring trenches on the Western
Front ran from the English Channel to the Swiss border, sometimes
separated by a thousand yards or more, sometimes by only a few
yards. Whatever the distance "no-man's land" was a wasteland of
deep, flooded shell holes, tangled barbed wire and mines, in which
the wounded often lay unreachable and the dead remained unbur-
ied. On both sides, no-man's-land was dominated by machine guns,
snipers, artillery, and riflemen. Patrols at night were constant, with
inevitable losses. Attacks by massed troops, after an artillery bar-
rage lasting for days, were bloody and seldom led to any significant
breakthrough.

The trenches were narrow, dusty, and unsanitary in the summer,
agonizingly cold and wet in the winter. Troops suffered from trench
mouth and trench foot, from dysentery, lice, vermin, and rat bites. In
wintertime they got frostbite, and in summertime heat prostration.
In every season, the stench of rotting, unburied corpses, unwashed
men, and raw sewage was overwhelming. British trenches were con-

sidered cleaner than French ones—the French were, to the British, shockingly indifferent to even the most primitive standards of personal hygiene and sanitation. The German trenches were considered to be the most elaborate, with deep underground dugouts and higher parapets to protect against sniper fire. In all the armies, soldiers mined, filled sandbags, and dug supporting trenches and ditches to drain the trenches day and night in all weather. They lived in mud so deep that it could snatch the boots off a man's feet as he walked.

Nineteen-sixteen would be the year that ended any hope of a short war. The year's losses were beyond the human imagination: 400,000 French casualties in the Battle of Verdun; 420,000 British and over 200,000 French casualties in the First Battle of the Somme. Alan Seeger would be the last of the soldier poets to write about the war in a spirit of enthusiasm. After him, the poet's task would be to describe what no one wanted to imagine and to speak what no one wanted to hear.

ALAN SEEGER'S YEARS AT HARVARD were not marked by any particular distinction. Although he was nominated for class poet, he lost to Edward Eyre Hunt, whose poetry is scarcely remembered, while the class ode was composed by T. S. Eliot. Seeger was something of a bookworm despite the flamboyant poetic pose. He haunted the libraries, translated verse, and worked on poetry that reads very differently from his war poems, much of it touched by a certain exotic quality that reflects his childhood in Mexico.

> I know a village in a far-off land
> > Where from a sunny, mountain-girdled plain
> With tinted walls a space on either hand
> > And fed by many an olive-darkened lane
> The high road mounts, and thence a silver band
> > Through vineyard slopes above and rolling grain,
> Winds off to that dim corner of the skies
> Where behind sunset hills a stately city lies. . . .
> Tall and luxuriant the rank grass grows,

That settled in its wavy depth one sees
Grass melt in leaves, the mossy trunks between,
Down fading avenues of implicated green.

What, one wonders, is "implicated green"? But never mind, this
is poetry of a very different kind from the best known of his war
poems that would make Seeger famous after his death. In his youth-
ful poems, bright flashes remind one of Rupert Brooke's poems
from the South Pacific:

Watch the white ever-wandering clouds go by,
And soaring birds make their dissolving bed
  Far in the azure depths of summer sky,
Or nearer that small huntsman of the air,
The fly-catcher, dart nimbly from his leafy lair.

It is hard not to like the "white ever-wandering clouds," or the
sudden specificity of the fly-catcher, or to wonder where Seeger's
muse would have taken him had he survived the war.

Except for Jack Reed, he does not seem to have made many close
friends at Harvard; nor did he look back upon those four years with
any special nostalgia. He might have said of Harvard, *I came, I saw,
I was forgotten.* Even those who were sympathetic to Seeger, like
his aspiring fellow poet Hunt, were puzzled by him. But in fact,
although Seeger cultivated a poetic image, he was more than able to
hold his own with his friend Jack Reed, whose politics were already
flamboyantly radical. Seeger was much better informed about the
world than he appeared to be.

Tantalizingly, one of Seeger's roommates in his last year at Har-
vard was T. S. Eliot, which cannot have been an easy fit, given Eliot's
prissy neatness and Seeger's erratic habits. Eliot's review of Seeger's
collected poems in 1916 is what might charitably be described as
faint praise: "Seeger was serious about his work and spent pains over
it. The work is well done, and so much out of date as to be almost a
positive quality. It is high-flown, heavily decorated and solemn, but
its solemnity is thoroughgoing, not a mere literary formality."

Eliot by then had already revolutionized poetry with the publication of "The Love Song of J. Alfred Prufrock," the first broadside of the modernism that would go on to shatter all the rules of poetry, literature, and art. His judgment that Seeger's poetry was "so much out of date as to be almost a positive quality" was cruel, the *almost* a pointed thrust to the heart with a sharp knife, about as hostile as it can get from one Harvard man writing about another who is a dead war hero and a fellow poet. Was it in some way influenced by the time they spent as roommates in 1910 at 42 Apley Court, an expression of some remembered irritation or exasperation felt by a would-be Boston brahmin at the untidy habits of a bohemian poseur? Or was it just an awkward attempt on Eliot's part to find a kind word to say about the kind of poetry he himself had repudiated?

GRADUATION IS OFTEN the most difficult moment for anyone attending a college or university, except for those who already have a defined career path or a profession. Alan Seeger was no exception. He drifted out of Harvard with no idea of his next step except to be a poet, and, more vaguely, to pursue "truth and beauty." He spent the summer at MacDowell, the artists colony in Peterborough, New Hampshire. One of his fellow guests rhapsodized about his appearance, "the handsomest man I had ever seen. . . . He looked like a young sun-god, who had stepped down from Olympus, and . . . he acted like one too." This reads very much like descriptions of his contemporary Rupert Brooke, but Seeger, unlike Brooke, seemed withdrawn and distant. He was not a good mixer, even among fellow writers.

His parents exhibited commendable patience with his lack of direction, enabling him to rent a furnished room in Greenwich Village to live the life of a poet and artist, which was as problematic then as it is now. A poorly paid editorial job at a small arty magazine did not work out. Seeger was unable to compromise his artistic principles or lower his lofty and unrealistic standards. He was a misfit, living hand to mouth. His biographers credit him with an irresistible attraction to women. Certainly he was tall, handsome, and of dramatic appearance, but unlike Rupert Brooke he does not seem to have felt the need for a passion for any one woman in particular. His former classmates John Reed and Walter Lippmann lived nearby on Washington Square and remained close friends with Seeger, but both of them were busy launching successful careers. He was adrift, unable to get his poems published or to settle on what to do with himself. At times he seemed to his friends to have "no ambition other than reading, falling in love, and writing poetry." He was poor, living on the occasional check from his father and loans from his friends, but poverty did not seem to weigh on him.

Perhaps Seeger's most significant relationship during this time was his friendship with an older man, John Butler Yeats, an Irish artist and father of the Nobel Prize–winning poet William Butler Yeats. Yeats had arrived in New York City in 1907 and eventually moved into a boardinghouse at 317 West 29th Street run by the three Petitpas sisters, who also ran a modestly priced restaurant, Café Petitpas, which was much frequented by Village artists and writers. Yeats was a convivial man who had given up the law for a successful career as a portrait painter. He was a gifted raconteur and a sympathetic judge of talent, who may have perceived that Seeger had genuine ability long before anyone else did. He also had the patience to draw Seeger out—after all, he himself was the father of six children, including the poet W. B. Yeats, the painter Jack Yeats, and two daughters who studied under William Morris, so the artistic temperament was nothing new to him.

Perhaps the best portrait of Seeger in his Greenwich Village period is the painting by John Sloan, *Yeats at Petitpas'*, now in the National Gallery of Art in Washington, D.C. Sloan was a member of the Ashcan School of painting, which favored impressionistic renditions of gritty urban reality over more genteel subjects. Sloan's painting of a dinner at the Petitpas sisters' café, probably made in 1910 or shortly afterward, is unusual for him. It is a bright, colorful, even cheerful depiction of "a lively gathering" artfully composed, with careful portraits of all the people attending it, dominated by John Butler Yeats, Sloan's friend and mentor. Yeats held forth at such dinners almost every night, but in the painting he appears to be making a sketch of Sloan—perhaps his tribute to their mutual admiration society.

For a dinner of bohemians, everybody looks rather tidy and well dressed, a hint that however radical their opinions and art might be, they still wanted to be perceived as respectable members of the upper middle class. From left to right, they are the literary critic Van Wyck Brooks, John Butler Yeats, and Dolly Sloan, the artist's wife; one of the Petitpas sisters, standing and serving what appears to be a plate of fresh fruit; the novelist Robert Sneddon; the celebrated miniature painter Eulabee Dix; Sloan; Fred King, editor of *Literary Digest*; and Vera Jelihovsky Johnston, wife of the Irish scholar and translator of the *Bhagavad Gita* Charles Johnston and a niece of the theosophist Madame Blavatsky. These names will not necessarily ring a bell for the modern reader, but they were well enough known then, substantial people in the decade before the First World War.

A tenth figure sits hunched in the corner, a shock of black hanging over his eyebrows, seated away from the table behind Yeats's left shoulder, leaning on his hand and looking vaguely toward the floor. Clearly he is not engaged in the conversation, perhaps not even listening to it. It is Alan Seeger, who by this time seemed like the shadow of John Butler Yeats, omnipresent and silent—it must have seemed to Sloan unrealistic *not* to include him, but in contrast to his treatment of the other figures, he did not waste time painting an exact portrait of his face. Sloan merely sketched with a few deft brushstrokes Seeger's features, half concealed by the hand and the hair, whereas all the others are done with exactitude and care. The regularity of Seeger's features is suggested, but he floats in the background, wearing what appears to be a brown corduroy jacket, the only man at the table not wearing a tie.

Whether intentionally or not, Sloan had captured Seeger at this point in his young life. None of his poems had been published; the only people who had read any of it were his friends Reed and Yeats. Others did not share Yeats's enthusiasm for the young poet, who "sometimes made a disagreeable impression on people" and was often rude and curt. Not surprisingly, his parents were worried about him, but not until the chaos and anti-Americanism of the Mexican Revolution drove them out of Mexico and back to New York City were they forced to confront his apparently aimless lifestyle in Greenwich Village. At a loss for any solution, they gave in and agreed with his plan to go to Paris in 1912.

If the Seegers truly believed that sending the prodigal son to Paris would offer a solution to his inability to choose a profession and make himself self-supporting, they must have been exceedingly naïve. Most likely it was a comparatively inexpensive way of kicking the can down the road in the hope that something would come along to propel Alan into a career. Then, as would be the case for another half century, there was an enduring Anglo-Saxon upper-middle-class belief that sending a young man to live in Paris for a time was a good way for him to "find himself," and with at least a chance he might stumble across something there that would inspire in him a desire for a career.*

Paris, however, did no such thing. Seeger remained single-mindedly devoted to the life of a poet, now in a shabbily furnished room on the Left Bank. Like many another American, he was enchanted by Paris—it made his poverty endurable. He was thrilled by the vivacity and joie de vivre of the French. He frequented the cafés on the Left Bank, where you could sit for hours nursing a single cup of coffee. He walked for hours in the crowded, busy streets, where people seemed so much more alive than in New York. He wrote about it with enthusiasm, as if he were describing Baghdad or Cairo:

What bright bazars, what marvellous merchandise,
Down seething alleys what melodious din,
What clamor, importuning from every booth:
At Earth's great mart where Joy is trafficked in
Buy while the purse yet swells with golden Youth!

To be young and alive in Paris was no doubt intoxicating, and judging from the last two lines, it clearly intoxicated young Seeger. Exactly how he lived, and what he did in the two years of his "golden Youth" that he spent in Paris is hard to say. One of his biographers, Irving Werstein, refers to numerous young women in his life: "He always had a Mimi, Gaby, Louise, or Renée clinging to

---

* The author spent several months in Paris in 1954, his father having operated on much the same theory as Mr. Seeger's.

his arm, girls flocked to him . . . his life was poetry, laughter, wine, and love." This may have been so, but since Seeger didn't keep a diary at this point, it's also possible that some of it should be taken with a grain of salt—people often exaggerate the amount of fun they had during their youth in Paris when they grow older; since Seeger was killed in 1916, others may be doing it for him. There must surely have been rainy days, lonely times, times when he ran out of money, even times when he lost faith in himself. Nevertheless, he would probably have subscribed to Oscar Wilde's comment that when good Americans die, they go to Paris. This had been true in the late eighteenth century, when Thomas Jefferson lived there; it was true in the nineteenth century, and it would remain true in the twentieth. Seeger celebrated it in the poetry that he wrote there. "Happiness engulfed him," someone who knew him then observed, and certainly his poems reflect a very different persona from that of the withdrawn, slightly morose and sometimes rude young man who had lived in Greenwich Village:

> But, having drunk and eaten well, 'tis pleasant then to stroll along
>> And mingle with the merry throng that promenades on Saint Michel. . . .
> All laughing lips you move along, all happy hearts that know-
>> ing what
> Makes life worth while, have wasted not the sweet reprieve of
>> being young.

"The sweet reprieve of being young" is good, and although the poem seems a little pedestrian—"merry throng"—it is certainly sincere. Above all, what those two years from 1912 to 1914 *did* instill in Seeger was a passionate devotion to France. He was not alone; many other young Americans in Paris felt the same. They tended to know each other, and almost all of them were engaged in one form or another of the arts, trying to find a voice, in flight from various degrees of American puritanism, parental oversight, and orderly career planning. It sounds very much like Paris during Hemingway's time there, after the end of World War I, a mixed crowd of young people trying to enjoy themselves and make their mark in the arts at the same time. Seeger was noticed among them not only for his height, his poetic appearance, and his poverty, but also for his high spirits—a big change from his Greenwich Village days.

Perhaps he had a premonition, or some awareness of the possibility, that the assassination of the heir to the Austro-Hungarian throne and his wife in Sarajevo on June 28, 1914, was more than just another tragic Balkan political event. For whatever reason, Seeger was galvanized into making a new effort to get his poems published. The headlines also prompted him to declare to his friends that if war came he would enlist at once to defend France. Unable to find anyone in Paris who would publish his poems, Seeger went to London, with no better results. It must have been depressing indeed to trudge from publisher to publisher in London trying to get someone to even *read* his handwritten poems, let alone publish them. When he learned that his father was coming over to London, ostensibly on a business trip but surely also to see how his son was doing, Seeger stayed on, while the headlines about the crisis in Europe grew darker.

The meeting was a happy one for both of them. Alan had cleaned up his act—he was no longer a surly, sulky, unwashed New York City bohemian. He had not yet found a self-sustaining career or managed to get his poetry published, but Paris had had a civilizing effect on him, and his father was pleased. They had spent very little time together in the years since Alan's family had moved to Mexico, but in England they reconnected, and clearly enjoyed each other's company. "We passed three days of such intimacy as we had hardly had since he was a boy in Mexico," his supremely patient father wrote.

Their reunion coincided with a rapid acceleration of events in Central Europe. On July 25, Austria-Hungary rejected Serbia's reply to her ultimatum, and on July 28 Austria-Hungary invaded Serbia, triggering off in quick succession full Russian mobilization, then Germany's. Alan Seeger hastened to return to Paris, but a last-minute tip about a small publisher of poetry from someone in London made him travel first to Bruges, despite the fact that the German Army was massing on Belgium's border. Somehow he persuaded a reluctant but sympathetic Belgian publisher to read his manuscript, and he left it in his hands before taking the next train to Paris.

IN PARIS, AS IN THE REST OF FRANCE, the orderly process of mobilization had begun—the first poster announcing it had gone up at four p.m. on August 1, between the Place de la Concorde and the rue Royale, where it is still preserved. All over France men between the ages of twenty-one and thirty-five converged on the railway stations to go to their *garnison*. There they would be kitted out and armed, 2.9 million of them from the reserves and the territorials who had completed their three-year military service, which, together with those currently serving, would give France an army of nearly four million men.

A number of foreign residents volunteered to serve in the French Army, but however enthusiastic they were, the Americans presented a special problem. Giving their allegiance to a foreign power would potentially deprive them of their U.S. citizenship, but joining the French Army would not make them French citizens, so if they enlisted, they risked becoming men without a country. The French were equal to the challenge: enlisting in the fabled French Foreign Legion would require taking an oath not to France but to the legion, the motto of which was *Legio Patria Nostra*, "The Legion Is Our Fatherland." The term of enlistment for Americans was reduced from seven years to the duration of the war.

The legion was both a part of the French Army and separate from it. Anybody who met its physical requirements could join, except for French citizens. It was otherwise not fussy about your nationality, your real name, or your background. If you could make it through the brutal training at Sidi Bel Abbès in Algeria, you were a *légionnaire*. Despite the romantic allure of service in the legion as portrayed in novels like Ouida's *Under Two Flags* and Christopher Wren's *Beau Geste*, service was tough and hard, discipline and living conditions harsh.

In the big picture, finding a place for about a hundred young Americans who wanted to fight for France would not affect the war much one way or another, but the French were shrewd enough to recognize a propaganda coup when it was handed to them. No Americans wanted to volunteer for the *German* Army, but France stood for something else: *la gloire*, civilization, beauty, democracy, the idea that France is "every foreigner's second country."

Nobody felt this more strongly than Alan Seeger, who came back to Paris to find a city almost emptied of its men and to learn from the *patron* of his favorite café that many of his fellow expatriates were drilling in the courtyard of the Palais-Royal. He rushed to join them and was quickly pushed into the ranks by Charles Sweeny, a West Pointer who would go on to become a sergeant in the legion and the first American to be commissioned as an officer in the French Army. It was a strangely mixed bunch, including a prize-fighter, a stunt pilot, two young men who had fought, or claimed to have fought in the Mexican Revolution, several Harvard graduates, a taxi driver, a jeweler's engraver, the son of a fencing master, and a big game hunter who dealt in ivory, all of them united by the determination to fight for France.

As General Alexander von Kluck's First Army advanced into Belgium on August 4, 1914, the opening movement of the Schlieffen Plan, there was no time to send volunteers for the French Foreign Legion all the way to Algeria for training at Sidi Bel Abbès, so an attempt was made to improvise a training center for them at Rouen, in Normandy. But that was considered too close to the fighting for comfort, so it was moved to Toulouse, in southwestern France. At this point, the volunteers came from almost every country in the world; the Americans in Paris represented only a small portion of the legion's recruits. Almost every non-French volunteer who wanted to fight for France was told to sign up with the legion— after all, turning foreigners into soldiers had been the legion's purpose since it was created in 1831. Seeger and his compatriots chafed at the wait, but given the existential crisis facing France as the Germans swept through Belgium, it is remarkable that the French War Ministry and the Ministry of Foreign Affairs were able to organize both the training facilities and the paperwork for the volunteers in less than two weeks.

On August 21 the Americans signed their enlistment papers and were given three days in which to put their affairs in order.

On August 25 they marched in a somewhat untidy column of civilians to the Gare Saint-Lazare to entrain for Rouen—sixty-eight out of the hundred had turned up; the others had changed their mind. A photograph shows them being led by a young man waving the American flag—judging by his height, he may have been Alan Seeger. There are descriptions of crowds cheering them, of young women embracing and kissing them, of people pelting them with flowers and chocolates, but the photograph of them crossing the Place de l'Opéra shows only a couple of puzzled bystanders and a man passing by on a bicycle.

Reality set in for the Americans as they were crowded into packed, dilapidated railway carriages with hundreds of other volunteers from almost every country in the world and shipped to Rouen. There nobody knew what to do with them. Like soldiers of every army, they learned "to hurry up, then wait." At Rouen, they encountered the chaos of war: the city was crowded to overflowing with British wounded, Belgian soldiers who were separated from their unit, civilian refugees, and French reinforcements, all of them exhausted, many of them drunk. The multiethnic twelve hundred volunteers for the legion were billeted in schools while the authorities tried to decide what do with them. At last, hungry, dirty, unshaven, and disheveled, they were herded into boxcars and sent to the Perpignan Barracks in Toulouse—about as far from Rouen as you can get while remaining in France—to begin their training as *légionnaires*.

The rules of the legion are time-honored and rigid. The NCOs are promoted from the rank and file, while the officers are almost always transferred from the French regular Army. Discipline is fierce, and trainees are pushed to the limit of their endurance and beyond. The legion normally fought in faraway places like Indochina and Morocco; its home was in Sidi Bel Abbès, not in France. Only in the most extreme national emergency was the Foreign Legion brought to France, the last time having been the Franco-Prussian War of 1870 and the civil insurrection in Paris that had followed the French defeat: the legion had played a role in the brutal suppression of the Paris Commune. The normal horrors that recruits to the legion faced in training were exacerbated by the difference between the tough, hard-bitten veterans, for whom the legion was their only allegiance, many of them fleeing from worse, and these idealistic young men who had joined not out of necessity but out of idealism and love of France.

Perpignan Barracks was a rude awakening for the Americans. However miserable they had been on the ninety-hour journey from Rouen to Toulouse, barrack life was worse: filthy straw mattresses infested with bedbugs, stiff clodhopper boots, miserable food, and all the complications of the legion uniform, with its nine-foot-long blue sash, the correct wearing of which was a proud legion tradition. Within a few weeks the Americans would be transformed into *légionnaires*, but for the moment they were kept together as part of Battalion C of the *2ᵉ régiment de marche*, rather than being plucked out and sent to the front as replacements. This was fortunate. Men usually fight better when they are among their own, and the American *légionnaires* were no exception. They did long route marches wearing heavy packs, gradually building up to twenty miles or more, despite the fact that the legion didn't issue socks, so their feet were lacerated with blisters. They learned to strip and fire their rifles, although the French Army was less concerned with marksmanship than with proficiency and enthusiasm in the use of the bayonet. The army believed in the fighting value of the famous *furia francese*, the summit of which was the bayonet charge carrying all before it, something which was already being rendered obsolete by massed German machine-gun fire.

The illusion that the *attaque à l'outrance* was still the key to victory lingered in the French Army and to a lesser degree in the British. But the French victory in the Battle of the Marne in the first week of September 1914, which saved Paris at the cost of more than 250,000 casualties, made it clear that what mattered now was firepower— huge quantities of massed heavy artillery and carefully sited machine guns sweeping the ranks of infantry as they advanced. After the Marne battle, both sides, exhausted and shaken by the sheer quantity of casualties (France would suffer more than 950,000 casualties in 1914, almost a quarter of her army, of whom over 300,000 were killed), settled down to dig themselves in, the opposing lines of trenches from the Swiss border to the North Sea.

The war of movement had ended: the Germans had failed to take Paris, the French and the British had failed to drive them back from Belgium and northeastern France, which contained the bulk of French industry. The Western Front became a giant stalemate for the next four years which would take the lives of over four million men. Inexorably, geography, strategy, and the moral imperative placed the Allies in the attacking role, the Germans in that of defense—they held almost a quarter of France, with much of her industry and mining, and all but a tiny bit of Belgium. The sacrifices that the French had made at the Marne and that the British had made at Ypres and Mons could be justified only by making the Germans give up what they had seized by force.

The failure of the Schlieffen Plan, which the German Great General Staff had spent twenty-three years perfecting, ensured a long war of attrition, instead of the quick knockout punches first against France, then against Russia, that Schlieffen had intended. Although nobody foresaw the outcome, least of all the Germans, the war would be won not by the strongest and best-led army but by those countries with the most resilient political and social system. Czarist Russia would collapse, as would Austria-Hungary, the Ottoman Empire, and the kaiser's Germany, while the democracies would survive, despite unimaginable losses.

NONE OF THIS WAS OBVIOUS in the autumn of 1914. Alan Seeger, in the final week of training in Toulouse, paused to write a letter to his mother. (Another contrast between the eager young Americans and the old *legionnaires*: it is hard to imagine any of those hard-bitten fugitives from justice or from domestic life writing a letter to his mother.) Seeger told her that they had learned in six weeks what the ordinary recruit in peacetime took two years to learn. He then went on to describe with ecstasy what his days were like: "We rise at 5, and work stops in the afternoon at 5. . . . The early rising hour is splendid for it gives one the chance to see the most beautiful part of these beautiful autumn days in the South."

He did not mention the wretched food, the blisters on his feet, the stiff uniform, the hostility and depredations of the regular *légion-*

*naires* toward the starry-eyed newcomers, or the savage tongue-lashings from the noncommissioned officers. He might have been describing a summer camp. Like many people who join the armed forces, he fell in love with it—he was among friends, he had a purpose in life at last, he was putting his manhood to the test, and he believed in the rightness of the cause, "doing my share for the side that I think right," as he put it.

Ten days later he wrote to her again, this time from Aube, east of Paris, close to the Marne, thrilled that he was apparently about to go into action. He could hear the big guns firing in the distance, from near Reims. "But imagine how thrilling it will be tomorrow . . . marching toward the front with the noise of battle growing continually louder before us. . . . The whole regiment is going, four battalions, about 4,000 men, you have no idea how beautiful it is to see the troops undulating along the road in front of one, in *colonnes par quatre* as far as the eye can see, with the captains and lieutenants on horseback at the head of their companies."

Indeed, the sight must have been impressive, even to a more experienced soldier's eye. The legion, like the rest of the French Army, was still wearing trousers of madder red and sky-blue tunics with polished brass buttons. Camouflage was not the point—there was no intention of taking cover or using stealth. The aim of the bayonet charge was to terrify the enemy, not to sneak up on him unawares. In the Boer War, from 1898 to 1902, the British Army had finally given up the red coat in favor of khaki for active service, but the French continued to cling to the red trousers as a national symbol of bravery, defiance, and courage, so much so that in 1913 the minister of war declared, *"Le pantalon rouge, c'est la France!"* (The red trousers, they are France!) No wonder Seeger ended his letter home, "I am happy and full of excitement over the wonderful days that are ahead." Few men can ever have gone to war with more enthusiasm.

It would be an understatement to say that Seeger's elation was premature. The Battle of the Marne had been won, the trenches were already being dug, and as autumn faded and winter arrived, he experienced all the brutal discomforts of trench life. It was "anything but romantic," he confessed. His enthusiasm for the war remained undiminished, however. Of sentry duty at night he wrote: "The sentinel has ample time for reflection. Alone under the stars, war in its cosmic rather than its moral aspect reveals itself to him. . . . He feels, with a sublimity of enthusiasm that he has never known before, a kind of companionship with the stars."

One doubts that many men in the French Army on sentry duty that winter shared his feeling about "companionship with the stars," but Seeger was not only a poet, he was a true believer, a more enthusiastic patriot for France than the French themselves. He bore without complaint the hardships of the winter in the trenches, relieved only by the constant artillery duels between the French and German guns. At some point, perhaps in February, he experienced his baptism of fire repelling a German attack on his length of trench. This time he did not write home about it but instead captured it in the first of his war poems.

## The Aisne

We first saw fire on the tragic slopes
Where the flood-tide of France's early gain,
Big with wrecked promise and abandoned hopes,
    Broke in a surf of blood along the Aisne. . . .

Craonne, before thy cannon-swept plateau,
    Where like sere leaves lay strewn September's dead,
    I found for all dear things I forfeited
A recompense I would not now forego [*sic*].

There where, firm links in the unyielding chain,
Where fell the long-planned blow and fell in vain—
    Hearts worthy of the honor and the trial,
We helped to hold the line along the Aisne.

✣  ✣  ✣  ✣

THAT SEEGER EXPERIENCED hand-to-hand combat for the first time at Craonne is ironic, as in 1917 that town would be the epicenter of French Army mutinies, when over 60 percent of the army's combat divisions mutinied after the bloody failure of General Robert Nivelle's offensive at the Chemin des Dames. The mutineers did not march on Paris—they simply stopped fighting. On parade they bleated like sheep about to be slaughtered. Their anthem was called "La Chanson de Craonne," written to the tune of a popular prewar hit, "Bonsoir m'amour." Soldiers were strictly forbidden to sing it. (They sang it anyway.) A reward, never collected, was put up for the identity of the man who wrote the lyrics, and it was prohibited from being played or recorded in France until 1974!

*Adieu la vie, adieu l'amour,*
*Adieu à toutes les femmes,*
*C'est bien fini, c'est pour toujours,*
*De cette guerre infâme,*
*C'est à Craonne, sur le plateau,*
*Qu'on doit laisser sa peau,*
*Car nous sommes tous condamnés,*
*C'est nous les sacrifiés.**

The fact that it was there, near the ruins of Craonne, which had been pulverized by German artillery, that Seeger finally got the opportunity to fight at close quarters with the enemy, is one of the odd coincidences of the war. He would surely have been shocked by the song, still more by the mutinies. His poems and his letters reflect, to the very end, a willingness to die and an unshakable confidence in the justice of the cause he had chosen. He freely welcomed "that chance to live the life most free from stain / And that rare privilege of dying well."

The fighting, the constant shelling, the large and small miseries of trench life did nothing to diminish Seeger's enthusiasm. He noted without complaint his numb feet, his frozen canteen, his bed of dirty straw, his longing for an attack to relieve the boredom, "to face the barbed wire and the mitrailleuse [machine gun], anything

---

* "Good-bye to life, good-bye to love, good-bye to all the women, It's all over now, we've had it for good with this awful war. It's in Craonne, on the plain, that we're leaving our skins, we've all been sentenced to death, we are the ones they're sacrificing."

for a little freedom and function for body and soul." Like many
another soldier, he came to realize that "the matter of eating" was

> the supreme if not the only event of the day. . . . Every
> morning at 8 o'clock a squad of men leaves the trenches
> and returns before daybreak with the day's provisions—
> bread and coffee, cheese and preserved foods, such as
> cold meat, pâtés, sardines, etc. . . . In the evening anoth-
> er squad leaves immediately after sundown. Every one
> waits eagerly to hear the clink of the pails returning in
> the dark. It is a good meal, a soup, or stew of some kind,
> as hot as can be expected in view of the distance from
> the kitchen fires, coffee and wine, and we all gather
> about with our little tins for the distribution.

Seeger, sustained by his passion, dreaming of victory, wrote:

> The army of deliverance, we would march through
> the narrow streets of the ancient city [Reims], the first
> stage of our long victorious advance would be accom-
> plished, and amidst the benediction of a ransomed
> people our hearts would dilate with that supreme emo-
> tion that life can offer, that emotion idealized on the
> fields of France, of her revolution and empire, whose
> name is that of the winged figure that her soldiers love
> to picture at the head of their victorious battalions—
> *la Gloire!*

This is heady stuff. Seeger never lost his passion for France or
for combat, even as the tidal wave of slaughter began to make oth-
ers feel that they were being killed to no purpose except to con-
tinue a war that nobody knew how to end. The poets after him
would record the horrors and the pointlessness of the war. He was
the last (at any rate in the English language) to celebrate its glory.
Because his best remembered lines of poetry, "I have a rendezvous
with Death / At some disputed barricade," have a certain melan-

choly ring, readers tend to ignore the theme of the bulk of Seeger's
war poems.

> Purged with the life they left, of all
> That makes life paltry and mean and small,
> In their new dedication charged
> With something heightened, enriched, enlarged,
> That lends a light to their lusty brows
> And a song to the rhythm of their tramping feet,
> These are the men that have taken vows,
> These are the hardy, the flower, the elite . . .
> For us, we battled and burned and killed
> Because evolving Nature willed,
> And it was our pride and boast to be
> The instruments of Destiny.

By 1917 no soldier would "thrill to the rhythm of marching feet"
or imagine that he was the instrument of Destiny. Poetry came to
be one of the few ways in which the horror, brutality, and mind-
less cruelty of the war could slip through the hands of censorship.
Poetry was simply not thought important enough to matter. Hence
Siegfried Sassoon was able to get away with his sometimes caustic,
bitter, and savage poetry.

The belief in a good cause—indeed, the belief that there was *any*
cause—died in 1916 at Verdun (365,000 French casualties) and the
Somme (420,000 British casualties, 250,000 French). It was replaced
by a growing suspicion that the old were sacrificing the young out
of sheer unwillingness to negotiate a compromise peace. Yet Seeger
kept the faith up to the very end of his short life.

His experiences were a constant succession of combat at close
range for six to ten days at a time, then of rest and drill before going
back to the line. While Seeger's letters to his mother play down the
risks, those to his father are somewhat more frank. "I was shot a
few days ago coming in from sentinel duty. I exposed myself for
about two seconds at a point where the communication trench is
not deep enough. . . . The ball just grazed my arm, tore the sleeve of
my capote and raised a bump on the biceps which is still sore, but

the skin was not broken and the wound was not serious enough to make me leave the ranks."

Once the French Army stopped the German advance on Paris at the Battle of the Marne, the Germans retreated just far enough to form a cohesive line and dig themselves in. They naturally chose the highest ground they could find, and since they were thrown back on the defensive, they took the time to construct an elaborate trench system, including deep dugouts reinforced with concrete and carefully sited machine gun nests. By contrast, the Allies dug in as close as they could to the German line without doing much in the way of planning. They thought of their trenches as the jumping-off points for attacking the Germans, with the aim of breaking through the German front line to resume open warfare. The Germans, for their part, were for the moment content to hold them back while inflicting constant losses on them. The British commanders in chief, Sir John French and Sir Douglas Haig who succeeded him, were both cavalrymen, convinced that once the infantry had made a break in the German line, the cavalry could surge through it and win the war. The French generals were rightly skeptical, but they still cherished the equally erroneous belief that the Germans would fly before "cold steel," the beloved bayonet charge, despite ample evidence that German artillery and well-placed machine guns could dominate the battlefield.

Most unusually for a soldier, Seeger was a regular contributor to the New York *Sun*, writing long, thoughtful pieces about the war, daily life in the trenches, and pleas for American support for France. He would have made a first-rate war correspondent or a good propagandist. His description of a parade behind the lines is a perfect example of the latter:

> "Présentez—armes!" went from captain to captain.
> Again the flash of the 4,000 bayonets. And while the
> battalions stood there, silent, motionless, the band
> broke out into the "Marseillaise." At the first bars
> of the familiar strains even the horses felt the wave
> of emotion that rippled over the field and whinnied
> in accompaniment.

The horses feeling emotion as the "Marseillaise" is played is a master touch.

Seeger was keenly observant, determined to learn his new profession, and level-headed. He also would have made a good officer, except that in the legion all the officers were French. He was in fact that most *rara* of *aves*, a major war poet who *wasn't* an officer. He was not the only one, and he benefited from the fact that in the French Army, the social distance between officers and men, while still wide, was nothing like the unbridgeable class gap between British "Other Ranks" and their officers. However muddy and grimy they might get in the trenches, officers had an orderly to brush their uniform clean and shine their leather at the end of the day, and to make up their bed even if it was in a dugout. They also had more privacy, whereas the men were packed next to each other in shallow holes dug in the wall of the trench. Sometimes if they dug too deep, they found themselves sleeping next to what remained of a long-buried corpse. It is hard to imagine how Seeger was able to write poetry, long, thoughtful pieces for the *Sun* and, at the invitation of his Harvard classmate Walter Lippmann, for *The New Republic*, and letters to his family. His buoyant good spirits never would leave him.

Indeed, Seeger is so cheerful that from time to time one suspects him of irony, but there is not an ironic bone in his body. Nor did he need to shock. Whatever he saw, he described it flatly, simply.

He wrote nothing like Ernest Hemingway's terse description of death and dying in the war: "But that night he was caught in the wire, with a flare lighting him up and his bowels spilled out into the wire, so when they brought him in, alive, they had to cut him loose." Instead, Seeger left it to the reader to imagine what it was like to crawl toward the enemy's line in the dark over ground strewn with dead bodies. Either you got it or you didn't—it was all the same to him.

> A shell surprised our post one day
>     And killed a comrade at my side.
> My heart was sick to see the way
>     He suffered as he died.

Not a word *de trop*. Seeger also mirrored or prefigured Hemingway's contempt for those who had not seen war close up:

Now turn we joyful to the great attacks
Not only that we face in a fair field
Our valiant foe and all his deadly tools,
But also that we turn disdainful backs
On that poor world we scorn, yet die to shield—
That world of cowards, hypocrites, and fools.

Seeger had the combat soldier's respect for the enemy. At a time when the newspapers overflowed with propaganda stories about German war crimes and atrocities,* Seeger describes Germans as the "valiant foe." It is the civilians on his own side he hates. Despite pain, fear, and daily suffering, he was where he wanted to be: "Amid the clash of arms I was at peace."

Nothing we know about Seeger suggests the kind of emotional and sexual entanglements that marked Rupert Brooke's short life. So far as we can tell, Seeger's relationship with his family was loving, and we know of no serious heartaches or murderous jealousy caused by the women in his life. The fact remains that "amid the clash of arms," he *was* at peace. Except for his poetry—the manuscript of what he called his "Juvenilia" had been kept safe by the publisher he had visited in what was now German-occupied Belgium, who took it to the American consulate in Brussels, from whence it would eventually make its way back to Seeger—little bound him to the world. He had no job, no home of his own, and almost no possessions. Like many other young men, he had made the army his home. He was valued there. His fellow American *légionnaires* were his friends, and he had no ambition to be promoted or decorated. In his own quiet way, he was happy. He had a purpose

---

* That is not to say that German war crimes and atrocities did not exist. The German Army's treatment of Belgian civilians was of a *Schrecklichkeit* (frightfulness as a policy) that prefigured World War II and included reprisals in which men, women, and children were shot.

to his life at last, beyond that of getting his poems published, which still proved impossible.

Seeger's life moved in more or less the same orderly way as that of men on both sides of the trenches. A week of danger and heart-stopping nighttime patrols in no-man's-land, a week in the reserve trenches, still very dangerous and subject to constant artillery fire, sniping, and sudden attacks, followed by a week of *repos* behind the lines. Seeger disliked these periods of "rest" since far from resting, the troops were kept busy with pick and shovel, filling sandbags, repairing the parapet, and digging new dugouts. Even during the week of "rest," his time was not his own. There were drills and parades. The troops were marched to an improvised shower to bathe and renew the endless struggle to rid themselves and their uniforms of lice.

At one point his platoon was quartered in the cellar of a ruined château that had been destroyed by gunfire and then looted. By some miracle the library had been preserved. He mailed his sister a leather-bound early edition of the first volume of Jean-Jacques Rousseau's *Confessions*, printed in Geneva in 1782. On the flyleaf, he wrote to her in pencil a description of his life: "It is an altogether curious sensation to recline here in an easy-chair, reading some fine old book, and just taking the precaution not to stay in front of the glassless windows through which the sharpshooters can snipe at you from their posts in the thicket of the plateau, not six hundred meters away. . . . I am going swimming in the Aisne this afternoon for the first time. In fine health and spirits."

The French Army continued to move Seeger's regiment back and forth along the line, apparently unable to decide whether to use it in one of the great assaults that it was planning. A certain amount of what the British Army called "wastage" took place—that is, a constant daily level of men being killed to no purpose by sniping, artillery fire, and on patrol in no-man's-land. But the army mounted no grand attacks on a big scale of the kind that Seeger dreamed of being engaged in. He did not want to die in some minor incident. "If it must be, let it come in the heat of action. Why flinch? It is by far the noblest form in which death can come. . . . The cause is worth fighting for. . . . We are all in fine form, fit and eager for the assault. I think it will come soon. *Le jour de gloire est arrivé.*"*

Seeger might not have been familiar with the proverb "Beware of what you wish for, you may get it." What he wished for would not come as soon as he wanted, but it was on the way. The military decisions that would take the lives of almost half a million French soldiers and a quarter of a million British took place in the ordinarily cautious mind of General Erich von Falkenhayn, chief of the Great German General Staff, an austere and coldly forbidding figure. In August 1914 he had had a sudden bout of indecision that helped undercut the Schlieffen Plan and cost the Germans the chance of taking Paris.

Now in 1915 Falkenhayn, appalled by the stalemate on the Western Front and determined not let the German Army be weakened by attrition, sought a place to attack that the French would have to defend. It should be on terrain that ensured that the French would be bled to death in attack after attack until their casualties reached a level at which France would collapse. He chose Verdun as the place that the French could not, for reasons of geography and history, give up. If the German Army took Verdun and the high ground around it, the French would have to attempt to retake it. No French government, no French general, could survive the loss of Verdun. Falkenhayn was not wrong, but he underrated the French determination to hold Verdun, and the ghastly losses he would be inflicting on his own army in one of the longest, bloodiest battles of the twentieth century, until the Battle of Stalingrad in World War II.

In May 1915 Seeger's battalion was moved to a section of the line near Reims, in the Champagne, where the front lines were so close that he could hear the Germans' conversation. The French and the Germans exchanged friendly insults and comments about the news, but that did not prevent the daily routine of bombs, shells, and

* A line from "La Marseillaise": "The day of glory has arrived."

sniper fire from both sides—the inevitable "wastage" of casualties even when there was no attack.

Seeger was perhaps the only World War I poet who made life in the trenches sound idyllic:

> Meanwhile [at dawn] the distribution of food takes place. A hot sup of coffee awaits the soldiers returning from *petit poste* [isolated outposts in front of the trench] in the morning. The soldier also "touches" his day's ration of wine, which, heated with a little sugar, makes an excellent sleeping potion. But most precious is the little measure of amber "taffia," or sweet rum, that is doled out only in the trenches and at the front.* There is nothing like it for reviving the spirits after a night in the cold. . . . How insipid beside it seems all the refinements of comfort that peace permits!

This description stands in vivid contrast to the experience depicted in detail in the vast bulk of books written by other participants in the war, all of which portray it as beyond rational description, a nightmare of hurt, pain, suffering, fear, and humiliation, intensified by life in the open, exposed to the elements, tormented by lice, fleas, and rats.

SEEGER'S BATTALION WAS MOVED SEVERAL TIMES, as if nobody was quite sure what to do with it. This reflected indecision at a much higher level. The attempt to drive the Ottoman Empire out of the war by landing at Gallipoli had merely resulted in another increasingly costly stalemate. A major attempt was underway to support beleaguered Serbia by a landing at Salonika, in Greece. A British attempt to take Baghdad was stalemated. The Russian Army, cut off from any help from the Allies by the failure to take the Dardanelles

---

* In the British Army, a tot of rum was doled out to troops before an attack.

and open a year-round shipping route through the Black Sea, was falling back in disarray, with catastrophic losses.*

Everywhere the Allies looked, they saw failed opportunities, shortages of manpower, and demands for more men, shells, and supplies than could be met. General Falkenhayn's grim assessment of Germany's position was matched by those of his Allied counterparts. The British were intent on training their "New Army" of almost a million volunteers (and on not feeding them into existing units as replacements, to avoid wastage), while in France General Joseph Joffre, the French commander in chief, drew up plans for a major offensive in the Champagne and Artois, intended, like so many before it, to break the German line.

The movements of Seeger's battalion were determined by the shifting demands of the planned offensive. Seeger could tell from the pace of the training and the reorganization of the legion that a major attack was being prepared. The first and second regiments were combined into one and made a part of a twenty-thousand-man Moroccan Division, along with the Algerian Tirailleurs† and the Zouaves, both regiments with a colorful colonial past. The Tirailleurs were recruited from Algerian tribesmen, while the Zouaves were by now mostly recruited from French settlers in Algeria and Morocco. (The French, like the British, had a certain sentimental admiration for the exotically uniformed armed forces of countries they had colonized.) Seeger's fellow Americans were dwindling, some killed or wounded, others transferred.

In August, Seeger was offered the "privilege" of transferring from the legion to a French regiment. He was sorely tempted and took nearly two months to make up his mind, but in the end he remained loyal to the legion. Still, he was realistic about his presence there. His was, he wrote in his diary, "a regiment made up almost entirely of the dregs of society, refugees from justice and rogues, command by *sous-officiers* who treated us all without distinction in

---

* The commander in chief, Grand Duke Nicholas, was replaced—disastrously—by his nephew, Czar Nicholas II.
† Roughly speaking, *tirailleur* means "sharpshooter," but by now they were light infantry.

the same manner that they were habituated to treat their unruly brood in Africa."

Seeger's entire division moved north on September 16. His battalion "marched away after dark in the rain," their rifles decorated with bouquets of flowers from the townspeople, and entrained in boxcars, about forty men to a car. Even Seeger complained about the discomfort. After an awful night, they marched on through all the preparations for a grand offensive, passing vast quantities of artillery, ammunition, and supplies, hastily constructed sheds marked *blessés assis* (lightly wounded) or *blessés couchés* (gravely wounded), and masses of tented camps.

Joffre's planned offensive had grown by leaps and bounds. It would now consist of almost 1.2 million men, about two-thirds French and one-third British. The British had agreed to attack reluctantly, but the need to maintain Allied unity was paramount, and the secretary of state for war, Field Marshal the Earl Kitchener, eventually ordered Field Marshal Sir John French to cooperate with Joffre. At this stage of the war, "the brass hats" (officers) still maintained that military decisions should not be made or influenced by "the frock coats" (civilians). But the awe in which the other members of the cabinet had once held Kitchener—and the generals—was ebbing and indeed had almost completely ebbed in the minds of David Lloyd George and Winston Churchill.

A similar awakening was taking place in France, as the number of casualties rose higher and higher, with nothing much to show for them. Georges Clemenceau's remark that war is too important to be left to the generals, although made two years later, was a thought that was already spreading through political circles in Paris and London. Despite these doubts, however, the offensive went forward, largely in hopes that it would relieve the pressure on the Russians.

Seeger was impressed by the preparations as he and his regiment marched toward the front line—everyone, he reported, was "in good spirits and full of excitement" at the prospect of seeing action, and was cheered by the noise of heavy artillery firing to the north. (As it happened, much of it was German.) The attack, he thought, would be "a grandiose affair": its "immediate object" would be "Vouziers and the line of the Aisne," but its larger object was "to expel the Germans from Northern France entirely." If Seeger, a mere foot soldier, could guess its goals, so could the Great German General Staff. The Germans had put down more barbed wire, sinking some of it in trenches to make it harder to cut. They had increased the number of dugouts to one every twenty meters to protect troops from the inevitable artillery barrage, and they had placed machine guns in dugouts, protected with steel plates, so they could traverse at ground level the lines of enemy soldiers as they advanced.

Seeger spent the next week digging *boyaux* (zigzag trenches) with pick and shovel by night, while under fire, for the attacking troops to make their way up to the front line. Meanwhile a tremendous artillery duel went on overhead day and night. This was the beginning of the immense artillery barrage that was intended to destroy the German frontline trenches.

Whatever others may have thought, Seeger was full of enthusiasm. When on September 19, 1915, his company commander read aloud to the men Joffre's order announcing the great attack, Seeger wrote, "The German positions are to be overwhelmed with a hurricane of artillery fire and then great assaults will be delivered all along the line. The chances of success are good. It will be a battle without any precedent in history." He was right about that.

Seeger's curious gift for cheerfully combining the dreadful realities of war with benign descriptions of the weather and the landscape continue throughout his diary. On September 21 he wrote: "About twenty heavy shells fell yesterday evening . . . near the park where we are bivouacking. Went out to watch them burst; no serious damage. Went up to work after supper. The dead and the wounded were being carried in litters through the streets of Suippes. . . . The fine weather is continuing, and it was a beautiful moonlight night, but frosty."

On the twenty-third a German shell buried three men in dirt. Seeger helped to dig them out, only to find when they were finally uncovered that they were dead. On the twenty-fourth he learned that the attack was for the next day. Far from feeling trepidation, he exulted, "[I] expect to march right up to the Aisne, born on an irresistible élan. I have been waiting for this moment for more than a year. It will be the greatest moment in my life. I shall take good care to live up to it."

Seeger's 1915 diary ends with this entry, and the volume that followed has never been found. But in a letter to his mother, almost 3,500 words long, he described the battle in detail. (He had already sent her a short message to tell he was alive, but it unfortunately did not reach her before the newspapers at home had mistakenly listed him among the American dead.) Seeger's enthusiastic account to her must be read in the context of what was undeniably a catastrophic Allied failure.

The British attack in the north never broke through the German front line. The result was pithily summed up by the commander of the British Fourth Army, General Sir Henry Rawlinson, in a message to the king's private secretary for the eyes of the king: "From what I can ascertain, some of the divisions did actually reach the enemy's trenches, for their bodies can now be seen on the barbed wire." Despite the first use of poison gas, which actually blew back into the British trenches, the British suffered almost sixty thousand casualties in one day, including 80 percent of the first twelve attacking battalions, for no meaningful gain in ground. The three divisions of cavalry that were to have exploited the breakthrough never saw action.

Unfortunately, the French attack in the south *did* break through German lines just far enough to allow the French cavalry to charge. Seeger witnessed the event, describing it to his mother as "a magnificent spectacle," with rather more enthusiasm than it merited. "Suddenly the long unpicturesque *guerre de tranchées* [trench warfare] was at an end," he wrote, "and the field really presented the aspect of the familiar battle pictures—the battalions in manoeuvre, the officers, superbly indifferent to danger, galloping about on their chargers." Splendid sights though there may have been, the Germans had moved their artillery back and from there opened a withering fire on the squadrons of French cavalry, annihilating them. In four days, the French suffered 190,000 casualties, most of them victims to superbly accurate German artillery fire.

Seeger did not spare his mother. He described in detail crossing (with bayonet fixed) the first line of German trenches, "filled with their dead," seeing "his best comrade" seriously wounded at his side, then lying in open field all night under ferocious enemy shell-fire. In the morning, another assault on the German second line failed—nobody came back but a few of the "walking wounded"—and Seeger spent the next four days under relentless shelling, his regiment having been "decimated." In the end, he had to confess to his mother that Joffre's offensive had failed, despite what he described as "many splendid moments." He consoled himself with his pride at fighting for France, and he glowed with pride when his division was reviewed by King George V, President Henri Poincaré, Field Marshals Kitchener and French, and General Joffre.

Those on the reviewing stand cannot have enjoyed the day as much as Seeger did. The king was thrown from his horse and injured. Field Marshal French was about to be replaced by General Sir Douglas Haig in view of the poor planning, bad timing, and confusion of the British attacks at Loos. Joffre would soon be promoted to the rank of Marshal of France and moved out of his command because of the high casualties in the failed offensive. And Kitchener's star had greatly dimmed. Then in June 1916, when he and his staff were aboard the HMS *Hampshire* en route to Russia, the ship hit a German mine and sank. Kitchener's death was greeted with barely disguised sighs of relief by his fellow cabinet members.

Seeger's division, once it was brought back to strength, would be placed in the *corps d'attaque*. That is, it would be among the elite first units to lead the attack in the next offensive, which in the meantime spared them "the monotony of long periods of inactive guard in the trenches such as we passed last winter." In the meantime, Mrs. Seeger apparently wrote to express her concern at the danger her son was in, which prompted a rather stiff reply from him. "Your letter naturally made me unhappy," he wrote, "for it is only in thinking of you that any possible doubt can rise in my mind about having done well in coming here. . . . I can only say that I am perfectly content here and happier than I could possibly be anywhere else."

✝ ✝ ✝ ✝

SEEGER SPENT THE AUTUMN AND WINTER OF 1915–16 in comparative comfort and safety. Joffre was drawing up plans for a new offen-

sive in the spring and was determined to safeguard his *corps d'attaque*.
Seeger was given a week's leave to spend in Paris, about which he
merely reported to his mother cautiously that he had "a very good
time," without any details.

The Paris in which he spent his leave was still recognizably the same
city he had loved before the war. Restaurants were open, and food was
plentiful if you could afford it. (Seeger was receiving a little money
from his father—not much, but the dollar went a long way against the
franc.) There were still pretty and fashionably dressed young women
on the streets, and the theaters and cabarets were full, unlike London,
which was becoming progressively grimmer and where rationing was
ever more strictly enforced. Paris made an effort to remain *gai Paris*: in
fact, it was almost a patriotic duty that it remain *la ville lumière*.

Seeger's mother was worried about him, and he wrote to calm her
down. "We probably shall not see action again before spring. Then
there will be a *foudrayant* [thunderous] attempt to drive the Germans
out of their positions, for which I hope more success than the pre-
vious ones." As it happened, his prediction was exactly what Joffre
and Haig had in mind for the Somme, but it ignored, as they did, the
possibility that the Germans would attack first.

Two days after Christmas, Seeger received from his mother "two
boxes of guava jelly in perfect condition—as if they had come from
Paris instead of Cuba." No doubt the gift was intended to remind
him of his childhood days in Mexico.

Shortly after the New Year he fell ill, with either bronchitis or
the flu, or both, and was hospitalized, for the first time since he had
joined the legion. He was evacuated to a hospital in the glamorous
resort town of Biarritz, on the Bay of Biscay—something of a lucky
break, since it was a luxurious place. There he slowly recovered from
severe breathing difficulty and a high fever. And it was there that he
wrote his most famous and prophetic poem.

IT PAINED SEEGER DEEPLY that he was in hospital and on conva-
lescent leave during the Battle of Verdun, which he rightly thought
would be the turning point of the war. The German attack had
begun on February 21, 1916, delayed by appalling weather, with two

days and nights of the heaviest artillery barrage of the war, "A storm, a hurricane, a tempest growing ever stronger, where it was raining nothing but paving stones." The Germans employed a new tactic: they advanced in small parties of heavily armed *Stosstruppen*, or storm troopers, taking advantage of the terrain, rather than in long lines of men marching forward with fixed bayonets like the French and the British. The storm troopers,* small units often under the command of a senior NCO, would emerge after an artillery barrage and attack the British from behind as they advanced. The Germans also had a new weapon, the "flamethrower," which shot a long stream of flaming oil and tar, similar to napalm. It was as if all the horrors of war were concentrated into one small area, in a battle that would last for six months, with combined casualties of almost a million men.

The intensity of the fighting was unimaginable, and almost unendurable. Over 65 million shells were fired during the battle, some of them from the largest guns ever used in land warfare. Corpses by the thousands went unburied, chewed up by the relentless artillery fire. "The pounding was continuous and terrifying," wrote one French soldier, "the air was unbreathable, our own soldiers, the wounded and the blinded, crawling and screaming, kept falling on top of us and died drenching us with their blood." A French officer, having endured four days and nights "soaked in icy mud—under terrible bombardment, without any shelter," reported that he taken 175 men into the battle and "returned with thirty-four, several half mad."

Yet the French held on. Falkenhayn's hope of bleeding the French Army to death came close to success several times, but he was bleeding the German Army to death too, and both sides were locked in a struggle from which neither could withdraw, in a landscape denuded of every sign of life, poisoned by explosives and gas. Nothing was visible but reeking shell holes, in which the wounded drowned helplessly. The battle would be ended only by the largely British offensive on the Somme in July, intended to relieve the exhausted French.

Short of breath and weakened—in the age before antibiotics, there was no cure for Seeger's illness except rest—he still looked forward to being well in time for the next big offensive in the spring.

---

* Hitler would take over the name for his *Sturmabteilung*, or brown-shirt SA.

It was "the only thing that really matters," he wrote to a friend. In a less warlike mood, he wrote to his sister Elsie that "love is the sun of life. The soul that draws near to it is beautiful as Venus, whose rays, so close it is, are never seen but mingled with the sun's own." He fell in love with one of his nurses, which spurred him to write love sonnets to her—a sharp contrast to "I Have a Rendezvous with Death," which he was writing at the same time. He wrote to his sister:

I lay this votive offering, to record
How sweet your quiet beauty seemed to me. . . .
My creed is simple: that the world is fair
And beauty the best thing to worship there,
And I confess it by adoring you.

This love affair—if that was what it was—was almost certainly never consummated. Seeger's sonnets to the young woman are admiring but without any hint of eroticism, and she herself later wrote of him, after he became posthumously famous: "During the 'off-duty' time I used to sit in the garden and read and he used to come and talk to me, and we would go for walks together. I had no idea, then, who he was, except that he was in the Foreign Legion, which in itself was a glamorous thing to be, but I liked him and enjoyed being with him." This does not sound like a grand passion, at least on her part. Ironically, one of the best of these sonnets is addressed to her because Seeger had been waiting for her and she did not show up for a walk together.

Seeger's feelings may have been stronger than hers, or perhaps she simply knew better than to give her heart to a young man whose chance of survival was near zero. In one of the last of his love sonnets, he writes movingly about her refusal to sleep with him:

Well, seeing I have no hope, then let us part;
Having long taught my flesh to master fear,
I should have learned by now to rule my heart,
Although, Heaven knows, 'tis not so easy near.
Oh, you were made to make men miserable
And torture those who would have joy in you.

In these sonnets, Seeger demonstrates something that had not been seen much in English poetry since the time of Andrew Marvell: a wry, witty description of love and lust, at once poignant and self-mocking.*

Seeger was invited to complete his convalescence in the home of a wealthy Frenchwoman, a friend of his family. "I don't believe there is a finer site in Biarritz," he wrote his mother. "The house too is the very ideal of comfort and luxury. Fancy me after a year and a half of sleeping with my clothes on in trenches and haylofts, sleeping now in a most voluptuously soft bed in a pink and white room, with a tiled bathroom adjoining. . . . [I]n the morning around ten o'clock I press a button and a maid comes, opens my shutters and brings me café au lait and toast and jam." In April he was given another month's leave in Paris, where he not only enjoyed himself but recovered at last the manuscript of his poems that he had left in Bruges—a persistent source of worry off his mind. "I took my fill of all the pleasures Paris can give," he wrote. "I lived as though I were saying goodbye to life."

SEEGER RETURNED TO HIS BATTALION IN MAY 1916, but as he was well aware, the great battle of Verdun was still raging 150 miles to the southeast, insatiably devouring lives on both sides. He guessed that his battalion would be part of the joint Anglo-French offensive to relieve the pressure on Verdun, where French divisions were being fed into the battle in rotation, to the detriment of morale. Seeger may have been one of the very few men in the trenches to reflect on the beauty around him. "We are in the depths of the spring forest; violets and lilies of the valley bloom in the beechen shade; cuckoos and wood-pigeons croon in the heavy foliage," he wrote to a friend, although the idyll was interrupted by occasional sniper or artillery fire. His daily schedule gives some idea of what it was like to be a soldier in the trenches, as opposed to an officer. The *reveil* (reveille) was at three-thirty a.m., formation and inspec-

---

* "Had we but world enough and time, / This coyness, lady were no crime. . . / The grave's a fine and private place, / But none, I think, do there embrace."

tion at four. Work (digging and filling sandbags) continued until ten a.m. Then came "soup and *repos* until 11:30, and then work again until 5." Nights were spent doing sentry duty or, more dangerously, patrolling no-man's-land, or performing the never-ending task of adding more barbed wire in front of the trench.

However beautiful the surroundings, it was a life spent in the mud and filth of a trench, exposed to the elements, and tormented by rats and lice. No matter, Seeger's essentially optimistic nature always shines through. He wrote to a friend of a sudden, unexpected artillery bombardment: "a terrific *rafale* [storm] of shrapnel began bursting right in our midst. . . . Cries to lend a hand. A sergeant and seven men had been touched. The most serious case was Sergeant Colette, a splendid fellow whom everyone liked. They took him away on a litter, but he died before reaching the ambulance. . . . The soldier's life has its hard moments, but the bright side is not lacking either—good health and good comradeship, the allurement of danger, joys of the open air."

Nobody was better than Seeger at making the best of a bad thing. His sunny view of the war sets him apart from almost everybody who wrote *anything* about it. To a man, the British war poets who followed Rupert Brooke expressed their disgust at the waste, the senseless killing, and the savagery; they raged at the incompetence of the generals and at the inability of the politicians and diplomats to find a way out of the mess they created. Brooke wrote about the war with enthusiasm but died before it could be put to the test. Seeger was alone of those who fought in order to find fulfillment. He is a long way from the bleak anger of Siegfried Sassoon's "Attack":

Lines of grey, muttering faces, masked with fear,
They leave their trenches, going over the top,
While time ticks blank and busy on their wrists,
And hope, with furtive eyes and grappling fists,
Flounders in mud. O Jesu, make it stop!

✢ ✢ ✢ ✢

SEEGER WAS SO BORED by the lack of action that he took to patrolling his stretch of no-man's-land alone. Admittedly it was wooded and hilly and therefore offered some cover, but it was still a risky thing to do. He sought ways of performing some feat that would win him a Croix de Guerre, but none happened; he was tempting fate for no reason. He wrote long letters to his *marraine de guerre* (war godmother), a uniquely French institution, in which a woman adopted a soldier as a pen pal and sent him cards, letters, packages of food, and little gifts. It was thoroughly respectable, indeed it was the outgrowth of a Catholic charity and of several major newspapers. Hundreds of thousands of soldiers put their name and their army mailing address in the newspapers asking for a *marraine*. Seeger's *marraine* sent him a cigarette lighter and a little pocket flask, and his correspondence with her is somewhat franker than that with his mother. He shared his great disappointment with her: he had been asked to write and recite a poem commemorating the Americans who had been killed fighting with the French armed forces on Declaration Day (now Memorial Day), but due to a misunderstanding, he received leave to do so for July 4 instead of May 30, so he missed the chance of reading his poem aloud in Paris. "It would have been such an honor and pleasure to have read my verses there in Paris," he wrote her. "I counted on seeing you and getting a moment's respite from the hard life here."

The war on the Western Front was at that moment still stalled in the titanic stalemate at Verdun, the French at the limit of their endurance, the Germans beginning to realize that General von Falkenhayn's plan to bleed the French Army dry had led to the military equivalent of a mutual suicide pact. Farther north, preparations were being completed for the Anglo-French offensive on the Somme, which would produce the greatest bloodletting of them all, a battle that would include not only a more ambitious use of poison gas but a new British secret weapon, the tank. As if both sides were letting out a gigantic sigh in anticipation of a greater and bloodier battle to come, Seeger's "Ode in Memory of the American Volunteers Fallen for France," which as he told his *marraine* he never got a chance to deliver, reads a bit like the last attempt to shed glory on the fallen dead.

Seeger's exuberant faith in France and his enthusiasm for the war remained undiminished.

Yet sought they neither recompense nor praise. . . .
Nay, rather, France, to you they rendered thanks
(Seeing they came for honor, not for gain),
Who, opening to them your glorious ranks,
Gave them that grand occasion to excel,
That chance to live the life most free from stain
And that rare privilege of dying well.

His was truly a voice that would not be heard again. He looked forward to what was to come.

"The prospects of an early *relève*, of a change of scenery and participating in a big action, make these days very exciting," Seeger wrote his *marraine* in mid-June, and on June 21 he reported that his regiment was on the move for "an unknown destination." He enclosed what would be his last poem, adding that he would be twenty-eight years old the next day.

On June 24 he wrote to tell her that after four or five sweltering, claustrophobic hours in a boxcar, he started off "in the heat of the day on what was without exception the hardest march [he] had ever made. . . . There were 20 kilometers to do under the blazing sun and in a cloud of dust. Something around 30 kilos on the back. . . . The battlefield has no terrors after trials like these that demand just as much grit and often more suffering."

The "big push," as the British called the offensive on the Somme, began in the early morning of July 1. "In the first hour alone a quarter of a million artillery shells were fired by the allies against the German lines—some 3,500 shells each minute." It was the worst bloodletting of the war, the darkest day in the long history of the British Army. Line after line of British troops marched to their deaths, bayonets fixed, many of them killed by artillery and machine-gun fire before they could even reach the frontline trenches from which they were supposed to attack.

It is possible, even likely, that Seeger did not know of the catastrophe to the north. The battlefield was over forty miles wide, and although the French met with stiff resistance, their artillery fire was better directed, and their tactics were less rigid than the British. Seeger's battalion was held in reserve for two days, near the

German-occupied village of Belloy-en-Santerre. One can imagine his growing impatience at being so close to the fighting yet still a spectator. At last, on July 4, Seeger's battalion was ordered to move forward and attack. A fellow *légionnaire* reported that he was "beaming with joy." A friend saw him wave as he moved forward and remembered that he was "the tallest man in his section," not an advantage when under fire. "His head was erect, and pride in his eyes, I saw him running forward, with bayonet fixed."

In the next moment, he was hit by machine-gun fire and fell. His body would be found and buried in a mass grave the next day. It has not been identified since—the ground was so torn up by German artillery that the grave was obliterated.

EVERYTHING SEEGER YEARNED FOR happened after his death. His poems were published in book form by Scribner in 1916, to all the praise that he had never received in his lifetime. He was posthumously awarded the Croix de Guerre and the *médaille militaire*, and in 1925 an immense heroic bronze statue resembling Seeger was erected on the Place des États-Unis in Paris. The sculptor modeled the face from photographs sent by Seeger's father. Seeger's name is engraved among the twenty-three American volunteers who died for France fighting in the French Foreign Legion, and excerpts from his "Ode in Memory of the American Volunteers Fallen for France" are engraved on either side in French and in English. He could hardly have aspired to more.

Passionate devotion to the war's purpose might well have died with him. For the Western Allies, Verdun and the Somme erased all that. The war became like some huge natural disaster on a colossal scale that would grind on remorselessly for another two years because nobody could find a way to stop it. Another American who volunteered to serve in a foreign army, although as an ambulance driver, described it bluntly: "You will die like a dog for no reason," wrote Ernest Hemingway.

Seeger was the last poet of that war to have sought and found glory.

# Chapter 6

# ISAAC ROSENBERG
## *Painter and Poet*

Your eyes have looked through death at mine.
You have tempted a grave too much.

*—Isaac Rosenberg, "Girl to a Soldier on Leave"*

**M**OST OF THE BETTER-KNOWN BRITISH WAR poets were officers, many of them from public schools (which in England are private, exclusive, and expensive) and from the universities of Oxford and Cambridge. For a person of a certain class and education, receiving a commission was almost automatic. All of them had undergone a certain amount of rudimentary military training at school. It was still generally believed that men of a certain class, upbringing, and accent would know how to give orders to those of a class lower than their own, and that they would be obeyed.

The social gap between officers and men in the British Army remained wide, and it was *intended* to be wide. They were expected to lead their men fearlessly, to set an example, to walk into machine-gun fire without flinching, armed with nothing more than a revolver and a cane. The walls of England's public schools and university colleges all exhibit plaques with seemingly endless lists of the names of young men killed in World War I, dwarfing by comparison those who would be killed from 1939 to 1945. Alistair Horne's account of the Battle of the Somme is titled *Death of a Generation*, and as far as the upper-middle-class was concerned, it was true: the best and the brightest of that generation were scythed down in the mud of Flanders and northeastern France.

"Rank hath its privileges," and officers did wear finer uniforms. Their clothes and kits were looked after by soldier-servants, they ate better food, and those who chose to do so went to brothels reserved for officers, marked with a blue light instead of the ones marked by a red light for "Other Ranks." They were decorated more often than were the troops, and they received separate decorations: the Military Cross and the Distinguished Service Order for officers. The Military Medal and the Distinguished Conduct Medal were for NCOs and Other Ranks. Only the very rare Victoria Cross—628 awarded in 1914–18—was shared.*

The strict discipline and rigidly enforced class distinction of the British Army made service "in the ranks" a kind of punishment that in some ways was harder to bear than the military danger.

One of the greatest of the British war poets was Isaac Rosenberg, who never rose higher than the rank of private. He joined up less out of patriotic zeal, like Rupert Brooke and Alan Seeger, than because he had no other option. Rosenberg hated it all, the routine anti-Semitism, the bullying—he was slight, short, frail, and timid, a natural target—and the manifold miseries of trench life. He was a poor soldier, his appearance on parade was seldom satisfactory, and he was always losing bits and pieces of his kit. He had no illusions about the army, the war, or his own place in that "land of ruin and woe" he was entering. He did not seek glory and did not expect to get it. "I never joined the army for patriotic reasons," he wrote Edward Marsh. "Nothing can justify war. I suppose we must all fight to get the trouble over." This is a long way from Rupert Brooke's view.

Rosenberg was born in Bristol in 1890. His parents, Dovber and Hacha, had fled from Russian Lithuania, partly because of endemic and increasingly violent state-sponsored Russian anti-Semitism, which among many other woes confined the Jews to the Pale of

---

* The Victoria Cross is awarded for valor to persons of any rank in the British Armed Forces for conspicuous courage and daring. Only 1,358 have been awarded since it was created in 1856 by Queen Victoria. It is Britain's highest and most privileged award. The VC is so rare that the last medal sold on auction went for over £400,000. (By comparison, the U.S. Medal of Honor has been awarded 3,525 times since 1862.)

Settlement in what is now Poland, Belarus, and Ukraine. Partly, too, they wanted to avoid seven years of military service for Dovber, in an army that neither recognized nor respected even such basic requirements of the Jewish religion as kosher food and Saturday worship. Shortly after their marriage, the Rosenbergs had moved surreptitiously to Moscow in an effort to avoid conscription for Dovber, who opened up a modestly successful kosher butchery, but the authorities soon closed it down, then seized and arrested him, since as a Jew he had no right to live in Moscow, outside the Pale.

Once he was released from prison, he made his way to Siberia, but no matter how far he fled, the police continued to track him down. As corrupt and inefficient as the vast czarist bureaucracy was, the police hunted down Jews living outside the Pale with all the single-minded determination of Inspector Javert in Victor Hugo's *Les Misérables.* Dovber eventually managed to return to Lithuania and from there crossed the border into Germany. From Hamburg he took passage to Britain, leaving his wife and infant daughter behind. He had wanted to go to the United States, but he could not afford the fare.

If Dovber had ever supposed that the streets of England were paved in gold, he would have been quickly disappointed. After failed attempts to find work as a pants presser and a butcher, he became an itinerant peddler, which he would remain for the rest of his life. He changed his first name to the more English-sounding Barnett, but he remained an impoverished outsider, living on the fringe of a society that was not his own. He was something of a gullible innocent as well, a lower-class Jewish embodiment of Prince Myshkin in Dostoyevsky's *The Idiot.* It would be a mistake to think of Barnett Rosenberg as uneducated, however—he was a devoted student of the Torah and a fervent Tolstoian, but he was unable to raise himself out of abject poverty. In a portrait of him painted by his son Isaac, his face is lean, his left eyebrow is raised quizzically, and his expression that of an intelligent man asking himself how he got into such a mess. He looks more like a scholar than a peddler who hawked his wares from door to door, only one step above a tramp.

Given these circumstances, it is remarkable how quickly young Isaac Rosenberg's talents were recognized. His family lived in a state of misery and deprivation that reminds one of Gorky's *The Lower Depths* or Dickens's description of the London slums in *Oliver Twist*. Hannah Rosenberg (she had changed her first name from Hacha shortly after arriving in England) looked back on her life in the Pale of Russia with as much nostalgia as she permitted herself. Despite giving birth to six children (one of whom was stillborn), there was no love lost between her and her husband. Hannah was sharp-tongued and strong-willed, her husband weak and ineffectual, a *yeshiva bocher* stranded in a foreign country, only just able to support a family. Theirs had been, as was then the custom among Orthodox Jews in the Pale, an arranged marriage. He had not been the man she wanted to marry, and she had not brought with her the dowry he and his family had expected.

In England, Barnett schlepped from one village to another as a peddler selling notions—thread, needles, pins, small bolts of cloth—from a pack on his back to housewives and davening over the Torah by candlelight at night. As miserable as that life might be, he seemed to prefer it to being at home and subjected to his wife's tongue-lashings. He had made his way to England without her and their first child, Minnie, and did not seem eager for them to join him there. Hannah followed him anyway. She took a room in Leeds, which had a large Jewish community, supported herself precariously by doing embroidery, and enlisted various Jewish charities to track down her husband. Once she found him, they lived for some years in Bristol, where Isaac was born, one of twins, the first of whom was stillborn. Isaac was not expected to survive either—he was so small and scrawny, the odds were against it—but he did.

Only a few months after his birth, the Rosenbergs moved to London's East End and found lodging in one room over a rag and bone shop. They shared the premises' one toilet with the owner and his family, their lodgers, and the men sorting the rags and bones. It would be difficult to imagine a more squalid and impoverished life. Barnett spent at least six months of the year on the road and never managed to send home more than a few shillings a week. Eventually they managed to move to better quarters, but only because Hannah rented rooms to lodgers and thus managed to eke out a miserable sustenance on her own rather than depending on her feckless husband.

Thus Isaac grew up in a world of poverty, discrimination, and domestic disharmony, with parents who, when they spoke to each other at all, spoke Yiddish. For long periods, Hannah would not speak a word to her husband, or even sit down at the table to eat with him, while he absented himself for weeks at a time and grew, perhaps thankfully, progressively more deaf. Nonetheless Isaac benefited from the excellence and toleration of the British school system, which far from excluding his religion embraced it as a means of persuading Eastern European Jews to overcome their suspicion of secular schooling. Shy, withdrawn, and not fond of sports, Isaac was sent to a Hebrew school at an early age. He learned Hebrew by rote and without enthusiasm, and by the time he was grown up, he had forgotten most of it. Unlike his father, he was not particularly religious; nor did Judaism as a religion interest him much. It would nevertheless leave a mark on his poetry, giving it from time to time a certain Oriental splendor, as in:

The gates of morning opened wide
On sunny dome and steeple.
Noon gleamed upon the mountain side . . .
Thronged with a happy people.

This is clearly a vision, not of the grim and dreary East End of London in which Isaac grew up, but of an imagined Jerusalem, the holy city that Jews had prayed to return to for nearly two thousand years.

From an early age, Isaac showed a gift for drawing rather than for poetry. Despite the family's poverty, they provided him with scraps of paper and pencils, and he often sat quietly at the table sketching portraits of his siblings. The notion that secular education was compulsory (and free) had not dawned on Isaac's parents, who had come from a country where for a Jew every contact with the state came in the form of a brutal threat or a demand. But once "the attendance officer" appeared, the Rosenbergs were happy to comply. The Jewish respect for education—combined with the assurance that there would be no effort to convert their children to Christianity—was enough to persuade them.

By the age of eight, Isaac was in grammar school, where he almost immediately attracted the attention of his headmaster, Mr. Usherwood, who recognized and encouraged the boy's talents. Usherwood not only provided Isaac with foolscap and crayons to take home but arranged for him to take art courses after school hours. He also increased Isaac's knowledge of the larger world outside the narrow ethnic one of his early childhood—it was not just art that interested him but the English language. He wrote fluently and devoured poetry at a level well beyond his age.

Had he come from a different social level, he might have been instantly recognized as university material, but the British educational system, mirroring the class distinctions that determined so much of British life, rigorously separated boys into "academic" and "technical" schools at an early age, the latter being what we now call vocational—that is intended to prepare them for a trade or a manual skill. Besides, the Rosenbergs needed Isaac to start contributing toward the family's income at fourteen, the "school leaving" age.

Isaac was fortunate in that his talent as an artist attracted attention early, first among his teachers, then among well-to-do Jewish ladies of a certain age in north London, for whom his mother Hannah did dressmaking, embroidery, and alterations. His drawings singled him out. Even his earliest ones show a remarkable degree of talent—his ability to draw what he saw, to handle perspective, to reproduce shade and highlights, was not something he had been taught or had learned; he had had no opportunity to study the work of great artists. It was a natural gift, something he was born with. Given the Orthodox Jewish theological ambivalence toward portraiture and the visual arts, it is remarkable that Isaac's father, a deeply observant student of the Torah, encouraged the boy's habit of drawing on every piece of paper he could find. Indeed, some of Isaac's best work are portraits of his father.

It is possible that in a household that was ruled by Hannah and her eldest daughter, any objections on Barnett's part were simply overruled or ignored, particularly since he was absent much of the time. All of Isaac's drawings display a bold firmness of line that is amazing in one so young and untaught. There are no signs of hesitation or second thought. There is a certain clumsiness and an unfinished quality to most of the drawings, signs of a lack of formal training, but the firmness of line impressed everyone who saw his sketches. So much so that it took some time before it became apparent that Isaac had another talent.

Isaac was different from the rest of his family, and from most of the other boys at school as well—dreamy, absorbed in his art, bad at games, conscious already that there was a whole world of culture from which he, as a poverty-stricken East End Jew, was virtually excluded. His sister Minnie seems to have understood this better than anyone else in his family. She took him to Whitechapel Public Library and introduced him to Morley Dainow, the librarian, who became Isaac's next mentor and opened up to him the world of literature and poetry. Dainow was a man of great culture and tact. He not only discerned in Isaac a thirst for poetry but encouraged him to write it, offering him advice, but never in an overbearing way. He recognized that Isaac had that peculiar combination of shyness and pride that sometimes accompanies the artistic temperament, and that too much criticism might stifle his creativity. Isaac himself would write a little later to another sympathetic admirer, "You mustn't forget the circumstances I have been brought up in, the little education I have had," which suggests that he understood his weaknesses very well and also how hard he would have to work to catch up with those who had been sent to an academic school rather than a technical one.

Dainow was a man of conventional taste in art and literature, but remarkably Whitechapel, next to its library, had an art gallery that contained works by Reynolds, Hogarth, and Rosetti, among others. The gallery was enough to give Isaac a growing sense of how much he still needed to learn, while the library offered him all the poetry he could read. Clearly the boy had a strong degree of intellectual curiosity for his age, and he read far beyond what Dainow would have thought was necessary for him to catch up. In fact, under Dainow's guidance, Isaac was swiftly acquiring the knowledge he would need to go to a university, even though he had no chance of attending one.

No doubt life in a small, cramped, crowded flat did not make it easy for Isaac to concentrate on his drawing or his poetry, however sympathetic his family was toward the cuckoo in their nest. People who knew him as a boy describe him as moody and sullen, as well he might have been given the yawning gap between his aspirations and his prospects. Even when he was ten, Isaac's gift for drawing was recognized at school, as it was at home, but in both places the expectation was that it would lead to a job in commercial art when he left the school at fourteen, so he was placed in a class to learn "art metal work," which mostly involved learning how to prepare engraved plates for rotogravure printing, a trade for which Isaac had no enthusiasm.

In the meantime, the Rosenberg family plunged from one misery into another. Peddling as a trade was coming to an end, as shops were opening up even in small villages. Better transportation was making it possible for country people to go to a nearby town and shop at a Woolworth for the kind of goods Barnett was peddling. His meager earnings declined to almost nothing, while his wife and his eldest daughter struggled to do enough embroidery to feed the family—labor which led to Minnie's near-blindness. Whatever small sums Barnett could amass from to time, he sent to his father in Latvia, who was also in dire straits. At one point Hannah's family sent Barnett enough money for a ticket to New York, in the forlorn hope that he might find those streets better lined with gold than those of London had proved to be. He went there but found no gold and returned to London. From that time, Barnett and Hannah lived as if they were divorced. Barnett faded into the background, having finally demonstrated by his failed voyage to New York his inability to succeed at anything.

By the time Isaac was twelve, his talent, both for drawing and for writing, was evident. Possibly with Usherwood's help, he submitted essays to contests and won one sponsored by the Royal Society for the Prevention of Cruelty to Animals. He began to compose poems. Like somebody in danger of drowning who reaches for a lifesaving hand, Isaac developed early on a gift for attracting the attention of older, wealthier people who admired his talent. It is impossible to say at what point he became aware of it, or to realize that it might be enough to rescue him from his family's sinking ship or from the poverty-stricken despair of London's East End Russian-Jewish community, refugees from the land of the pogrom, the knout, and the Cossacks. As ineffectual as Barnett might be, Hannah was energetic, determined, and shameless at pushing Isaac forward to those who bought her embroidery. Many of them lived in middle-class comfort in North London, Jews who were assimilated by a generation or two. Among them were Rabbi Asher Amshewitz and his wife Sarah, whose son John was a painter and would grow up to become a well-respected member of the Royal Academy. When Hannah visited the Amshewitzes, she sometimes brought Isaac with her, to give him a chance to show his drawings to John Amshewitz. Unfortunately that backfired: Amshewitz, impressed by one of the drawings, offered Isaac half a crown* for it. That offended Isaac, who had been looking for advice rather than for what he mistakenly assumed was charity.

For as long as he could, Isaac attended the Arts and Crafts School in Stepney Green after school. He saw himself as a painter rather than a poet. He sought out and found friends who, like him, were poor, young, Jewish, and trying to become artists or poets, although he was the only one who was both. Standoffish and easily embarrassed as he was, his friends were important to him, as were the evenings he spent in the library or at art school. To one of the first of the many patrons who appeared in his life, he wrote with appealing frankness, "I really would like to take up painting seriously, I think I might do something at that; but poetry—I despair of ever writing excellent poetry. I can't look at things in the simple, large way that great poets do." Nor did Rosenberg have Rupert Brooke's ability to write, with apparent ease, line after felicitous line of poetry. He labored hard over every line, striving for the right effect. It would take the war to liberate his muse. Perhaps no other poet would describe in such searing visions the horrors of trench warfare, and at least two of his last poems are regarded by many as among the finest to come out of that war.

When he reached the age of fourteen, he was expected to begin working and help support his family, so he was apprenticed as

---

* To put this in perspective, two shillings sixpence in 1900 would be worth over $20 today.

an engraver of printing plates at Carl Hentschel, Ltd. The job involved standing over hot vats of the acids used to etch the plates. He hated the work, which was as unhealthy as it was poorly paid and depressing.

He increasingly sought out evening courses in which he could improve his ability to draw and paint, while at the same time he read his poems to anyone who would listen. His meager pay enabled him to attend art classes at Birkbeck College in Chancery Lane, where his work won several prizes, and later at the London County Council School of Photo-Engraving and Lithography in Fleet Street, which was also attended by Paul Nash, who would become perhaps the most talented and original of British official war artists in *both* world wars. Nash would write that the purpose of the school was avowedly practical: "You were there to equip yourself for making a living." That was surely true, but at the same time, for a few hours a day, the school liberated Isaac and other art students (all young men; the only women there were figure models) from the tedium of his work and from the dark, noisy, crowded confines of the family flat.

The presence of other talented young people bolstered Isaac's shaky self-confidence, as did the prizes his work won, but he was still far from earning a living as a painter, still less as a poet. His painting attracted attention, however, and it is easy to see why: his pictures have a boldness that his early poems lack. Isaac's mentor John Amshewitz had obtained for him a permit to paint in the National Gallery. His copy of Velasquez's portrait of Philip IV caught the eye of a fellow painter, Mrs. Lily Delissa Joseph, who was not only rich but had a brother, Solomon J. Solomon, who was a successful painter and a member of the Royal Academy. Solomon painted vast historical subjects (Samson being bound by the Philistines at the order of an enraged, bare-breasted Delilah, for instance) and fashionable portraits. He would go on to become a camouflage expert in the war with the rank of lieutenant-colonel.* Solomon, in short, had everything that Isaac lacked—money, fame, respect and assimilation in the gentile world and the British class system.

---

* Solomon was an uncle of the American playwright and theater director Moss Hart, author of *Act One*.

Solomon's sister Lily Joseph was no mere dabbler herself. Her paintings were regularly exhibited at the Royal Academy; she was an early convert to Impressionism and a determined suffragette as well. Although Isaac described her, in an unpublished work of fiction, as "rosy and buoyant," in one of her self-portraits she looks somewhat sallow, but she has sensuous full lips, marked by a pronounced Cupid's bow, and lively, intelligent eyes.

Mrs. Joseph was not lacking in self-confidence. Expressing her admiration for Isaac's copy of the Velasquez portrait, she suggested that he try painting in the same sober palette that she used. This kind of advice from a stranger might easily have offended him, but after further conversation, it became clear to him that she knew what she was talking about. He was impressed enough to do a painting of Hampstead Heath in the rain, using the colors she had suggested, and he brought it to her house to show her.

Several of the works that Isaac painted under Lily's influence bear a striking resemblance to Monet's paintings of the London bridges, although whether he was aware of them is not known. The brushstrokes are heavier, with weight like those of Van Gogh, and the colors are subdued to the point of being almost monochromatic. But the brushstrokes have a lot of energy, even violence—could they indicate a suppressed resentment at having to paint to someone else's ideas?

Certainly Isaac appreciated the attention he was getting from Lily Joseph, but entering into her world was difficult for him. An invitation to dinner obliged him to borrow the right clothes and to face a bewildering array of silverware and food he was not accustomed to eating. Each course was presented by servants in white gloves, for the Josephs lived in the full bloom of Edwardian upper-middleclass formality.

Lily, whose will was as fierce as that of Isaac's mother, showed his work to her sister, Mrs. Henrietta Löwy, and to their friend Mrs. Herbert Cohen, both of whom were generous with scholarships and donations. She enlisted them as supporters of Isaac. Mrs. Löwy's daughter Ruth, a student at the Slade School of Art, would later marry the book publisher Victor Gollancz. This formidable trio of art-minded ladies introduced Isaac to a Jewish world very different from his own, people who were wealthy, well educated, influential, assimilated, and cultured, while still remaining Jews. At the apex of this world were such grandees as the merchant bankers Lord Rothschild and Sir Ernst Cassel, whose friends (and grateful clients) included King Edward VII and Winston Churchill. Despite a certain degree of anti-Semitism in Britain, one of its most popular and successful prime ministers had been Benjamin Disraeli, raised to the peerage by a grateful Queen Victoria as the Earl of Beaconsfield. The first Jewish member of Parliament had taken his seat in the House of Commons as early as 1770.

The three women guided Isaac toward the Slade, paid his fees for the first year, and gave him an allowance. It would have surprised them, and no doubt Isaac as well, to know that he would be remembered more as a poet than as a painter. His attendance at the Slade was in many ways a life-changing experience. Here too his new-found patrons applied the full force of their connections. His originality as a painter might have won him a place at the Slade without these backers, but with them, plus Lily's brother Solomon J. Solomon, he could hardly fail.

The Slade was in any case a more liberal institution than the staid and much larger Royal Academy of Art, which had been founded more than a hundred years earlier by George III. The Slade was more modern not only in its taste but in its choice of students, a significant number of whom were young women. The school at least recognized impressionism, post-impressionism, and cubism, even if it did not embrace them, and many of its students were rebels who looked across the Channel at those daring new ways of painting. A certain swaggering bohemianism and social flair were the house style. The student body included the young Lady Diana Manners, a daughter of the eighth Duke of Rutland, who would go on to lead a glamorous life as a society beauty and hostess (lovingly caricatured as "Mrs. Stitch" in Evelyn Waugh's *Scoop*); she would marry the dashing political figure and diplomat Duff Cooper. Also enrolled were Phyllis Gardner, who would one day have a passionate love affair with Rupert Brooke, and Dora Carrington, an associate member of the Bloomsbury Group, who despite marriage and affairs with numerous men and women had a lifelong unconsummated but devoted relationship with Lytton Strachey.

Rosenberg—poor, shabby, serious, and ever so slightly on guard against being condescended to—felt out of place. It was not enough that he had talent; *everybody* here had talent. Nor was the fact that he was both a poet and a painter so unusual. The surgeon and painter Henry Tonks, who taught at the Slade and would eventually become Slade Professor of Fine Art, once remarked that "a painter who is not a poet ought to be put in the stocks." A sensitivity toward *all* the arts was expected of Slade students, along with a certain amount of boisterous high spirits. But Rosenberg was too poor to be part of the social life—he could barely "afford a halfpenny for a cup of coffee at Lockhart's, a cheap tea-room near the Slade," and he disliked being "treated" by other students since he could not return their hospitality.

Rosenberg's output of drawings and paintings remained high, and it seems to have met with qualified approval by his teachers, but things did not run smoothly between him and his benefactors. A certain awkwardness is apparent in his correspondence with them, a resistance to any criticism of his work, together with resentment at being so dependent on their generosity. The tension shows up in his letters to Mrs. Cohen (hers to him have not survived), about which one of his biographers, Jean Liddiard, writes that "the difficult relationship of patron and protégé . . . difficult to sustain at the best of times, was frayed in this case by Mrs. Cohen's insistence that she participate more fully in his work." Isaac's reply is somewhat inarticulate but begins with a bold statement of fact, "I am very sorry to have disappointed you," and goes on to regret that she doesn't like a picture he has painted. (She regards it as "unfinished.")

By his second year at the Slade, his allowance seems to have been reduced or cut off altogether, and there had clearly been a break between Isaac and his patrons, since he wrote to Mrs. Cohen, "You can call me rude, ungentlemanly, ungrateful, etc.—but you know it is only my honesty in not concealing what I think that leaves me open to this." Despite Isaac's poverty, he went to extraordinary lengths to pay back two pounds that he thought he owed her, so as not to feel further obligated. Isaac had complete confidence in his artistic abilities but an extreme social inferiority complex, an unfortunate combination that left him unable to charm, pretend, or persuade. The only way he could deal with Mrs. Cohen's no doubt well-meaning interest in his painting was to break off with her entirely, thus sacrificing not only her financial support but that of her friends as well.

Rosenberg then applied to the Jewish Educational Aid Society, which fortunately paid for his next two years at the Slade. He even managed to sell a few drawings that he had submitted to exhibitions—the amounts of money were negligible, but they made a huge difference to Isaac, and he was able to rent a small, makeshift studio in which to attempt larger paintings. But it was poetry on which he now wanted to make his mark, not painting, and nothing is harder to do. A friend introduced him to a "printer-publisher," Israel Narodiczky, on the Mile End Road in Stepney, who had a weak spot for artistic waifs and strays. He agreed to publish fifty copies of *Night and Day*, a twenty-four-page pamphlet of Isaac's selected poems, for two pounds. Perhaps because most of Narodiczky's output was in Yiddish or Hebrew, the pamphlet is full of errors and omissions, which Isaac attempted to correct on the copies he gave away. (None were sold.)

Although Isaac lacked Rupert Brooke's gift for networking, he did his best to attract attention to his poems and, to a lesser degree, his painting. He wrote to the prolific Anglo-Jewish playwright and novelist Israel Zangwill (creator of the phrase "the melting pot" and a man greatly admired by Theodore Roosevelt), enclosing some of his poems, with a letter of almost comic self-abasement: "If the poems do not merit any part of the time you may do me the honour to bestow on them, then [my] presumption is the more unpardonable, but though I myself am diffident about them, one has, I suppose, whether one has reason or not, a sort of half-faith; and it is this half-faith—misplaced or not—that has led me to this course." This obsequiousness echoes the bathos of "Approbation from Sir Hubert Stanley is praise indeed," but of course Isaac was not aiming for humor.

There is no record that Isaac's letter to Zangwill led to anything, but his paintings caught the eye of that indefatigable dowsing rod of talent Edward Marsh. Marsh not only bought one of Isaac's more ambitious paintings, *Sacred Love* (a small colorful painting of a naked young man and a half-clothed young woman), but hung it in a prominent place in the guest bedroom of his flat, where it was admired by Rupert Brooke, among others. Marsh, despite a phenomenal workload and a social schedule that would have exhausted a lesser man, became the friend and adviser to painters and poets he admired, and once he discovered that Isaac was not only a talented painter but also an ambitious poet, he took him under his wing.

Marsh was one of the most pertinacious and meticulous editors of all time. He "diabolized" (to use his own word for the process) poetry and prose alike with the care of a surgeon, cutting, questioning the use of a word, correcting punctuation, filling page after page with deft and tactfully phrased comments and suggestions. Winston Churchill, W. Somerset Maugham, Rupert Brooke, D. H. Lawrence, and Siegfried Sassoon would all benefit in varying degrees from Marsh's eagle eye and firm judgment. He did the same for Isaac Rosenberg's poetry. Isaac did not enjoy the process any more than he had enjoyed Mrs. Cohen's comments on his painting, but he reacted a good deal less defensively, perhaps because Marsh knew how to criticize without too sharp a sting. Besides, what young writer is not flattered by someone paying such close attention to his work? Indeed, Isaac's first letter to Marsh begins, "Thanks for your criticism which of course I agree with." That said, Isaac did not hesitate to reject Marsh's advice when he did disagree with it, and he seems to have recognized that Marsh's taste in poetry was less daring than his taste in painting.

Without becoming a full-fledged patron, Marsh helped Isaac out by buying his paintings with an occasional check. Marsh had only a civil servant's salary, but he received a tidy private income thanks to being a descendent of Spencer Perceval, the only British prime minister to be assassinated* and in whose honor Parliament had established a substantial settlement. Marsh set about widening Isaac's horizon by sending him the first of the five anthologies of "Georgian" poetry that he was to edit between 1911 and 1922. Isaac was greatly impressed by the work of Gordon Bottomley, all but forgotten now but then a rising star, and James Elroy Flecker, a much-admired poet and friend of both T. E. Lawrence (the future

* In the House of Commons in 1812.

Lawrence of Arabia) and Rupert Brooke. "I know little of these men, and from that little I know how much I miss by not knowing more," Isaac wrote Marsh, thanking him for the book. The first volume of *Georgian Poetry* contained five of Brooke's best early poems, including "The Old Vicarage, Grantchester," as well as poems by Walter de la Mare, D. H. Lawrence, and John Masefield, among others. For Isaac, it was practically a crash course in modern poetry, as no doubt Marsh intended it to be.

It is also interesting that most of the poets in the anthology knew or knew of each other. Flecker and Brooke had been friends at Cambridge. T. S. Eliot and Siegfried Sassoon were friends and admirers of Walter de la Mare. John Masefield would eventually be named poet laureate on the recommendation of Edward Marsh to Prime Minister Ramsay MacDonald. Wilfrid Wilson Gibson was not only close to Rupert Brooke, but would become one of Brooke's literary executors. And Harold Monro, another Cambridge man, opened the Poetry Bookshop, where Brooke recited his poems to an audience that included the American poet Amy Lowell and above which Gibson and several of the Georgian poets lived. John Drinkwater rented a cottage in the same rural Gloucestershire village as the American poet Robert Frost, where Brooke was a frequent visitor.

Isaac Rosenberg could hardly fail to notice that none of these poets were Jewish, and that almost all of them had been to the same kind of school or university, and that they were connected in one way or another to the English world of letters and to the rather smaller but still significant world of English poetry. The bucolic strain of much Georgian poetry, with its idealization of pastures, hedgerows, thatched cottages, and country life, was as foreign to him as the East End of London would be to them.

Even Marsh could only do so much for Isaac, whose alienation and latent inferiority complex had increased since his older sister Minnie's marriage and departure for South Africa. His health had deteriorated too. He coughed a lot and was short of breath—the doctors told him he had "a weak chest," and needed rest and a change of climate. The Jewish Educational Aid Society agreed to send him to the seaside town of Bournemouth for a couple of weeks, which he described as "a big sanitarium" with an "invalids' garden," but as soon as he returned to London, the coughing returned. It is hard to say what the problem was. It could not have been tuberculosis, since that would have been easily diagnosed. More likely it was a chronic case of severe asthma, for which the air of London, thickened by the smoke from several million coal fires, could not have been less salubrious. Ironically, just as Isaac was beginning to make an impact with his paintings, he was obliged to leave England for his health— not to the countryside, where he would have felt displaced, but to South Africa, to stay with his sister Minnie and her husband in Cape Town, to escape from another winter in London.

Distant as it was, South Africa was not quite as exotic a destination as it might seem. It had a large and mostly Orthodox Jewish community dating back to the sixteenth century. From the mid-nineteenth century on, it had been swelled by immigrants, mostly from Eastern Europe. Anti-Semitism was certainly present, both among the Boers and the English, but South Africa, for its Europeans at any rate, had no equivalent to the poverty of London's teeming East End slums. Minnie's husband was a postal official, and Isaac's uncle, Peretz Rosenberg, was a well-respected rabbi in Johannesburg. These people were comparatively prosperous and well-established. Isaac hoped to sell some of his paintings, take on commissions for portraits, and give art lessons to pay for his board and keep, not an unreasonable plan. Marsh gave his blessing to it, as, more important, did Isaac's mother.

Isaac did not have much to bind him to England. His poetry reflects a rather tepid and almost certainly unconsummated love affair with Sonia Cohen, also a survivor of childhood misery. Sonia worked in the East End equivalent of a New York City garment district sweatshop, but apparently she appreciated poetry and was friendly with some of Isaac's fellow young artists. Isaac painted a rather demure portrait of her, in which she looks thoughtful rather than passionate, but his poems reflect his erotic longing, together with his disappointment, which was entirely realistic, that she was never going to return it. Whatever her feelings for him were, she seems to have been his soulmate rather than his lover. She would not have risked pregnancy for a man who was virtually penniless. With no home of his own and few prospects, he could not even get his shoes repaired without borrowing the money from one of his patrons. He was also profoundly self-involved. Even his most devoted biographer, Joseph Cohen, describes him at that point in his life as "solemn, preoccupied, over-assertive, difficult," hardly a combination of traits likely to win over a sensitive young woman.

At some point before leaving for South Africa, Isaac had a more serious affair with Annetta Raphaël, a woman older than himself, no doubt with more sexual experience; after the war, she would go on to become a respected painter and sculptress and co-found, with her artist husband Mario Mafai, the Scuola Romana. A major figure of expressionism, she would live until 1975, and her work would be exhibited all over the world. Raphaël's widowed mother, like Isaac's parents, had fled from Russian anti-Semitic persecution, and Annetta (whose name became Antonietta once she moved to Italy) was brought up in London, where she trained as an artist and was a part of the circle around the sculptor Jacob Epstein. Isaac's departure for Cape Town apparently ended their affair.

In the meantime Marsh continued to diabolize Isaac's work with his usual close attention and passion for detail. Isaac groaned and grumbled at the pages of closely reasoned advice that he received about every line of his poetry, but he paid attention. "I am not going to refute your criticisms," he wrote Marsh. "In literature I have no judgment—at least for style. If in reading a thought has expressed itself to me, in beautiful words; my ignorance of grammar etc, [*sic*] makes me accept that. I should think you are right mostly, and I may yet work away your chief objections."

Unlike Rupert Brooke, Isaac tended to work endlessly at his poems, making changes even after it was set in type. In "Midsummer Frost," the poem to which Isaac is referring above, the final version differs drastically from the earlier draft that Marsh read. Here is the first version:

### Midsummer Frost

A July ghost, aghast at the strange winter,
Wonders, at burning noon, (all summer seeming),

How, like a sad thought buried in light words,
Winter, an alien presence, is ambushed here.
See, from the fire-fountained noon there creep
Lazy yellow ardours towards pale evening,
Dragging the sun across the shell of thought.
A web threaded with fading fire.
Futile and fragile lure!
All Jul walks her floors that roof this ice,
My frozen heart the summer cannot reach,
Hidden as a root from air, or star from day.
A frozen pool whereon mirth dances
Where the shining boys would fish.

Amorous to woo the golden kissing sun,
Your flaunting green hoods bachic eyes
And flower-flinging hands,
Show quaint as in some frolic masker's whim,
Or painted ruby on a dead white rose.
Deriding those blind who slinked past God
And their untasked inheritance,
(Whose sealed eyes trouble not the sun)
With a thought of Maytime once,
And Maytime dances;
Of a dim pearl-faery boat
And golden glimmerings;
Waving white hands that ripple lakes of sadness
Until the sadness vanishes and the stagnant pool remains.
Pitiless I am, for I bind thee, laughter's apostle,
Even as thy garland's glance, and thy soul is merry, to see
How in night-hanging forest of eating maladies,
A frozen forest of moon-unquiet madness
The moon-drunk, haunted, pierced soul, dies.
Starved by its Babel folly, stark it lies,
Stabbed by life's jealous eyes.

The second version, after Marsh's suggestions, is drastically different:

## Midsummer Frost

A July ghost, aghast at the strange winter,
Wonders, at burning noon, (all summer seeming),
How, like a sad thought buried in light words,
Winter, an alien presence, is ambushed here.

See, from the fire-fountained noon there creep
Lazy yellow ardours towards pale evening,
To thread dark and vain fire
Over my unsens'd heart,
Dead heart, no urgent summer can reach.
Hidden as a root from air or a star from day;
A frozen pool whereon mirth dances;
Where the shining boys would fish.
My blinded brain pierced is,
And searched by a thought, and pangful
With bitter ooze of a joyous knowledge
Of some starred time outworn.
Like blind eyes that have slinked past God,
And light, their untasked inheritance,
(Sealed eyes that trouble never the Sun)
Yet has feel of a Maytime pierced.
He heareth the Maytime dances;
Frees from their airy prison, bright voices,
To loosen them in his dark imagination,
Powered with girl revels rare
And silks and merry colours,
And all the unpeopled ghosts that walk in words.
Till wave white hands that ripple lakes of sadness,
Until the sadness vanishes and the stagnant pool remains.
Underneath this summer air can July dream
How, in night-hanging forest of eating maladies,
A frozen forest of moon unquiet madness,
The moon-drunk haunted pierced soul dies;
Starved by its Babel folly, lying stark,
Unvexed by July's warm eyes.

A whole world of scholarship is devoted to tracing the different versions of Isaac's poems. Most of those that were published during his lifetime were corrected or revised by him in pencil; the copy would then be sold or, more often, given away. So the "final" version of each one represents a scholarly compromise. Had he survived the war, he might have gone on revising them, and no doubt Marsh would have gone on suggesting changes. Myself, I prefer the earlier version of "Midsummer Frost" to the later one, but that is just a question of personal taste. For me, Isaac's war poems have a directness and simplicity that his earlier poems lack, as if the shock and sheer horror of trench warfare focused his talent.

Isaac had a surer touch with drawing and painting than he did with poetry, although with these too he sometimes spoiled what he had done by changing it, often to answer criticism. In much the same way that Rupert Brooke's poetry was made to seem outdated by the work of modernist poets like T. S. Eliot and Ezra Pound, Isaac's paintings were soon eclipsed by the work of more "advanced" English artists like Paul Nash, Wyndham Lewis, and Stanley Spenser.

Isaac's voyage to South Africa was a major watershed, at once an attempt to flee from the stifling closeness of his life at home, to put behind him what seems to have been the more important of his two love affairs, and to experience a brighter and more colorful landscape than London's stained brick and fog—and to regain his health.

Cape Town was a thriving, fast-growing metropolis by 1914, with a population of about 200,000. (It is well over 2 million today.) It had a bustling business district, trams, and considerable importance as a port city. The Jewish community was substantial (although nothing like that of Johannesburg). People looked to London, three weeks away by ship, as the center for all that was fashionable, and for culture and art. Isaac, as someone who had studied at the Slade, had a brief moment of celebrity in Cape Town, in part stage-managed by his sister Minnie, who had always been good at promoting her artist brother.

In no time he acquired, thanks to Edward Marsh, a commission to paint two of the children of Sir Herbert Stanley, a rising figure in the British colonial service. He was invited to give a lecture about art and the artist, to an audience that was surely somewhat baffled by his references to painters they had never heard of and whose works they had never seen. It was later reprinted, together with two of his poems, in *South African Women in Council*, "a woman's magazine . . . where it looks very odd among the recipes and hints on preserving fruit." Isaac dismissed most of the great artists whom his listeners had been taught to admire and, as he wrote to Marsh, drew their attention instead to "[Augustus] John, Cézanne, Vangoch [*sic*], Innes, the early Picasso, (not the cubistic one) Spencer Gertler Lamb, Purvis [*sic*] de Chavannes Degas." Of the Futurists, among whom he counted himself, he said, "Theirs is the terrible beauty of destruction and the furious energy in destroying. They would burn up the past; they would destroy all standards. They have wearied of this unfair competition of the dead with the living."

One sees his point. In every age artists have rebelled against being judged by the work of old masters, although it seems doubtful that his audiences would have agreed with him. Considering what was shortly to come, the phrase "the terrible beauty of destruction" is somewhat prophetic. Isaac would soon experience at first hand more destruction than he could ever have wanted to see.

At first Isaac was overwhelmed by Cape Town. "There's a lot of splendid stuff to paint," he wrote Marsh. "We are walled in by the sharp upright mountain and the bay. Across the bay the piled up mountains of Africa look lovely and dangerous. It makes one think of savagery and earthquakes—the elemental lawlessness." His enthusiasm soon waned. Whatever its other virtues, Cape Town was lacking in artistic ferment. He found the people mired in "gold dust, diamond dust, stocks and shares, and heaven knows what other flinty muck." The Dutch who had settled in South Africa very early in the seventeenth century had aspired to create an isolated agricultural utopia, but like the American South, it soon came to depend on slavery. The sheer vastness of the land meant that the Dutch could always trek beyond the reach of governance, even after the British acquired the Cape Colony.

In the late nineteenth century, the world's largest deposits of gold and diamonds were discovered there, which led to a savage war with

Great Britain and the eventual transformation of South Africa to a modernizing industrialized country of great wealth. Speculation on shares of gold or diamond mining companies became more important than farming in the remote hinterlands with slave labor. After the end of the Boer War in 1902, Cape Town and Johannesburg were places where it was possible to get rich quickly, so it was hardly surprising that Isaac Rosenberg found people to be more interested in "flinty muck" than in modern art.

Isaac had not been in Cape Town more than a month—just time to complete his portrait of Sir Stanley's children—when the faraway event that was to change his life took place, the assassination of the Archduke Franz Ferdinand and his wife, on June 28, 1914, followed by the fatal series of mobilizations that culminated in the German invasion of neutral Belgium. "But the neutrality of Belgium is just a scrap of paper" (*un chiffon de papier*), the German chancellor protested when the British ambassador told him that the United Kingdom was declaring war on Germany. That scrap of paper would cost millions of men their lives.

Isaac was not prompted to any degree of enthusiasm by the news from home. "I despise war and hate war," he wrote Marsh, who as Winston Churchill's private secretary was in the thick of things at the Admiralty. "Now is the time to go on an exploring expedition to the North Pole; to come back and find settled order again." As the months went by, Isaac continued to write poems and paint. His health improved. He felt no urge to enlist; nor was it necessary, since Britain had as yet no conscription. The publication of his lecture introduced him to a whole new set. The daughter of the speaker of the Union Assembly was so impressed by his poetry that she invited him to spend a couple of weeks near her family's home in the leafy, upscale Cape Town suburb of Rondesbosch.

He wrote home in ecstasy at the luxury of his surroundings: "I'm here in Rodensbosch having a happy time . . . living like a toff. . . . Early in the morning coffee is brought to me in bed. . . . I shan't make your mouth water by describing my wonderful breakfasts—the unimaginable lunches—delicious teas, and colossal dinners." He was distressed by the state of his one pair of shoes—the holes in the soles grew larger every day. Even more humiliating, every night they were picked up from outside his door and reappeared in the morning with the cracked uppers polished to a gleaming shine.

His sister Minnie had been reluctant to see him go, but she understood that it was too good an offer to turn down. There in Rodensbosch, with its neat gardens and flamboyant flower beds, Isaac was exposed to an alternative future. He could be a successful painter of portraits and landscapes, with a sideline in serious poetry, among well-to-do people with a cultivated interest in the arts, a provincial celebrity in a world where his Jewishness wasn't held against him. After all, almost a third of the major gold and diamond mines were owned or controlled by South African Jews of European origin. Otherwise, he could go home to a much less certain life, with no guarantee of where his next meal was coming from.

He described the war to Marsh as "a perfect nuisance," and like most people, he assumed it would be over quickly. The notion that it would drag on for four years of bloodshed, costing many millions of lives, had not occurred to him or anyone else except Field Marshal Kitchener, who predicted exactly that and called for a volunteer army of at least a million men.

In the autumn of 1914, the armies settled down to the miseries of trench warfare on the Western Front, while on the Eastern Front the Russian Army was defeated at the Battle of Tannenberg (over 250,000 Russian casualties, among them its commander, who committed suicide rather than report the defeat to the czar) and withdrew to a defensive line. Isaac, on the other hand, experienced perhaps the most enjoyable period of his life. He had escaped from the failure of a love affair, from the tension between his parents, from the pressure of poverty, and from the competition to succeed in the superheated London art world. In the benign climate of Cape Town, his health returned, and a degree of optimism flickered faintly through his correspondence with Marsh and his family. A certain lyricism crept into his poetry, smoothing out the occasional harshness. He sounded like a happy man.

But he had already made up his mind. Despite the middle-class comfort of his life in Cape Town, "a creature of the most exquisite civilization, planted in this barbarous land," he was making plans for his return. He hoped to be back in England, he wrote his parents, "about the time of the warm weather—about March or so." He sailed for home in February 1915, his voyage marred only by the fact that most of the paintings he had done in South Africa were dropped overboard as they were being loaded onto the ship. Such once-in-a-lifetime pieces of bad luck seemed to plague Isaac throughout his life.

Luckily, his mind was set on other things, among them a plan to write a play in verse about Moses—an extraordinarily ambitious project for a young man. He returned to Britain to find the family's situation unchanged. His mother and father were still not on speaking terms, and they were all still crowded into a small flat. Since his poverty was as complete as ever, he had no option but to live at home with his family. "Estrangement and hostility hung heavy in the atmosphere of the household," Joseph Cohen comments in his biography of Isaac, remarking that in a note to Hannah (they no longer talked), Barnett Rosenberg compared her to "leprosy." Isaac reassumed the hopeless task of attempting to mediate between his parents. In the circumstances it is extraordinary that he was able to write and paint at all, but as usual he persevered. He submitted his poems to the editors of many magazines and showed his drawings and paintings to Edward Marsh. Marsh had a great admiration for Isaac as an artist and bought as many of his pieces as he had room for. When it came to Isaac's poetry, however, his admiration was always combined with detailed criticism. He was a born editor and did not spare Isaac's feelings. "If you do find time to read my poems," Isaac wrote Marsh with a rare hint of resentment, "and I sent them because I think they're worth reading, for God's Sake! don't say they're obscure. The idea in the poem I like best I should think is very clear."

Isaac's attempt to explain the idea in the poem to Marsh nevertheless is completely obscure. It begins: "That we can cheat our malignant fate who has devised a perfect evil for us, by pretending to have as much misery as we can bear, so that it withholds its greater evil, while under that guise of misery there is secret joy," and goes on from there into obscurer depths. Marsh struggled with "The Blind God," but it was not just its obscurity that perplexed him. He remained the arbiter of neo-Georgian poetry, with its lyricism and its very English dislike of abstract ideas and attempts to define (or defy) God. He was the least prejudiced of Englishmen, but without the subject ever quite emerging clearly between them, it was Isaac's Jewishness to which he objected. Wrestling with the ideas of who or what God is, and of what our relationship with Him should be, was not something Marsh was interested in or that he could edit out of Isaac's poetry, as "The Blind God" makes clear.

## The Blind God

Streaked with immortal blasphemies,
Betwixt His twin eternities
The Shaper of mortal destinies
Sits in that limbo of dreamless sleep,
Some nothing that hath shadows deep.

The world is only a small pool
In the meadows of Eternity,
And men like fishes lying cool;
And the wise man and the fool
In its depths like fishes lie.
When an angel drops a rod
And he draws you to the sky
Will you bear to meet your God
You have streaked with blasphemy?

Marsh had those two vital characteristics of an editor, patience and a real respect for talent, even when it took a form that was not at all his cup of tea. He and Isaac did not quarrel, and Marsh continued to buy drawings and small paintings from Isaac and to "diabolize" his poems. The importance to Isaac of the occasional small check from Marsh is best described by himself in his thank-you letter: "I love poetry—but just now the finest poem ever written would not move me as [much as] the writing on that cheque."

There is an engaging frankness to Isaac's letters as he struggles to describe exactly what he feels without any plea for sympathy. The relatively small amounts of money he was receiving from Marsh he put into getting his poems printed, using Israel Narodiczky again, for a pamphlet with the title *Youth*. Narodiczky was helpful and generous, charging Isaac only two pounds ten shillings for one hundred copies, exactly what Marsh had paid Isaac for three drawings. But again, since most of Narodiczky's work was in Hebrew or Yiddish, there were numerous errors. Still, seeing his poems in print was a huge boost to Isaac's self-esteem, as was his sale of several poems, if only for a few shillings, to *Colours*, a glossy, upmarket avant-garde art magazine, despised by Wyndham Lewis and Ezra Pound.

In the meantime Isaac was beginning to think about his verse play *Moses*. It was a challenge to his imagination, since we do not know anything more about Moses than the Old Testament tells us. Reading the fragments that he eventually produced, it is hard to imagine what Marsh made of them. "The royal paunch of Pharaoh dangled worriedly, / Not knowing where the wrong," does not sound like the kind of thing Marsh would have wanted to include in *Georgian Poetry*. Nor would it likely appeal to "an aesthete with a strong sense of tradition, and of the English tradition . . . the self-appointed custodian." But among his other virtues Marsh was curious, and tolerant of other people's artistic ambitions.

Having some of his poems printed enabled Isaac to send them out to people who might review them, or at least *read* them. One was Sydney Schiff, a prolific author under the pseudonym Stephen Hudson and a wealthy patron of the arts, whose friends and protégés over the years would include Proust, Picasso, Diaghilev, Stravinsky, Aldous Huxley, T. S. Eliot, James Joyce, and Osbert Sitwell. Schiff was like a Jewish version of Edward Marsh, and before long Isaac was in frequent correspondence with him, enclosing more poems and an outline of *Moses*, which even Schiff found hard to follow. Like Marsh, Schiff was sympathetic to artists, and his life was a kind of one-man foundation, connecting artists with each other and writers to magazines that might publish their work. He seems to have known everyone and read everything, although he moved in a very different set than Marsh. Moreover, he did not share Marsh's ability to be the vital "spare man" of society, witty, gossipy, politically well informed, and perfectly dressed at every dinner party, charming everybody from members of the Royal Family on down.

In April 1915 came the news of Rupert Brooke's death, which temporarily shattered Marsh's composure. Isaac did not like Brooke's "begloried sonnets," as he called them, and was mildly jealous both of Brooke's fame and his close relationship with Marsh. In fact, his letter to Marsh about Brooke's death was notably short and lacking in warmth, which he must have realized, since he wrote some days later to apologize. Marsh, although distraught with grief, forgave Isaac, but the blaze of patriotic fervor that Brooke's death and his war sonnets aroused seems to have turned Isaac's mind toward enlisting despite the fervent Tolstoyan belief in pacifism of his parents and his own doubts about the war.

To some extent, Isaac's thoughts about enlisting were practical: he was still living at home with his parents, increasing their impoverishment by being another mouth to feed. Small sums from Schiff and Marsh could not change that, and even an attempt to go back to his old job preparing lithographic printing plates failed. It was as if his only way forward were to join up. All around him even the most improbable people were enlisting, or else they were taking on the many social and physical burdens of declaring themselves conscientious objectors, which he was not. He had written to Marsh that he hoped "Kaiser William will have his bottom smacked" on the outbreak of war, but at the same time he hated the *idea* of war, and he rightly feared that *this* one would merely produce a "bath of blood" with no outcome worth fighting for. The pressure to enlist was enormous in 1915. Kitchener wanted an army of a million men—nothing smaller could hope to defeat the Germans or help the beleaguered French, whose casualties from August 1914 to the spring of 1915 exceeded 650,000. Still, the government remained unwilling to impose conscription, which was regarded as a deeply un-British institution.

True to his own convictions about the war, Isaac kept on drawing and writing, while attending a school that taught the printing trade. He barely eked out an existence by selling a drawing from time to time to Marsh or by begging small "loans" from Schiff, which neither of them expected could ever be repaid. It cannot have been easy; it was at the height of the "white feather" period, in which women jeered at apparently fit young men who were not in khaki and handed them white feathers, symbolizing cowardice, while men physically threatened them. Isaac, with his usual blunt honesty, tried to explain his situation to Schiff. Marsh, still mourning Brooke and working at the right hand of Winston Churchill, may not have been in a mood to listen to Isaac's explanations. "I can only give my personal and if you like selfish say that one's individual situation is more real and important to oneself than the devastation of fates and empires especially when they do not vitally affect oneself." Even the patient Schiff gently reproached Isaac for his self-pity. Getting his poems published anywhere remained difficult. Ezra Pound, ever on the lookout for poetic talent, had sent "Youth" to his friend Harriet Monroe in Chicago for *Poetry Magazine*, albeit with a lukewarm and mildly anti-Semitic comment, but with no result.

Throughout the autumn of 1915, Isaac hesitated between enlisting and not enlisting. The war dragged on. Germany used poison gas for the first time at the Second Battle of Ypres, killing six thousand Canadian soldiers in ten minutes. A German U-boat sank the passenger liner *Lusitania*, taking 1,198 civilian lives. The landings at Gallipoli took place, which would cost over a hundred thousand British and Commonwealth lives and strip Churchill of his post as first lord of the Admiralty. The Battle of Loos, a military disaster, killed fifty thousand British troops, including two generals, and the few British soldiers who managed to reach the German front line were killed. In the East, a German offensive cost the Russians Poland and untold thousands of lives; it impelled the czar to take personal command of the army, with disastrous consequences for himself and Russia. Germany began bombing England by night with zeppelins. There was not the faintest ray of hope that the bloodbath would ever end. A recruiting poster of the day read, "It is far better to face the bullets than to be killed at home by a bomb—join the army at once & help to stop an air raid." It was not this bleak message that convinced Isaac, however. It was sheer need. He had run out of options for providing for himself. In the army, he would at least be fed, housed, and paid a shilling a day.

Even then Isaac nearly failed. His lungs were weak, his physical condition was poor, and he was too short. He would have been rejected as unfit for military service had not the government, desperate for cannon fodder, just revised the physical requirements sharply downward. It created "Bantam battalions" of men who were too short to meet the previous height standard of five feet three inches. To enlist, he had to sneak out of his parents' flat with a toothbrush and two books in his pockets (John Donne's poems and Sir Thomas Browne's *Religio Medici*), in order to avoid a scene with his mother, who was adamantly opposed to military service. He requested service in the Royal Army Medical Corps as an alternative to killing, but it was infantrymen the army needed, and in any case Isaac had no medical experience or training,

Isaac was dispatched to an army recruit depot at Bury St. Edmunds, about seventy miles northwest of London. From there he wrote to inform his parents that he had signed up—news that precipitated a dramatic explosion at home. His mother "raged and sobbed and would not be comforted. . . . At one point she seemed near collapse." Even Isaac's father, who was inured to his wife's storms of emotion, was "angry, perplexed and helpless." The Rosenbergs focused their fear and rage on Edward Marsh, but for once Marsh could do nothing. Isaac had signed up for general service, a guaranteed ticket to the trenches and no power could undo that fatal signature.

At Bury St. Edmunds, it began to dawn on Isaac what he had let himself in for. "I have just joined the Baantams [*sic*] and am down here amongst a horrible rabble," he wrote Marsh. "Falstaff's scarecrows were nothing to these. Three out of every 4 have been scavengers, the fourth is ticket-of-leave."* To Schiff, he wrote rather more frankly (presumably he did not want to sound too critical of the British Army to Marsh) "about having to eat out of the same basin as 'some horribly smelling scavenger who spits and sneezes into it.'"

For weeks no uniforms or towels were issued to the recruits, so Isaac was obliged to dry himself with the handkerchief he had brought with him. He was wet, cold, half-starved, and savagely picked on by officers, noncommissioned officers, and his fellow recruits for being a Jew. His fellow Bantams were noisy, physically

---

* *Ticket-of-leave* is an old-fashioned term for parole. By 1915 it had come to describe men whose prison sentence would be suspended if they agreed to join the army.

violent, uncultured, and as filthy in speech as in their personal hab-
its, while Isaac was withdrawn, fastidious, silent, and timid, a natu-
ral target for every bully. Theft was common, and the fact that Isaac
spent what little free time he had reading books or writing poetry
stirred up a certain amount of class resentment. Eventually he man-
aged to win a degree of acceptance by giving away most of the con-
tents of the food packages his mother and his sister Annie sent him,
and by drawing portraits of his barrack mates.

Still, Isaac remained deeply, numbingly miserable and lonely. Even
in civilian life, Isaac had not been a good mixer, and it was more
difficult still for him in a barrack room. Although he was working
class, he did not share the rowdy, jeering lower-class resentment of
those of his barrack roommates toward those who were in author-
ity. Throughout his young life he had been among other Jews. Even
in places like the Slade, where Jews were a minority, most people
had been tolerant or at least hid a fairly low level of social anti-
Semitism. Here in the recruit depot, he was the only Jew in his bar-
rack, a figure at once exotic and despised. He turned to his poetry as
an escape, and as one of his biographers astutely points out, one of
the first poems he wrote at Bury St. Edmunds, "The Jew," conveys
his feeling of isolation in a hostile world.

> Moses, from whose loins I sprang,
> Lit by a lamp in his blood
> Ten immutable rules, a moon,
> For mutable lampless men,
> The blonde, the bronze, the ruddy,
> With the same heaving blood,
> Keep time to the moon of Moses,
> Then why do they sneer at me?

The last line says it all about Isaac's reaction to barrack life. He
had never been particularly interested in Judaism or the history of
the Jews—his ambition was to be a major English poet. But now his
thoughts turned again toward the idea of a verse play about Moses,
not the familiar, older Moses who talked almost as an equal with
God and led the Jews out of Egypt, but Moses in Egypt, a powerful

giant of a man, at home in Pharaoh's court yet not a part of it, a man capable of murder.

> While the new lips my spirit would kiss
> Were not red lips of flesh,
> But the huge kiss of power.
> Where yesterday soft hair through my fingers fell
> A shaggy mane would entwine,
> And no slim form work fire to my thighs.
> But human Life's inarticulate mass
> Throb the pulse of thing
> Whose mountain flanks awry
>
> Beg my mastery—mine!
> Ah! I will ride the dizzy beast of the world
> My road—my way.

Isaac's Moses is an epic warrior like Achilles, whose future is determined not only by God's inscrutable demands but by his own yearning for power. In short, he was everything that Isaac was not, lying on his cot of rough boards at the recruit depot, scribbling away at his poems on scraps of paper despite the brawling, noisy, stinking, sneering presence of his mates.

The recruits drilled and marched in their threadbare civilian clothes, and they learned to come to terms with a world in which everything had to be done double time and every shouted order obeyed. Unlike his mates, Isaac was not used to heavy physical labor, but shoveling coal was the army's traditional way of breaking a recruit's will. It was also the best preparation for a soldier's life in the trenches, where he would have a pick or a shovel in his hands more often than his rifle. Even while he was still wearing his civilian shoes, he developed big sores on his heels, once his boots were issued—big, heavy army clodhoppers with thick soles and steel studs, made of leather as stiff as a board. Isaac's feet were reduced to an appalling state—he marched "in terrible agony." Nobody had told him that the boots had to be soaked in oil to soften them up. No one had shown him how to bring them to the required mirror-like spit-shine afterward. He had no gift for producing a razor-sharp crease in his breeches or in winding his puttees perfectly. He was isolated from the camaraderie in which these secrets were passed on from one recruit to another, or from a friendly corporal. He was on his own, bewildered by the threatening shouts of the drill sergeant and the curt contempt of the rare officer who deigned to notice him.

To make matters worse, he slipped and fell while running and cut his hands. Sent to the military hospital, he received even less food and little in the way of treatment. In a rare burst of resentment, he wrote to Schiff, "The doctor here, Major Devoral, is a ridiculous bullying brute and I have marked him for special treatment when I come to write about the army." Much of what Isaac received he gave away. "With cigarettes I could make myself more liked," he wrote Schiff, "and eatables I'd like myself." The hospital was even harder to bear than the barrack. "There is not a book or paper here, we are not allowed to stir from the gate, have little to eat, and are not allowed to buy any even if we have money—and are utterly wretched." He did not tell his mother he was in the hospital for fear of worrying her even more.

Once his hands and feet began to heal, Isaac's lot improved a bit, thanks to Marsh and Schiff, who sent him cigarettes, chocolates, paper, and watercolors, as well as the occasional pound or two, with which he was able to buy a better pair of boots. Isaac's spirits rose a bit once he was in uniform and issued a rifle. Though he was still bullied and exhausted, he felt he was becoming a soldier. His serious demeanor, his quiet, studious nature, and his constant reading and drawing whenever he had a moment to himself unexpectedly paid off when his sergeant offered to put his name in for promotion to lance-corporal, a "one-striper," the lowest rank of noncommissioned officer. Somewhat perversely, Isaac turned the promotion down; whether he was unwilling to become a part, however small, of the military command structure, or he did not want to give orders is not known. Being made a lance-corporal this early in his training would have singled him out as a possible candidate for an officer's commission—it was usual to give a soldier a stripe before putting his name in for a commission. So accepting the promotion might radically have changed his life, although it would not have improved his chance of surviving. Second lieutenants had the highest rate of casualties of any group in the war, since they were expected to lead their platoon, boldly walking casually into rifle and machine-gun fire, setting an example for their troops.

Isaac's group of volunteers was originally called the 12th (Bantam) Battalion of the Suffolk Regiment. Although the British Army was expanding at a dizzying rate, it kept in place the division of troops into the traditional regiments, some of which went back nearly four hundred years. Each one, whatever its seniority and place in the line of battle, was a small military world unto itself, with its own fiercely guarded traditions, battle honors, peculiarities of dress, and close ties to a county or a city. The Suffolk Regiment had been founded in 1685 as the Duke of Norfolk's regiment of foot; its home, the site of its regimental depot, was Gibraltar Barracks in Bury St. Edmunds, Suffolk. It had fought in every corner of the globe and served with distinction in every part of the British Empire.

In peacetime, a regiment might consist of two battalions, each of 977 soldiers and noncommissioned officers, and thirty officers and warrant officers. Each battalion was commanded by a lieutenant-colonel. In wartime, a regiment might expand to twenty-five or more battalions, each theoretically a duplicate of the others. Inevitably, as the number of battalions grew apace, the strong regional identity of the regiment (the Suffolks recruited from Suffolk, the Royal Welch Fusiliers from Wales, etc.) became diluted. Isaac, like most of his mates, had never been in Suffolk in his life. His battalion might have a handful of senior officers and warrant officers who were of local origin, but as a rule, only the first two battalions of a regiment retained its original deep roots. Still, once a man had been in a regiment long enough, he usually developed a strong loyalty to its identity. He might not know or care what division or corps he served in, but he knew he was "a Suffolk," or a South Wales Borderer, or a Duke of Cornwall's light infantryman.

Isaac had hardly had time to polish his Suffolk cap badge (Gibraltar Castle with its key, surrounded by oak leaves and surmounted by the crown) before his partially trained battalion was transferred to the South Lancashire Regiment and moved to Farnborough, to become part of the Fortieth Division.

Isaac managed to get home for Christmas in his ill-fitting uniform—a photograph taken at the time shows him looking pale and thin in a badly wrinkled tunic that is several sizes too large. He enjoyed a four-day leave that seems to have taken place without Sturm und Drang on the part of his mother, doubtless helped in part by his not telling her that his battalion would soon go overseas. He saw old friends and made the first step toward printing, at his own expense, his verse drama *Moses*.

For Isaac, life in the 12th South Lancashires at Aldershot was no improvement. He was stuck with the same miscreants as before, and he caught cold from sleeping on the damp floor of the barrack. The level of violence and theft among his barrack mates was, if anything, worse; the food was inedible and in short supply. One slight glimmer of hope was the fact that the second-in-command of the battalion was Jewish, and his family had heard of Isaac. With *Moses* almost completed, Isaac began to write poems about his life in the army, and almost immediately he found the voice that would lift him to the first rank of the British war poets. "Marching" captures that most familiar occupation of the soldier with brutal realism:

> My eyes catch ruddy necks
> Sturdily pressed back—
> All a red-brick moving glint.
> Like flaming pendulums, hands
> Swing across the khaki—
> Mustard-colored khaki—
> To the automatic feet.

The earlier striving for poetic effect, the complicated metaphors, the attempt to leap in one bound to the kind of poetry Keats wrote— all this is gone. With the "ruddy necks," the hands swinging across the khaki, the "automatic feet" (a wonderful phrase), Isaac struck a new note of simplicity that conveys the rhythm of feet marching at the regulation 116 beats a minute. This new approach did not appeal to Marsh, who was trying to push Isaac in the other direction. At the same time, Marsh was struggling with the War Office to straighten out the amount that was supposed to be deducted from

Isaac's pay (a shilling a day) to go to his family, as well as the amount they had been supposed to receive on his enlistment (eleven shillings six pence).

The level of violence in the battalion was a constant threat, and the men were close to starvation. There was talk of mutiny. There were even rumors that a few men had tried to break out from camp and been bayoneted. The fact that Isaac was receiving parcels of food from home, in addition to being a Jew, made him a target for ugly threats and outright robbery, but he was saved by the army itself. It finally came to grips with the low standards of the Bantams in the Fortieth Division, weeded out the worst offenders, and transferred the remainder of Isaac's battalion to the 11th King's Own Royal Lancaster Regiment, which had a proportion of regular soldiers and NCOs. Discipline was strict, even harsh, but that had the advantage of ensuring that there was little or no unrest in the barracks, while food was better and more plentiful. Unfortunately for Isaac, he now attracted attention more because of his dreamy absentmindedness and lack of spit and polish than by the fact that he was Jewish.

More painful than the conditions in which he lived was the fact that so little of his poetry was published. He spent his time making handwritten copies of his poems and sending them out to poets he admired, a few friends, and of course, Marsh and Schiff. As far as the world at large knew, he might as well not have existed. A Whitechapel friend and fellow poet, John Rodker, now living with Sonia Cohen, one of Isaac's old flames, sent a few of Isaac's poems to Harriet Monroe, of *Poetry Magazine* in Chicago, with the result that "Marching" would be published later in 1916. But otherwise fame continued to elude Isaac, who kept on sending scraps of poems to an increasingly critical Marsh. Isaac had a gift for annoying his patrons. His description of the plot for *Moses* could hardly have been more off-putting for a fastidious reader like Marsh: "The plot is droll. There is a famine in Egypt caused by the superabundance of slaves who eat up all the food meant for the masters. To prevent this, all the back molars of the slaves are drawn, so they eat less. The plot works around this."

The description may have been partly responsible for Marsh's negative view of *Moses* when he read the printed version. He gave

Isaac "a piece of his mind" about the verse play. Then he wrote to the poet Gordon Bottomley, who admired Isaac, that it was "truly magnificent in parts . . . but as a whole it's quite ridiculously bad." He described it to Bottomley as "a farrago," and admitted that he had written to Isaac "with the utmost brutality."

Compared to the vast and ghastly events taking place on the far side of the Channel, Marsh's reaction to *Moses* may have been a tempest in a teacup, but those very events may have led him to underate Isaac's war poems. Isaac resisted attempts to cast him as a second Rupert Brooke. He did not particularly respect Brooke's war poems; nor did he share Brooke's rosy view of England or his love of the English countryside. Marsh's view of Isaac's poetry was doubtless not improved by Isaac's rejection of patriotism as a motive for enlisting, still less by the constant pressure from his family to improve his wretched living conditions. Isaac's energetic elder sister Annie was holding Marsh's feet to the fire and would spend the rest of her life acting on her brother's behalf, typing his poems and demanding that his status as "fit for active service" be reconsidered. Long after his death, she would protect his poetry and ensure that he had a proper gravestone.

Through the spring of 1916, Isaac's battalion drilled and trained relentlessly. He correctly guessed that firing with live ammunition was a sign that the Fortieth Division would soon "be ready for the front." His opinion about the army had not changed. He still deplored "how ridiculous, idiotic, and meaningless" it was, "and its dreadful bullying, and what puny minds control it." He had managed to get *Moses* printed, together with several of his poems, in a bound pamphlet with a cover price of one shilling, or four shillings sixpence for a hardbound copy. (A decent example of the former now goes for about $3,000.) He managed to get six days' leave at last (he had missed getting leave for Passover because he was "confined to barracks" over a minor offense), during which he managed to conceal from his family that he would soon be shipped out, for fear of worrying them.

Shortly after his return to camp, the king inspected the first of the Bantam battalions. Isaac had missed seeing Marsh in London because he spent too long at the printer making last-minute corrections, but he wrote to Marsh telling him that he expected to be "off at last, tomorrow or Mon." He joked that the king "must have waited for us to stand up for a good while. . . . At a distance we look like soldiers sitting down, you know, legs so short." Whether Marsh was amused is unknown—his respect for the royal family was complete—but since he continued to correspond at frequent intervals with Isaac, sent him parcels of food, and read all the scraps of poems Isaac mailed him, there was clearly no break between them, even if he did think Isaac's poetry was going in the wrong direction.

In what may have been a piece of bad timing, Isaac wrote a card to his sister Annie to tell her he was about to be sent to France and mailed it to her office. If he had hoped to get away without a family scene, he was disappointed. She asked for a day off from work and took the train to Aldershot, but she was able to talk to Isaac only through the wire fence surrounding the camp. She begged him not to go, told him he was not fit, and demanded to see the medical officer who had examined him. Isaac wouldn't let her do it. (It is doubtful it would have changed anything.) "I stood there begging him not to go," she wrote later, "He said goodbye and vanished into the distance. I just stood at the fence feeling as if somebody had given me a good hiding."

The next day he embarked for France.

# CHAPTER 7

# ISAAC ROSENBERG'S LIFE AND DEATH IN THE TRENCHES

T HE BRITISH ARMY'S NORMAL PRACTICE WAS TO give battalions more training once they were in France under the eyes of seasoned noncommissioned officers and warrant officers who had been in the trenches. As the Battle of the Somme began in 1916—the big push intended to relieve the pressure on the French Army—the need for more men temporarily halted this acclimatization to the finer points of trench warfare. Isaac's battalion was sent straight to the front, to sink or swim.

Isaac's experience as a soldier, coupled with his ability as a painter, makes his war poetry unique. Rupert Brooke wrote elegiacally about war before he had experienced it; those poets who followed Isaac—Sassoon, Robert Graves, Wilfred Owen—wrote with intense fury and immense sadness about the waste and stupidity of it all. Their enemy was not the Germans but their own generals, for the inept waste of their soldiers' lives.

For his part, Isaac brought to the war an artist's sharp eye for the humble detail. He did not lament the cruelty and the suffering—he *described* it precisely, so the reader could not avoid it. It is almost a shame that he did not become an official war artist, like many of his Slade contemporaries. He might have produced pictures like those of Goya, indelible images of human suffering. Being a war artist might also have spared his life. The war artists worked in dangerous places, but they were not exposed to the myriad dangers and horrors of trench warfare, and they were commissioned as officers.

But Isaac's bad luck remained unchanged. Regulars looked down on his battalion since its Other Ranks were men who until recently would have been turned down as unfit for service. Meanwhile within it, he was humiliated for being Jewish, for being a bookworm, and for being timid, as well as poorly turned out. In addition, his health, never robust, declined sharply living in the open. As a soldier, he could not carry a drawing pad or paints, and he was forced to write poems with a pencil, on whatever scraps of paper he could find. At one point, the officer censoring his battalion's mail home returned Isaac's letters unsent because he "could not be bothered with going through such rubbish" as Isaac's poems. It is hard to imagine how Isaac could have fallen any lower, yet his letters reflect a quiet determination to do his best, and there is no hint of despair or self-pity in them. He did not wax enthusiastic about the opportunity for close combat with the enemy, as Alan Seeger did, but he did not flinch from it either.

To a friend he wrote:

> *We made straight for the trenches, but we've had vile weather, and I've been wet through for four days and nights. I lost all my socks and things before I left England and hadn't the chance to make it up again, so I've been in trouble, particularly with bad heels; you can't have the slightest conception of what such an apparently trivial thing means. We've had shells bursting two yards off; bullets whizzing all over the show, but all you are aware of is the agony of your heels.*

To Marsh he sent his first poem after embarkation, "The Troop Ship."

Grotesque and quietly huddled
Contortionists to twist
The sleep soul to sleep,
We lie all sorts of ways
And cannot sleep.
The wet wind is so cold,
And the lurching men so careless,
That, should you drop to a doze,

Winds' fumble or men's feet
Are on your face.

This may have been one of the poems that the officer who cen-
sored Isaac's letters dismissed as "rubbish," but in fact it represents
a new and more realistic poetry about the war. It addresses not the
great theme of patriotism but an ordinary soldier's forlorn attempt
to sleep on the deck of a crowded troop ship, despite the cold, wet
wind and the boots of his fellow soldiers. It is a tiny fragment of
the reality of war, shorn of glory, simply a moment of numbing dis-
comfort and misery. The poem is almost as simple and direct as
Kipling's, except that Isaac is totally lacking in military spirit and
regimental pride. He has as little interest in the King's Own Royal
Lancaster Regiment as it has in him.

Rosenberg's company was put into a forward trench at once, in
pouring rain that turned everything to "sucking, stinking mud."
Isaac stood, lay, slept in mud, his misery increased by the fact that he
had lost his socks and had to write to his mother asking her to send
some, thereby revealing to her that he was overseas. It says much
about the strength of Hannah's hold over her family that Annie too
had been unable to tell her mother she had seen Isaac just before he
embarked. Nobody in the Rosenberg family wanted to provoke *that*
storm of emotion!

The pain in his feet from going without socks and the discomfort
of wearing wet clothes for days and nights on end concerned Isaac
more than the random artillery shells that exploded near him or the
occasional sniper's bullet whizzing overhead. This too was a theme
in accounts of trench warfare on both sides: long periods of sodden,
lice-infested misery and boredom alternated unpredictably with sav-
age moments of terror. Nonetheless Isaac kept up his correspon-
dence, soothing Marsh, writing to Harriet Monroe. Thanks to Ezra
Pound sending her a few of his poems, Isaac was now in the odd
position of having them published in Chicago rather than London.
He still kept trying to calm his mother and writing his poetry under
unimaginably difficult conditions. His three most famous poems
date from this period, including "Break of Day in the Trenches,"
the poem for which he is chiefly remembered.

The darkness crumbles away.
It is the same old druid Time as ever,
Only a live thing leaps my hand,
A queer, sardonic rat,
As I pull the parapet's poppy
To stick behind my ear.
Droll rat, they would shoot you if they knew
Your cosmopolitan sympathies.
Now you have touched this English hand
You will do the same to a German.
Soon, no doubt, it will be your pleasure
To cross the sleeping green between.
It seems you inwardly grin as you pass
Strong eyes, fine limbs, haughty athletes,
Less chanced than you for life,
Bonds to the whims of murder,
Sprawled in the bowels of the earth,
The torn fields of France.
What do you see in our eyes
At the shrieking iron and flame
Hurled through still heavens?
What quaver—what heart aghast?
Poppies whose roots are in man's veins
Drop, and are ever dropping;
But mine in my ear is safe—
Just a little white with the dust.

This is a long way from Rupert Brooke's view of the war, or even Alan Seeger's. There is no hint of glory or sacrifice, still less of eagerness to face death. The dead, on both sides, are the victims of random murder on a mass scale, no more heroic than the victims of an accident. The most despised denizen of the battlefield, the ubiquitous rat, is at the center of the poem, with its "queer, sardonic" expression as it moves from one side's trenches to the other's, feeding indifferently on the dead. This is the war, expunged of patriotism, glory, and heroism, a world of violent death, mud, rusted barbed wire, and suffering. Isaac quickly picked up the laconic language of understatement that every British soldier used to describe the indescribable. "We had an exciting time today," he wrote Marsh. "There were quite a good many sent to heaven and the hospital I carried one myself in a handcart to the hospital (which is often the antechamber of heaven)."

Despite a slight reduction in the warmth of his relationship with Marsh, Isaac kept up a frequent correspondence, sending him scraps of poems and even occasional drawings. The Rosenberg family continued to deluge Marsh with pleas to have Isaac removed from the trenches, but it has to be said that Isaac himself never asked Marsh to intervene. In his own quiet way, he was as determined to stick it out as Alan Seeger had been, although without supposing that any glory would attach to his suffering. It is remarkable how many letters Isaac managed to write, not only to Marsh but to Schiff, to his family, and even to his old flame Sonia, whose husband would soon be sent to prison as a conscientious objector.

In addition to writing to Edward Marsh on Isaac's behalf, Annie now typed his poems and sent them back to him for corrections and changes; as inefficient as the British Army might be at providing hot food in the trenches, the General Post Office managed to deliver twelve million letters and a million parcels a week to soldiers, many of them in the front line. Letters back and forth took only a couple of days to arrive, not counting the time it took to censor the outgoing mail. Writing itself was a challenge—candles were in short supply, and writing paper was available only from the YMCA behind the lines. Isaac wrote mostly in pencil, crouched over a camp fire at night when he was lucky enough to be near one.

Annie's campaign to rescue Isaac via Marsh seems to have had a certain effect on his life. He was examined for fitness several times, but every time he was declared fit, despite his "weak chest," poor physique, and scarred feet. In those days, a soldier had to be close to death to be declared unfit for service. "I am sorry for your Hebrew bard," wrote one of Marsh's friends in the War Office, to explain that he could do nothing and to suggest that Marsh write privately to the adjutant of Isaac's battalion, asking if Isaac could not be given a desk job. Reluctantly Marsh did so—this was not the kind of thing he liked doing, but Annie was remorseless—only to be told that Isaac

1. Rupert Brooke.

2. Mrs. Brooke with two of her boys, Rupert on the left.

3. Rupert Brooke in costume for *Comus*, wearing the tunic that was "so short and tight he couldn't sit down."

4. King's College, Cambridge.

5. The Old Vicarage, Grantchester.

6. The Olivier sisters, on the beach in Cornwall, 1914: Margery, Brynhild, Noel, and Daphne.

7. Ka Cox.

8. Élisabeth van Rysselberghe.

9. Phyllis Gardner,
self-portrait.

10. Tuatamata.

11. Cathleen Nesbit.

12. Lady Eileeen Wellesley.

13. Edward Marsh and Winston Churchill.

14. Lytton Strachey, portrait by Dora Carrington.

15. Rupert Brooke.

16. Rupert Brooke in uniform of the Royal Naval Division, with his mother, 1914.

17. Rupert Brooke's grave site.

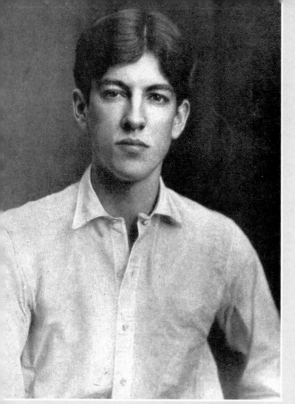

18. Alan Seeger, at Harvard.

19. Alan Seeger, in uniform, in the French Foreign Legion.

20. John Sloan, *Yeats at Pepitas'*, ca. 1920. Alan Seeger is third from the left, out of the lively conversation and lost in thought.

21. Isaac Rosenberg,
self-portrait.

22. Isaac Rosenberg, pencil sketch
of himself in a trench.

23. Isaac Rosenberg in uniform,
ca. 1915.

24. Isaac Rosenberg,
"Hark, Hark the Lark."

25. Isaac
Rosenberg,
*Sacred Love*,
the painting
Edward Marsh
bought, and
which was
admired by
Rupert Brooke.

26. Robert Graves, after the war.

27. Robert Graves as an officer of the Royal Welch Fusiliers, 1914.

28. The Sassoon family in the mid-nineteenth century, in Bombay: the patriarch David Sassoon, seated; standing left to right his sons, Elias, Albert Abdallah, who would open the family business in Britain, and Sassoon David Sassoon, already dressed in European clothes.

29. Trinity College, Cambridge, Boat Club Ball, June 1906,
Siegfried Sassoon in front.

30. Siegfried Sassoon as a lieutenant in the Royal Welch Fusiliers.

31. Painting of Sassoon, by Glyn Warren Philport, 1917.

32. Craiglockhart.

I am making this statement as an act of wilful defiance of military authority, because I believe that the War is being deliberately prolonged by those who have the power to end it.

I am a soldier, convinced that I am acting on behalf of soldiers.

I believe that this war, upon which I entered as a war of defence, has now become a war of aggression and conquest.

I believe that, if the purposes for which I and my fellow-soldiers entered upon this war had been so clearly stated that it had been impossible to change them without our knowledge, the war would have been at an end.

I have seen and endured the sufferings of the troops and I can no longer be a party to prolonging these sufferings for ends which I believe to be unjust and unjust. evil

I am not protesting against the military conduct of the war, but against the political errors and insincerities for which the fighting men are being sacrificed.

On behalf of those who are suffering now, I make this protest against the deception which is being practised on them. Also I believe that it may help to destroy the callous complacence with which the majority of those at home regard the continuance of agonies which they do not share, & which they have not sufficient imagination to realise.

— June 15th.

I believe that the purposes for which I and my fellow-soldiers entered upon this war should have been so clearly stated that it had been impossible to change them without our knowledge; and that, had this been done, the objects which actuated us would now be attainable by negotiation.

33. Draft of statement against the conduct of the war, April 1917, written in Sassoon's pocket notebook.

34. Wilfred Owen and Mme. Léger at a lecture by Laurent Tailhade, Bagnères, August 1914.

35. Wilfred Owen in uniform in the Manchester Regiment.

36. Wilfred Owen and
Laurent Tailhade,
1914.

37. Wilfred Owen
and Arthur
Newboult, during
his mother's visit to
Edinburgh, July 1917.

had once again been declared fit. Isaac himself did not complain, but in a sketch on the back of a letter to a friend, he drew himself squatting in the bottom of a trench in the pouring rain wearing his steel helmet, with a ground sheet pulled around his shoulders, looking thin to the point of emaciation, with an expression of resignation on his face. There is an empty marmalade tin by his feet. It is a quick pencil sketch, but once again it reminds us of his skill as a draftsman.

Isaac was shifted in and out of the front line, not because of Marsh's intervention on his behalf, but because he was the kind of soldier most of his commanding officers wanted to get rid of. One of them, who happened to be Jewish, remarked many years later, "The continued transfers of Rosenberg are a symptom of his 'unsoldierliness.' Units always tried to get rid of their unsatisfactory soldiers. . . . This does not mean that Rosenberg was a bad man, a bad poet or anything except that he was not the type . . . who could make a soldier or even look like one." He often had a button undone, a shoulder strap unfastened, his cap badge unpolished, or untidy puttees. Nobody disputed his bravery or his willingness to work hard, but he never managed the indispensable trick of *looking* like a soldier that is so dear to the heart of every sergeant-major. He was assigned to the divisional work battalion, backbreaking manual labor in the mud. Then he was reassigned to a field company of the Royal Engineers for the even less enviable task of hauling barbed wire by mule-drawn limbers at night into no-man's-land, dirty, dangerous work, since the noise and the mules were only too likely to attract the attention of German artillery. It was about this work that Isaac wrote one of his most famous poems, "Dead Man's Dump," as the steel-shod wheels of the limbers swerved from the muddy path and ran over bodies, British and German, that had been collected there for burial.

"Dead Man's Dump" offers a view of the war as it was, shorn of glory, as brutal as the famous ice-cold last lines of Randall Jarrell's "The Death of the Ball Turret Gunner" in 1945:

Six miles from earth, loosed from its dream of life
I woke from black flack and the nightmare fighters.
When I died they washed me out of the turret with a hose.

With the same unblinking eye, Isaac wrote of the last scream of
a soldier newly dead as the wheels of the limbers run over his chest,
squeezing out the remaining air from his lungs.

> The wheels lurched over the sprawled dead
> But pained them not, though their bones crunched. . . .
> They left this dead with the older dead,
> Stretched at the cross roads.
> Burnt black by strange decay,
> Their sinister faces lie,
> The lid over each eye . . .
> And our wheels grazed his dead face.

The image of wheels grazing the face of a man who might have
been alive only half an hour before has few equals in the poetry
of the war; the sound of the crunching of the bones is Isaac at his
unflinching best. No other poet comes this close to the reality of
war. It is scarcely surprising so few of his poems were published
in his own lifetime, yet even more surprising that some of them
sneaked past two layers of censorship, the first by the junior officers
of his own battalion, the second at the vast shed erected in Hyde
Park, London, where over 25,000 people, most of them women,
labored in shifts to sort and censor the mail from the front.

Isaac was soon back in the trenches. Late in 1916 the Battle of
the Somme was winding down, having cost over a million casual-
ties on both sides. The British Army was preparing for yet another
big push, this time an attack intended to relieve the Ypres Salient in
Flanders, which would cost the lives of nearly half a million men on
both sides. Even the least fit men were being ruthlessly combed out
of safe jobs to replace the dead and wounded. The war had passed
into a stage of mutual exhaustion, both sides having sacrificed so
many lives that they were unable to give in.

The big picture looked pessimistic for the Allies. In Russia, the
abdication of the czar early in 1917 produced chaos on a hitherto
unimaginable scale, enabling the Germans to move substantial
numbers of men west, and bringing Field Marshal Paul von Hin-

denburg and his overbearing chief of staff, General Erich Luden-
dorff back, to command the German armies in the West. At sea,
Germany moved toward unrestricted submarine warfare, sinking
all ships regardless of their nationality—a move that was intended
to bring Britain to her knees but would instead bring the United
States into the war. In the Middle East, the Ottoman Empire was
showing signs of collapse as the British Army, under the energetic
command of General Edmund Allenby, fought its way north from
Egypt to take Jerusalem. Meanwhile the desert Arabs, led by Law-
rence of Arabia, pushed the Turks back from their vast empire to
the south.

The German Great General Staff and the kaiser took a suicidal
gamble that Germany could win the war before the Americans—
mostly untrained and as yet poorly equipped—entered the war in
large numbers. The Turks played another and more sinister losing
card, perpetrating the first modern genocide: nearly a million and a
half Armenians, a Christian minority, men, women, and children,
were systematically either shot or herded brutally into the Syrian
desert to die of exhaustion, starvation, and dehydration, their bod-
ies left unburied to disintegrate in the sun.

The Central Powers faced—or feared they faced—extinction.
On the Western Front, the Germans retreated to the Hindenburg
Line, so well prepared with concrete pillboxes and dense belts of
wire that attempts to attack it would prove sacrificial. They set about
preparing for their own attack, intended to split apart the French
and the British Army and end the war before the Americans arrived
in quantity. The use of new and novel weapons on both sides had
done little or nothing to break the bloody stalemate. The tank, a
British innovation, failed to break the German line effectively. The
use of ever more sophisticated and deadly poison gases increased
suffering on both sides but failed to prove decisive. Both sides
fought on, while each battle, Arras, Messine, Ypres, Passchendaele,
cost many hundreds of thousands of deaths. By now, both of Isaac's
brothers were in France.

Isaac's feet continued to torment him, and his health was deterio-
rating. He described his situation to Marsh half-humorously:

*The other night I awoke to find myself floating about with the water half over me. I took my shirt off and curled myself up on a little mound that the water hadn't touched and slept stark naked that night. But that was not all of the fun. The chap next to me was suddenly taken with Diarrhoea and kept on lifting the sheet of the Bivouac, and as I lay at the end the rain came beating on my nakedness all night. Next morning, I noticed the poor chap's discoloured pants hanging on a bough near by, and I thought after all I had the best of it.*

Artillery shells and night patrols did not seem to bother Isaac as much as the possibility of his poems going astray. He sent scraps of them home as often as possible, to be typed by his sister Annie. They sent them back and forth for correction, then to Marsh for his usual diabolization, which his friend Christopher Hassall described accurately as "minutely carping criticism based on good will." Isaac, like so many other poets and writers, bore these comments with equanimity, patience, and only an occasional mild objection. At one point, he attempted to cheer up his benefactor Sydney Schiff, who was depressed by the war, pointing out that "we [the soldiers] manage to keep cheerful out here in the face of most horrible things but then, we are kept busy, and have no time to brood." Isaac's doughty common sense and good humor are apparent in most of his correspondence.

In September 1917, after over a year in the trenches, he was at last granted two weeks leave to go home and be cosseted by his family. Unfortunately he missed seeing the two people he most wanted to see—Schiff was away (but sent him a pound note to spend on his leave), and Marsh was in France with Winston Churchill, who had by now been made minister of munitions and had summoned Marsh back to his old job as his private secretary.

On the termination of Isaac's leave, he returned to the front. The attempt to break out of the Ypres Salient had by then failed, at the cost of over 400,000 British casualties, and plans were already being drawn up for another big push. Isaac's return to the front was a symptom of Britain's shortage of manpower under the pressure of such overwhelming losses. Even those who were manifestly unfit except to an army doctor were being conscripted to serve in the infantry.

In the autumn of 1917, Isaac was diagnosed with influenza and hospitalized, as were both of his brothers. He was able to receive parcels of books and resume his correspondence, but he recovered in time to be sent back into the line. That was toward the end of the Battle of Cambrai, the first in which the tank was used on a large scale. On the first day of its use, the results were satisfying: advances of up to five miles. By the second day, however, more than half the tanks had been destroyed or put out of action. The battle settled down into another drawn-out bloodletting, dominated by well-placed German machine-gun fire and devastating artillery barrages. It ended with more than 100,000 British casualties (and 54,000 German), for no worthwhile gain of ground. The tanks' success on the first day had been enough to result in the ringing of church bells all over the United Kingdom to celebrate a victory, but that only made all the more bitter the dawning realization, by the end of the second, that nothing much had been accomplished except another terrible list of casualties. The effective surprise weapon turned out to be not the mechanically unreliable tank but the German storm troopers, small groups heavily armed and trained to cling to the terrain and bypass strong opposition.

Isaac's health continued to deteriorate, but no matter how often the doctors examined him, they continued to pass him as fit, despite impassioned and herculean attempts on the part of his sister Annie to have him moved to a clerical job behind the lines. He had heard that a Jewish battalion was being formed for service in the Middle East, where at least the climate would be dry. He mentioned it in a letter to Marsh, whom Annie had been tormenting on her brother's behalf. "I see my sister has been on the warpath again," he wrote to Marsh, "and after your scalp in her sisterly regard for me. I have now put in for a transfer to the Jewish Batt—which I think is in Mesopotamia now. I should be acclimatized to heat after my S. African experience. I'll let you know if I get it." As usual, Isaac did not press his own case and made fun of Annie's attempts on his behalf. He does not seem to have made any serious effort with his own officers either. As it happens, Marsh *could* have got Isaac transferred, had he pressed hard enough. Transferring a man to a heathier climate where he could continue to fight was an altogether different proposition than taking him out of the line and putting him in a safe clerical job, which Annie was begging Marsh to do.

So Isaac stayed at the front and was moved into the First Battalion of the King's Own Royal Lancaster Regiment. That would have been unthinkable only a few months earlier, since the first battalion of any regiment usually got the pick of available men, regulars, and the most soldierly. Isaac fell into none of those categories, but the bloodletting at Arras and Cambrai made it necessary to fill the ranks with whatever men were available. From March 19 to 23, 1918, the Germans attacked the British near Arras in relentless hand-to-hand fighting, forcing the Royal Lancashires back out of their trenches until the Germans too were forced to return to their own lines.

Isaac managed to find an inch of candle and wrote a quick letter to Marsh. "We are very busy just now and poetry is right out of our scheme," he noted, but he nevertheless managed to include his last poem, "Through These Pale Cold Days," which he described as "a slight thing," but it shows that his mind was still set on joining the Jewish Battalion in the Middle East. It is typical of Isaac to describe ten days of hand-to-hand fighting as being "very busy just now." He never wanted to describe the slaughter and the killing to his family or to Marsh; he sought neither pity nor glory.

Through these pale cold days
What dark faces burn
Out of three thousand years,
While underneath their brows
Like waifs their spirits grope
For the pools of Hebron again—
For Lebanon's summer slope.
They leave these blood stilled days
In dust behind their tread
They see with living eyes
How long they have been dead.

The Germans attacked again in force on March 28, the day Isaac wrote the letter. The fighting and shelling went on day and night. A neighboring battalion was completely wiped out, and Isaac's own battalion lost more than seventy men in one day. On the night of March 31, his platoon was sent out to patrol no-man's-land. The soldiers crept forward between coils of barbed wire, crouching among unburied, shattered corpses, as they inched forward in and out of shell holes full of stinking mud and worse. Somewhere in the shrieking chaos, Isaac and five other soldiers close to him were killed, possibly by a single explosion, since the body parts were not recovered until years later, by which time the fragments were impossible to identify.

The fragments that could be found were thrown into a mass grave, and when a suitable stone was put up in Bailleul Road East Cemetery in 1926, Plot V, Saint-Laurent-Blangy, Pas de Calais, Isaac's was marked with his name and serial number and a Star of David. At the top were the cautionary words, "Buried near this spot," since there were no identifiable remains. At the bottom of the stone are the words he would most have wanted: "Artist and Poet."

One of his finest drawings, bought by Edward Marsh in 1913, is "Hark, Hark, the Lark," showing four ecstatic nude figures greeting the song of a lark. It was placed in Marsh's guest bedroom, where Rupert Brooke admired it. Shortly before Isaac's death, he returned to the same theme in a poem about a soldier leaving the front line for a period of rest and hearing the lark's song:

Dragging these anguished limbs, we only know
The poison-blasted track opens on our camp—
On a little safe sleep.
But hark! joy—joy—strange joy
Lo! Heights of night ringing with unseen larks,
Music showering our upturned list'ning faces.

For forty-three years his sister Annie fought a vigorous and ultimately successful battle to have Isaac's work published and to gain for his poetry the recognition it deserved.

Marsh, for all his doubts about Isaac's poetry—he much preferred his art—continued to press for its publication. So did a number of other influential cultural figures, particularly Edith Sitwell, the formidable poet and flamboyant literary celebrity, and her brother Osbert. T. E. Lawrence was also a huge enthusiast and proselytizer for Isaac's poetry—he had carried Rosenberg's *Moses* in his saddlebags on his camel in the desert. So was T. S. Eliot. But the main force in lifting Isaac out of obscurity was his sister Annie, who devoted her life to the challenge of getting his poems published. Not until 1937, however, would his collected works, edited by Ian Parsons, be published, leading the distinguished critic F. R. Leavis to describe Isaac in *Scrutiny* as "a genius." Even so, sales were disappointing; fewer than five hundred copies of the collection were sold in the United Kingdom. Isaac's reputation for bad luck was dramatically confirmed when a bomb destroyed the London warehouse of Chatto and Windus, putting the book out of print. W. B. Yeats left Rosenberg out of his compilation *The Oxford Book of Modern Verse.* Annie was undeterred, and largely thanks to her, Isaac's place among the war poets and in English literature was finally firmly established.

In a supreme irony, Annie died in 1961, "a frail little old lady." When walking along the promenade at Brighton, "a gust of wind blew her into a moving cement mixer below her," in which she was horribly mangled and died, as tragic and as wasteful a death as her brother's.

# CHAPTER 8

# ROBERT GRAVES
## *"The Necessary Supply of Heroes*
## *Must Be Maintained at All Costs"*

G IVEN THE RAPIDLY ESCALATING NUMBER OF casualties, it may seem amazing to the reader today that the British public remained so ill informed about the realities of trench warfare, or that the troops did not complain more, at least when they went home on leave. Part of this can be explained by the national habit of ignoring what one does not want to know and by the famous stiff upper lip, reinforced by the popular songs like "Pack up your troubles in your old kit bag." The troops themselves did not want to be thought of as shirkers or whiners in a nation where the correct answer to the question "How are you?" is "Mustn't grumble."

They did not want to scare their loved ones by trying to describe the indescribable, much of which in any case was too awful to be believed. The photo magazines, newsreels, and television footage that brought the horrors of the Vietnam War (and subsequent wars) home in graphic detail did not yet exist, so the public was spared images that might have shocked them. The memoirs and novels that described the horrors of the war did not begin to be published until the 1920s, by which time almost everyone had already reached the conclusion that the war had been a huge mistake, even though few agreed about whose fault it had been.

Most of Isaac Rosenberg's poems were not published until long after 1918, or they were published in such obscure magazines that they attracted little attention. By 1917, in any case, they were over-shadowed by poems in which incandescent anger at the suffering of the soldiers, the ignorance of the public, the incompetence of the generals, and the obstinate refusal of the politicians to negotiate terms was the main theme.

Nor were the principal poets at this stage of the war easy to ignore or dismiss. Like Rupert Brooke, they were officer material, some of them well-connected public school men, some decorated heroes who had survived serious wounds, brave and efficient infantry officers who were nevertheless determined to show the war for the cruel, shameful, and wasteful descent into hell that they knew it to be. They were not conscientious objectors or pacifists opposed to all war—they were simply opposed to *this* one. In our time, we do not think of poetry as inflammatory, still less as subversive, and it is hard to think of *any* poet since the First World War whose work produced a major shock wave among the general public. But by 1917 poetry had become a weapon in the hands of those who opposed the war. It is a long way from Rupert Brook's patriotic sonnets in 1914 to Siegfried Sassoon's angry, sarcastic, defiant poem "Base Details" in 1917:

> If I were fierce, and bald, and short of breath
> I'd live with scarlet Majors at the Base,
> And speed glum heroes up the line to death.

Sassoon's lines contain no hint of Brooke's enthusiasm for a heroic death, or Seeger's thirst for glory, or even Rosenberg's stoic acceptance of the horrors of trench warfare. The poet, rather, took aim at all those on his own side whose feet were not in the mud of a trench—the generals, the staff officers, the press, the politicians, even the general public, all whom applauded the front line soldiers without any real understanding of the horror, misery, and pain they suffered, or the sheer pointlessness of their deaths.

By this stage of the war, the principal war poets were not newcomers to trench fighting. Two of the most famous, Robert Graves and Siegfried Sassoon, joined up as soon as they could, in 1914, responding to the call as Rupert Brooke had done. These junior officers were exactly the young men who formed the backbone of the officer corps of the British Army: middle-class, well educated, physically fit, enthusiastic, brave, and willing to take enormous personal risks and to lead their men in battle. If these young men no longer believed that the war had a purpose, or that the generals and the government knew what they were doing, still less cared about the lives of the soldiers, then perhaps the war was a mistake, a grotesque, self-inflicted human catastrophe on a scale so colossal that no purpose could possibly justify it, the modern-day equivalent of Cronus devouring his own children. One of the more distinguished soldier poets, Robert Graves, when he came to write *The Greek Myths* in the mid-1950s, paid special attention to Cronus, surely not by accident.*

The life expectancy of a young infantry officer was brief. Until late in 1916, he would still wear well-polished field boots and riding breeches, a Sam Browne belt and a cap with a gleaming badge. One or two embroidered "pips" (stars) on his sleeves would indicate his rank. Enemy riflemen and machine-gunners could hardly mistake such officers or miss them as they tried to advance nonchalantly in front of their platoon or company, armed only with a revolver and possibly a cane or swagger stick. The issuing of steel helmets late in 1916, although strongly resisted in some of the swanker regiments, led to an attempt to make junior officers less obvious targets. In some regiments, the pips were moved to the epaulets. Officers sometimes wore a leather jerkin, puttees, and short lace-up boots like those of their men, and some even carried a rifle like their soldiers, so they no longer stood out from a distance as officers. But the casualty rate did not diminish. They were still expected to walk cheerfully into massed rifle and machine-gun fire despite artillery barrages and poison gas.

The price of leadership on the battlefield was often death. Painted or carved in stone, the list of young men in their twenties who were

---

* In Robert Graves's youth, a working knowledge of "the classics," Greek and Latin, was still deemed essential for anyone intending to attend Oxford or Cambridge. That attitude still persisted faintly in 1954, when I went up to Magdalen College, Oxford, after serving in the Royal Air Force. When Karl Leyser, the senior dean of Magdalen, asked me what I was proposing to study, I replied, "Modern languages, French and Russian." He gave a dramatic sigh, then said briskly, "Why didn't you save us a lot of time and trouble and go to Berlitz instead?" From his point of view, the only foreign languages worth "reading" at Oxford were Greek and Latin.

killed between 1914 and 1918 stretches from floor to ceiling in every public school, college, chapel, and educational institution in Britain. At my own college in Oxford, Magdalen, the list of those killed in the 1914–18 war numbers 207, versus *nine* killed in World War II. Over 20 percent of all Oxonians who graduated in 1913 and 1914 were killed, the highest death rate of any group in Britain.

Although he was in some ways not typical of this group, Robert von Ranke Graves joined up without hesitation the moment war was declared. Like so many others his age, he was due to go up to St John's College, Oxford, in the autumn of 1914, having just graduated from Charterhouse, one of the nine great public schools of England. But on the outbreak of war, he decided to enlist. Graves was spending the summer at his mother's house in northern Wales and sought the help of the secretary of the local golf club, who promptly called the adjutant of the nearest regiment, the Royal Welch Fusiliers,* and told him that an Old Carthusian was hoping to join the regiment. In keeping with the social order of the day, Graves, as a public school graduate, was immediately enrolled as an officer in training—no nonsense about serving in the ranks. He began his service on August 11, just seven days after Britain declared war. He assumed, as did almost everybody else, that the war would be over by Christmas and worried only that he might miss the fun.

Like Rupert Brooke at Rugby, Graves had been in the Officer Training Corps at Charterhouse and therefore assumed he knew more about the basics of soldiering than he really did. He knew still less about the traditions and peculiarities of his regiment. After three weeks of "square bashing" (intensive drilling), he had a subaltern's pip on each sleeve and was commanding fifty reservists— tough working-class Welshmen from the hills who were part of the

---

* The Royal Welch Fusiliers is one of the more storied regiments of the British Army. Dating back to 1689, the unit retains proudly the archaic spelling of *Welch* with a *c*. Fusiliers wear five black ribbons on the back of the unform collar in commemoration of the queue that British redcoats wore in the eighteenth century. Its privates are addressed as "Fusilier." The regimental mascot is an exotic, long-horned white Himalayan goat, which is led on parade by the "goat-major," the goat wearing a silver headdress, with its horns gilded, and ranked as a lance corporal. It was the Royal Welch Fusiliers that charged the Americans at Bunker Hill.

"special reserve," a new name for what had once been the "militia." They had been called up to do their annual two weeks of training with their local regiment—something of a lark, as opposed to their regular work as miners or farm laborers—only to find that once war had been declared, they were back in uniform for the duration. They were understandably "browned off" (British Army slang for disgruntled); nor were they happy about obeying orders from a young man who had just turned nineteen and spoke no Welsh. Graves coped somehow. He was tall, resourceful, and strong, and although his company commander described him as "unsoldierlike and a nuisance," he soon fell in love with his regiment, a feeling that prevents *Goodbye to All That*, his 1929 memoir of his service in World War I, from being a relentless account of horrors.

He spent several months on detachment at the thankless task of guarding interned German and Austro-Hungarian civilians—and recovering those of his fusiliers who had deserted and gone home. He was then ordered back to the regimental depot to be smartened up before being sent to France. Ironically, his unsoldierly appearance kept Graves temporarily from the slaughter, as much as he wanted to go. He had had his uniform made by the wrong tailor, his shirt was the wrong shade of khaki, and never having had a valet, he had not required his soldier-servant to bring his Sam Browne belt, boots, and buttons up to the required mirror-like shine. Because of his lack of interest in flat racing,* he was also judged unsportsmanlike, another major strike against him.

Graves was in limbo. Then by chance a fusilier who was a well-known boxer and was giving a demonstration of his skills gave him the opportunity to put on a borrowed pair of shorts and boxing gloves. Graves knocked the champion out in three rounds—he had been a very successful boxer at Charterhouse, as well as a formidable rugby player, and had a badly broken nose to prove it. The fact that an officer, however unsoldierly his appearance, had boxed with a professional and won proved Graves's sportsmanship, and he was rewarded by being sent out on the next draft to France, early in 1915.

Throughout all the horrors to come, Graves was sustained by his

* Racing at a track, as opposed to steeplechase racing, which goes over fences.

natural courage—he was one of those rare people who simply do not appear to feel fear. He relished every bit of it, from the ceremony of eating a raw leek (the Welsh national vegetable and symbol), to the roll of drums on St. David's Day, to the priceless porcelain trophies on the table of the officers' mess that had been looted from the Summer Palace in Beijing in 1860. This is not unusual. In the brutal circumstances of war, people cling to their unit or their ship—it identifies them. In the famous phrase of the Indian Army of the Raj, "The regiment is your mother and your father." During a long and extraordinarily productive life (he lived to ninety and published more than 140 works) Graves retained his affection for the Royal Welch Fusiliers to the end, and in 1939 he even wrote two successful historical novels about a sergeant in the regiment during the American Revolutionary War. In anybody else's hands, they might have been potboilers—and they were, in fact, written in a hurry for money. Nevertheless they were well reviewed and are still very readable.

Graves's passion for his regiment can partly be explained by its history but partly also by his uncertainty about his own identity. He sometimes claimed to be Irish—his grandfather was a Church of England bishop in Ireland, although as part of the "Protestant ascendency," he would hardly have been considered Irish by the Irish themselves. He was sometimes considered Welsh because his mother owned a house in Wales, and sometimes he seemed German because his mother was a niece of the nineteenth-century German historian Leopold von Ranke. But he always remained deeply and essentially English, no matter how many summers he and his siblings spent in Bavaria. Graves was the butt of many jokes and sometimes outright suspicion because of the "Von Ranke" in his name. But despite a lifelong fascination with other cultures and a yearning to connect himself to Celtic mythmaking, he remained as English in his poetry and person as Rupert Brooke.

If Brooke had impressed people by his beauty, Graves impressed them by his size (he was six foot two), his strength, and his physical vitality. Even in advanced old age, he was a striking figure. By that time of his life, his reputation as a poet had been exceeded by his fame as a weaver of myths and by his magnetic personality—he had become, with his leonine head and bushy mane of white hair, a cult figure to whom celebrities made pilgrimages, including movie stars like Ava Gardner and Alec Guinness. Toward the end of his life, he was appointed Oxford Professor of Poetry (an honor not entirely dissimilar to that of poet laureate). His first lecture was a media event, attended by film star Ava Gardner as well as a mass of journalists and press photographers. J. R. R. Tolkien, Oxford don and author of the worldwide best seller *The Lord of the Rings*, was also present; he commented acerbically, but with good humor, that Graves was "entertaining, likeable, [with] a bonnet full of wild bees. . . . [He] looked like Siegfried/Sigur in his youth, *but* an ass, it was the most ludicrously bad lecture I have ever heard." By then Graves, like so many figures of British culture, had been canonized by longevity, particularly since he had wisely declined all the honors that would surely have been his for the asking. Instead he preferred to hold forth as a kind of living tourist attraction on the Spanish island of Majorca.

Graves was born in the quiet, middle-class, leafy London suburb of Wimbledon, home since 1877 of the All England Croquet and Lawn Tennis Club. At the beginning of *Goodbye to All That*, he describes, without nostalgia or regret, a whole secure bourgeois life. The maids and the nanny had tiny rooms without carpets or linoleum upstairs. The drawing room downstairs was crammed with all the bric-à-brac of Edwardian England. The easy chairs were placed in a half circle around the fire for a reading of *The Taming of the Shrew*, accompanied by lemonade, petits-fours, and cucumber sandwiches. (Both his parents were teetotalers.) It was a serene world, about to be engulfed almost as thoroughly as Pompei.

On his father's side, the Graves family traced itself back to Cromwell's conquest of Ireland, and beyond that to a French knight who landed in England with Henry Tudor, Earl of Richmond, to overthrow Richard III. On his mother's side, he descended from a long line of Bavarian minor gentry. The Graves men were, even by the standards of the day, enormously procreative—Robert Graves's grandfather, the Right Reverend Lord Bishop of Limerick, had eight children, and his father, Alfred Graves, had ten, by his first and second wives.

Alfred Graves was inspector of schools, an important post in the civil service, as well as a minor poet and songwriter. He had a special interest in Gaelic poetry and became a respected cultural figure in Ireland, and he was named a Welsh Bard at the National Eisteddfod of Wales, a rare honor for somebody who was not Welsh. Thus, although he was stoutly English, Robert Graves had a swirl of conflicting cultures going through his mind, as well as a driving ambition to become a poet. His father was a prodigiously productive poet, writing enormous amounts in what little spare time he had, and so he had more sympathy for his son's ambition than most fathers would have had.

The oppression hanging over Robert Graves's head as a boy was not the possibility of war but the need to go to boarding school. He was perfectly happy spending alternate summers in Bavaria and Wales, where he struggled successfully to overcome a fear of heights by climbing dangerous cliffs. The Graves family was a happy one, centered around the children. Graves had no desire to leave it for school, anticipating correctly that he would hate it, and that at the end of it he would have to go up to Oxford, which he would hate even more. He was a chick with no desire to leave the nest.

Unlike Rupert Brooke, whose years at Rugby School were the happiest of his life, Graves's years at Charterhouse* were miserable, despite his buoyant temperament and daunting physique. He had won a scholarship, but that and the fact that he was always short of pocket money led to his unpopularity. In addition, he was innocent and prudish about sex, wore ready-made clothes instead of tailored ones, and bore as his middle name Von Ranke at a time when the kaiser's high-handed behavior was beginning to make Germany unpopular in Britain. A rumor spread that Graves was not only German but a German Jew, making him doubly unpopular. He was also brilliant and hardworking and made no effort to conceal that

---

* Charterhouse, founded in 1611, is one of the largest public schools in England, boasting among other things the biggest war memorial in England, which lists the names of the seven hundred Old Carthusians who were killed in World War I.

at a school in which most of the boys affected a languid indifference to work. He was a "swot," in fact, a boy who worked hard, excelled, and made no attempt to hide it.

Graves's claim that he was Irish did not improve matters. On the contrary, it brought down on his head the hostility of an older boy who really *was* Irish, and who subjected him to every kind of physical and mental abuse, including making fun of Graves's innocence and prudish distaste for foul language and sex talk. Complaining to those in authority would have marked him as a whiner, or still worse a tattletale, and brought him even greater contempt and punishment. He yearned to run away but hadn't the courage to—and no doubt didn't want to disappoint his father.

In the middle of his second year at Charterhouse, he wrote to his parents begging them to take him away from the school, and describing some of the indignities he had suffered. Predictably, this backfired; his parents felt obliged to visit his housemaster and show him the letter. Their visit did not go unnoticed, and the result was that Graves was treated as an informer and virtually stigmatized. Effectively isolated, he began to write poems, even though that further added to his unpopularity. Warned off playing rugby by the school doctor because of a heart murmur, Graves took up boxing instead, rightly guessing that that might discourage some of the bullies. Boxing would become an important part of his life, but more important than that, he decided to become an agnostic, despite the piety of his parents, and fell in love with another boy—a relationship that was intense, but almost certainly unconsummated.

Ironically, in view of his war service, Graves was the principal opposition speaker in a debate on the proposition that "This house in favor of compulsory military service"; Graves's side lost by a landslide. He also resigned from the Officer Training Corps. Perhaps the best thing that happened to Graves at Charterhouse was the friendship he formed with one of the younger masters, George Mallory. A member of Rupert Brooke's circle at Cambridge, Mallory introduced him to the work of contemporary poets and to that ubiquitous promoter of poetic talent Edward Marsh, who, like Mallory, at once recognized that Graves was potentially more than a mere schoolboy poet.

Mallory also introduced Graves to the world of serious mountaineering, teaching him how to climb the most difficult and dangerous cliffs in Britain. Mallory was a world-famous mountaineer who in 1924 would die trying to reach the summit of Mount Everest.* He introduced Graves to many of the most dangerous climbs in Britain, some of them a thousand precipitous feet high. They could be mastered only by inserting the toe of a boot or the fingers of one hand into the tiniest of crevices in the rock face. Graves reveled in the danger and wrote about it with cool precision. "About half-way up we reached a chimney. A 'chimney' is a vertical fissure in the rock wide enough to admit the body; whereas a 'crack' is only wide enough to admit the boot. One works up a chimney sideways, with back and knees; but up a crack with one's face to the rock." On one occasion, on a sheer cliff face with a drop of several hundred feet, Graves was knocked unconscious by rocks dislodged by the climber ahead of him. Luckily he was saved by his rope. Graves's courage, physical endurance, and calm in the face of danger were about to be put to an even greater and longer test. As he was climbing precipices in Wales, Britain declared war on Germany. The schoolboy trying not to think about his first year at Oxford was suddenly plunged into adult life.

ONE OF THE VIRTUES OF *GOODBYE TO ALL THAT* is that at first it reads like a comic novel about the life of a young officer in a crusty old regiment, rather like Evelyn Waugh's *Officers and Gentlemen*, but it soon takes on a darker tone. To his disgust, Graves was posted from the base camp near the port city of Le Havre to gain some experience in the trenches in a rival Welsh regiment, the Second Battalion of the Welsh Regiment, which he described as "tough and rough" and which had been in constant combat since 1914 "losing its fight-

---

* Mallory's sun-bleached and desiccated body was discovered and identified two thousand feet below the summit in 1994. That of his climbing partner Andrew Irvine has never been found. The question of whether they reached the summit before they fell has never been resolved.

ing strength five times over."* His platoon was made up of underage boys and overage men, both of which groups had lied about their age to enlist. The youngest was fifteen, the oldest sixty-three. What the older soldiers thought of being commanded by an officer who had just turned nineteen is unrecorded but easily imaginable.

After twenty-four hours of slow travel in a decrepit railway carriage, Graves, six other young officers, and forty men were marched by stages at night toward the front line, under increasing artillery fire. What looked like an impressive spectacle from a distance soon became a near and frightening one as shell fragments began to whiz through the air. They followed their guide, a mud-stained private of the Welsh Regiment, and paused in a ruined pharmacy to be issued gas masks (which would prove woefully inefficient) and field dressings. Officers and men alike were burdened like packhorses with equipment. Graves carried a full pack plus his revolver, field glasses, wire cutters, a trench periscope, a compass, and much else. At the noise of each explosion, like everyone else he first flung himself down in the mud, but soon he learned that he was wasting his strength without improving his chances. A muddy road gave way to a muddy path, then to a shallow muddy trench cut in the clay. Graves discovered to his disgust that he was walking on a living carpet of mice and frogs that had been caught in the trench and were unable to get out.

There was no way to escape the mud. Troops slept in shallow, muddy burrows dug in the side of the trench. They ate squatting on the mud floor of the trench. When not on sentry duty, they were kept hard at work with pick and shovel deepening the trench, digging new communications trenches, putting down more barbed wire, and filling sackcloth sandbags with mud to build up the traverses. Officers messed in a dugout in the side of the trench, its earth ceiling reinforced with timber; a muddy army blanket drawn over the entrance hid the light of a lantern. It was a troglodyte existence, occasionally interrupted by sudden death or an unexpected attack as each side tried to exert its dominance over no-man's-land.

---

* Given a battalion strength of 900, this means the loss of about 4,500 men killed, gravely wounded, or missing between August 1914 and May 1915.

Graves, who would very shortly establish a reputation for fear-lessness, spent his first night on the fire step beside the sentry, cautiously peering over the parapet into the dark. "A German flare shot up, broke into bright flame, dropped slowly and went hissing into the grass just behind our trench. . . . Instinctively I moved. 'It's bad to do that, sir,' he said, as a rifle-bullet cracked and seemed to pass right between us. 'Keep still, sir, and they can't spot you. Not but that a flare is a bad thing to fall on you. I've seen them burn a hole in a man.'" At stand-to, at dawn, Graves found a man apparently sleeping. He turned his flashlight on him and ordered him to get up, barely noticing that one of his feet was bare. Graves shook him and then realized that the man "had taken off the boot and sock to pull the trigger of his rifle with one toe; the muzzle was in his mouth." He had blown off the back of his head. Suicide in the trenches was not uncommon. The foul living conditions and constant danger took their toll, and it sometimes required only a piece of bad news from home to break a man's nerve.

Graves found, as so many did, that peering toward the enemy trenches at night was not only dangerous—the Germans had fixed rifles at any point from which they might expect to detect a movement—but also dismaying. If you looked at no-man's-land long enough, it was easy to imagine you saw movement and to imagine that a night attack was beginning. He breakfasted in the dugout company headquarters on eggs, bacon, coffee, toast, and marmalade, with his CO and fellow company officers, a cheerful and informal group. One morning he met a nineteen-year-old sol-dier who had just left Rugby School (Rupert Brooke's beloved alma mater) and reported that he had shot a German before breakfast, "Sights at four hundred.'" It was not only the Germans who were good at sniping.

Graves was experiencing his debut under fire when he learned about the death of Rupert Brooke. He wrote as quickly as he could,

---

*    It is a tribute to the quality of the rifles of both armies that an aimed shot at four hundred yards over open iron sights was possible, even by a soldier who was not a trained sniper with a telescopic sight. Military technology had made even the most ordinary of weapons far more deadly than ever before, multiplying the casualties.

on May 22, 1915, to Edward Marsh to tell him how grieved he was, "for your sake especially and generally for all us who know what poetry is." He told Marsh he was surprised that he was not frightened: "I swear to you, Eddie, it's a true bill, that a violent artillery duel going on above my dug-out two nights ago simply failed to wake me at all though I was conscious of the whole place rocking, but, when this had ceased, I was awoken by a very persistent lark which hung for some minutes over my platoon trench, swearing at the Germanoes." He sent Marsh a few lines of poetry describing his experience of war in almost comic terms, a vivid contrast to the high-flying emotion of Brooke's war poems:

Or you'll be dozing safe in your dug-out—
A great roar, the trench shakes and falls about;
You're choking, choking—then, hullo!
Marjorie's walking gaily down the trench
Hanky to nose (that powder makes a stench!)
Getting her pinafore all over grime.
Funny, she died ten years ago.
Ah, this is a queer time.

The ability to summon up a sudden image of the past after a violent, near-death experience is very much a mark of Graves's poetry, together with the hint that he doesn't take all this horror altogether seriously. Perhaps more than any of the other soldier poets, he made every effort to be a good officer and a credit to his regiment—for which he had a profound affection, not always reciprocated—while composing poems that undermined the conventional view of the war. Graves was still smarting that he had been attached to a battalion of the Welsh Regiment, which he found inferior in smartness and discipline to his own, but he ended his letter to Marsh on a buoyant note: "Tomorrow we go, they say, into some trenches where we and the Bosches [*sic*] are sitting in each other's pockets, the whole placed mined and counter-mined, complete with trench-mortars, gas and grenade throwing parties, so now for a little sleep. Yours in the muses."

Even when Graves was withdrawn from the front line for a time, his description of trench life is chilling: "Everything here is wet and smells. The Germans are very close; they have half the brick-stacks, we have the other half." The trenches at this point passed through what was once a brickyard.

> Each side snipes down from the top of its brick-stacks
> into the others' trenches. This is also a great place
> for German rifle-grenades and trench-mortars. . . .
> A corpse is lying on the fire-step waiting to be tak-
> en down to the grave-yard tonight: a sanitary-man
> killed last night in the open, while burying lavatory
> stuff. . . . His arm was stretched out stiff when they car-
> ried him in. . . . It stretched right across the trench.

His fellow soldiers shook the dead man's hand as they passed him, making boisterous jokes to the corpse. Most of the men, he pointed out, were miners, "accustomed to death," with a trademark working-class mixture of pessimism and cheerfulness, intensified by a natural dislike of authority and total mistrust of anybody who wasn't sharing the danger. They would follow their own officers anywhere, provided they showed courage under fire, but had no confidence in the staff or the generals and still less enthusiasm for the war or any expectation that they would survive it. When the general commanding their division inspected them with tears in his eyes after a failed attack, a grizzled sergeant remarked, "Bloody lot of use that is, busts up his bloody division, then weeps over what's bloody left."

When Graves was finally reunited with the Second Battalion of his own regiment, his blimpish seniors treated him with contempt. Junior officers were spoken of as "warts" and were forbidden to even address their superiors or to speak at table. They were not allowed to drink whiskey and in general were treated like new boys in boarding school—a familiar, but uncomfortable situation for Graves. The battalion had been in India for many years before the war, and the subalterns were expected to ride well, though few did. When they were out of the trenches, they trained on a makeshift polo field every afternoon, on a packsaddle rather than riding one, with crossed stirrups, agonizing at the trot.

Graves actually looked forward to going out at night on patrol—anything was better than the riding school. Besides, a display of courage was the only way to attract favorable attention. Unlike the Welsh Regiment, whose attitude toward the Germans was live and let live, the Second Battalion of the Royal Welch Fusiliers sought to exert dominance over no-man's-land every night, to which the Germans responded by doing the same. When patrols met, the fighting was brutal, silent, and hand-to-hand. The Germans finished off British wounded with a Bowie knife cut to the throat, which made less noise than a pistol, while the British armed themselves with a cosh (a leather sap filled with lead pellets) or a knobkerrie (a stout stick like a shillelagh, with a lead weight at the end). Both were designed to bash in an enemy's skull. The aim was to reach the German outposts and if possible to bring back a prisoner, or at least the collar badges off a dead German, so that the battalion would know what regiment it was facing.

On his first night with the Second Battalion, Graves was sent out on patrol with a sergeant. "Wriggling flat along the ground" like snakes, they made their way through their own wire to a gap in the German wire, lying flat and motionless, faces pressed against the dirt every time they heard a sound and every time the Germans sent up an illuminating flare that lit the ground in front of their trenches with a harsh magnesium glare for minutes at a time. At one point, Graves reached out and accidentally "placed his hand on the slimy body of an old corpse." This was indeed a kind of baptism by fire. For a time it insulated Graves from fear and horror, but it did not prevent these cumulating emotions from affecting his mind—it merely delayed the inevitable reaction. In the meantime, it gave him a valuable reputation for personal courage that made his life in the battalion marginally more bearable. He was a poet, after all, and despite his robust appearance and broken nose, he was a young man of great sensitivity and strong emotion, not at all the reckless daredevil he attempted to be.

GRAVES HAD REJOINED THE ROYAL WELCH just in time to become part of the ill-fated Battle of Loos, the big push of the British Army in 1915, and the first time the British used poison gas on a large scale. Nobody in higher command was enthusiastic about the attack, for the ground ahead was unfavorable and the enemy trenches elaborate and strongly held on high ground that would be difficult to reach. But as was so often the case on the Western Front, the British need to do something to placate the French—coupled with the belief of cavalrymen like the British commander in chief Sir John French that the war would be won by "fighting spirit of the cavalry" rather than by artillery and machine guns—led to a battle that seems in retrospect to have guaranteed high casualties for little or no gain. In this view, the function of the infantry was to seize the enemy trenches and enable the cavalry to break through and advance into open country. How the cavalry were to do so across ground that was muddy, pockmarked with shell holes, and crisscrossed with wide bands of barbed wire and deep trenches was a question left unanswered, such was the faith that the moral power of *l'arme blanche* (the cavalry saber) deployed en masse would carry all before it.

The Battle of Loos (September–October 1915) has been fought over by historians as fiercely as it was on the ground. The three-week bloodbath cost the British nearly sixty thousand casualties, including four major-generals. The preparations had been elaborate— the British had dug mines deep under the German front lines, to explode them at the beginning of the attack. But the ground chosen was unpropitious, a bleak landscape of mines, slag fields, quarries, a brickyard, and flooded shell craters. The Germans had spent almost a year fortifying it with Teutonic military ingenuity: impenetrable fields of barbed wire, countless concealed machine gun nests, a maze of trenches reinforced with concrete dugouts, plus a formidable earthen fortress known as the Hohenzollern Redoubt. Graves's company commander, a polite, competent and normally uncommunicative regular captain, upon handing his officers their orders for the attack, sardonically remarked that they didn't make much sense but it didn't matter, since "we'll get killed whatever happens."

Planning for the attack, which would involve over 120,000 men, was hampered from the beginning by the rivalry between the commander in chief of the British Expeditionary Force (BEF), Field Marshal Sir John French, and the commander of British First

Army, General Sir Douglas Haig. Sir John was a short but swash-buckling hero with a hair-trigger temper; he was a brilliantly suc-cessful cavalry commander and a notorious womanizer who had been promoted beyond his competence. At sixty-two, he still had a certain swagger—he wore a khaki hunting stock with a gold stock pin instead of a collar and tie. His attitude toward security was cheerfully negligent, as he confided even the most closely guarded military secrets to one of his mistresses. Haig, on the other hand, was a dour and deeply religious Scot, a "scientific" soldier, a born intriguer married to a lady-in-waiting to the queen, which gave him back-door connection to the king. Neither man spoke French. Haig had been close to French for years—French saw himself as Haig's mentor—and Haig had even loaned French a considerable amount of money. French was a habitual overspender, while Haig's family owned the famous Haig & Haig distillery company, making him a wealthy man.

By the autumn of 1915, French was physically exhausted and volatile—Haig compared him to a fizzy soda water bottle always ready to pop its cork. He left much of the planning for the British attack to Haig. French held back under his own command a reserve of two divisions, which he did not want to commit to battle until the initial attack had succeeded, at which point it was hoped they could deliver the final blow that would break through the German lines and open the way for the cavalry. Haig had been impressed by the plan to use poison gas and smoke shells immediately prior to the attack, but he does not seem to have taken into account the possi-bility that the wind would blow in the wrong direction. His plan of attack simply assumed that his troops would be advancing toward trenches in which the enemy was choking to death and blinded.

Looming over both men was the immense figure of the secretary of state for war, Field Marshal the Earl Kitchener, victor of Omdur-man, former governor-general of the Sudan, commander in chief of India, British agent and consul-general of Egypt (the equivalent of the viceroy of India), perhaps the most revered soldier in Brit-ain. His stern face with its mighty mustache graced the ubiquitous recruiting poster, bearing the legend, "BRITONS, He [Kitchener] wants you, Join your country's army! God save the King." It was

Kitchener who had created "the New Army" of volunteers and pre-
vented them from being fed piecemeal as replacements into exist-
ing battalions. In this case, however, he had allowed several of his
new battalions to serve in the battle, despite the animosity between
himself and Sir John French. Kitchener thought French had neither
the temperament nor the talent to command the BEF, while French
thought Kitchener mad. French was incensed that Kitchener wore
his uniform as a field marshal when visiting the BEF since his role
as secretary of state for war was a civilian one. Both French and
Haig were dubious about the suitability of the ground ahead of the
army for an attack, but Kitchener's keen awareness of the possibil-
ity of a Russian collapse and of growing French doubts that Britain
was willing to cooperate in a major offensive on the Western Front
persuaded him to overrule them.

These lofty considerations were unknown to the men in the
trenches. The attack began, and Robert Graves remembered being
awed by the artillery barrage, which in the course of five days
hurled nearly 300,000 shells at the German lines. But as much as
it impressed Graves, the results were negligible. Haig had assem-
bled over nine hundred guns, but they were spread out over a long
front of over eleven thousand yards rather than being concentrated
at one point. As the British went over the top from their frontline
trenches, he was relying on gas to neutralize the defenders and on
"smoke candles," instead of more effective smoke shells, to blind
the German machine-gunners. Three hundred thousand shells may
sound like a lot to us, and it sounded like a lot to Graves, but a year
later, at the First Battle of the Somme, the artillery barrage by the
British consisted of 1.7 million shells over one week.

In addition, almost 30 percent of the shells fired at Loos in 1916
were duds. Their failure to explode would present a serious haz-
ard to advancing infantry as they stumbled over them. Due to the
nature of the ground, and poor or inexperienced staff work, many
of the British guns were poorly sited and proved unable to cut the
German barbed wire or to reach German artillery or the massive
concrete bunkers in which German troops could shelter. As a result,
German losses from the British artillery barrage were so small that
the commander of the Sixth Army, General the Crown Prince Rup-

precht of Bavaria, at first refused to believe that it was the preliminary to an attack.

Many of these problems stemmed from the relative inefficiency of British artillery as compared to that of the Germans, and to the shortage of shells, which would soon become a scandal that would almost bring down Asquith's government. A more important problem was General Haig's mistaken conviction that gas, not artillery, was the decisive weapon—that those Germans who survived the artillery barrage, when they emerged from their dugouts, would die or choke on it, or surrender. But at this stage of the war the Germans had more effective protection against gas than the British did.

Moreover, the efficacy of gas was hugely dependent on the weather. Prodigious efforts had been made to lug 5,100 heavy cylinders of chlorine gas, totaling 150 tons, as close as possible to the front line. Each bulky cylinder weighed over 160 pounds. With their pipes and valves attached, they were almost impossibly hard to slog through a maze of narrow, muddy trenches at night. Nor did they inspire confidence in those who had to carry them; many of the cylinders were badly corroded, while others leaked dangerously, giving off an alarming stench, and their release valves were flimsy and easily damaged.

The attack was to take place according to a rigidly orchestrated sequence: the end of the artillery barrage would be followed by a forty-minute discharge of the "accessory," as the gas was referred to for the purpose of security. Thereafter smoke candles would be lit, and the men would leave the assault trenches and attack. As far as the "accessory" was concerned, Robert Graves's company commander, when asked whether he believed it would be successful, replied briskly, "We're sure to bungle it. Take those new gas-companies—sorry, I mean accessory-companies—their very look makes me tremble. Chemistry-dons from London University, a few lads straight from school, one or two N.C.O.s of the old-soldier type. . . . Of course they'll bungle it. How could they do anything else?"

Even leaving aside the "accessory" and the need for the troops to wear a suffocating tube helmet pulled down over the face, the advance was not likely to be rapid. Each man was to carry two hundred rounds of ammunition, a rifle and bayonet, heavy tools (a pick or a shovel) in a sling, emergency rations, a water bottle, field dressing, and if available, a pair of wire cutters. The notion that the advance was a "charge" in any sense of the word is misleading. Everything took place as if in slow motion: heavily laden, terrified men climbed clumsily, with considerable difficulty, out of sodden assault trenches on makeshift ladders. Those who were not shot on the parapet stumbled forward through thick, greasy mud and tangles of barbed wire under a deadly rain of razor-sharp shell fragments. (Steel helmets had not yet been issued, so head wounds were frequent.) Then they encountered massed rifle and machine-gun fire. German machine-gunners fired from low, concealed nests, often hitting whole lines of men in the ankles or lower legs as they emerged from the assault trench and stood up. Their dead or wounded bodies would impede the advance of the men behind them.

On the eve of battle, Graves's battalion marched back to leave off their spare kit and greatcoat. The officers spent a raucous evening in the dining room of a nearby château, which Graves describes as a grotesque reenactment of the Last Supper, with the general commanding one of the supporting divisions in the Christ role at the center of the table. "It's going to be a glorious balls-up,"* one of the division's senior staff officers predicted, pointing out acidly that the general was a silly old woman who didn't know where his own division was and couldn't even read a map properly. For once, junior officers (captains and below) were allowed to order whiskey—as a rule, they were obliged to drink beer—before the battalion was marched back by night through massed cavalry to the assault trenches, "cold, tired and sick, and not at all in the mood for a battle." Graves and his fellow officers tried to catch a little sleep in an abandoned railway siding in the pouring rain, waiting to support the Middlesex Regiment, and for the gas attack on which so much had been staked.

"All we heard . . . was a distant cheer, confused crackle of rifle fire, yells, heavy shelling on our front line, more shouts and yells, and a

---

* *Balls-up* is the universal British military equivalent of the American *fuck up,* as in SNAFU, "situation normal, all fucked up."

continuous rattle of machine-guns," Graves would write. It was followed by a stream of walking wounded, then by men "yellow-faced and choking," whose brass buttons had been turned verdigris-green by the gas. Then came the stretcher-bearers carrying the heavily wounded through the narrow trenches under a hail of fire from the German artillery. "What's happened?" Graves shouted, but the only answer he got was "Bloody balls-up!"

The gas attack had been a disaster. Although the wind conditions were all wrong, the gas companies had been ordered to proceed with the release of the gas nevertheless, "at all costs." As it turned out, they had not been provided with the right size wrenches to open the valve on their gas cylinders, so they had to scrounge for adjustable ones. When they were found, and the gas was released, it hung like a cloud in front of the British troops, or wafted back and pooled in the assault trenches without reaching the Germans. The Germans shelled the assault trenches, breaking open many of the cylinders, at which point the gas companies panicked and ran.

Those troops who managed to get far enough forward to attack were decimated, stopped by the German barbed wire that the artillery barrage had failed to destroy—ordinary fragmentation shells had no effect on it—and by relentless German machine-gun fire. The new British hand grenades—which were to be ignited by a system very much like a match striking a match box—failed in the rain, further hampering the assault. Later, the staff examining the battlefield with binoculars could tell how close British troops had come to the German front line by the long rows of British dead, particularly the kilted Highland infantry, who were immediately identifiable by their bare legs.

Graves's description of the first day of the Battle of Loos—it would haunt him for the rest of his long life—is a litany of horrors, and his telling it the deadpan tone of a detached observer, rather than with indignation and disgust, makes it all the more terrifying. He describes trenches full of bodies, their overwhelming "gas-blood-lyddite-latrine smell," and the agony of the wounded who were unreachable in the barbed wire: "[Captain] Samson lay groaning about twenty yards beyond the front trench. Several attempts were made to rescue him. He had been very badly hit. Three men got killed in these attempts. . . . In the end his own orderly managed to crawl out to him. Samson waved him back, saying that he was riddled through and not worth rescuing; he sent his apologies to the company for making such a noise." That night, when Graves went out to bring in the wounded, he saw Samson's body. Wounded in seventeen places, the man had jammed his fist into his mouth deep enough to silence his own cries of pain. Graves remarks on the attitudes of many of the dead, stiffened into grotesque shapes while bandaging wounds, crawling, and cutting wire. The constant rain rendered the unbearable even more miserable.

The casualties were appalling. Those of the Argyll and Sutherland Highlanders were not untypical, seven hundred casualties out of perhaps nine hundred men; fourteen officers were killed out of the sixteen who went over the top. In the next few days, the British attempted to repeat the attack, with declining success and mounting casualties, going out night after night to bring in the remaining wounded and the dead. With his usual keen eye for detail, Graves noted that the dead who were too close to the German wire to move "continued to swell until the wall of the stomach collapsed; a disgusting smell would float across," often causing him to vomit, although that did not prevent him from noticing that the "color of the dead faces changed from white to yellow-grey, to red, to purple, to green, to black, to slimy."* He kept himself going by drinking a bottle of whiskey a day, leading to a dislike of it later in life.

Loos was a disaster that was hard to hide, although by the standards of later British disasters, it was small—over 60,000 British casualties to no more than 20,000 German, for no significant gain in ground. It led to the removal of Field Marshal Sir John French from command of the BEF and to his replacement by General Sir Douglas Haig. French had mentored Haig, underestimating his ambition and his ability to go behind his chief's back at 10 Downing Street and the palace. Haig managed to convince everybody who mattered that the British would have won the Battle of Loos

---

* Another writer, Ernest Hemingway, who served as an ambulance driver in Italy in 1918, remarked on much the same thing in his short story "A Natural History of the Dead."

had Sir John French committed the reserves more quickly, and had he stayed back at his headquarters instead of moving closer to the fighting; there German artillery had severed his communications, leaving him unreachable at key moments in the battle. French was short-tempered, nettlesome, and volatile. His face turned purple when he was contradicted.

Haig, by contrast, was self-contained, cold, and absolutely convinced of his own righteousness and moral authority—not by any stretch of the imagination a lovable man, nor one who aspired to be. But far from learning anything from the disaster of the Battle of Loos, he would merely repeat it on a larger and larger scale over the next three years, multiplying the casualties at a dizzying rate.

Both Sir John and Sir Douglas were suspicious of the French and kept in mind the British government's concern that while the BEF must of necessity cooperate with its ally, it was in no circumstances to take orders from the French high command. Not until the spring of 1918, when General Ludendorff's last-ditch great offensive, the Kaiserschlacht, intended to defeat the Allies before the Americans arrived in force, nearly separated the British from the French army, would the Allies finally agree to the appointment of an Allied commander in chief, or "generalissimo," in the person of General Ferdinand Foch.

ON OCTOBER 3, Graves's battalion was withdrawn from the fighting at Loos, which had settled down into desultory skirmishes and artillery barrages. He was transferred to the even more punctilious First Battalion of the Royal Welch Fusiliers. On visiting another company's mess, he found a copy of *The Essays of Lionel Johnson*. Johnson was a respected turn-of-the-century English poet and essayist who died young; he was a homosexual and an alcoholic of considerable charm, a friend of Oscar Wilde and W. B. Yeats. His work has been described as *"fin du siècle* and decadent," but to the contemporary reader it may merely seem lush and overwrought.

It was the first book Graves had seen in France that was neither a military manual nor a trashy novel. Curious, he glanced at the flyleaf and saw that it belonged to one Siegfried Sassoon. Glancing around to see who might be its owner, he had no difficulty in locating him at once. The tall, languid, handsome young subaltern had a face that was ever so slightly exotic in appearance and the hands of a concert pianist. Graves got into conversation with him, and they left the mess together to find a quiet place to talk.

Graves, with his rugby player's physique, his broken nose, and his gift for boxing, was sensible enough not to talk about poetry with his fellow officers. None of them would have regarded reading it, let alone writing it, as a suitable occupation for a soldier. Partly because of his willingness to crawl out into no-man's-land looking for trouble at night, partly because he had joined the regiment's special reserve so early on in the war, Graves had been promoted to acting captain—three pips—over older and wiser officers. Sassoon was still a lowly subaltern with a single pip and had not yet seen action, but the subject of poetry instantly bonded them to each other.

Sassoon had published at his own expense a few slim volumes of poetry, enough to attract the attention of Edward Marsh, while Graves was in the process of putting together a volume of his war poems. Sassoon was a dedicated and daring rider, both as a fox hunter and as a steeplechase rider, and as such he was viewed as an acceptable young officer. Yet he was a member of a famous Jewish family—the Sassoons were so rich and so assimilated that, like the Rothschilds, they were hardly even thought of as Jewish anymore. The Sassoons were friends, financial advisers, and bankers to King Edward VII. One of them was military secretary to General Sir Douglas Haig and would go on to become a Conservative member of Parliament, while Siegfried's aunt Rachel Sassoon Beer was editor and part owner both of *The Observer* and *The Sunday Times*. Although Sassoon's father had been disinherited for marrying a Gentile, he was still well-to-do. Siegfried* had been brought up as a Christian and was educated at Marlborough School and Clare College, Cambridge. He did not regard himself as Jewish. Nor did his fellow officers—at any rate, in his superlative *Memoirs of an Infantry Officer*, he does not mention a single anti-Semitic remark or slur, even after he

---

* His name does not signify any connection to or sympathy with Germany. His mother was merely a fervid admirer of Wagner's operas.

became perhaps the most famous and controversial junior officer in the British Army.

A further, if somewhat muted and subterranean, bond was homo-erotic. Graves's erotic experiences, such as they were, had focused on other young men, in particular a boy three years younger than himself at Charterhouse, for whom Graves had an intense, although unconsummated passion. A schoolboy romance with a younger boy, however innocent, was frowned upon and led to an unpleasant interview with the headmaster, but nothing worse—the friend was later accused of soliciting, and for a time it frightened Graves off pursuing further romances with men. Sassoon too was attracted to young men but remained for the moment innocent. They were not at first admirers of each other's poetry, but it made a huge difference that they could at last talk to each other about literature and art, rather than sports and the latest West End shows.

"He is a strange person, full, of ideas and originality," Sassoon wrote cautiously to Edward Marsh about Graves shortly after their first meeting, over tea and buns in nearby Béthune. Sassoon made every effort to be a perfect officer—his tailoring and his demeanor were everything the First Battalion of the Royal Welch Fusiliers could expect. By contrast, Graves dressed carelessly by the stan-dards of his regiment and slouched. He was big, clumsy, outspoken, and full of effervescent and unpopular ideas, which he had no hesi-tation in expressing in a loud voice, to the dismay of older and more senior officers.

Although Graves was nearly ten years younger than Sassoon, he had been in the field for many months and had the combat expe-rience that Sassoon still lacked. They differed about almost every major figure in English literature, beginning with Milton, whom Sassoon admired and Graves dismissed with contempt. Graves also made fun of fox hunting, which was still at the time the center of Sassoon's life—that, and the bucolic English upper-middle-class rural life that went with it. Nevertheless, they became fast friends and would remain so for many years, with one lengthy lapse. There may have been a sexual element in the relationship. Graves thought Sassoon had physical feelings for him, while Sassoon alternately admitted and denied it. The likelihood is that for Graves, it was

the continuation of his schoolboy passions, and for Sassoon too a
natural impulse, although both men would eventually adopt a het-
erosexual lifestyle. Graves would enjoy, if that is the right word, a
dizzyingly complicated and even mildly scandalous heterosexual
love life and father eight children.

They showed each other bits and pieces of their poetry. Graves's
work was in transition from the precocious cleverness of his school-
boy verse to harsh descriptions of life and death in the trenches,
made more striking by his skill and his gift for making the last line
of a poem an unexpected, brutal blow to the reader. Sassoon was
still writing about the war with romantic lyricism and had not as
yet moved to savage anger intended to shock the reader. Still under
the spell of Rupert Brooke, he thought Graves's poetry too "real-
istic," while Graves thought, correctly, that Sassoon would change
his tune after experiencing life in the trenches. They would both
become unwilling to see the war as an opportunity for noble sacri-
fice, following the example of Brooke, or even as justifiable. Indeed,
Sassoon would eventually attempt to become the war's most public
and celebrated martyr.

THE PROGRESS OF THEIR POETRY—they had, until their meeting,
both been modestly self-published, but the war would make them
famous—mirrored the progress of the war. Graves began with con-
ventional war poems, like this one about troops returning from
their time in the front line:

> and we go
> Miles back into the sunny cornfield where
> Babies like tickling, and where tall white horses
> Draw the plough leisurely in quiet courses.

This kind of lyricism soon gave way to lines such as those describ-
ing the searing vision of a dead German:

> To-day I found in Mametz Wood
> A certain cure for lust of blood:

Where, propped against a shattered trunk,
In a great mess of things unclean,
Sat a dead Boche; he scowled and stunk
With clothes and face a sodden green,
Big-bellied, spectacled, crop-haired,
Dribbling black blood from nose and beard.

This was a radically different view of the war than poetry had offered so far. Graves was determined that his readers should understand what the war that was being fought on their behalf was really like, in lines that have a certain martial tread:

"Fall in!" A stir, and up we jump,
Fold the love letter, drain the cup,
We toss away the Woodbine* stump,
Snatch at the pack and lift it up. . . .
Where are we marching? No one knows.
Why are we marching? No one cares.

Graves's poems have a jaunty tone, with inevitable barbed last lines to puncture the reader's illusions:

But the boys who were killed in the battle
Who fought with no rage and no cant,
Are peacefully sleeping on pallets of mud
Low down with the worm and the ant.

Graves was naturally brave and had managed to turn himself into a much more competent officer than he looked, despite his doubts about the war. His devotion to the Royal Welch Fusiliers was nothing short of obsessional. Like Evelyn Waugh in the next world war, he wrote spirited and comic satire about his military superiors and their narrow view of the world, while at the same time longing to be accepted as one of them. He was like a boy who entered one of England's great public schools—Marlborough, in his case—

---

* Cheap brand of English cigarette, mostly sold in packets of five.

resentful of the humiliations, bullying, and physical intimidation being inflicted on him by his elders, but eager to take his place in the school hierarchy.

SIEGFRIED SASSOON'S TRAJECTORY as a young infantry officer was more dramatic than that of Graves. With his immaculate appearance, perfect manners, and undoubted skill and courage as a horseman, he had fewer problems fitting into military life in a crack regiment than Graves, and not so many rough edges. Still, he sought to burnish his image, perhaps as a preemptive defense against anti-Semitism, by rash and risky acts of bravery in the field. Merely being in the front line was dangerous enough, but Sassoon sought out every opportunity to patrol no-man's-land by night, earning himself the admiring nickname "Mad Jack."

Hardly anybody could have tried harder to fit in as an infantry subaltern. Like Graves, Sassoon instantly embraced the ethos, the customs, the traditions, and the peculiarities of the Royal Welch Fusiliers. If nothing else, the hunting field had prepared him for a world in which every small detail of dress mattered to an excruciating degree. One of the books he brought with him to war was Robert Smith Surtee's *Mr. Sponge's Sporting Tour*, a classic mid-Victorian novel of fox hunting. He had transformed himself, apparently without conscious effort, into a horsey, sporting English country gentleman with a passion for cricket, a persona that he kept throughout a long and in other ways flamboyantly unconventional life, which would include affairs with the composer and matinée idol Ivor Novello, Prince Philip of Hesse, the actor Glen Byam Shaw, and the prolific author and gardener Beverley Nichols, as well as a stormy marriage, fatherhood, and conversion to Roman Catholicism.

The nomadic Sassoon family had a gift for adapting themselves to whatever country they happened to be living in, since fourteenth-century Spain. By the mid-nineteenth century, they were fabulously rich Baghdadi Jews, bankers, traders, and tax collectors on behalf of the Ottoman sultans. They then expanded to Egypt, British India, and China, adding opium trading to their list of profitable businesses. Wherever they went, they built on a grand scale, including the first skyscraper on Shanghai's Bund (now a luxury hotel), while adhering to strict Orthodox Judaism. A photograph of David Sassoon, the mid-nineteenth-century patriarch, with three of his sons, in Baghdad, shows him seated as if on a throne, swathed in sumptuous embroidered silk robes. With his full, thick white beard and silk turban, his slippers with long, curved toes coming to a sharp point, he is a figure straight out of *The Arabian Nights*. Two of his sons are dressed similarly, like exotic examples of Middle Eastern fantasy. The third wears a well-cut European suit and a stiff, high white collar, clearly in preparation for the Sassoon family's intention of expanding their business to Britain, where they would soon rival the Rothschilds and intermarry with them.

Siegfried's father, Alfred Sassoon, broke with the family tradition. Rather than pursue a career in business or public service, he chose a life more out Puccini's *La Bohème*, becoming a sculptor on an ambitious scale and a gifted amateur musician. Although he led a busy life in London society, he preferred the Paris artistic world. In other respects as well he differed from his family. He fell in love with and married a daughter of the Thornycroft family, bluff, hearty English squires, leavened by a pronounced artistic streak. Theresa was not only beautiful and a talented painter—she attended the Royal Academy and had paintings exhibited there—she was also a deeply religious Christian. Her family accepted, not without some misgivings, Alfred Sassoon as her husband, but his family did not accept her. In fact, his mother cut him off from her share of the family fortune and formally declared him dead. She sat shiva for him, the Jewish ritual seven days of mourning, and cursed any children who might come out of his marriage.

Nonetheless it was, at first, a love match. Alfred was hardly penniless, while Theresa's family were well-to-do and generous. Both of them were artistic and high-spirited, and Alfred had no objections to being married in a High Church Anglican ceremony or to having his children brought up as Anglicans. Certainly physical passion was not lacking, for Theresa gave birth to three boys in quick succession, the middle one being Siegfried. Alfred was able to buy and renovate Weirleigh, a vast, mullioned, crenellated Victorian monstrosity of a house in then-rural Kent, with a spire like that of a church. It had nine bedrooms and the usual cramped quarters in the attic for servants, who included a nanny, a cook, a kitchen maid, and three housemaids, not to speak of the outdoor servants—a head gardener, two undergardeners, the groom, and two stableboys—not an unusual number of servants in mid-Victorian times. Weirleigh's saving grace was seven acres of land, part of which Theresa transformed into a famously beautiful garden (another of her talents). It provided a paradise for three active boys to grow up in.

But Alfred's roving eye brought the marriage to an early end. He was, as the phrase went, a ladies' man and fond of good company as well. Living in rural Kent, taking tea with his neighbors and attending church on Sunday did not interest him. Before the children were hardly more than infants, he yearned for life in London society and in the Paris artistic demimonde, perhaps all the more so because he already knew he was suffering from tuberculosis. It was then still an incurable disease, and he knew he might not have many years left to enjoy himself. In any case, he left the family, and the break was final. Whenever he visited the children, Theresa locked herself up in the living room and refused to see him or acknowledge his presence. This was doubly painful because Alfred seems to have been a loving father—his children adored him. He brought them extravagant presents, enjoyed playing with them, and inspired Siegfried to share his love of cricket, the quintessential English sport. Siegfried also inherited his mother's passion for horses (she was a superb horsewoman), her interest in gardening, her artistic sensibility, and her love of music, which both his parents shared.

As with most English boys of his class, his nanny played an out-of-proportion role in his life. Nanny Mitchell, although a strict disciplinarian, provided him with solid support in a household that was all too obviously divided by a failed marriage. So, increasingly, did Tom, the stableman, coachman, and head groom. Eventually Tom would take on the role of father figure, teaching the boy to ride, introducing him to the world of fox hunting, and acting as his cricket coach. Within limits, it was a perfect childhood for an adventurous boy who loved the countryside, a small, self-contained world dominated by Nanny Mitchell. It was made all the more tightly embracing because Theresa disliked schools and did not want to be separated from her children. As a result, they were educated at home by a succession of private tutors, to whom would eventually be added a Fräulein to teach French and German, and a retired sergeant to teach boxing and fencing. This idyll would continue until 1894, when Nanny Mitchell retired, and Alfred Sassoon died. Urged on by her own family, eventually Theresa decided that her children would have to endure the common fate of English upper-middle-class boys: they would board at a prep school, then attend a public school.

Between the tutors and Theresa's determination to shape her favorite among her three sons into what she wanted him to be, Siegfried might easily have grown up spoiled. Fortunately for him, boarding school provided a counterbalance. His prep school was a fairly benign experience, although the transition from a home life centered almost entirely around himself and his brothers to boarding in a dormitory with a dozen other boys cannot have been easy. Still, the school was only a few miles from Weirleigh, in familiar country, so visits home, although not frequent, were easy. Siegfried did well in school, and managed to pick up another sport to which he remained devoted for the rest of his life, golf. He was also stimulated to write poetry—it was the *rhythm* of the words that intrigued him more than the meaning of the phrases. Of all the war poets, he would have the surest touch with the ebb and flow of words, no matter what the subject was, and his poetry almost begs to be read aloud.

Marlborough College, one of the great public schools of England, was an altogether bigger challenge, a railway journey of at least five hours from Siegfried's home in Kent, with pupils numbering in the hundreds, vast grounds, and a confluence of many buildings. The town of Marlborough, on the coach road between London and Bath, is supposedly the burial place of the legendary wizard Merlin, and the school itself, although not founded until 1843, is on the site of an ancient castle and a Neolithic burial mound. Originally intended as a boarding school for the sons of churchmen who could not afford the fees of Eton or Harrow, Marlborough had, and still has, a certain reputation for earnestness, although not without the usual degree of "physical discomfort and ritual bullying" of all public schools at the time.

Siegfried as an adult would remember mostly the habitual indignities of public school life—humiliation and intimidation at the hands of masters, brutality and mockery at the hands of older boys. He would have none of Rupert Brooke's passionate conviction that his time at Rugby had been the happiest of his life. Perhaps it was impossible for Siegfried to overcome the years when he had been the focus of his mother's attention and his schooling had been in the hands of nannies and tutors. At Marlborough he never quite fit in to the turbulent life of a big boarding school. Moreover he made the discovery that he was sexually attracted to young men, despite the constant warning and vigilance of the masters against the slightest sign of homosexuality; needless to say, there were no locks on the doors of the toilets, and bathing was rigorously supervised. Unlike Rupert Brooke, he remained physically innocent. Perhaps to distract himself from desires he could not express, he resumed writing poetry with single-minded determination, spurred on by one of the masters who regularly offered a prize of half a crown for the best poem written by a boy of his form.

Siegfried's career at Marlborough was something less than stellar academically. He did not do well at mathematics or the classics, or indeed at anything that failed to interest him. He missed a lot of class time because of illness—first measles, then two serious bouts with pneumonia, one of which nearly killed him. Theresa came to the school and looked after him herself, surely unusual, and withdrew him for a long period of recuperation. But there is no suggestion that he was delicate, for he played field hockey, a game almost as violent as rugby, and, with greater enthusiasm, cricket. His ambition to become a poet would not have struck any of his masters at Marlborough as sensible or realistic, and his poems, mostly fairly banal ones about school life, were regularly turned down by the school magazine, although he did manage to get several about cricket published (apparently without payment) in the magazine *Cricket*. He left the school without regret—the headmaster's parting words to him were, "Try to be more sensible," a less-than-spirited farewell to a young man who would become, in less than thirteen years, perhaps England's most famous poet.

Siegfried went straight from Marlborough to a "crammer" for

nearly a year—a boarding school for a relatively small number of young men who needed to be coached (or crammed) for the Oxford and Cambridge entrance examinations, or for those of the army, the civil service, or the diplomatic service. The crammer, Henley House, had the great advantage of being less than ten miles from Weirleigh, an easy bicycle ride, and its atmosphere was more relaxed than school, since all twenty pupils were the same age. Moreover, there was no "fagging," the system by which each of the younger boys acted as the valet-servant of a senior pupil—and which more or less guaranteed a good deal of abuse.* There was neither corporal punishment nor a vast, unwritten body of school traditions of behavior and dress, the slightest breach of which, however innocent, would provoke anything from ridicule to a beating from an older student or a master.

Needless to say, the crammer was also missing the tense, suppressed adolescent sexual energy of a big boarding school. Its zeitgeist was more that of a comfortable country club, with a golf course, tennis courts, and a cricket pitch. Not surprisingly, Siegfried did well there. He made friends, passed his examination, and went up to Clare College, Cambridge, in 1905. He did not make this choice himself. The Sassoon family had always favored Eton and Oxford, so it is possible that Theresa was determined to make a break with the family which had disowned her marriage. Many members of her own family had attended Cambridge. In any case, it was she who chose Clare, the second oldest college in Cambridge and one of the most beautiful. It was then a comparatively small college, and she may have thought Siegfried would be more comfortable there.

His Thornycroft relatives urged him to read law at Cambridge. Perhaps that was unfortunate. The subject was not one in which he had the slightest interest, and it was also fact-based, learned by rote, at which he did poorly. It lacked fantasy or romance, and it did not excite his imagination. In any case, he had no intention of becoming a lawyer. He managed, not without difficulty and despite the disapproval of his Thornycroft relatives, to switch from law to

---

* For those who are interested in English public schools, the prototypical bully is the brutal, cowardly Flashman in *Tom Brown's School Days*.

history, but here too he found the narrow focus unappealing. He did not dislike Cambridge, but he made no impact there. He set his hopes on winning the Chancellor's Medal for poetry—a considerable distinction—but that effort failed. After less than two years at the university, aware that he could not possibly expect to pass the second-year examination, he decided to leave and assume the life of a country gentleman at home. His mother raised no objection— one guesses that she wanted him to be home more than to have a stellar university career. Siegfried's Thornycroft uncle and the long-suffering trustee of his small estate might have deplored his retreat into a life of fox-hunting, breakneck steeple-chasing, golf, and cricket, but that was what Theresa had always wanted.

Siegfried stepped into the world in which so many of Dickens's characters dwelled, those who could write under profession "private income." He was not idle, far from it, for he wrote poetry steadily and in enormous quantity. He collected books, as he had done since his schooldays with discriminating taste, and he indulged himself in having small editions of his work privately printed, with exquisite attention to detail—he had an unexpected gift for book design and typography. What was more, he had an uncommon flair for public relations that contradicted his persona as a bluff, modest, hearty horseman and country bumpkin. Relying mostly on his Thornycroft relatives and his mother, he managed to get his slim volumes of verse into the right hands in London, where they attracted a certain amount of attention. As early as 1908, only a year after his leaving Cambridge, his narrative poem *Orpheus in Diloeryum* excited the interest of Edmund Gosse, who praised its "richness of fancy and command of melodious verse."

Gosse was a major figure in art, poetry, music, and literature. He had known Browning, Tennyson, and Swinburne and helped popularize Ibsen in England. Wealthy by marriage, he was a prolific writer. From his prestigious sinecure as librarian of the House of Lords Library, he reviewed for *The Sunday Times*, and he was almost as gifted a talent-spotter as Edward Marsh. He would play an important role in the careers of James Joyce, W. B. Yeats, and Sassoon. Siegfried had at last found someone at the center of London's cultural world who would read his poetry thoughtfully and offer him advice and criticism (not by any means always accepted) and, more important, promote him.

Like a magnet, Gosse attracted Siegfried to London, where he soon made friends with the editors of several magazines, partially overcoming a certain amount of bashfulness. His poetry and prose poems in this period seem a little lush and old-fashioned, but that was in part because he lacked any experience in life. Even though he was becoming more acutely aware of his own homosexuality, he remained, as he put it coyly in an anguished confessional letter to the utopian socialist and proselytizer of homosexual freedom Edward Carpenter, "entirely unspotted," despite his attraction for his own sex and the antipathy he felt toward women.

Siegfried's correspondence with Carpenter represented a significant turning point in his life. It is hard to imagine a greater contrast than that between Sassoon and Carpenter, a passionate vegetarian and sexual liberationist who dressed in knickerbockers and homemade sandals, lived openly with a working-class man, popularized the idea of "the simple life" (a phrase he had coined) and the abolition of social classes, was a friend and disciple of Walt Whitman, and corresponded with everyone from Gandhi to Isadora Duncan. Fiona MacCarthy once described Carpenter rather cattily, but not inaccurately, as "the gay godfather of the British left."

Sassoon's friendship with him forced him to face his own sexual nature more frankly, although he remained, in an expression that did not then exist, firmly closeted. Almost inevitably, Siegfried was introduced to Edward Marsh and began to move toward life in London, away from his mother and his horses. He joined a modest club, which gave him a place to stay, and eventually he sought a pied-à-terre in the same building as Marsh's, decorating it with more extravagance than he could afford. One feels him tentatively beginning to spread his wings. The self-publication of *The Daffodil Murderer*, a parody of John Masefield's enormously successful bathetic verse-tragedy *The Everlasting Mercy*—he printed a thousand copies— brought Siegfried at last some degree of fame and served to introduce him to others in the London social and artistic world, like Max Beerbohm, "the inimitable Max," and eventually, thanks to Marsh, to Rupert Brooke.

To Marsh's disappointment, the meeting with Brooke came to nothing. Brooke had just returned from his trip to the South Seas with poems of a *farouche* vividness that made them the talk of London. Sassoon felt he was being patronized by his glamorous fellow poet in Marsh's flat where Brooke was staying. Brooke was at his most Byronic that morning, with bare feet, a mane of carelessly brushed gold hair, and a bucketful of charm. Sassoon's attempt to win Brooke over, young poet to young poet, as it were, by denigrating Rudyard Kipling, fell flat when Brooke professed an admiration for Kipling that he did not necessarily feel, and the two never met again. Perhaps it did not help that Brooke was an anti-Semite or that he failed to mention *The Daffodil Murderer.*

Marsh had better luck exposing Siegfried to the Ballets Russes. The poet was overwhelmed by the dancing, the performers, including the great Nijinsky, and the avant-garde music of Rimsky-Korsakov, Debussy, Ravel, and Stravinsky. Siegfried was unmoved by Marsh's taste for modern painting and was not yet able to take the daring leaps in his poetry that Rupert Brooke had taken in Polynesia—and that would soon be taken to even further lengths by T. S. Eliot, Ezra Pound, and William Carlos Williams. It would take the overwhelming experience of war in the trenches to shock Sassoon into writing poetry with the sharpness of a weapon.

For financial reasons—he was by then seriously in debt—Sassoon had to return to his quiet life in Weirleigh, having enjoyed a touch of fame in London, where he had made a number of influential friends. No doubt his mother was pleased to have him home, but he must have felt some disappointment. Fortunately perhaps for him, world events soon solved the problem of what he was to do with himself.

A LACK OF PURPOSE marked Siegfried's life. At the age of twenty-eight, he was still sexually innocent. He was a prolific poet, but most of his poetry was self-published, yet he had no profession beyond that of a poet, nor did he want one. He was slim, athletic, and good-looking but still living at home with his mother. Apart from his patriotic feelings, the war may have come as a relief; it presented him with an immediate purpose, as well an experience that might enrich his poetry. It cannot have escaped his attention that Rupert Brooke, who was already a celebrity, had traveled halfway around the world and lived as an adventurer in the South Pacific, while he himself was still living quietly at home, playing cricket and riding to hounds.

A poet, like any other writer, needs material, and Siegfried had none. Almost eagerly, he joined the army a few days *before* Great Britain declared war on Germany. He took what was for someone of his class the extreme step of enlisting in the ranks, instead of seeking a commission. His first impulse, not surprisingly, was to join the cavalry, and possibly because it was the nearest cavalry regiment, he signed up as a trooper in the Royal Sussex Yeomanry. On August 4, 1914, he was already in uniform. He had brought his favorite hunter, Cockbird, with him—it was common for officers joining a cavalry regiment to bring their own horse, but very uncommon indeed for a trooper to do so. He was soon living in a tented camp in Lewes, learning parade ground and mounted drill, as well as looking after his own horse and bringing every piece of leather and brass in his possession to a mirror-like gloss. For someone who had always had Tom the stableman and two stableboys to look after his horses, his tack, and his boots, this cannot have been an easy transition. It could not have been made easier by the fact that many of the officers knew him as a well-to-do young sportsman, while to his fellow troopers he seemed like a rich toff who was slumming. His initial enthusiasm for life in the ranks took a blow when he realized that there was no way his beloved Cockbird could carry the weight of a cavalry trooper's saddle and equipment (nine stone, or 126 pounds), so he had to sell the horse to an officer. Not surprisingly, within a couple of weeks he was writing to Edward Marsh about the possibility of getting a commission.

Then an accident in the field—he decided to jump a few fences and had a serious fall in which he broke his arm so badly that it required the insertion of a metal plate—kept him home recuperating for nearly five months, time enough for him on second thought to apply for a commission. A neighbor, a retired military man, got him into the special reserve of the Royal Welch Fusiliers. Like most officers of the Royal Welch Fusiliers, he had no connection with

Wales—it was the rank-and-file who were locally recruited—and until he joined it, he had still less idea of its long history or traditions. He had the good sense to go to the best uniform tailor to have his made. He found the experience very much like ordering hunting clothes from E. Tautz, and he received fatherly advice from the tailor about his khaki shirts: "You can't have them too dark." This turned out to be true, for when another young officer appeared beside Siegfried in the adjutant's office, the adjutant glanced disdainfully through his monocle at the man's shirt and greeted him with the comment, "Christ! Who's your tailor?"

From the very first, Siegfried fit in with the Royal Welch. Public school and the hunt field had shaped him for the role of a second lieutenant, despite his shyness and the feeling that he was a fraud. Most of the young officers around him in the dreary industrial wasteland outside Liverpool, where the Royal Welch training depot had been established, were twenty-one years old or less, some of them just out of school. Siegfried was twenty-eight, enough of an age difference to make him seem like a wise elder even though they were all the same rank. Training was hard, mostly parade ground drill, in the belief that troops who learned to achieve perfection in drill would have the same discipline and instant obedience to orders under fire. When it came to training, square bashing, the crisp crash of boots in perfect unison, was thought to be the answer to everything, and the Royal Welch was second to none in its high standard of drill.

The camp itself was utterly dreary. It consisted of rows of hastily assembled tin-roofed huts, standing in the lee of smoke from the Bryant and May match factory and a TNT factory that spewed noxious chemical fumes. But for those young officers who could afford it, Liverpool offered the many comforts of a grand hotel. Siegfried described the camp as "a soldier manufactory," which is exactly what it was. At intervals, drafts of officers and men were "passed out," having completed their training, and sent overseas as replacements for the growing number of Royal Welch battalions in France or the Middle East. By the spring of 1915, young men were being commissioned who would never have been considered officer material before the war, so some effort was made to turn them into "officers and gentlemen," as well as teach them drill, musketry, and military law.

Siegfried at first shared his cramped, "cell-like" little room with a reticent married civil engineer who spent his evenings playing solitaire instead of socializing in the officer's mess. Far from being the snobbish, bullying monsters that Robert Graves would describe in *Goodbye to All That*, the senior officers of the camp were elderly and stranded far from the comforts of the Royal Welch regimental depot in Wrexham, Wales, with its glittering silverware and precious porcelain.

Siegfried was far from unhappy there. As for Robert Graves, service in the Royal Welch Fusiliers would become for him a lifelong obsession. Whatever his feelings about the war, his affection for his regiment was real and intense. He loved even the makeshift officers' mess, where young officers in training sat at two long tables, joined by a head table for the senior officers, and where the food was served by deferential old soldiers in white jackets wearing the ribbons of long-ago campaigns from all over the world. In his own way, Siegfried was a snob and looked down on young officers who had not been to a public school, whose manners were uncertain, and whose shirts were the wrong shade of khaki.

Siegfried cheered up when his roommate was changed, the civil engineer having been sent to the front. Dick, as he chose to call this next roommate in *Memoirs of a Fox-Hunting Man*, had graduated from Sandhurst, the British equivalent of West Point, and was his social equal. He was far more accomplished at drill, musketry, map reading, and the responsibilities of an officer than Siegfried was.

Although Siegfried chose to change his name when writing about him, it is clear that he fell in love at first sight with David Cuthbert Thomas, and equally clear that while they became close friends, the relationship was unconsummated. Thomas may not even have been aware of the intensity of Siegfried's attraction. It was perhaps the first passionate love affair of Siegfried's adult life, and although undeclared and unrequited, it had a major effect on him.

Thomas was not a fox-hunting man, but he enjoyed hearing Siegfried talk about it. He was a keen cricket player and a golfer, and they seem to have hit it off. However Siegfried's description of his roommate makes it evident how strong his feelings were. Dick, he would write, "had the obvious good looks which go with fair hair and firm features, but it was the radiant integrity of his expression which astonished me." Siegfried let himself go, describing his new friend: "His was the bright countenance of truth; ignorant and undoubting; incapable of concealment but strong in reticence and modesty. In fact, he was as good as gold." His companionship "was like perpetual fine weather," although no doubt it was disappointing, if not excruciating, for Siegfried when Thomas "wound up his watch, brushed his hair, and said his prayers morning and evening." The relationship became even closer when they were sent on a course to Cambridge and shared a room at Pembroke College. Perhaps ironically in view of what was to come, the previous occupant's name was on the staircase—it was "Paradise."

CHAPTER 9

# SIEGFRIED SASSOON
## *"Brother Lead and Sister Steel"*

S IEGFRIED SASSOON WAS STILL IN CAMBRIDGE, AT a course at the Officers' School of Instruction, when he learned that his younger brother, Hamo, had died of his wounds on a hospital ship after the evacuation of Gallipoli, that failure which cost the British almost 300,000 casualties. That campaign's only important consequences were the rise of General Mustafa Kemal, who would become the founder of modern Turkey as Kemal Atatürk, and the temporary end of the hitherto charmed political life of Winston Churchill, whose brainchild it had been.

Even on the subject of his brother's death, Siegfried's war poetry was still modeled after Rupert Brooke's, conceiving the war as an adventure and worthy cause. He had as yet not experienced it. He and his roommate David Thomas went out to the front together, enduring the usual bumpy Channel crossing, then the interminable changes of trains and nights in rotten transit camps. In November 1915 the "army schools" where troops and junior officers were instructed in the practical realities of trench fighting did not yet exist. They went straight from square bashing and musketry practice in the U.K. into the trenches, without being taught the hard lessons in combat that might keep them alive or make them efficient killers. Siegfried and David were both happy to be posted together to the First Battalion of the Royal Welch, which had a higher proportion of regular officers and NCOs and consequently a superior level of esprit de corps and crisp efficiency than the battalions formed after the war began. *All* Royal Welch Fusiliers believed they constituted an elite, but the First and Second Battalions were the elite of the elite, their regimental spirit of an older vintage, steeped in battles that had taken place long before most of the present recruits had been born. The two subalterns were spared much of the snobbish disdain that Robert Graves was still encountering: Thomas, because he was a graduate of Sandhurst, that is to say a professional officer, and Siegfried, because his exploits as a point-to-pointer (long-distance cross-country rider) validated him as a sportsman and a gentleman, so they were treated with some degree of courtesy.

Siegfried settled into the life of a platoon commander easily enough. At first, his concern was for the constant filth and discomfort of life in the trenches, as opposed to the danger. He quickly got used to leading glum, sodden working parties into no-man's-land at night to shore up defenses. "Went on a working party . . . started up half a mile of light-railway lines through marsh, with sixty men. Then they carried hurdles up the communication trenches, about three-quarters of a mile, which took two hours. Flares went up frequently; a few shells, high overhead. . . . The trenches are very wet." The next three nights were similar, but on the fourth night he adds that he "came home soaked. . . . Beastly night for the men, whose billets are wretched." Siegfried would differ markedly from many of his fellow officers in his constant concern about the discomfort of his men, and their miserable food and living conditions. Most officers tended to ignore those factors. In one of his first war poems written from the front, Siegfried described their existence as no previous poet had:

I see them in foul dug-outs, gnawed by rats,
And in the ruined trenches, lashed with rain.

He had not yet turned against the war. This poem expresses a combination of pity and revulsion rather than anger, and no glorious deaths.

He pushed another bag along the top,
Craning his body outward; then a flare
Gave one white glimpse of No Man's Land and wire;
And as he dropped his head the instant split
His startled life with lead, and all went out.

No heroism here. The poem describes a working party laboring in the slush and mud and freezing cold, and a soldier killed suddenly by a sniper. His death, during an ordinary working party, is meaningless, part of the unglamorous routine of trench warfare, a far cry from Alan Seeger's thanks for the "rare privilege of dying well." Sassoon seems to have understood almost at once that the war had become a giant killing machine, that dying well was unlikely or impossible.

That did not prevent him from doing his job, or at any rate learning it, or from hoping to win praise from his superiors and perhaps even a decoration. Above all he treasured his place in C Company, low as it was, and the friends he made there. From the first, he fit in. He liked and respected his company commander, who was a civilian at heart. Sassoon would later write affectionately about him and about his fellow subalterns, disguising their names in *Memoirs of an Infantry Officer,* which hovers unsteadily between a memoir and a novel. He balances the horror of the trenches with the close, cozy comradeship of candlelit evenings in the dugout and shared food packages from home. "Already we were quite a happy family," he wrote thirteen years later and, there is no doubt, sincerely.

He had not yet experienced combat at close quarters, but he led enough working parties into no-man's-land to understand the feelings of his men as they slogged through the mud at night. They were, he thought, Christ-like in their suffering. In "The Redeemer," he wrote of one of them.

> He faced me, reeling in his weariness,
> Shouldering his load of planks, so hard to bear,
> I say that he was Christ, who wrought to bless
> All groping things with freedom bright as air,
> And with His mercy washed and made them fair.
> Then the flame sank, and all grew black as pitch,
> While we began to struggle along the ditch,
> And someone flung his burden in the muck,
> Mumbling: 'O Christ Almighty, now I'm stuck!"

This poem is from an interim stage of Siegfried's work, still written in a slightly self-conscious style, but the subject matter is grimly realistic. His poetry was not yet savage, as it would soon become, written in white hot anger at the politicians who were prolonging the war rather than seeking an end to it, the generals who didn't care for their soldiers' lives, the public at home that accepted lies rather than face the truth, and even fellow officers who talked big but cadged safe jobs away from the front. He wanted people to see the war as it was, in all its ugliness and random brutality. No other British war poet would write a poem about a fellow officer who boasted of killing German prisoners but in fact shirked the fighting and went safe home:

> And here you are
> Still talking big and boozing in a bar.

Not even Robert Graves could match the sinister nastiness of Sassoon's "The Kiss," a deceptive title for a poem that epitomizes the ultimate fact of war, killing, with a brutal simplicity that rivals Kipling's matter-of-fact way of describing the realities of war* and that might have been intended in part to mock him:

> To these I turn, in these I trust;
> Brother Lead and Sister Steel.
> To his blind power I make appeal;
> I guard her beauty clean from rust.

> He spits and turns and loves the air,
> And splits a skull to win my praise;
> But up the nobly marching days
> She glitters naked, cold and fair.

> Sweet Sister, grant your soldier this;
> That in good fury he may feel
> The body where he sets his heel
> Quail from your downward darting kiss.

---

* "With the bullets kickin' dust-spots on the green." —"Gunga Din"

The poem is even more chilling than the lecture on bayonet fighting that both Sassoon and Graves described at the army school they attended in France. "Sets his heel" (in the second-to-last line) refers to the lecturer's stern admonition to stamp your heel hard on the body of the man you have just stabbed to help you withdraw your bayonet. "The star turn in the school-room was a massive sandy-haired Highland Major whose subject was 'The Spirit of the Bayonet,'" Sassoon wrote. "He spoke with homicidal eloquence. 'The bullet and the bayonet are your brother and sister. . . . Stick him between the eyes, in the throat, in the chest. . . . Don't waste good steel. Six inches are enough. What's the use of a foot of steel sticking out at the back of a man's neck? Three inches will do for him; when he coughs [blood], go and look for another.'"

Siegfried's particular specialty was to write brilliant parody that at the same time pulsates with righteous anger, and to describe things intended to provoke outrage and disgust in the reader. Nothing in his previous poetry had predicted this ability; nor would he revert to it after the war was over. He advanced toward it step by step as he moved from the comparative security of being a transport officer—who looked after a battalion's horses, a job for which he was eminently qualified—to being a platoon commander in the trenches. He had appreciated the safety and comfort of the horse lines, but he also felt a certain degree of guilt at his own good fortune and was relieved when his new commanding officer told him that he was rather wasted in the job—a conclusion Siegfried himself had reached.

The winter of 1916 was a critical one on the Western Front. To the south, the Battle of Verdun ground on remorselessly, having already taken the lives of nearly half a million French and Germans. It was not a time to be overseeing the care of the battalion's horses. The preparations for the First Battle of the Somme were in full swing, intended to relieve the pressure on the French, but British and French casualties would exceed 600,000. For Siegfried, one attraction of serving in the front line was that he would rejoin David Thomas. But by the brutal irony of warfare, David, while commanding a work party two days before Siegfried rejoined the company, was hit in the throat by a bullet. The battalion medical officer had warned him not to move his head, but he reached into his pocket for a letter from his girlfriend and died instantly. Siegfried returned to his company just in time to see David's body lowered into a shallow muddy grave bundled up in a sack, the ultimate desecration of such bright beauty and promise.

Thomas's death produced in Siegfried rage, grief, a passionate desire to hurt the enemy, and thirst to win a decoration. He took unnecessary risks, led patrols at night out into no-man's-land armed with a pistol and a knobkerrie, his tunic pockets full of grenades, hoping to find and kill a German. He courted death and acquired a reputation as a daredevil. Winning a decoration was, as it happened, very difficult to do in the First and Second Battalions of the Royal Welch Fusiliers—all temporary young officers in the Royal Welch were carefully told that they must not expect to be decorated. Awards for heroism were reserved for regulars, since they represented important milestones in a professional officer's career. Nevertheless Siegfried, after risking his life to go out into concentrated enemy fire to bring in a seriously wounded man lying disabled in a shell crater, was recommended for a Military Cross.

He had yearned for action, and in a rapid blur of events, he got it when, as his friend and fellow poet Robert Graves reported:

> He distinguished himself by taking, single-handed, a battalion frontage which the Royal Irish Regiment had failed to take the day before. He went over to the top with grenades in broad daylight, under covering fire from a couple of rifles, and scared away the occupants. A pointless feat, since instead of signalling for reinforcements, he sat down in the German trench and began reading a book of poems which he had brought with him. When he finally went back, he did not even report. Colonel Stockwell, then in command, raged at him. The attack . . . had been delayed for two hours because British patrols were still believed to be out. "British patrols" were [merely] Siegfried and his book of poems. "I'd have got you a D.S.O., if you'd only shown some sense," stormed Stockwell.*

---

* The Distinguished Service Order (DSO) is a decoration for officers for bravery, second only to the Victoria Cross.

There is good reason to believe that Graves's version of the event is more facetious than true, that in fact Siegfried only just missed getting a DSO, or at the very least a bar to his Military Cross

From July to November 1916, the First Battle of the Somme, perhaps the most wasteful land battle ever fought, ground on remorselessly, ultimately producing almost half a million casualties on the British side, more than 200,000 for the French, and over 500,000 for the Germans. It failed to produce a decisive Allied victory. The most it did for the Allies was deeply shake the German Army, which would not recover its fighting élan on the Western Front until the great German breakthrough of 1918. But it squandered the volunteer army that Kitchener had built up so carefully before his death. A whole generation of Britons died in the mud of the Somme, with consequences that were still felt in the Second World War.

No soldier could fully take in a battle of this size. Perhaps the only officer who could was General Haig, but he tended to look at it through the rose-colored glasses of the high command. At the company level, all that men could do was glimpse the German front line, obscured as it was by smoke, and the men suffering to their immediate right and left. "The battle winks and thuds in blundering strife, / And I must lead them nearer day by day, / To the foul beast of war that bludgeons life," Siegfried wrote. Perhaps no poet captured the reality of that war better than he did, in fiercely descriptive lines, as realistic as a photograph.

At dawn the ridge emerges massed and dun
In the wild purple of the glowering sun
Smouldering through spouts of drifting smoke that shroud
The menacing scarred slope; and, one by one,
Tanks creep and topple forward to the wire.
The barrage roars and lifts. Then, clumsily bowed
With bombs and guns and shovels and battle gear
Men jostle and climb to meet the bristling fire.
Lines of grey, muttering faces, masked with fear,
They leave their trenches, going over the top,
While time ticks blank and busy on their wrists.

ALTHOUGH THEY WERE NOW SERVING in different battalions, Graves and Sassoon remained close. Graves was the first to be wounded, just before his twenty-first birthday in July 1916. Shell splinters hit him in the hand, the groin, and the leg; the most serious one pierced his lung. He was taken to a dressing station, where the battalion medical officer decided he would not survive the night, and he was left for dead. The next day he was discovered to be still alive and was taken screaming in pain by stretcher, then ambulance, to the nearest field hospital, and from there by train to a hospital in Rouen. In the meantime, his commanding officer reported him dead and wrote a letter of condolence to his family.

The news of Graves's death was published in the casualty list in *The Times*, prompting Siegfried to write, "I thought I had found a lifelong friend to work with, so I go my way alone again." Then Siegfried contracted trench fever (caused by bites from infected lice), and was sent home to recuperate in Oxford, at Somerville College, which like many of the other colleges had been transformed into a hospital.

After he recovered, he spent time at Graves's cottage in Harlech, where they worked on their poems. Earlier in their friendship, it had been Graves who had the combat experience, and Siegfried who thought Graves's war poetry was too bitter. Now the situation was reversed: Siegfried was the one with a decoration, and his war poetry was sharp as a knife, devoid of any lyric trappings.

> "Good-morning, good-morning!" the General said
> When we met him last week on our way to the line,
> Now the soldiers he smiled at are most of 'em dead
> And we're cursing his staff for incompetent swine.
> "He's a cheery old card," grunted Harry to Jack
> As they slogged up to Arras with rifle and pack.
>
> But he did for them both by his plan of attack.

Siegfried spared no one, not even mothers who mourned their sons, still less the politicians and the press. He was determined that people should see the war as it was, without the false comfort of heroic death.

You smug-faced crowds with kindling eye
Who cheer when soldier lads march by,
Sneak home and pray you'll never know
The hell where youth and laughter go.

WHILE SIEGFRIED WAS RECOVERING from trench fever in Oxford, he met one of his most devoted admirers, Lady Ottoline Morrell, a literary hostess and a glamorous magnet to artistic talent and genius of every kind. A half-sister of the sixth Duke of Portland, Lady Ottoline had a notoriously open marriage to a member of Parliament, a substantial fortune, and a reputation as a formidable man hunter. Her lovers included the philosopher and mathematician Bertrand Russell, with whom she exchanged nearly four thousand letters, and they may also have included the artists Augustus John and Henry Lamb, as well as Lytton Strachey's muse, the painter Dora Carrington. Moreover, she is thought to have been the inspiration for D. H. Lawrence's Lady Chatterley, perhaps because the last love affair of her life was with her head gardener.

Her beautiful Tudor house in Garsington, just outside Oxford, was the center of the intellectual set who opposed the war. Lady Ottoline, a large woman with a taste for flamboyant and eccentric clothes—in photographs she resembles a ship-of-the-line in full sail—pursued Siegfried with determination, despite every indication that he was not attracted to women. More important, she introduced him to her friends who were pacifists, conscientious objectors, or simply people disgusted by the gruesome sacrifice taking place across the Channel, close enough so that on some days, when the wind was blowing in the right direction, the ceaseless thunder of heavy artillery could be heard as far away as Garsington.

Harsh treatment of conscientious objectors, however highly placed, was commonplace in Britain. Indeed, Bertrand Russell, though heir to an earldom, would be sent to prison in 1917 for his public comments about the war. But while it was one thing for a civilian to repudiate the war, it was quite another for a decorated serving officer, who could be court-martialed, imprisoned, or at least theoretically, shot. It was at Garsington where Siegfried first contemplated making a stand against the war in a more direct way than through his poetry. He was not, nor did he ever claim to be, a conscientious objector; he simply wanted to cut through the sentimentality and patriotic clichés about the war and draw attention to the suffering of the soldiers. The short time he spent at Lady Ottoline's house, exposed to people who had thoroughly repudiated the war, certainly moved him toward what he anticipated would be martyrdom.

He passed his long leave the way he wanted to; he hunted, wrote a prodigious amount of poetry, played golf, and spent as much time as he could in the English countryside. He even managed to keep up his growing friendship with Lady Ottoline without ever quite succumbing to her advances, no mean feat. But his poems reflect a growing anger at civilians, both those who profited from the war and those who sentimentalized it. His mood alternated paradoxically between a desire to go back to the front and anger that the war was still going on. Like many another soldier, he found it difficult to live among civilians who did not understand, or *want* to understand, the horror of the war that was being fought ostensibly on their behalf.

At the same time, Siegfried missed the comradeship, the shared misery and danger, and the intense emotion of battle. The death of David Thomas, as well as so many of the men he had commanded, haunted him, as did bouts of guilt over the number of Germans he had killed seeking revenge for Thomas's death.

> You can't believe that British troops "retire"
> When hell's last horror breaks them, and they run,
> Trampling the terrible corpses—blind with blood.
>> O German mother dreaming by the fire
>> While you are knitting socks to send your son
>> His face is trodden deeper in the mud.

This passage echoes Siegfried's own experience of lifting a dead young German soldier's head out of the mud and cleaning off his face with his sleeve, only to glimpse, as he and his men fell back, that it had been trampled in the filth of the trench. The horrors in Sassoon's poetry are not products of his imagination: they are snapshots of the brutal reality, which he was unable to escape and determined to share.

It did not help that after his sick leave, the army, having passed him as fit for service, was in no hurry to send him back. He languished for weeks at the depot near Liverpool in miserable discomfort. "The third winter of the war," he wrote, "had settled down on the lines of huts with calamitous dreariness; fog-bleared sunsets were succeeded by cavernous and dispiriting nights when there was nothing to do and nowhere to do it." The occasional dinner at a grand hotel in Liverpool produced in him a combination of guilt and disgust. He was sustained for some weeks by the company of Robert Graves, who was also awaiting return to the trenches, and by a constant stream of lavish presents and extravagantly phrased letters from Ottoline Morrell. Still, he was relieved when he was finally sent back to France, to what he described as "the Purgatory" of the Fifth Infantry Base Depot at Rouen, to await posting.

The journey there was long and dispiriting. He slept miserably on the deck of a troop ship—somebody stole his new trench coat while he slept. The depot, when he got there, consisted of drafty tents erected in frozen mud. The first thing he saw after he reported to the adjutant was a soldier who had stripped himself half naked and was howling in confused rage. "The man's been under detention for assaulting the military police," a sergeant explained, "and now 'e's just 'ad news of his brother being killed. Seems to take it to 'eart more than most would. 'Arf crazy, 'e's been, tearing his clothes off and cursing the war and the Fritzes. Almost like a shell-shock case, 'e seems."

Time did not improve Siegfried's depressing first moments at the depot. Even the officers' mess was no more than a drafty tent, its only decoration a bulletin board with the names of officers who were being sent up to the lines and notices about soldiers who had been shot by firing squad for cowardice. Junior officers spent hours drilling in the freezing cold in "the Bull Ring" or lounging in canvas chairs in the officers' mess playing cards and listening to sentimental records on the gramophone. Siegfried was already depressed by the news that he would probably be posted to the Second Battalion of the RWF instead of the First, where he had made his mark, but he hit a nadir when he was diagnosed with *German* measles. He was assigned to a tent that was already overcrowded with six sick officers in a hospital for communicable diseases surrounded by barbed wire like a prisoner-of-war camp, where he spent ten days of excruciating boredom and discomfort.

He was relieved when his posting finally came, even though it was to the Second Battalion, which was resting behind the front line after taking heavy losses. He had looked forward to joining Robert Graves there, but Graves had been invalided home. In addition, the ambience of the Second was still very much as Graves would later describe it in *Goodbye to All That*. Having served for many years in India before the war, the Second was still dominated by stiff-upper-lip senior officers who spoke of the junior officers as "warts" and who behaved like pukka-sahibs. Not even the fact that Siegfried had won a Military Cross did him much good here.

PREPARATIONS FOR THE BATTLE OF ARRAS had been going on for some time in early 1917. The purpose of the British attack was to draw the attention of the Germans away from what was intended to be a more powerful French offensive along the Aisne River. But as the weaknesses of the French Army became apparent, the diversionary "sideshow" increased in importance. In the French high command, the dashing and overconfident general Robert Nivelle had replaced the phlegmatic general Joseph Joffre as commander in chief—he was promoted over the head of the cautious but more competent general Philippe Pétain. Nivelle not only looked the part, he spoke English fluently, thanks to an English mother, and was thus able to diminish the natural reluctance of the British to cooperate with their ally, still less to fit in with French plans. Only the most deluded of optimists, however, could have imagined that a combined Franco-British attack to the north and the south of the Somme battlefield would result in a decisive Allied victory.

The situation for the Allies was bleak. The abdication of the czar had led to mass desertions from the Russian Army. Romania's offensive against the Germans and the Austro-Hungarians had collapsed, the Ottoman Army had been victorious at Gallipoli and still spasmodically threatened the Suez Canal. Nivelle's planned offensive was something of a desperate throw of the dice, which the British felt themselves unable to resist without altogether jeopardizing the Alliance.

The Germans could hardly ignore the immense preparations for a major battle—the British alone dug miles of tunnels in the expectation of blowing up many sections of the German front line. They would fire nearly 3 million rounds of artillery over a twenty-four-mile front. Field Marshal Paul von Hindenburg and his chief of staff, General Erich Ludendorff, two hard-headed military realists, having won a whole series of triumphant victories in Russia, had been brought west to take command of the German Army and acted swiftly. They built a long line of heavy fortifications well behind their own front line and suddenly withdrew the German Army to it, abandoning the ground they had fought to hold and turning it into a wasteland. Every village was pulverized, every well polluted, every road and bridge destroyed, every tree chopped down. This literally scorched earth was littered with booby traps that exploded when touched, over which the British would find it almost impossible to advance. That the Germans were willing to give up ground they had fought to defend for over three years, at a loss of hundreds of thousands of lives, and withdraw behind the Hindenburg Line (as the Allies named it) should have served as a warning to the BEF that it was advancing into a trap, but it failed to. Even more threatening, the new German line was fortified with buried concrete bunkers occupied by elite storm troopers.

With supreme irony, the British attack had been scheduled for April 1, 1917—a date that provoked a combination of mirth and foreboding—but was postponed until April 9 because of the unexpected retreat of the Germans. By the time the Second RWF was thrown into the battle five days later, it had already deteriorated into "a murderous mix-up," as Sassoon put it, flashes of which appear in his prose and poems. "I can remember a pair of hands (nationality unknown) which protruded from the soaked ashen soil like the roots of a tree turned upside down; one hand seemed to be pointed at the sky with an accusing gesture. . . . Floating on the surface of the flooded trench was the mask of a human face which had detached itself from the skull." The image might almost have been painted by Salvador Dali. Charged with leading a bombing attack on a German tunnel, Siegfried tripped over something, his flashlight revealing "somebody half hidden under a blanket." Supposing it to be man asleep, he gave him a kick and cursed him, only for his flashlight beam to settle on "the livid face of a dead German whose fingers still clutched the blackened gash on his neck." Years later Siegfried would still have nightmares about the Battle of Arras.

In an act of courage that ought to have earned him another decoration, he advanced under fierce fire into a section of the Hindenburg Line, carrying a sack of grenades. He was ahead of his small bombing party when he came upon a Cameronian[*] corporal throwing grenades at the Germans. Sassoon joined him, then went off to explore a sap off the trench, raised his head to see what he could, and felt "a tremendous blow" to his back. He fell, briefly unconscious, against a mud wall. In fact, he had been shot by a German sniper: the bullet passed through his chest and exited from his back, leaving a serious wound. His sergeant—a kind of uniformed Jeeves, always calm and in control in any situation—found him, helped him back to the main trench, and dressed the wound. Now that his men were coming up, Siegfried stayed there trying to organize a new attack until he received an order not to advance farther. He handed over command to another officer and walked back to the command post, where he was congratulated on his "courageous action," To his chagrin, he would not be recommended for a decoration.

In spite of Siegfried's intense disgust at the war and his anger at how the lives of the soldiers were being wasted by military incompetence, he was not then and would never be a pacifist, in the true meaning of the word. He was not fearless (very few people are), but he was capable of mastering his fear, and hand-to-hand combat gave him an intense excitement and aroused him to undertake numerous acts of bravery, at the risk of his life. Paradoxically, his anger at the brass hats was in part fueled by the feeling that he had not received the decorations

---

[*] A soldier of the Queen's Own Cameron Highlanders, the 79th Foot, a kilted infantry regiment.

he thought he deserved. Unlike T. E. Lawrence, who attempted to refuse all the decorations he was awarded,* Siegfried sought them and was embittered when they failed to be awarded. Indeed, his feelings toward the army were like those of a jilted lover, a combination of resentment, anger, and thwarted love. Whether the act of notoriety that would shortly make him famous could have been squelched had he received a bar to his Military Cross or the Distinguished Service Order for his action in the Hindenburg trench, we can never know, but it was certainly an ingredient, as he admitted himself.

He made his way by slow, wearying, painful steps through one army medical facility after another until he finally arrived at a military hospital for officers in London, his mind seething with relief at being alive as well as resentment of the war. Once there, he wrote poems at a furious rate, including one that recreated his own experience in the tunnel at the Hindenburg Line, an unflinching description of the moment that would haunt him for the rest of his life.

His anger was intensified by the dawning realization that the Battle of Arras had been yet another futile and costly waste. It had cost the British 160,000 casualties for no worthwhile gain in ground. The army had made no breakthrough; those cavalrymen who had attempted to advance over the broken ground were slaughtered. Tanks, poison gas, deep mines filled with explosives tunneled under the German front lines that were ignited as the attack began, intense air warfare in the skies above, new infantry tactics—none of it had made a significant difference. It was another colossal stalemate.

Farther south, the French attack had been equally futile and costly, with casualties of nearly 190,000. Coming after the huge bloodletting at Verdun and the rosy optimism of General Nivelle, the pointless slaughter had a disastrous effect on French military and civilian morale. Nearly half the French regiments on the Western Front mutinied. They did not leave their lines or march on

---

* Lawrence did not turn them down—it is impossible to turn down a decoration once it has been awarded and gazetted. But he never wore the ribbons or used the initials (he was officially Lt. Col. T. E. Lawrence, CB, DSO), and after the war, he refused to accept them when, over breakfast at Buckingham Palace, the king attempted to pin them to his uniform, to His Majesty's confusion and embarrassment.

Paris—they simply refused to attack and responded to orders from their officers by baaing like sheep being led to the slaughter.

Nivelle was sacked and replaced by Pétain, who wisely addressed the complaints of the soldiers and reduced the number of executions by firing squad to the bare minimum. Fortunately for the Allies, German losses had been high enough that even the monumentally self-confident Ludendorff was deeply depressed. Had he attacked the French at that moment, it might have ended the war, but neither the German soldiers nor the high command was capable of it. Far away in Russia, the Provisional Government's attempt to coordinate an attack with Nivelle's offensive led to the virtual collapse of the Russian Army as troops voted for peace with their feet, abandoning their lines to go home en masse, while the political situation in Russia deteriorated toward the October Revolution.

Sassoon knew none of this; nor could even have guessed it, but he was determined to make a statement that went beyond his poetry to make the public face the reality of what the soldiers were suffering. The publication in 1917 of a collection of his poems—many of them about the war, despite the deceptively bucolic title *The Old Huntsman*—made him briefly famous, but poetry was not enough to change the course of events. Encouraged by Ottoline Morrell and aided by Bertrand Russell, Sassoon struggled to write a prose declaration of protest that would be impossible to ignore.

By then, plenty of people were writing against the war, among them Bertrand Russell, but none of them was a serving officer with a military decoration. Siegfried was well aware that his protest would provoke enormous attention and might lead to his being court-martialed or imprisoned (as Russell would be), possibly even executed for cowardice.* Siegfried had many motives for making his protest. The new Russian government had released treaties revealing the extent of gains in territory to which both countries had agreed, which Siegfried (and many others) took as a cynical divvying up of the spoils, undercutting the British claim that it was fighting a war of self-defense and international morality. His compassion for the

---

* During the First World War, the British Army executed 306 men for cowardice, none of them officers.

suffering of his fellow soldiers moved him as well, as did his grow-ing conviction that the British government was prolonging the war instead of trying to negotiate an end to it.

Although Russell was among those to whom he showed drafts of his protest, Siegfried neither needed nor accepted much in the way of editing. Russell introduced him to a pacifist member of Parlia-ment, who agreed to read his statement aloud in the House of Com-mons, thereby ensuring that it would be published, but having come this far, he paused before releasing it. This was not from caution; on the contrary, Siegfried wanted to make sure that the army could not ignore his protest, and therefore he decided that at the end of his leave, he would deliberately fail to report. Being absent without leave was the equivalent of desertion, a court-martial offense.

In May 1917 he was sent to continue his recovery to the palatial house of a titled, elderly, aristocratic couple who had made it avail-able for convalescent officers. Set in the English countryside, not far from his own home, Chapelwood Manor was in some ways an ideal refuge for Siegfried, whose love of the country was deep and genuine. But not even the beautiful garden, the orchard, and the home farm could calm him for long. His mind remained mired in the trenches, and the slightly dotty spiritualism of his hostess and the fact that she and her husband believed completely in the justice and morality of the war infuriated him. Although he was pleased by the reviews of *The Old Huntsman* (Virginia Woolf reviewed it favor-ably for the *Times Literary Supplement*), he was disappointed that the anti-war feeling of many of the poems did not cause as much of a scandal as he had hoped. By the summer of 1917, even the most patriotic and conventional readers were beginning to be dazed by the sheer scale and horror of the war and concerned that it might go on forever, perhaps blunting the shock value of Siegfried's poems.

He passed his protest around, garnering praise from Lady Otto-line and her friends and, predictably, cautious warnings not to pro-ceed further from everybody else. The one person with whom he did *not* share it was Robert Graves, who was recuperating from his wound on the Isle of Wight. Doubtless he knew that Graves would object. Sassoon did, finally, warn Graves of what he planned to do at the last moment, when it was already too late to stop him. The subsequent events have been somewhat obscured by the fact that Graves sought to put himself at the center of them, while Sassoon sought to play down or deny his role.

Meanwhile Siegfried received an offer to be made a cadet training officer at Cambridge University, a job which would have kept him in uniform, but spared him a return to the horror of the trenches. He turned it down. In his quiet, polite English way it was martyrdom he wanted, not the compromise of a noncombatant post and personal safety.

Siegfried delayed his return to the RWF depot until he received a telegram from the commanding officer ordering him to report at once. Instead, Siegfried wrote his CO a letter explaining his situation, one that, no doubt, he had been turning over in his mind for some time. The letter combines firmness of purpose with a fine sense of military politeness. It was clearly not written in haste.

> *I am writing you this private letter with the greatest possible regret. I must inform you that it is my intention to refuse to perform any further military duties. I am doing this as a protest against the policy of the Government in prolonging the War by failing to state their conditions of peace. . . .*
>
> *My only desire is to make things as easy as possible for you in dealing with my case. I will come to Litherland immediately I hear from you, if that is your wish.*
>
> *I am fully aware of what I am letting myself in for.*

Showing an unexpected talent for promotion and publicity, Siegfried sent out a torrent of mimeographed copies of his statement, making it all but impossible to ignore.

> I am making this statement as an act of willful defiance
> of military authority, because I believe that the War
> is being deliberately prolonged by those who have the
> power to end it. I am a soldier, convinced that I am
> acting on behalf of soldiers. I believe that this War,
> upon which I entered as a war of defense and liber-
> ation, has now become a war of aggression and con-

quest. I believe that the purposes for which I and my
fellow-soldiers entered upon this War should have been
so clearly stated as to have made it impossible for them
to be changed without our knowledge, and that, had
this been done, the objects which actuated us would
now be attainable by negotiation.

I have seen and endured the sufferings of the troops,
and I can no longer be a party to prolonging those suf-
ferings for ends which I believe to be evil and unjust.

I am not protesting against the military conduct of
the War, but against the political errors and insinceri-
ties for which the fighting men are being sacrificed.

On behalf of those who are suffering now, I make
this protest against the deception which is being
practiced on them. Also I believe that it may help to
destroy the callous complacence with which the ma-
jority of those at home regard the continuance of the
agonies which they do not share, and which they have
not sufficient imagination to realise.

The statement is in many ways curiously wrong-headed, despite
the care with which Siegfried wrote it and the attention Bertrand Rus-
sell paid to it. From today's perspective, the war was wrong because
of its size and its cruelty, not its origins. The United Kingdom had
declared war because Germany violated the neutrality of Belgium,
of which the United Kingdom was one of the original guarantors.
The restoration of Belgium was still the most critical of Britain's war
aims. The fact that the British had later made promises to their allies
and that they planned to add to their own empire does not seem all
that surprising or reprehensible. Perhaps shrewdly, Sassoon did not
criticize Haig or the British high command for the wasteful battles
and indifference to high casualties; rather he laid all blame for the
suffering of the soldiers on the government and the politicians.

Siegfried returned to the depot, and if he expected to be greeted
with manacles, he must have been disappointed. The rather more fiery
commanding officer was away, and he was greeted by the acting CO,
Major John Macartney-Filgate instead. This kind and gentle officer—

Siegfried described him as "a man of great delicacy of feeling"—treated the matter more like a breach of good manners than a court-martial offense and sent Siegfried back to his hotel in Liverpool to await further orders. Perhaps Major Macartney-Filgate had been moved by a letter from Robert Graves suggesting that Sassoon should be ordered to appear before a medical board rather than court-martialed.

At this point, Siegfried committed the deeply symbolic act of tearing the ribbon of the Military Cross off his tunic and throwing it into the River Mersey. He did not throw the decoration itself into the river. In his fictionalized account of the incident, he would write that "the poor little thing floated away as though aware of its own futility," and he regretted that it did not make a satisfactory splash.*

To Siegfried's surprise, his refusal to resume his military duties did not at first produce a dramatic reaction. Perhaps he underrated the first instinct of the RWF, which was to avoid at all costs any scandal involving its own officers. It was not Siegfried's protest against the war that caused any kind of disapproval. Rather, it was his decision not to appear before a medical board, for which a Royal Army Medical Corps full colonel had traveled all the way from London to Crewe. It was an embarrassment for the regiment and inappropriate behavior on Siegfried's part for an officer and gentleman.

At this point Robert Graves showed up. He had begged his doctors to declare him fit so he could leave Osborne, on the Isle of Wight, to persuade Siegfried to appear before the medical board. The army, Graves told him, would never allow him "to become a martyr to a hopeless cause." He would simply be locked up in an insane asylum for the duration of the war. In the end Siegfried backed down, not because he had changed his mind about the war but rather, one suspects, because he was and would remain throughout his long and emotionally complicated life always very conscious of his status as

---

* Many accounts of Sassoon's life describe him as having thrown the decoration itself into the Mersey. But many years after his death in 1967, it was found in an attic (together with his revolver and his identity disks), which would seem to prove that he was at one point not only invested with it but went to the trouble of keeping it. It is now in the Royal Welch Fusiliers Museum in Caernarvon Castle, Wales.

an officer and a gentleman. Being shot or imprisoned would be one thing; being committed to a mental hospital, quite another.

Graves may or may not have stage-managed the medical board appearance, once Siegfried agreed to attend it, but he certainly acted as the star witness, bursting into tears as he related his friend's suffering. The result was something of a standoff. The board concluded that Siegfried was suffering from "shell-shock," a catch-all term for what was then officially referred to as "neurasthenia."* Siegfried agreed to be sent for treatment to a "convalescent home" for officers. He would not be charged with desertion or cowardice; nor would he lose his commission or his rank.

If the War Office thought this would end the matter quietly, it was mistaken. Siegfried's statement had been read aloud in the House of Commons, and once it was printed in *Hansard*, the traditional transcript of parliamentary debate, newspapers all over the country reprinted it, mostly with unfavorable comments. Siegfried's fellow officers were kinder. Many of them shared his anger at the pointless waste of their soldiers' lives and the government's apparent willingness to let the war drag on indefinitely, but they thought his decision to publish the statement was inappropriate.

Graves was ordered to escort Sassoon to Craiglockhart War Hospital, outside Edinburgh, but as was typical of Graves, he missed the train, so Siegfried made his way there alone. He was not cheered by what he found. Craiglockhart was an old "hydro," a vast, sprawling Victorian hydropathic hospital, from the days when hydropathy—treatment by bathing the patient in hot or cold water—was a popular remedy for a whole variety of ills that we would now treat with medication or psychotherapy. The ground floor was chilling but impres-

---

* *Neurasthenia* had been variously (and vaguely) described since the mid-nineteenth century as a relatively mild mental illness, often attributed to overwork or stress physically affecting the nervous system. In Victorian times, it was thought to afflict women, but in the First World War it was used to describe men who had lost their nerve. At one time, Freud supposed that it might be caused by coitus interruptus or masturbation. Symptoms included dizziness or fainting spells. Both Virginia Woolf and Marcel Proust were diagnosed as neurasthenic. *Shell shock* was thought to be caused by repeated concussions to the brain from explosions and from the stress of battle. It is now referred to as post-traumatic stress disorder, or PTSD.

sive, in the style of a decaying grand hotel. Upstairs the army had built a warren of small and cheerless rooms that housed, two to a room, about 150 officers who were judged to have lost their nerve. The doors had no locks, and the walls were so thin that Siegfried could hear the cries and muffled groans of men who were suffering from nightmares. The purpose of the hospital was to get these officers back to the front as soon as possible—of the 1,800 treated there, almost 800 would be sent back, although some of the more serious mentally ill patients, those who were mute, partially paralyzed, or unable to stop trembling, had to be moved to mental hospitals. Siegfried's feelings about being sent there are best captured in some of the poems he wrote there:

Where men are crushed like clods, and crawl to find
Some crater for their wretchedness, who lie
In outcast immolation, doomed to die
Far from clean things or any hope of cheer.

It did not help that most of the men there were emotionally damaged and he was not. He was there as the result of taking a principled stand rather than having a breakdown. To his discomfort, the general feeling about the patients was that they were shirkers, trying to wangle their way out of service at the front, or weaklings. These were men he would have despised in ordinary circumstances, and he struggled to make the best of his time there. He resented the lack of privacy, which made it difficult for him to write poetry.

Part of the treatment was to get the men "out of themselves" in supposedly therapeutic organized activities, such as sports, exercise, and every imaginable hobby, from photography to making model boats. Although no effort was spared to keep the patients cheerful and busy, there was no disguising Craiglockhart's purpose. Officers who had "lost their nerve" were receiving treatment that would enable them to be sent back on active duty—and most likely killed. The patients were by no means confined to the hospital and its grounds, and Siegfried was able to go on long walks and soon took up golf again, a game at which he excelled.

The wretched food and the unwelcome company depressed him, but fortunately he came under the care (and to some extent the spell) of Captain W. H. R. Rivers, a Royal Army Medical Corps psychologist who became something like his gentle but firm father-confessor. Rivers was no ordinary army doctor. He was a fellow of St. John's College, Cambridge, a distinguished and adventurous anthropologist, and a groundbreaking psychologist. As a doctor, he had studied in Germany and was familiar with the work of Freud and Jung. He was at once a scientist and a man of the most refined sensibility, with a keen appreciation of the arts. It would have been difficult, perhaps impossible, to find a doctor better suited to understanding or "treating" Siegfried. They had informal conversations, rather than strict Freudian analytic sessions, and quickly became friends, overcoming the fact that it was Rivers's job to talk Siegfried out of his anti-war convictions and send him back to the front, where he would very likely be killed. Rivers himself was quietly skeptical of the war and sympathetic to Siegfried's anger at the sufferings of the soldiers. He also shared Siegfried's growing interest in socialism—at the end of

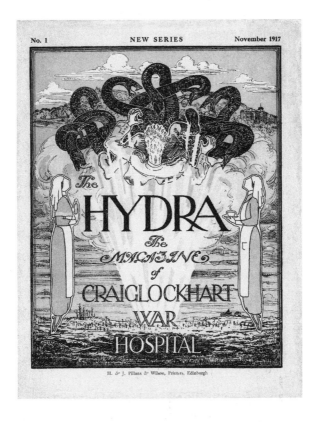

River's short life, he would be named a Labour Party parliamentary candidate, although he died before the election. He was almost certainly, like Siegfried, a repressed homosexual by inclination.

In any case, Siegfried's feelings for Rivers went far beyond the ordinary transference of a patient to his analyst. Siegfried would later write that he found "peace in the pools of his spectacled eyes and a wisely omnipotent grin." Rivers's task was simplified by the fact that it was moral indignation that had sent Siegfried to Craiglockhart, not "lack of moral fiber," the military euphemism for cowardice. Both men, patient and doctor, struggled with guilt: Siegfried because he was safely out of the war in which so many of his friends were dying; Rivers because he was treating Siegfried in order to send him back into the war. They both seem to have recognized this paradox with ironic good humor.

Although Siegfried's anti-war statement might seem to have fizzled out, now that he was shelved out of the way at Craiglockhart, it had made him far more famous than his poetry could have done. His friend Edward Marsh brought the matter to the attention of Winston Churchill, recently returned to power as minister of munitions after a four-month spell as a battalion commander at the front, a self-imposed punishment for his part in the failed Gallipoli campaign. Indeed, later in life Churchill would claim he had saved Sassoon from execution. That is unlikely, but it indicates that Siegfried's legend had begun to outgrow the man, rather like that of T. E. Lawrence, who was to become his friend. To those who were against the war, Siegfried became a hero and a martyr, while even many who did not agree with him, like Churchill, admired him—seldom has someone been better able to have it both ways. Despite his relationship with Rivers, Siegfried found life at Craiglockhart—he called it "Dottyville"—barely tolerable. There was nothing to prevent him from walking out and going down to London, as some of his pacifist friends urged him to do, but that would put Rivers in the position of having to take action to bring him back, a betrayal of trust with a man Siegfried liked and admired.

Siegfried found his fellow patients "very unexciting and pathetic," but he was not under any kind of confinement or security. He managed to get out and meet an astounding variety of people in Edinburgh, including the astronomer royal for Scotland, the vice chancellor of Edinburgh University, and Lady Margaret Sackville, an admired and prolific poet and a great beauty who was for many years the mistress of Ramsay Macdonald, a future Labour prime minister. Rivers had secured for Siegfried a temporary membership in his club in Edinburgh (the Scottish Conservative Club, although Rivers was neither). In fact, Siegfried was by no means isolated or socially deprived. His only obligations were to meet with Rivers three times a week and to be back at Craiglockhart before ten p.m.—not exactly the equivalent of prison life. He wrote a prodigious quantity of poems there, some of his best, and he was free to have visitors, including a rather trying visit from Lady Ottoline, who was still under the fading illusion that she might seduce Siegfried into a more intimate relationship.

Unbeknownst to Lady Morrell, he had by that time met a fellow patient, a young as yet unpublished poet, who would become one of the major figures in his life.

# CHAPTER 10

# WILFRED OWEN

## *"My Subject Is War, and the Pity of War"*

I T IS HARDLY SURPRISING THAT SIEGFRIED SASSOON was looking for a father figure—after all, his own father had virtually abandoned the role when Siegfried was only four years old—or that he found one in Dr. Rivers. What is more paradoxical is that Siegfried also wished to *be* a father figure, although perhaps not consciously. His empathy for his troops, and his anger at their suffering, were a reflection of this wish. As young as he was, many of them were younger, and despite his rank, education, and upbringing, he was a sympathetic figure, as opposed to a class-bound martinet, as so many officers were.

What was more—which also commanded the men's respect—he was good at his job, his courage was widely admired, and he was efficient and fair-minded. He sought to improve their condition in any way he could, and he risked his life on numerous occasions to bring in the wounded and the bodies of the dead. Unlike many officers, he never hesitated to share the backbreaking and dangerous labor of repairing wire at night or carrying heavy loads of ammunition, bombs, or gas cylinders up to the front line. Indeed, it was concern for his men that had been the chief motive for his declaration in the first place.

But the divide between Siegfried and the other patients at Craiglockhart was deep. They were there because they had lost their nerve, or because of the emotional wear and tear of war. Some had had a single, unbearable experience that they were unable to forget or repress, like a young officer who had been gathering the bits and pieces of one of his men who had been blown up by a trench mortar round and found himself picking up a perfectly intact eyeball to drop into the sandbag. Siegfried, on the other hand, was there because of what he had written. The relationship between him and Rivers was so complex and subtle that it lies at the center of the Regeneration Trilogy, a Booker Prize–winning series of novels by Pat Barker that was published between 1991 and 1995.* In these novels, the sessions between Siegfried and Rivers are not a dialogue aimed at converting Siegfried, like those between Rubashov and his interrogators in Arthur Koestler's *Darkness at Noon*. Nor did Rivers disagree with Siegfried's view of the war. Rather, he understood that as long as the war went on, Siegfried could not live with himself unless he went back to the front to share his men's suffering. If he could not *end* the war—the notion that he could have by his protest was at once naïve and vain—he would have to resume his place in it. Session by session, at least three times a week, the two men struggled with the questions of death, duty, and sacrifice. They were perhaps more than a bit in love with each other, although Rivers was too professional a doctor to let his feelings show. Their conversations were not strictly Freudian, but they were set against the terrifying reality of Britain at war—the fierce punishment of pacifists, deserters, and conscientious objectors; the repression of homosexuals; the everlasting miseries of class distinction; and the war itself, consuming thousands of lives daily and leaving behind it a trail of broken spirits and bodies, unimaginable wounds and unmitigated pain and misery.

Siegfried did not make friends at Craiglockhart, except for one or two golfing partners, so he does not seem to have been aware that a fellow poet was present there, still largely unpublished. Second Lieutenant Wilfred Owen had been sent to Craiglockhart for treatment of neurasthenia. An unassuming figure, he was short and stocky, with a ghostly mustache and slicked-down hair parted in the middle. He went out of his way not to attract attention to himself—certainly Siegfried never noticed him.

On the other hand, Owen had no difficulty in recognizing Sas-

* The novels were *Regeneration* (1991), *The Eye in the Door* (1993), and *The Ghost Road* (1995).

soon, who was not only very tall, with dashing good looks, but more important to Owen by far, an acclaimed, *published* poet. It must have taken a good deal of determination for Owen, who was shy and withdrawn at the best of times, to finally screw up his courage to knock on Siegfried's door and introduce himself. He had wisely bought several copies of *The Old Huntsman* for Siegfried to sign— what author can resist somebody who has actually bought several copies of his or her book? What's more, Owen had read the book carefully. His admiration for it was apparent and sincere enough to thaw Sassoon's initial mild impatience, coupled inevitably with class consciousness; class distinction, then as now, was the minefield of English social life. Owen was lower middle class, with a slight grammar school accent, while Siegfried was born in the highest reaches of the upper middle class, a public school man who had attended Cambridge and whose relatives were rich, well connected, and well placed. By contrast, Wilfred Owen's father was a railway stationmaster and his family tree was studded with shopkeepers and tradesmen. In addition, Owen was something of a mother's boy, as was Sassoon himself. (It takes one to know one.)

Despite all this, Owen managed to bring up the fact that he was an aspiring poet, and when they met again, a week later, he brought along an armful of manuscript for Siegfried to read. By that time, Siegfried's attitude toward Owen had softened. He must have realized that Owen was a besotted admirer of his work and a man badly in need of a mentor. He rapidly dismissed Owen's earlier work, which was as lyrical as his own had been, as well as much of his latest, which consisted of imitations of Sassoon's own ferocious, angry war poems. But he discerned at once that Owen was an extraordinarily gifted poet who badly needed both encouragement and editing. He may or may not have told Owen that he must be prepared "to sweat your guts out," but there was never any doubt that Owen would be more than willing to do that, and over the next few weeks they became not just friends, but something very much like lovers.

On Owen's side, the admiration was intense and undisguised—he positively *gushed* about Siegfried in his letters to his mother and father. On Siegfried's side, it was more cautious and slower to grow, but both of them had an interest that went far beyond each other's poetry. Each must have realized almost at once that the other was homosexual, and that they were attracted to one another. Owen had almost certainly had by this time a number of sexual experiences in Bordeaux with men who sold themselves in the street or under bridges—he rather daringly alluded to that, although in carefully coded language, in a few of his poems.

For his part, Siegfried had had a number of "crushes" on young men of his own class at school and at Cambridge. But beyond a strong mutual attraction, it is unlikely that anything physical took place between them at Craiglockhart. Siegfried was determined to avoid a sexual relationship with anyone, and he was still trying to fight off Lady Ottoline. In any case, Craiglockhart was hardly the place for intimacy, since there were no locks on the doors and Siegfried did not yet have a room of his own. Moreover the shadow of the Oscar Wilde case hung darkly over military life—the penalty for sex between male officers involved the loss of one's commission, disgrace, and a possible prison term.

UNLIKE SASSOON, Owen had not come to the war quickly or with any illusions about what he was letting himself in for. The notion of the war as a grand adventure did not occur to him. He had been teaching English in Bordeaux and did not join up until October 1915, by which time it was socially uncomfortable to be an apparently fit young man still wearing civilian clothes. The war had already become a gigantic killing machine, with no end in sight. Owen had unexpectedly achieved the life he wanted in France, or as near to it as he could get, and was reluctant to give it up.

Wilfred Owen's family was respectable but comparatively poor. On his father's side, he descended from a long line of craftsmen and shopkeepers in southwestern England, making their way generation by generation toward the lower rungs of middle-class status. On his mother's side, there were somewhat more inflated claims to gentry, unsupported by much in the way of facts, and a family tree that included clockmakers, shopkeepers, printers, and a prosperous timber merchant. Wilfred's younger brother Harold, whose three-volume autobiography is the source of much ambiguity about the family's status, sometimes claimed Welsh ancestry and sometimes vehemently denied it, depending on whether the Celts were being looked on as more or less romantic and adventurous than the English at any given time. In fact, both sides of the family came from the counties bordering southeastern Wales and were of solid English stock. Quite apart from the skilled tradesmen on both sides of the family, there must have been a flickering artistic streak, since Wilfred Owen became a gifted poet and his brother Harold a painter.

Owen's mother Susan grew up in fairly comfortable circumstances at Plas Wilmot, the house that her grandfather, Edward Salter, a successful joiner,* had built but did not live to inhabit. It stood on the outskirts of Ostwestry, a picturesque and thriving town in Shropshire, the history of which goes back to Arthurian legend. The town remains a treasure trove of ancient buildings and historic sites. Given the number of medieval timber-framed buildings in Ostwestry, Edward Salter would have had ample scope to learn his craft, and the house he built for himself, although unpretentious, displays plenty of paneling.

Salter's young widow had to farm the property to keep her family fed. Both Wilfred and his brother Harold would write about Plas Wilmot as if it were one of the stately homes of England, but in fact it was a modest working farm, with a barn, several acres of fields, and a small formal garden. Susan and her sisters were born and grew up there, until she accepted the hand of Tom Owen, a sturdy young man from a family with fewer pretensions to gentility—his father was a shoemaker, his mother the daughter of a butcher. He had sailed to India as a ship's boy at the age of fifteen, worked as a railway clerk there, and returned to become a railway clerk in nearby Shrewsbury. Harold portrayed his father as yearning for the sea and adventure, but there is no independent evidence of this, and judging from family photographs, he seems to have been a contented family man and devoted cricketer who rose steadily through the ranks of railway management.

---

* A joiner was a skilled wood craftsman who built paneled rooms, ceilings, doors, and trim.

Tom Owens was certainly determined to ensure that his boys—he and Susan had three boys and a girl—received a better education than he had, but public school and university were well beyond his means. Wilfred went to local private day schools with modest fees in Birkenhead, a grimy suburb of Liverpool, when his father became stationmaster there, and later in Shrewsbury, a more picturesque town (and an important railway junction) on the border of Wales. Again, Harold recalled life in Birkenhead as something like that of Oliver Twist in Fagin's slum garret, but neither Wilfred's biographers nor Wilfred himself seem to have felt that. Family photographs show everybody well dressed. A nursemaid in a starched white cap and apron is unmistakably present, although given the low wages of servants in Edwardian England, that does not necessarily imply wealth.

No doubt for Susan it was a big step down from Plas Wilmot (with three servants and a stableboy), but Tom Owen seems to have done his best for his family. He took young Wilfred on a holiday trip to France, and Susan often took her children to visit the substantial house of her sister in Wimbledon who was married to the prosperous owner of a number of pork butcher shops in London's East End. Both parents were religious, leaning toward what we now call evangelism; Sunday churchgoing and daily prayer were very much a part of their lives. If they did not live in Dickensian squalor, as Harold alleges, they were certainly poor by the standards of Susan's sisters. Throughout her adult life, Susan suffered from a combination of anxiety and ill-health, although it is not clear whether this was hypochondria or merely a result of living with four children in cramped, rented homes. In photographs with her young children, she appears attractive and smiling. In later life, she put on weight and her expression is more guarded. Her first two sons were healthy enough, but her third son, Colin, suffered from rickets and was obliged for some years to wear steel braces on his legs. Mary, her youngest child, was small and frail, almost dwarfish, with a head that was too large for her body.

Susan was a devoted mother—indeed, Mary would not have survived without her care—but she made no secret of the fact that her firstborn Wilfred was her favorite. He was serious; early on he became a voracious reader, and he shared her deeply religious nature. The bond between them was more than amply demonstrated by the sheer volume (and prodigious length) of his letters to her, running into the many hundreds, unabated even during his service in the trenches. By contrast, Harold was his father's favorite. Tom took him on long walks through the Liverpool dockyards, absorbing the sights, sounds, and smells of the ships unloading and loading. Whether Tom longed for a seafaring life as opposed to humdrum domesticity and a job as a railway clerk is open to doubt. If Harold is to be believed, his father yearned for the sea and encouraged people to address him as "Captain" in the dockside cafés he took the boy to on their walks together.

Strangely, many years later, when Tom visited Wilfred in Bordeaux, Wilfred told people that his father was a baronet who should be addressed as "Sir Thomas," and even more strangely his father joined in this mild social deception. Both boys seem to have had a strong streak of snobbery mixed with social anxiety, not an uncommon English characteristic and one they perhaps shared with their father. Susan too sought to claim her family's improbable descent from Anglo-Norman gentry and fantasized that her eldest son would become "Sir Wilfred Edward Salter-Owen," revealingly enough placing her family's name before that of her husband.

None of these attempts to gild the lily would have helped Wilfred much through his early years at school. The Birkenhead Institute was a private school for lower-middle-class children. It was a large step up from state-funded compulsory grammar schools for working-class children, with their emphasis on vocational training, and several steps down from more expensive preparatory schools that were intended to prepare pupils for entrance into a public school (a private, expensive, and socially exclusive boarding school), from which they would normally move on to Oxford or Cambridge. The fees of the Birkenhead Institute were modest, although they represented a considerable sacrifice for the Owens, but unlike a state school, the curriculum included Latin, then still a necessity for a university education and a broad range of the liberal arts.*

From the beginning, Wilfred was a model pupil. He was studious, well behaved, and had, according to his brother Harold who attended the same school, "the intense purposefulness of a serious student." He was not keen on sports and tended to hang about on the sidelines with a friend, Alec Paton, who was similarly studious. Harold, when he came to write about this almost sixty years later, took the view that the friendship between the two older boys was based on "mutual respect" rather than "any affectionate impulse," but since one of the major themes of the three volumes of his autobiography was to deny that Wilfred had been a homosexual, this may have been wishful thinking.

Far more likely, Wilfred's relationship with Alec was one of innocent, but powerful mutual affection. Oddly enough, rough though many of the boys were, Wilfred was never bullied. He seems to have had an uncanny ability to stay out of trouble. The 828 pages of Harold Owen's autobiography are a powerful testimony to sibling rivalry (and written when his brother Wilfred could no longer contradict him), but still they make it clear that Wilfred was his mother's favorite and that he expected deference from his younger siblings. He was disarmingly grown-up for a schoolboy, and at an early age he was already obsessed by poetry, although not yet writing it.

In 1907 Tom Owen finally received the promotion he had been hoping for: he became chief clerk to the superintendent of his rail-

---

* The existence of three different kinds of schools had the effect of reinforcing the ultimate British class barrier, language. Those who had attended grammar schools spoke "lower-class" English, further intensified by strong regional accents (e.g., Cockney in the East End of London, Brummie in Birmingham, or Scouse in Liverpool, not to speak of Scottish, Irish, and Welsh). Those who went to schools like Wilfred's spoke a more prim and proper English, and those who went to public school, then on to Oxford or Cambridge, spoke in the distinctly upper-class language and accent of the elite. When Sassoon first met Owen, he thought he had a grammar school accent, but it was not. I am good at recognizing class differences in the way people speak, even though, having been educated in part in the United States and Switzerland, my own accent is mid-Atlantic, and I am sometimes mistaken for a Canadian.

way. That necessitated a quick move from Birkenhead to Shrews-
bury, a small, prosperous provincial city on the Welsh border.
Unlike Birkenhead, which adjoins the port and the city of Liver-
pool, Shrewsbury was set on the peaceful Severn River and was
surrounded then by open, rolling countryside, a much nicer envi-
ronment for the Owen children, although Wilfred and Harold were
both upset by the suddenness of the move.

Wilfred was then approaching fourteen, then the school leaving
age, which brought into focus the question of what was to become
of him. In the end, he enrolled in the Shrewsbury Borough Tech-
nical College, with a view to becoming as soon as possible a proba-
tionary pupil-teacher. The advantage was that it would give him a
free education; the disadvantage was that it would prepare him for a
poorly paid career as an elementary school teacher in a state school,
a dead end for a bright and culturally ambitious boy with a passion
for poetry. Nor did he have a gift for doing well in examinations
that might have won him a scholarship to London or Reading uni-
versities and open up to him a more appealing career than teaching
multiplication tables to slum children.

By good fortune his mother, vastly more religious than his father,
came up with the notion that Wilfred might act as assistant to a
country parson and at the same time continue his studies with a
view to getting a university degree. The strength of Wilfred's reli-
gious belief was not in doubt; he was a passionate evangelical like
his mother, which is to say Low Church, as opposed to Anglicans,
who were High Church and flirted with Rome.*

Fortunately for Wilfred, the vicar of a small rural church in
Dunsden, Oxfordshire, not far from Reading, was looking for just
such an assistant. After an exchange of correspondence, Wilfred
made the journey to Dunsden for a weekend and more than satis-
fied the vicar with what Harold would call "his quiet gentleness and

---

* Since its inception under Henry VIII, the Church of England has been split
between those who wanted to bring it closer to Rome and those who wanted to cleave
more closely to orthodox Protestantism. Under the Tudors, those who went too far in
either direction were often executed. By the mid-nineteenth century, it merely affected
a churchman's career.

dark shyness," as well as his sound evangelical belief. Wilfred would be paid "a token salary" and would receive free room and board, in return for which he would perform "parish visiting" and act as the vicar's assistant. Wilfred would have time to continue his studies, in the hope of attaining an M.A. Perhaps just as important he would have a place to pursue them, since hitherto he had shared a tiny, unheated attic room with Harold, with a single table and lamp.

What remained unsettled was the vicar's expectation that Wilfred would be studying in order to enter the Church. Although Wilfred was guileless, he would have perceived at once that revealing that he felt no vocation for the Church would be a mistake, and he therefore left the matter open. He would be serving in effect as an amateur assistant curate, while studying for a degree and pursuing his dream of becoming a poet. For the moment, however, the job solved the problem of what he was to do, in a way that satisfied even his father, and put him on the path to independent adulthood.

Inevitably, the Reverend Herbert Wigan became a significant factor in Wilfred's life. Wigan was no jolly foxhunting country vicar in the Surtees tradition. He was serious, stiff, and formal, and he quickly came to rely on his eighteen-year-old assistant, who was in some respects even more serious-minded than the vicar himself.

Wilfred's position changed his life radically. From a small, crowded house in Shrewsbury, shared with five other people and a maid, he found himself living in a vast Victorian vicarage, with a formal dining room, a library, a sitting room, at least four bedrooms, and four servants. Wigan was personally abstemious, but he had a private income and was used to living comfortably. Wilfred found it was necessary to expand his wardrobe and to learn such upper-middle-class usage as calling the midday meal "lunch" instead of "dinner," the evening meal "dinner" instead of "tea," and to dress for dinner, that is, to wear a dinner jacket and white bow tie if guests were present. Every morning a maid brought him a jug of hot water for shaving, made his bed, and carefully looked after his modest wardrobe.

One of the rare photographs of Wilfred at Dunsden shows him in a neat, well-tailored glen plaid suit of plus fours, with leather buttons and brightly polished shoes, looking more like a country gentleman than an assistant curate. He is standing next to what appears to be a bicycle, which might explain the knee breeches and the long socks. He had his own bedroom, but at first Reverend Wigan was not overly accommodating about giving him his own room in which to study and write. As kind as Wigan appears to have been, life at the vicarage was not satisfying. Wilfred was obliged to conceal his growing passion for poetry—particularly the poems of Keats—and to endure long, silent meals, frequent prayers, and Bible readings, a dull life for an adolescent, particularly one whose faith was ebbing.

Almost two years passed before Wilfred was able to confront the vicar with his unwillingness to take holy orders. This produced a crisis both in the vicarage and at home. The sheer dullness of life at the vicarage was one factor, and the difficulty of finding the time to write poems—an activity of which Wigan in any case disapproved—in between prayers, parish duties, and Bible readings was another. Wilfred felt that he was being suffocated, and after his inevitable confrontation with the vicar over his loss of faith, he returned home and fell ill from a lung ailment that may have been more in the nature of a crisis of nerve. He was home with his parents again, he had no profession, and his only prospect was as an elementary school teacher, a career that he emphatically did not want.

His brother Harold was in much the same position, but he solved it by going to sea as an officer cadet on a big steamship line. Perhaps inspired by Harold's escape, Wilfred rather courageously took his fate into his own hands and found himself a job as a teacher of English at a Berlitz school in Bordeaux. Berlitz was not fussy about formal degrees; a working knowledge of French and a quick study of the Berlitz method, which consisted mostly of conversation rather than rote learning, was enough. The pay was miserable, and the hours were long—Berlitz squeezed the most out of its teachers, who were called *Professeur* whatever their qualifications or lack thereof. But for the first time in his life, Wilfred had a taste of freedom. At Dunsden he had been subject to the vicar's close attention and obliged to pay respect to a degree of religious belief that he no longer shared, but in Bordeaux he was on his own.

He had never been to a boarding school, or to a university, or spent more than a day at a time in a big city. Now he had not only escaped from home, and his mother's close attention to his spiritual well-being, he had also escaped from England and was earning his own income, however meager, in a foreign country. Even living in cheap rented rooms, with the usual inadequate French plumbing and demanding landladies, he was free at last to drink a glass of wine. (Except for breakfast, what meal in France, however cheap, is without wine?) He could sit up all night scribbling poems and reading, skip going to church on Sunday, or nurse a café au lait on a café terrace and watch the world go by. He suffered from occasional bouts of illness, rarely alleviated by the peculiarities of French medicine.

He kept up a perfect torrent of letters home, most of them addressed to his mother. Their tone is alarmingly like that of love letters. After reporting in some detail about his problems with constipation and the odd (and ineffective) French remedies for it, Wilfred wrote to his mother of the photograph of her that he carried with him:

> *I see that justly proportioned face composed, yet with benignancy bright and active in the eyes; the mouth is set; and yet it ever smiles a gentle smile; With what firmness sits the head upon shoulder-throne! And lo! The arm, seemingly as strong as a Titan's; and when used to succour and sustain, so strong in very truth! With the hand hanging in perfect grace, a lady's hand . . . and not far away, the Kitchen-room, and the whole house She reigneth in as a Queen.*

A few days later he sent a postcard to inform her of a nosebleed, and he told her that her card and letter, received as the doctor was taking his temperature, helped to calm him. Only a few days later he told her he was still "obstinately c-nst-p-t-ed" and to thank her for sending him copies of *Punch* magazine. She in turn wrote to tell him in detail of *her* symptoms, which spurred him to inquire for more details: "Your headaches seem interminable," he wrote, and the news of them made his "spirit mourn all Sunday." He urged her to "pillow yourself in bed; close down the blinds of your room, surround yourself with perfumes and flowers, feed on fish, milk, honey and wine; forbid any sound to reach you," and to delegate all household duties to his unfortunate sister Mary.

One guesses that what meant most to him was the experience of living in one of the great port cities of Europe, rich in architecture and history. He got along well with his fellow Berlitz "professors" and his pupils, but he was slow to develop a social life, which he was in any case too poor to afford. Of necessity, his French improved, his stomach began to adapt to meals in the cheapest of French restaurants, and he started to look beyond the seemingly endless Berlitz lessons, at one point even considering the possibility of establishing a Berlitz franchise elsewhere himself. In the end, he found a sideline by tutoring in English, which gave him a welcome, if ambivalent position in a middle-class family.

Curiously, the shots that killed Archduke Franz Ferdinand and his wife in Sarajevo on June 28, 1914, had no great or immediate impact on Wilfred Owen. He was involved in moving on (and mildly upward) as a tutor of English to another family, with whom he was to stay in their rented villa in Bagnères-de-Bigorre, a slightly fading summer resort town and spa in the Pyrénées, where his pupils would be a mother and daughter. News of his move set off alarm bells for his mother, for he would be living with a French family, one with a daughter, in or near a resort town, all of which seemed to threaten a moral disaster. Wilfred was at pains to calm her concerns. He had somehow managed to suggest that Mme. Léger was an actress, to his mother's horror, but he rushed to assure her that she was instead the manager of her husband's successful decorating business, and that she wore only a modest amount of makeup—like most French women, he was quick to point out. She was in her thirties, "elegant rather than *belle*: has shapely features luxuriant coiffure, but is much too thin to be pretty." As for Nénette, the daughter, she was only eleven. He rather spoiled the attempt to play down Mme. Léger's appearance to his mother by adding that her toilette was always "unimpeachable," that she could not stand "plain people," and that she had told him frankly that "she does not love her husband excessively," a hint that even he might have been able to perceive as a perfumed handkerchief dropped charmingly at his feet. As for her appearance, in a photograph of her sitting next to Wilfred at an open-air concert, she is, by modern standards, not too thin at all but svelte and elegant, with a striking profile and an expression that suggests a woman of considerable experience.

M. Léger too was charming, an amateur theatrical producer with many friends in the arts, who had wisely placed his substantial decorating firm in the more businesslike hands of his younger wife. He seems to have treated Wilfred more as a friend than as a tutor. As for Nénette, she was high-strung, difficult, argumentative, and undisciplined, but she swiftly became fond of Wilfred. She was something of a juvenile bluestocking, writing plays at the age of nine, and bonded immediately to Wilfred, so that he was in the surprising position of being surrounded by *two* adoring females. "All women, without exception, *annoy* me," he had written somewhat tactlessly to his mother, but now that he was living with the Léger family, his feelings about women softened.

In fact, Wilfred seemed to have stepped into the plot of a French domestic drama: the glamorous wife with a considerably older husband, the attractive but bratty daughter, the tight quarters of a modest summer villa, the shy and handsome young English tutor. Wilfred had indeed become a good-looking young man, despite having grown a narrow mustache that did him no favors, and parting his hair down the middle, which did even less. Madame took him off at once to buy rope-soled canvas espadrilles, required footwear for summer holidays in France. She also clearly lavished on him her considerable charm.

Wilfred's letters dealt with the war as if it were a remote event, although he mentions that he "receives glances from knitting women which not Madame Defarge could make more menacing."* This was not surprising since there was universal conscription for all men between the age of twenty and forty-five in France, and the sight of an apparently healthy young man in civilian clothes was bound to create hostility. The explanation that he was British solved this problem, when he was able to offer it—Great Britain and Russia were France's only two significant allies. Still, it was uncomfortable to be the only man of military age not in uniform. (M. Léger was too old.)

---

* Mme. Defarge is the vengeful *tricoteuse* in Charles Dickens's *A Tale of Two Cities.*

He toyed with the idea of volunteering as a stretcher-bearer, but Mme. Léger soon put a stop to that, and he seems to have been too busy listening to the confidences of Madame and Nénette to pay much attention to the war. For decades the French had planned that when war came, they would attack toward Alsace and Lorraine, and nobody doubted it. The loss of the two provinces to Germany at the conclusion of the war of 1870–71 was still the unrequited wound in the French national soul. Ever since their loss, the statues representing Alsace and Lorraine on the Place de la Concorde in Paris had been draped in black. The swift German advance through Belgium in August 1914 obliged General Joffre to abandon this plan and move the bulk of his forces north to cover Paris instead, at a cost of over half a million casualties,* including over 27,000 killed in a single day.

Wilfred reported that he continued to be "immensely happy and famously well" and was busy entertaining Nénette with drawings, playing the piano, making boats, acting out comedy, inventing stories, playing hide-and-seek, and the like. Going home to enlist simply does not appear to have occurred to him, his letters were mostly about Mme. Léger, his "amiable hostess." He continued to point out from time to time that Mme. Léger had no connection with the stage, just in case his mother was still concerned on that score, although she might have been more alarmed to learn that part of his duty was to take Nénette to church on Sundays—a Catholic church, of course. As the battle in Belgium was raging, with the British Expeditionary Force at last in action, the big news he confided in a long letter to his sister Mary was that he was about to meet a "a great French Poet," thanks to the Légers.

LAURENT TAILHADE IS HARDLY A NAME to conjure with in the English-speaking world, but before the First World War, he was a considerable presence in French literary life, both for his outsize personality and for his work. He was a friend and follower of such

---

* About 300,000 in the Battle of the Frontiers, at least another 200,000 in the Battle of the Marne.

major French symbolist poets as Stéphane Mallarmé and Paul Verlaine, a fierce satirist, a poet who lived to drive a stake into the heart of the French bourgeoisie. A fervent anarchist, he had gained notoriety by praising the act of a more committed fellow anarchist who had thrown a bomb into the Chamber of Deputies: *"Qu'importe la victime si le geste est beau?"* (Who cares about the victims if the act is glorious?) Tailhade asked, a line that was thrown in his face after he later lost an eye when an anarchist tossed a bomb into a restaurant where he was eating. His right hand had also been badly mutilated in a duel with a right-wing political opponent. Tailhade was that unusual combination of poet and man of action. Although twice married he was more or less openly bisexual.

The moment he met Wilfred Owen they became friends, or perhaps more accurately *guru* and *shishya* (teacher and disciple). The relationship was also a love affair of sorts, though probably not consummated. During the first few weeks, they saw each other frequently, and Tailhade, who was a "decadent" (in France this was a literary movement rather than a moral judgment) and an admirer of Oscar Wilde, opened Wilfred not only to a more exuberant poetic style but also to a more confident *personal* style. One senses the unfolding of his personality and an increasing self-confidence, despite poverty, the lack of a career, and the endless stream of letters home.

Tailhade had become a friend of the Légers, who moved in artistic circles, so when he lectured outdoors at the casino in Bagnères, they eagerly attended, taking Wilfred with them. M. Léger had organized a concert that preceded the lecture. Afterward the poet was invited to lunch, and he seems to have accepted almost instantly Mme. Léger's suggestion that he come and stay with them rather than remain in his hotel. The next day Wilfred visited Tailhade, then described his new friend to his mother with remarkable frankness, even allowing for Harold's later editing: "He received me like a lover. To use an expression of the Rev. H. Wiggins, he quite slobbered over me. I know not how many times he squeezed my hand; and, sitting me down on a sofa, pressed my head against his shoulder." This "imbues [me] with a sensation of happiness," he added. None of this seems to have alarmed his mother, perhaps because in a letter written only four days earlier, he had confided an even more startling piece of news, which was that Mme. Léger, many of whose most important decorating clients were in Canada, had proposed that Wilfred accompany her on her next visit there. That would not only put Wilfred in close daily shipboard contact with Mme. Léger, whom Mrs. Owen still suspected of being a moral threat, but expose him to the danger of being torpedoed by a German submarine.

The several weeks in which Tailhade and Wilfred pursued their friendship went unrecorded in his letters home, perhaps wisely on his part, although on Tailhade's, the seduction seems to have been more literary than physical. Tailhade was in poor health, and Wilfred might not yet have been ready for a sexual relationship with another man. Matters cannot have been helped by the presence of Mme. Léger and Nénette, both of whom were devoted to the young Englishman. In the end, Tailhade went back to Paris once the summer was over, and Mme. Léger sailed for Canada alone. What remains of Wilfred's correspondence contains vague references to some kind of bust-up in the "Affair Léger," but Harold's editing of his brother's letters seems to have been unusually drastic for this part of Wilfred's life.

On his return to Bordeaux, Wilfred stayed in the Léger house for some weeks. He hinted to his mother that "the Léger episodes have not taken the bloom off my innocency [*sic*]." More mysteriously, he remarked on "the seamy side of Madame Léger's cap," which makes her sound more like a *tricoteuse* à la Madame Defarge than the elegant and attractive woman she clearly was. One wonders if Mme. Léger tried to seduce Wilfred and failed.

The Berlitz school was closed, so Wilfred was obliged to troll desperately for students and take lodgings in Bordeaux. It was a precarious existence, but it at least left him independent, which he vastly preferred to going home to Shrewsbury in defeat. He seems to have made a broader range of friends, including a doctor who took him to see French surgeons operating on badly wounded soldiers without anesthetics. That failed to shock or disgust him— indeed, he made neat sketches of some of the wounds in a letter to Harold. The city of Bordeaux was crowded with Parisians, since the government had moved there when Paris had seemed threatened by the German advance. Lodgings were hard to secure, but Wilfred's letters are cheerful, even optimistic, and he soon had nine pupils, including a viscount and a wealthy manufacturer of perfumes.

In some respects, this may have been one of the happiest times in Wilfred's life. He was free and independent, writing great amounts of poetry, albeit unpublished. He felt no obligation to go home and join up, as he surely would have been urged to do in Great Britain, where in the streets total strangers insulted healthy young men not in uniform. Perhaps he picked up male prostitutes—Bordeaux is a major seaport, so every variety of sex was on sale—and may have confessed it to Robert Graves three years later, when Graves came to visit Siegfried Sassoon at Craiglockhart. But Graves may simply have been embellishing his conversation with Wilfred. How likely is it that Wilfred would have confessed such a thing, after all, to a total stranger in a taxi ride from the railway station to Sassoon's golf club for a late lunch? Be this as it may, Wilfred seems to have become, perhaps thanks to his relationship with Tailhade, more comfortable with his homosexuality and more aware that it was not just a phase he was passing through.

Still, Wilfred confided to his mother his yearning for a closer relationship with someone: "I begin to suffer a hunger for Intimity. At bottom it is that I ought to be in love and am not. . . . I lack any touch of tenderness. I ache in soul, as my bones might ache after a night spent on a cold, stone floor." This may be a reference to Tailhade, who despite his age had tried to join up and for the first time made Wilfred wonder, at first not very seriously, if *he* should enlist. He contemplated going home, but German submarine sinkings were making the home voyage dangerous.

Then out of the blue, the sister of the British consul in Bordeaux recommended him as a tutor to a well-to-do lady who was looking after her four nephews. Two of them were at Downside, one of the most prestigious Catholic public schools in England. It speaks volumes for Wilfred's reputation that the consul and his sister picked him for such an eminently respectable job. He moved with all his luggage into Mlle. de la Touche's house at Mérignac, then a countrified suburb of Bordeaux (now home to its airport). From there, he could travel by tram every morning to the city to give his English lessons, then return to tutor the boys in their schoolwork. He was treated like a houseguest, the boys, although high-spirited, liked and respected him, and he spent Christmas there—worrying his mother by attending a Catholic mass. When the sinkings at sea increased and Mlle. de la Touche decided not to risk sending the two older boys back to Downside until the spring, he stayed on as their tutor. Even Wilfred's mother could find no criticism to make of Mlle. de la Touche, an elderly gentlewoman who had been the governess of one of the sisters of King Albert I of Belgium.

Apart from tutoring the boys, Wilfred made a stab at a business career. First he attempted to secure a contract for tin-plated items (pots, pans, mess kits) for his wealthy uncle Ted at the French War Ministry. Then he tried to help his pupil M. Peyronnet, the manufacturer of perfumes, improve his export sales and to find new sources for perfume bottles, which had hitherto come from Germany. The tin plate project came to nothing (rich Uncle Ted was a continuous disappointment to the needy Wilfred), and for a time it looked as if he might go to Egypt on behalf of M. Peyronnet, but that fell through too. The British consul suggested that Wilfred take up a consular career, but that would require him to learn one more foreign language and have a "tea-party examination" (a personal interview over tea) with the foreign secretary. Clearly, Wilfred was looking for a more substantial career than giving English lessons. He did not consider life in the trenches as one of his options.

He wrote at length to his mother about his future, partly in response to his father's well-justified concern that his "present life was not leading anywhere in particular," and partly to say that while he remained willing to keep his ears open for a call to holy orders, he had not heard one yet. "There is *one* title I prize," he wrote his mother, "one clear call audible, one Sphere where I may influence for Truth, one workshop whence I may send forth Beauty, one mode of living entirely congenial to me." That title, although he did not mention it, was "poet."

At Eastertime, the boys were still in Mérignac and so was Wilfred, having been nursed back to health after a bout of flu by Mlle. de la Touche, who had been warned by her neighbor, a French admiral who clearly lacked the Nelson touch, that the Bay of Biscay and the Channel were more dangerous than ever. Wilfred's plan to return with them was delayed further by an attack of measles, which the doctor, with the characteristically misplaced self-confidence of French medicine, instantly misdiagnosed as sunstroke. Then Mlle. de la Touche decided not to risk sending her nephews across the Channel at all, throwing Wilfred into utter confusion.

In the end it was not until May 1915 that he returned home, after finding a tutor to replace himself for a few weeks in Mérignac. His journey was made possible by M. Peyronnet, on whose behalf he was to attend a British Industries Fair, presumably to report on the availability of British glass bottles and to set up a display of Peyronnet's perfumes. If he was uncomfortable about being in civilian clothes at a moment when posters everywhere urged young men to enlist, he did not mention it. He attended a patriotic meeting to hear Prime Minister Asquith speak, and may have seen Rudyard Kipling there, then surely the most widely read poet in the English-speaking world. Wilfred also spent several weeks at home in Shrewsbury working on an epic poem about Perseus, only fragments of which survive.

The war ground on mercilessly. In Gallipoli fierce fighting raged as the Turks attacked British, Australian, and New Zealand troops. At sea a German submarine sank the RMS *Lusitania* with the loss of over thirteen hundred passengers and crew. Violent anti-German riots broke out in big cities all over the United Kingdom, and huge battles were fought on the Western and Eastern Fronts, but not much of that was reflected in Wilfred's letters. Indeed he seemed almost eerily unconcerned.

By mid-June 1915, Wilfred was back in Bordeaux, this time in a comfortable lodging in town, from which he commuted to Mérignac to tutor the boys. Peyronnet was delighted with Wilfred's work in London and brought up the idea of Wilfred going to Egypt for him. Wilfred was willing enough but thought it unlikely he would get to Egypt to sell perfume so long as the fighting continued at Gallipoli. For the first time, he suggested to his mother that if the Egyptian trip did not come off by September, he might enlist in the army. He mentioned seeing a poster in his London hotel announcing that gentlemen returning from abroad might be given a commission in the Artists Rifles* and "will be sent to the front in 3 months." Wilfred told his mother that he still "didn't want the bore of training" and didn't want to wear khaki, but something in the announcement apparently lodged itself in his mind.

He spent the summer in Bordeaux, complaining of the heat, until the middle of September, when Mlle. de la Touche finally decided to send the boys back to Downside, thus subsidizing Wilfred's trip home. In mid-October he took and passed the medical examination for the Artists Rifles. The claim that he might be given a commission and sent to the front in three months was wildly at odds with the facts. It would be over a year of marching, drilling, and study before Wilfred would arrive in France in December 1916, exactly what he had hoped to avoid. Unlike young men who had served in the Officer Training Corps at public schools, Wilfred was starting from scratch, with no previous experience of military drill and discipline. He also lacked the assurance of public school and Oxford or Cambridge graduates that their education was enough to prepare them to command soldiers in battle.

On October 21, 1915, Wilfred was sworn in, kissed the Bible, and received his first typhoid inoculation. The initial training of the Artists Rifles was held in urban Bloomsbury, of all places. He found a room in a French boardinghouse on Tavistock Square, near which, he was delighted to learn, Charles Dickens had lived for six years. Here the conversation at mealtimes was mostly against the British, whom the French suspected as usual of holding back their manpower and letting the French do most of the fighting. Despite being France's ally, Britain was, as always, *l'Albion perfide*, perfidious

---

* The Artists Rifles was one of those uniquely English amateur solutions to a professional military problem. Formed in the late nineteenth century, it was a rifle regiment of volunteers from the arts: painters, sculptors, poets, musicians, and so on. They fought bravely in the Boer War. In the First World War, the regiment had several battalions at the front and others at home training officers who hailed from the arts and the professions. In the British Army, rifle regiments had emerged from the American Revolutionary War, because the rifled hunting weapons of so many Americans were superior in accuracy to the smoothbore muskets of the British infantry. Rifle regiments wore dark green uniforms instead of red, with black leather and buttons, and considered themselves the elite equals to the Foot Guards.

Albion. Wilfred's lodging was within a short walk of Harold Monro's Poetry Bookshop, where there were frequent readings. By October 25 he was in uniform and being drilled in Cartwright Gardens, struggling with his puttees and becoming accustomed to the smell of Kiwi boot polish, Brasso, and the castor oil that recruits used to soften their boots. Route marches took place routinely through the London streets, but he was free to enjoy life in London in his spare time. His uniform got him into the theater at half price to see a dramatization of Baroness Orczy's novel *The Scarlet Pimpernel.*

Soon Wilfred Owen was swept into the time-honored routine of training in the British Army. There were frequent moves to huts sleeping thirty or more men in windswept, newly built camps, and endless cleaning, polishing, and drilling. He was required to master a vast amount of military skills and law, so it was not until the beginning of June 1916 that he was finally commissioned in the Manchester Regiment and received his officer's uniform from the tailor. He was smart enough to order it from Pope & Bradley on Bond Street, a well-established military tailor, rather than buying it ready-made and risking the instant wrath of his commanding officer and the adjutant at the sight of a badly fitting uniform or the wrong shade of khaki. We do not know much about his life in those months, except that Harold Monro read and praised his poems and helped him edit them, and that he eventually moved into a rented room above the Poetry Bookshop. As an as yet unpublished poet, he found Monro's attention and qualified appreciation enormously important, and his bookshop a meeting place for all who were interested in modern poetry. Monro thought some of Wilfred's poems more than deserved a place in one of Edward Marsh's *Georgian Poetry* collections, which Monro published, but in the end nothing came of this idea, presumably because Marsh was not impressed.

Most of Wilfred's poems at the time were strained and romantic, written in self-conscious imitation of Keats, of whose work he was passionately fond. He had a natural gift for writing poetry— Monro was right about that—but most of it was lush and poetic in an old-fashioned way, at a time when Ezra Pound and T. S. Eliot were writing. It would take the brutal experience of war—and the fierce editing pen of Siegfried Sassoon—to harden and simplify

Wilfred's voice and turn his poems into those most often quoted from the First World War. For the moment, he was stuck in a penumbra of personal sadness and regret, not so much for love lost as for love not yet experienced, expressed in the "decadent" tones of Oscar Wilde, with "the purple shade" hanging over "the light blue sand":

> Thereby she set a weeping-willow tree
> To droop and mourn. Full dolefully it clung
> About the form, and moved continually,
> As if it sighed; as if it sometimes wrung
> Convulsive fingers in sad reverie,
> And ever o'er the light blue sand it hung
> A purple shade.

Any expectation that he might soon be sent into battle was dashed; instead, he was to be given much more training and assigned the most humdrum of military duties. A commission in the Manchester Regiment did not carry with it the pomp and circumstance of a commission in the Royal Welch Fusiliers, which made it seem like such an awesome experience to Robert Graves and Siegfried Sassoon in 1914. The Manchesters were a good, solid line regiment. During the Siege of Ladysmith in the Boer War, a detachment of First Manchesters, although surrounded, fought until there were only two men left alive. Both of them received the Victoria Cross. But the Manchesters had none of the glamour of more famous regiments, still less the swank of mess nights in full dress uniform, with the candelabra lit, the passing of the port decanter, and the regimental string band playing in the background.

Wilfred had no connection whatsoever to Manchester the city, but by the summer of 1916, newly minted second lieutenants were being sent as replacements to whatever regiments needed them most. The life expectancy of a second lieutenant on the Western Front in 1916 was calculated at six weeks, so a constant supply was needed. Wilfred joined the Fifth Battalion of the Manchester Regiment on June 18, 1916. It was stationed in a newly built camp near Guildford, in Surrey, only thirty miles from London. Unlike their officers, the men were mostly from Lancashire—tough, hardened miners and industrial workers, not easily acclimated to military discipline.

The transformation of a poet and a teacher of English into an infantry officer produced a miraculous change in Wilfred Owen. He had hitherto held an ambivalent place in the English class system. His father was merely a railway official, and his two years at the vicarage had been at least as compromised by his not having an M.A. or attending university as it was by not receiving the "call." Although he had been addressed as "Professor" at the Berlitz school in Bordeaux, it was not a real academic title. But once he reached Guildford with a star on each sleeve, he was undisputedly an officer and a gentleman. He was, he wrote his mother, "marooned on a Crag of Superiority in an ocean of Soldiers." He contemplated the men he would command without any initial affection. "The generality . . . are hard-handed, hard-headed miners, dogged, loutish, ugly . . . blond, coarse, ungainly, strong, 'unfatiguable', unlovely, Lancashire soldiers, Saxons to the bone." As an officer, he had a room to himself, and a soldier-servant to make his bed, polish his buttons, boots, and Sam Browne belt, and press his uniform. "My servant has nothing else to do but serve me," he wrote his mother, although that was not altogether everything—in battle his soldier-servant would advance beside Owen, bayonet fixed, and do his best to carry his messages. If Owen was wounded, his soldier servant was to get him back to his own front line. Owen was deferentially coached in the correct performance of his military duties by his "priceless" sergeant-major, and given a chance to command a platoon, a thrilling change from the humble task of giving English lessons in Bordeaux for a pittance.

No sooner had he settled in than he was posted to Aldershot for a musketry course (he proved an excellent shot), then back to Guildford for a course in gas warfare, endless route marches, and lessons in bomb-throwing with live hand grenades. Wilfred had ambitions to get himself transferred to the Royal Flying Corps to train as a pilot, but by now he was considered a useful infantry officer, so nothing came of it. In fact, he did not reach France until January 1917, just in time to participate in a series of hopeless attacks north of the Somme battlefield, over ground which he described to his mother, without exaggeration as "the Slough of Despond" and

"Sodom and Gomorrah . . . pock-marked like a body of foulest disease and the odor is the breath of cancer."

WILFRED'S INTRODUCTION TO THE FRONT was tolerable enough. He spent a few days at the enormous base camp of Étaples. From there, after a few days, in accordance with some incomprehensible system, officers were posted to the regiment and battalion where they were needed. Wilfred had a good soldier-servant to make him temporarily comfortable, although sleeping in a tent in midwinter in a vast sea of mud cannot have been as pleasant as he made it sound to his mother. He was very pleased to receive his orders to join the Second Manchester Battalion at the front—the soldiers were mostly regulars, experienced, professional officers and men. It took him the best part of two days and nights of intense discomfort to travel the forty miles to Halloy, near Beaumont Hamel, where the Second Battalion was recuperating from severe fighting that had reduced it to less than half its strength. The French railway system was in a state of advanced chaos due to the strain of the war. Wilfred had not had dry feet since landing in France. He was exhausted, filthy, and had had nothing to eat since leaving Étaples. He was, as he put it, "let down gently into the real thing: Mud."

He slept with two other junior officers, one of them of all things a noted watercolorist from the Artists Rifles, on the muddy stone floor of an abandoned farmhouse, while most of the men lay in half-ruined barns on lousy, muddy straw. "We eat and drink out of old tins," he wrote his mother, "we are never dry, and never 'off duty.'" His kit was now augmented by a steel helmet and a more up-to-date gas mask. Over the next three days, the battalion marched toward the front, "slowed down by the awful state of the roads, and the enormous weight carried." It was "beginning to freeze through the rain. . . . We were at the mercy of the cold, and, [despite] being in health, I never suffered so terribly as yesterday afternoon." When he was finally able to lie down on his damp, muddy bed in a tent, he heard, for the first time, the heavy, monotonous thunder of the guns.

It was British policy to dominate no-man's-land, which Wilfred described as looking under snow like "the face of the moon chaotic, crater-ridden, uninhabitable, awful, the abode of madness." Even without a great attack, this meant constant patrols at night and a steady stream of casualties from German snipers, machine-gun fire, and artillery, as well as from occasional friendly fire while returning to the British front line. Wilfred was "transformed" by "wearing a steel helmet, buff jerkin of leather, rubber waders up to the hips, & gauntlets," the last necessitated by the fact that there was never less than two feet of water in the trenches. Wilfred was not only *at* the front but in front of it, in an underground advance post in no-man's-land, with twenty-five men crammed tightly into a dugout, under constant (and accurate) German shellfire. "Those fifty hours," he wrote, "were the agony of my happy life." It took Wilfred half an hour to crawl to his other posts. At the dugout to his left, two sentries were "blown away to nothing." Wilfred kept his own sentries halfway down the mud steps to give them some protection from the bombardment, but one of them was blown down by an explosion and, Wilfred thought, probably blinded. He would later turn this incident into one of his first war poems, writing in a voice very different from before:

We'd found an old Boche dug-out, and he knew,
And gave us hell, for shell on frantic shell,
Hammered on top, but never quite burst through.
Rain, guttering down in waterfalls of slime
Kept slush waist high, that rising hour by hour,
Choked up the steps too thick with clay to climb. . . .
                    There we herded from the blast
Of whizz-bangs, but one found our door at last,
Buffeting eyes and breath. Snuffing the candles,
And thud! flump! thud! down the steps came thumping
And splashing in the flood, deluging muck—
The sentry's body; then his rifle, handles
Of old Boche bombs, and mud in ruck on ruck.
We dredged him up, for killed, until he whined
"O sir, my eyes—I'm blind—I'm blind, I'm blind!"
Coaxing, I held a flame against his lids
And said if he could see the least blurred light

He was not blind; in time he'd get all right.
"I can't," he sobbed. Eyeballs, huge-bulged like squids
Watch my dreams still; but I forgot him there
In posting next for duty, and sending a scout
To beg a stretcher somewhere, and floundering about
To other posts under the shrieking air.

This is poetry as unflinchingly reportorial as a film documentary, but also unforgiving. There is no heroism here, no higher purpose to the fighting, just an inescapable tide of misery, pain, and suffering, of which the unfortunate sentry's blindness is merely a small part.

By the beginning of February 1917, he had experienced much that would form his poetry over the next two years. He had been gassed—only with tear gas, but still terrifying—and had contracted dysentery. One of his platoon froze to death, and he had dealt with the impossibility of getting back any of his wounded while "marooned on a frozen desert," buffeted by high explosive. To his surprise, and to the envy of his fellow subalterns, he was sent away on a course for transport officers, but even out of the front line, he remained obsessed by the ugliness of it all. "Hideous landscapes, vile noises, foul language . . . everything unnatural, broken, blasted; the distortion of the dead, whose unburiable bodies sit outside the dug-outs all day, all night, the most execrable sights on earth." Even at the transport school, his blanket was frozen stiff by the morning.

By the beginning of March, Wilfred was back with his battalion. At one point, he injudiciously stepped over the parapet to get to the head of his party, only to hear the high-pitched *ping* of a rifle bullet passing just over his head. A few days later he fell down a fifteen-foot abandoned cellar in the dark while trying to find one of his men who was in a state of exhaustion. He hit his head on the way down and was taken to a casualty clearing station with a concussion. He may have been deep in the hole for a considerable period of time before he was found and pulled out. He lost his watch and his revolver. He suffered the side effects of concussion, nausea, vomiting, and high fever, but gradually he came around. He helped the overworked nurses to care for other officer patients, many of whom were worse off than he was, with terrible wounds and injuries. Between the sniper's bullet and the fall, he may have lost some measure of his original sangfroid.

Previously he had been behaving like the unshakable, reliable junior officer he was meant to be, but his composure may have slipped a notch. It was not improved when command of his battalion temporarily passed to the senior major, J. F. Dempster, whom Owen particularly disliked and described as "an arrogant snob." This was to become a festering wound. Dempster may have been put off by Owen's accent, which suffered from what Siegfried Sassoon would later describe as a faint taste of grammar school. Dempster may also have had a slight suspicion that Wilfred was homosexual, but for whatever reason, the two men disliked each other, which would have serious repercussions for Wilfred.

He was finally released from hospital at the beginning of April and returned to his battalion. The Germans had recently startled the Allies by withdrawing from their positions to the almost impregnable Hindenburg Line, leaving behind a vast, devastated wasteland, ingeniously booby-trapped, with roads, villages, houses, bridges, and even trees completely and methodically destroyed. The British struggled to keep contact with the enemy, taking heavy losses. Wilfred reported to his mother that it had taken him four days of chaotic travel to find his battalion, and that in the ruins of Amiens, he had paused to buy a postcard to send her and to purchase a small automatic pocket pistol. He noted that his "long rest has shaken [his] nerve." This was perceptive. He had just missed, by one day, a triumphant but costly attack by the Second Manchesters, which among others took the life of his friend Second Lieutenant Hubert Gaukroger.

Over the next few days, Wilfred took part in constant fierce fighting. He spent four days and nights under shellfire "without relief in the open, and in the snow," kept alive "on brandy [and] the fear of death." A man next to him got "a beautiful round hole deep in his biceps," the perfect "Blighty wound," just bad enough to send him back to England for rehabilitation but not to inflict loss of the limb. Wilfred, to his regret, received only a piece of shrapnel that ripped a hole through his trench coat and another that tore one of his puttees. He felt a certain degree of discomfort at giving orders to men who had been through even harder fighting. He may have had to endure a certain amount of sharply worded criticism from Major Dempster about the amount of time he had remained at the casualty, and perhaps at the number of days it had taken him to find his way back to the battalion.

Prolonged sleeplessness, constant shellfire, and the loss of a friend may have had their effect on Wilfred, but he seems to have done his job. He went twelve days without washing his face or removing his boots, attacking the entrenched Germans twice in one day, despite frostbitten feet and the most intense shellfire he had ever experienced.

At some point on or around April 10, a heavy German shell exploded only a few feet from where Wilfred lay, throwing him into the air. He landed among the scattered but still recognizable body parts of his friend Gaukroger, whose body had been "horribly disinterred" from its shallow grave by a previous shell. Wilfred may have spent several days lying in a shallow hole covered by a sheet of corrugated iron. This time the damage to his nerves was impossible for him to control. The brigade was withdrawn from the front line for a rest, but by then Wilfred's state of nervous exhaustion was unmistakable.

One of his superior officers in the battalion, perhaps the "odious" Major Dempster, may have accused him openly of cowardice, but in any case the battalion medical officer examined him, diagnosed him with "neurasthenia," and sent him to a casualty clearing station, having observed him "to be shaky and tremulous . . . and his conduct and manner were peculiar, and his memory confused." Wilfred's biographer Dominic Hibbard concludes that Dempster may have written this observation, but there is no knowing for certain. In any case, it lays it on a bit thick and was clearly intended to suggest that Second Lieutenant Owen had behaved in a cowardly fashion under fire, which was not the case, since he did not break down until *after* the battalion was withdrawn from the line.

Many officers and certainly almost all generals regarded shell shock as imaginary, a phrase intended to cover up or excuse cowardice* or

---

* In the Second World War, in the British armed forces, the official phrase used to describe cowardice was "lack of moral fiber," or LMF.

lack of guts. But by 1917 the British Army had seen enough shell-shocked officers and men to conclude that they needed treatment as opposed to punishment; the object was to get them well enough to resume their place in the front line as soon as possible. Unsurprisingly, officers were given better treatment than Other Ranks, but whatever the rank, a substantial degree of ambivalence and confusion on the subject prevailed. Those who were diagnosed with shell shock had their medical papers marked *W*, for "wounded," and they would therefore be awarded a wound stripe and a small pension. Those who had developed the symptoms of shell shock *without* having been under direct artillery fire had their medical file marked *S*, for "sick," and were entitled to nothing, however strong their symptoms. By 1917, treatment was mostly given at centers close to the front. Only the more extreme cases were returned to Great Britain.

Wilfred's case was marked *W*. Nobody doubted the seriousness of it except his commanding officer, but he did not receive much in the way of treatment. He was at pains, however, to assure his mother that he was well. "Do not for a moment suppose I have had a breakdown," he wrote her. "I am simply <u>avoiding</u> one." He nevertheless warned her not to "hawk this letter about"—the notion of being in the hospital without a *physical* wound was thought of as shameful at home. He also did not mention that a few of his fellow officer patients, and many more Other Rank patients, were there because they had shot themselves in the hand or the foot to get out of the trenches.

More surprisingly, he admitted to his sister Mary that he had been "shaky" when he first arrived at the casualty clearing station. It was not the German artillery that was responsible for his state of mind, he explained, but the fact that he had been living so close to his friend "poor old Cock Robin (as we used to call 2/Lt. Gaukroger), who lay not only near by, but in various places around and about, if you understand." Whether Mary understood this rather baffling reference to the trauma that had produced Wilfred's shell shock is difficult to guess. He hardly mentioned treatment in his letters home, except for a famous nerve specialist, "a kind of wizard who mesmerises when he likes." This might mean that the doctor practiced hypnosis, and it might account for the fact that lying among the scattered body parts of his friend Second Lieutenant Gaukroger was still so sharply on Wilfred's mind that he tried to describe it to Mary. In any case, he was not returned to his battalion, as his case was considered serious enough for him, in mid-June, to finally be moved to a hospital at Etretat, on the Channel Coast, and from there to a hospital outside Southampton, back in England.

FROM SOUTHAMPTON, he was posted to Craiglockhart War Hospital outside Edinburgh. Between trains, he took the opportunity to spend a day in London, shopping for a new cap at Peter Robinson's on Oxford Circus, one of London's first department stores, being measured for a new pair of riding breeches at Pope & Bradley, and having tea at the Shamrock Tea Rooms. One senses his satisfaction at being transformed overnight into a young officer and gentleman of leisure, in London for the day with money to spend. (He made far more money as a second lieutenant than he had ever earned as an English tutor.) At last he was freed from the constant thunder of the guns and the presence of sudden death. Perhaps the only bad moment was meeting, of all people, his nemesis Dempster, now a lieutenant-colonel, on New Bond Street as he emerged from the tailor, but neither showed his feelings toward the other.

Like Siegfried Sassoon, Wilfred's first glimpse of Craiglockhart was depressing. He described it as "a decayed Hydro," and it did not improve on closer inspection. The building had been converted to a military hospital by the War Department with a minimum of expense. Most of the officers housed there were burdened by a sense of failure and guilt at having broken down at the front. They were under treatment but also under suspended judgment, being tested for signs of recovery that would enable a medical board to declare them fit for service and send them back to rejoin the fight. A sign bearing the Sword of Damocles might have been hung over the entrance of Craiglockhart.

Wilfred thrived there better than most, perhaps because he had never experienced the forced communal living of a public school, or of life at Oxford or Cambridge. He had, at last, the leisure and degree of privacy to write poems, and he quickly became the editor of the hospital's magazine, the fortnightly *Hydra*, where some of his own poems were first published. An astonishing number of clubs, societies, and special interest groups proliferated at Craiglockhart, encouraged as a means of keeping the patients busy and drawing them out of their misery. They were dedicated to debating, photography, model yacht making, carpentry, theater, and every imaginable form of sport. Owen was an inveterate joiner and enthusiast for them. He was a founding member of the Field Club, which studied the area around the hospital geologically, botanically, and economically.

For Wilfred, being at Craiglockhart was like being an undergraduate, with Dr. A. J. Brock as his tutor. Brock did not have the personal magnetism or colorful career of Captain Rivers, who treated Sassoon, but he was nevertheless a considerable figure who corresponded with Sigmund Freud and evolved a whole theory of dealing with the trauma of shell shock that he called ergotherapy. He recommended a typically British combination of physical work, cold baths, avoidance of spicy foods, exercise, and intricate handicrafts, all of it intended to "make the patient face up to life . . . and the phantoms of the mind."

Except for the uniforms, the missing locks on the doors, and the number of people who woke up screaming, Craiglockhart might well have been one of the smaller Oxford colleges in Wilfred's description of it. "I feel a kind of reservation about all the pleasant things I do here," he wrote his mother, but went on to add, a little less cheerfully, "I have made no friends in this place, and the impulse is not in me to walk abroad and find them." He gave a very successful lecture to the Field Club on the subject "Do Plants Think?" He hammered out a copper bowl, visited a munitions work, took up swimming in the municipal bath, and studied German. In every way he sought to follow Brock's packed regime.

Owen began work on an epic poem on a classical theme, *Antaeus and Hercules*, suggested by Brock, and he even persuaded his mother to make the long train trip north to see him. Brock summed Wilfred up as being "an outstanding figure, both in intellect and in character," but his praise was a mixed blessing, since the sooner he felt Wilfred was cured, the sooner the medical board would send him back to France.

He still hoped to write poetry that would "Light up the Darkness of the World," but his star had not yet risen, though it was to do so very shortly.

# CHAPTER 11

# APOTHEOSIS

W ILFRED OWEN FIRST MENTIONED THE PRES-ence of a new star on his horizon on August 15, 1917. He had been busy acting, editing the hospital magazine, arguing with his mother by letter about whether Christianity and the war were compatible (he thought not, and he had hard words to say about the Archbishop of Canterbury, who did). So he may not have noticed at first the presence of Siegfried Sassoon. Wilfred had been reading, apparently by chance, some of Sassoon's poems and was deeply moved by them, so it must have appeared to him providential that its author so unexpectedly appeared. Wilfred observed to his mother that he would rather meet Sassoon than Tennyson, but the opportunity didn't come until a week later, when he screwed up his courage to call on Sassoon. At their first meeting, Sassoon treated Wilfred with a certain lordly condescension. Wilfred persisted, however, and their next meeting was warmer. They talked about poetry, and Sassoon asked Wilfred to help him decipher a handwritten fan letter from H. G. Wells, written in pale pink ink.

Wilfred was smitten, so much so that he sat down at once afterward to write a poem in Sassoon's style:

The Dead-Beat (True—in the incidental)
He dropped, more sullenly, then wearily,
    Became a lump of stench, a clot of meat,
    And none of us could kick him to his feet.
    He blinked at my revolver, blearily . . .

We sent him down at last, he seemed so bad,
    Although a strongish chap and quite unhurt.
    Next day I heard the Doc's fat laugh: 'That dirt
You sent me down last night's just died. So glad!'"

This is nasty stuff, and one could have guessed it was based on personal experience even without Wilfred's note that it was. Threatening a soldier with a pistol who was reluctant to move forward was common enough in both armies, indeed it is one of the reasons officers carry a pistol in the first place. But the tone of the poem—and the sting of the last line—sounds more like Sassoon than Wilfred. There is no note of pity or sympathy, only a sharp, pervading cruelty.

Sassoon was genially critical of the younger poet's work, dismissing many of the earlier sonnets as too lyrical, but he admired some of his more recent work. Wilfred described the meeting to both his mother and, unusually, in a separate letter to his father, urging Tom to read Sassoon's "The Death-Bed" as "a piece of perfect art," and telling him "there is nothing better this century can offer you."

He drowsed and was aware of silence heaped
Round him, unshaken as the steadfast walls . . .

Light many lamps and gather round his bed.
Lend him your eyes, warm blood, and will to live.
Speak to him; rouse him; you may save him yet.
He's young, he hated war; how should he die
When cruel old campaigners win safe through?

But death replied: "I choose him." So he went,
And there was silence in the summer night . . .
Then, far away, the thudding of the guns.

Within a week, he was writing to his mother, "Siegfried called me in to him, and having condemned some of my poems, amended others, and rejoiced over a few, he read me his last works, which are superb beyond anything in his Book. Last night he wrote a piece which is the most exquisitely painful war poem of any language or time.* I don't tell him so, or that I am not worthy to light his pipe." Wilfred was in the full throes of hero worship, while Sassoon, although he may have been better at concealing his emotions, was beginning to feel a powerful attraction for his handsome young admirer, critiquing and rewriting Wilfred's poems, who had sent home to his mother and sister for every scrap he had written.

Sassoon was all too often imperious. He kept Wilfred waiting for hours for lunch at his golf club while he finished his game ("a severe fleshly trial," Wilfred described it, since he had skipped breakfast). Then he made up for it by taking Wilfred for tea with the astronomer royal. (Sassoon seems to have known everybody.) He offered to get Wilfred a staff job in England, but although Wilfred, like Sassoon himself, dreaded going back to the trenches, he did not want special treatment. He positively gushed about his new friend to his mother, inevitably arousing her suspicion or perhaps her jealousy. "Sassoon I like equally in all the ways you mention," he replied to her. "The <u>man</u> is tall and noble-looking. . . . The <u>Friend</u> is intensely sympathetic. . . . He keeps all effusiveness strictly within his pages. In this he is eminently <u>English</u>. It is so restful after the French absurdities." (This is presumably a reference to Laurent Tailhade, the previous poet with whom Wilfred had been smitten.)

At first Wilfred appeared to Sassoon merely as a promising minor poet, with a sheaf of lyrical poems that seemed now, in the fourth year of the war, to be out of tune with reality and mired in

---

\* **Dreamers**

> Soldiers are citizens of death's grey land,
>> Drawing no dividends from time's tomorrows. . . .
> I see them in foul dug-outs, gnawed by rats,
>> And in the ruined trenches, lashed by rain,
> Dreaming of things they did with balls and bats,
>> And mocked by hopeless longing to regain
> Bank holidays, and picture-shows, and spats,
>> And going to the office in the train.

The last two lines somehow bridge war poetry like that of Sassoon with the modernist poetry of T. S. Eliot. Indeed, the spats are more than worthy of Eliot!

the past. Nor did Wilfred show evidence of the facile genius of Rupert Brooke, whose poems flowed like music, apparently written without effort, and yet had the solid power of being based on his own experiences. Wilfred had neither the tempestuous love affairs nor the voyage to the South Pacific as material to fall back on. His life experiences were undramatic as inspirations for poetry, and yet gradually Sassoon became convinced that he was in the presence of genius. The suspicion was confirmed when he read an early draft of "Anthem for Doomed Youth," the most famous poem that would come out of the war, by far and away the most anthologized.

Sassoon's changes to the poem are relatively minor, but significant, and it is easy to see how much Wilfred owed his new friend. Originally called "Anthem for Dead Youth," the poem's early draft is powerful but lacks the concentrated punch of the final version.

What passing-bells for you who die in herds?
  —Only the long monotonous [anger] of the guns!
And only the stuttering rifles' rattled words
  Can patter out your hasty orisons.
No wreaths for you, nor balms, nor stately choirs;
  Nor any voice of mourning, save our shells,
And bugles calling for you from your shires,
  Saddening the twilight. These are our farewells.

What candles may we hold to speed you all?
Not in the hands of boys, but in their eyes
Shall shine the lights of your goodbyes.
The pallor of girls' brows must be your pall;
Your flowers: the tenderness of comrades' minds;
And each slow dusk, a drawing down of blinds.

The last line remains moving, but the focus of the draft is outward ("you who die in herds"). Although the form is there, the poem seems disjointed. Its familiar final form, with major changes Sassoon made underlined, is incomparably stronger.

## Anthem for <u>Doomed</u> Youth

What passing bells for those who die as cattle?
—Only the monstrous anger of the guns
Only the stuttering rifles' rapid rattle
Can patter out their hasty orisons.
No mockeries for them, <u>nor</u> prayers, <u>nor</u> bells,
    Nor any voice of mourning save the choirs
The shrill <u>demented</u> choirs of wailing shells;
    And bugles calling <u>for them from sad shires</u>.

What candles may be held to speed them all?
    Not in the hands of boys, but in their eyes
Shall shine the holy glimmers of goodbyes.
The pallor of girls' brows shall be their pall,
Their flowers the tenderness of patient minds,
And each slow dusk a drawing down of blinds.

The last line is indeed the valedictory that epitomizes the sadness that followed the war, as the British mourned the loss of more than 750,000 men. Wilfred's war poems lack the ferocious anger and sarcasm of Sassoon's; he was perceptive enough to realize that and wrote of himself, "My subject is War and the pity of War. The poetry is in the pity." It is appropriate then that his words are incised on the black slate slab memorializing the war poets of the First World War in the Poet's Corner of Westminster Abbey.

It should not be imagined that the relationship between the two men was all one way. Sassoon recognized in Wilfred a greater poet than himself, but his own poetry also improved as the two men worked together. Still, it was Sassoon who remained in Wilfred's eyes "the great man," an impression no doubt influenced by class. Wilfred managed to persuade Sassoon to let him publish one of his poems in *The Hydra*, alongside an unsigned one of his own. It was surely the growing friendship between the two men that gave Wilfred the confidence to go out in company in Edinburgh and even to sit for his portrait, both in a charcoal drawing and a watercolor.* Although Sassoon warned Wilfred not to publish his poems too soon, he nevertheless went out of his way to bring the younger man's name to the attention of his set, both those involved in poetry and the smaller world of gay friends, many of whom were influential in the arts.

In mid-October, Sassoon's friend and fellow Royal Welch Fusiliers officer, Robert Graves, arrived for a brief visit. Graves bridged both worlds; he was a published poet *and* an active homosexual. (Although he would soon shock Sassoon by falling in love with a young woman, whom he would eventually marry, and go on to marry twice and father eight children.) Graves was one of those men who fill up a lot of space, both physically and psychically. More than that, he had reached the rank of captain, unusually for a young officer who was not a regular soldier, with three pips on his sleeve to Wilfred's one. He was fiercely opinionated, even argumentative on almost every subject under the sun. He both impressed and frightened Wilfred, whose ambivalent reaction to Graves and his sense of class envy are evident in his letter to his mother about the meeting.

> *He [Graves] is a big, rather plain fellow, the last man on earth apparently capable of the extraordinary, delicate fancies in his books. . . . No doubt he thought me a slacker sort of sub. S. S. [substitute Siegfried Sassoon] when they were together showed him my longish war-piece 'Disabled' (you haven't seen it) & it seems Graves was mightily impressed, and considers me a kind of* Find*! ! No thanks, Captain Graves! I'll find myself in due time.*

There is a slight tone of resentment in the letter. Wilfred may have been unhappy at having to share Sassoon with a poet whose work had already been published, or he may have felt that Graves was patronizing him. In fact, Wilfred was at the height of his powers. The poem that had impressed Graves is one of Wilfred's sharpest, and he had just completed his "gas poem," "Dulce et Decorum

---

* Unfortunately, Wilfred's mother disliked both and destroyed them after his death.

Est," which many consider the final statement on the sacrifice of a whole generation in the mud and blood of Flanders.

Bent double, like old beggars under sacks,
Knock-kneed, coughing like hags, we cursed through sludge,
Till on the haunting flares we turned our backs,
And towards our distant rest began to trudge,
Men marched asleep. Many had lost their boots,
But limped on, blood-shod. All were lame, all blind;
Drunk with fatigue; deaf even to the hoots
Of gas-shells dropping softly behind.

Gas! GAS! Quick, boys!—an ecstasy of fumbling
Fitting the clumsy helmets just in time,
But someone still was yelling out and stumbling
And flound'ing like a man in fire or lime—
Dim through the misty panes and thick green light,
As under a green sea, I saw him drowning.

In all my dreams before my helpless sight,
He plunges at me, guttering, choking, drowning.

If in some smothering dream, you too could pace
Behind the wagon that we flung him in,
And watch the white eyes writhing in his face,
His hanging face, like a devil's sick of sin;
If you could hear, at every jolt, the blood
Come gargling from the froth-corrupted lungs,
Obscene as cancer, bitter as the cud
Of vile, incurable sores on innocent tongues,—
My friend, you would not tell with such high zest
To children ardent for some desperate glory,
The old Lie: *Dulce et decorum est.*
*Pro patria mori.*

This turned out to be an enormously productive period for Wilfred, given the daily presence of a friend and fellow poet who urged him on. He was simply happy to have a sounding board for his poems other than his mother, although in the end it was still she that he sought most to please. He wrote six poems in one burst, including one of his strongest, about death, which begins: "Out there, we've walked quite friendly up to Death,— / Sat down and eaten with him, cool and bland."

To his mother, Owen described his new life at Craiglockhart, where he read his poems aloud "over a private tea" in Sassoon's room. Sassoon had at last managed to get a room to himself, thanks to Rivers. Owens also passed on the news that Sassoon had changed his mind and now thought Owen should get his manuscripts typed up for submission to a publisher. It is hard not to see this as the happiest time of Owen's life. He was relieved of responsibilities and was immensely productive. His work was being appreciated and taken seriously, if only by one person, and he was in love. His brother Harold scoured his letters so thoroughly after his death that it is impossible to tell whether Owen had a physical relationship with Sassoon,* but in every other respect it was the closest he would ever come to a love affair. "Spent all day [with Sassoon] yesterday," he wrote his mother ecstatically. "Breakfast, Lunch, Tea & Dinner."

It could not last. Wilfred was examined at the end of October and had no doubt that the medical board would find him fit for duty. His symptoms were under control, and his nightmares were less frequent, perhaps because he had channeled them into his poems. The need for young officers was greater than ever. In France, Haig's autumn campaign was eating up lives at a furious rate, and the outlook for the Allies had never seemed darker. The Russian collapse was now beyond repair or doubt, and the Battle of Caporetto cost the Italians over 300,000 casualties plus almost as many captured, a rout masterfully portrayed by Ernest Hemingway in *A Farewell to Arms*. The arrival of the Americans in force was delayed—it takes time to train and equip a whole army from scratch—while everywhere Germany and Austro-Hungary seemed stronger. Only in the

---

* The jury is still out on this subject and probably always will be.

Middle East was there a ray of hope as General Allenby's army captured Jerusalem, the first sign of the Ottoman collapse. Everybody was needed at the front, no matter how frail or damaged.

Wilfred and Sassoon spent their last evening together at the Scottish Conservative Club in Edinburgh, eating a good dinner, drinking "a noble bottle of Burgundy" and laughing uproariously over a volume of especially bad poetry. Sassoon had given Wilfred, as a parting gift, a thick envelope, which he opened in the club while waiting to take the midnight train. It contained a ten-pound note* and a letter of introduction to Robert Ross in London, the friend, editor, and devoted defender of Oscar Wilde and a literary luminary almost as well connected and admired as Edward Marsh. Ross was a friend of H. G. Wells, Arnold Bennett, and Osbert Sitwell, as well as a central figure in the homosexual literary and social world.

Sassoon must have hesitated before including the ten-pound note for fear it might be taken as an insult, but Wilfred responded with genuine gratitude.

> *Know that since mid-September, when you still regarded me*
> *as a tiresome little knocker on your door I held you as Keats*
> *+ Christ + Elijah + my Colonel + my father-confessor +*
> *Amenophis IV in profile. . . . I love you, dispassionately, so*
> *much, so <u>very</u> much, dear Fellow, that the blasting little smile*
> *you wear on reading this can't hurt me in the least. . . . And you*
> *have <u>fixed</u> my life—however short. I was always a mad comet;*
> *but you have fixed me. I spun around you a satellite for a month,*
> *but I shall swing out soon, a dark star in the orbit where you*
> *will blaze.*

This passage was prophetic, Wilfred Owen would soon outshine all other English First World War poets, the spokesman for a martyred generation. He ended his letter with a phrase he had used ear-

---

* To put this in perspective that would be the equivalent in buying power of almost $1,400 today.

lier to his mother to describe his relationship with Sassoon: "[We] knew we loved each other as no men love for long."

SASSOON'S LETTER TO ROBERT ROSS bore instant fruit. Wilfred and Ross became friends at their first dinner together, and Ross introduced the younger man to Wells and Bennett, both of whom would contribute to making his name better known. Soon enough he was back in the Manchester Regiment, with the Fifth (Reserve) Battalion. It was stationed in seaside Scarborough, which he had sometimes visited on summer holidays as a child, and where the officers lived in two hotels. Rather to his surprise, Wilfred was not sent to France immediately but was put in command of a "dozen batmen, 4 Mess Orderlies, 4 Buglers, the Cook (a fat woman of great skill,) two female kitcheners, and various charwomen!" His duty was to make things go smoothly for the seventy officers who lived there, a role somewhere between that of a majordomo and a butler.

He and his commanding officer disliked each other at first sight, but otherwise Wilfred seems to have been content with his humble domestic role, although he told his mother, not altogether humorously, that he lived in terror of the colonel's bath water being too cold or his dinner plate too hot. Wilfred had seen enough service in the trenches not to feel humiliated dealing with officers' complaints about the food, the servants, or the number of newspapers in the lounge. He still hoped for a second pip and a Military Cross to validate his combat experience and to justify the searing images in his poems. But for the moment he was content to live in safety in Scarborough, with time enough to write poetry.

More important, it was less than four hours by train to London, so he would eventually be able to resume his life and friendships in the literary world. In the meantime, he passed his spare time in Scarborough shopping for antique furniture and silver for his mother. (He had a discriminating eye.) Sassoon also passed as fit for active service and rejoined his battalion in Ireland, where the British military presence had been increased since the abortive Easter Rising of 1916. That return to arms would eventually take him to Palestine, then back to the Western Front, where he would be wounded by a bullet to the head.

Correspondence between Owen and Sassoon was not as frequent as one might have supposed, although Harold Owen may have destroyed some of the letters. But Wilfred was overjoyed to receive a letter from Robert Graves, to whom Sassoon had shown some more of Owen's poems. "Puff out your chest a little, Owen, & be big—for you've more right than most of us," Graves wrote. Curiously, Owen was swiftly acquiring a reputation as one of the most important soldier poets of his generation, although only a few of his poems had been published. It did not matter, because Harold Monro, Wells, Bennett, Sassoon, and Graves were already talking him up, so that a certain glow now attached to his name. Graves ended his letter with an exhortation: "You must help S.S. and R.N. and R.G. to revolutionize English poetry—so outlive this war."*

Wilfred mentioned that to his mother, in a letter written on the last day of 1917: "I go out of this year a Poet, my dear Mother, as which I did not enter it. I am held peer by the Georgians, I am a poet's poet. I am started. The tugs have left me, I feel the great swelling of the open sea taking my galleon." Almost immediately it began to come true. Invited to Robert Graves's wedding—which Sassoon did not attend out of pique that the bridegroom was deserting the homosexual world for marriage to a beautiful young feminist†—Wilfred was introduced to Edward Marsh, Sir Max Beerbohm, and other luminaries as "Owen, the poet," rather than as Second Lieutenant Owen. Shortly afterward *The Nation* published one of his poems, for which he received the first money he had ever been paid for a poem, a check for two guineas (forty-two shillings), a modest milestone.

He was indeed for the moment "a poet's poet," his fellow poets recognizing his budding genius, and he sensed that he was on the brink of a career. He buckled down to his somewhat humdrum job

---

* Siegfried Sassoon, Robert Nichols, and Robert Graves. Nichols is the least remembered of the three, but unlike Wilfred Owen he was already published. He is one of the sixteen war poets listed on the memorial in Poets' Corner, in Westminster Abbey.

† Nancy Nicholson was eighteen years old and attended her own wedding in a rage because she had not hitherto read the wedding vow, which contained the word *obey*.

of supervising the staff, keeping track of the liquor and cigarettes in the officers' bar, and drawing up the mess bills of officers who had been selected to go to France. There the new team of Field Marshal von Hindenburg and General Ludendorff were about to launch the last and most powerful German offensive, intended to cut off and crush the British forces in Flanders before American troops arrived in quantity. The Germans had withdrawn fifty divisions from the Eastern Front, as Russian resistance collapsed after the Bolshevik Revolution, and stationed them in the west. It was in the nature of a last, desperate gamble, despite the ponderous self-confidence of Hindenburg and Ludendorff. They nevertheless prudently named the battle the Kaiserschlacht, the Kaiser's Battle, thus assigning the blame, if it failed, to the kaiser rather than to themselves. The battle would rage from March to July 1918 and cost the Germans over 600,000 casualties, and the Allies over 800,000. It briefly brought Germany closer to victory than at any other moment in the war, despite the impending collapse of its Austro-Hungarian and Ottoman allies.

Returning to the front hung around Wilfred's neck like an albatross unless the war ended suddenly—he was dealing all day with officers facing the same grim future. Some of the new friends Sassoon and Robert Ross had introduced him to tried to find a secure place for him in the War Office or training troops. Wilfred did not prevent them, but neither did he encourage them. At some level he was reconciled to his future, although determined to enjoy what little pleasure Scarborough had to offer as long as possible. He was now in charge of a little café that had been opened for Other Ranks as well as running a hotel for seventy officers. As a result, he was endlessly busy and found it hard to get leave, perhaps a reflection of his commanding officer's dislike of him. "I suppose I may get leave in a fortnight or so," he wrote to his mother (he did not), "but there is a new rumor of my going to a Command Depot; which is where most Light Duty Officers 'end up,' doing physical drill, to fit them for serious warfare." One of the battalion's patrols, he added, had shot a man suspected of being a spy during the night, although why the Germans would have landed somebody to spy on Scarborough, where the Fifth (Reserve) Battalion of the Manchester Regiment was doing nothing more interesting than endless parade ground drilling, seems mysterious. For once Wilfred's prediction was correct. In mid-March he was ordered to report to the Northern Command Depot in Ripon, Yorkshire, from which he sent a plaintive postcard: "An awful Camp—huts, dirty blankets—in fact WAR once more. Farewell Books, Sonnets, Letters, friends, fires, oysters, antique-shops. Training again!"

He fell mysteriously ill, then recovered just as mysteriously. Most of the officers in his hut, he complained, were recently commissioned NCOs and fearful snobs, but he finally found a room he could rent in a cottage that was a five-minute walk from the camp. There he had the privacy to write and revise his poetry. His spirits were not raised by events in France, where the great German offensive had begun on a fifty-mile front, wiping out the gains that the British had made with such great losses in 1917, taking back the ground around where Wilfred had fought and suffered. British losses were enormous. Over 100,000 men were captured in the sweeping German advance. In Beaumont Hamel, "which already in 1916 was cobbled with skulls" and which Wilfred knew all too well, British soldiers were dying again in masses. Companies of underage boys were being sent the front, as well as "officers who had been wounded over and over again." He was quite aware that his turn must come very soon. The Germans pushed on relentlessly, despite their own severe losses, coming close enough to Paris to hit it with a long-range gun, shaking French morale as nothing had since 1914.

Against all odds, Wilfred finally got leave to spend two days in London, staying in the flat above that of Robert Ross. A poem of his had just won a prize in *The Bookman*—recognition was coming at last. He had more invitations to lunch and dinner than he could manage. Ross encouraged him to have his poems typed for submission to the publisher William Heinemann, and he introduced him to Captain Osbert Sitwell, a sympathetic member of the cultural establishment, and to Captain Sir Charles Scott Moncrieff, the future translator of Proust's *À la recherche du temps perdu*. Wilfred paid a visit to Scott Moncrieff at the War Office, to which he had been posted after receiving serious wounds. He and Scott Moncrieff may have briefly been lovers, and Scott Moncrieff did his best to find him a home posting as an instructor, but the need for officers at the front was simply too urgent. Wilfred felt "the first flickers of the limelight" as magazine editors at last sought his poetry, but he was conscious that he would very soon be sent back to the fighting.

In its inscrutable way, the army sent Wilfred back to Scarborough first, where he lived uncomfortably in a tent. By some miracle, he managed not to fall victim to the first wave of the Spanish flu that would take between 25 million and 50 million lives worldwide as the war ground on remorselessly toward its end.

In Scarborough, he learned that Siegfried Sassoon had been wounded, his battalion having been shipped from Palestine to Marseilles, then back to the front line in France.

SASSOON'S RETURN TO ACTIVE SOLDIERING had been even more inevitable than Owen's—after all, he had never been ill. He had simply proclaimed his opposition to the way the war was being fought and had been shunted off to Craiglockhart to shut him up. Rivers understood that Sassoon could not sit the war out in safety and adroitly arranged for the medical board to send him back to the Royal Welch Fusiliers. After a brief spot of leave, Sassoon returned to the RWF depot at Litherland, on the outskirts of Liverpool, where he slipped effortlessly back into the military routine. None of his fellow officers seem to have begrudged him his four months at Craiglockhart, or objected to the protest that had sent him there. He was received back with heartiness mixed with embarrassment, caused more by his getting his name in the news than anything else. The bulk of the Third Battalion of the RWF was in Limerick, part of the large garrison that was holding down Ireland in the wake of the Easter Rising in 1916, following which ninety people (including one woman) were condemned to death by court-martial, fifteen of them executed by a firing squad.

After another leave of twelve days, Sassoon joined the battalion in Limerick, saw a few familiar faces, and settled down to the peaceful routines of square-bashing, or drilling troops. He had never been in Ireland before and found it peaceful, lush, and friendly. He spent much of his time in the gentlemanly pursuit of fox hunting and enjoyed splendid teas with cold salmon and snipe. As a bold rider and keen fox-hunter, he was in his element. His problem was that he wanted to go back overseas (Ireland still counted as part of the United Kingdom) and into action. But despite several attempts to get himself posted to the Second Battalion of the RWF at the front in France, he was eventually posted to the 25th Battalion, in Palestine.

Every regiment of the British Army had ballooned in size during the war. The RWF had had three battalions in 1914 but grew to include no fewer than thirty-nine by 1918. It was typical of Sassoon to want to be back with the more prestigious First or Second Battalion, in both of which he had friends, and both of which were in action. He was not eager to die, but he yearned for the excitement and camaraderie of combat and feared that Palestine would provide neither.

He was seen off at the station by his friend Robert Ross and surrendered himself to the inevitable boredom and delays of army traveling, an interminable 1,466 miles, squeezed into a compartment with three other junior officers and all their kit. Like many other English poets, he luxuriated at his first sight of olive trees, the dusty hills, a "sunlit and joyous" Mediterranean landscape so different from his own.

By the time he spent a few days in a rest camp and boarded a ship bound for Alexandria, some of the excitement was wearing off. He found most of his fellow officers infuriating, with their card games, their drinking, and their tendency to play kitschy popular songs on the gramophone over and over again. Along the way, his watch was stolen, and his spirits sank until he took a train across the Suez Canal and traveled north along the coastline into the Judean hills. There the flowers and wildlife—combined with being in the Jewish heartland at last, the mysterious and exotic East from which the Sassoon family had so recently emerged—restored his equilibrium. His interest in the biblical landscape remained that of an English gentleman, however, curious but detached. He had been brought up as a Christian, having been cursed even before his birth by his maternal grandmother because of his father's apostasy, and while he retained a cordial relationship with many members of his father's family in adulthood—his Jewish aunt left him a considerable fortune—he had no interest in or curiosity about their religion or his own. (He would convert from Anglicanism to Catholicism toward the end of his life.) He could joke about it—when lending money to Robert Graves, he wrote, "Why keep a jewish friend unless you can bleed him?"—but it was not something he felt deeply about or that occupied his attention.

Unfortunately, Siegfried had missed the taking of Jerusalem by two months, and by the time he reached his battalion, they were engaged in nothing more exciting than repairing roads. A keen observer of nature, some of his best writing is about the trees and birds of the Judean hills north of Jerusalem. Long hikes and bird watching were his only relief to profoundly monotonous days—sweltering hot by day, freezing cold at night—apart from reading *War and Peace*, a copy of which he had bought, of all places, in Port Saïd, then the world's center for English-language pornography.

He was saved by another of those unexpected and mystifying moves with which military life is punctuated when his battalion was ordered back to France. Maps of Palestine were handed in, and tropical kit was canceled. The battalion marched down the endless, dusty roads it had been repairing back to Alexandria, for a spell in another deadly, boring transit camp in the desert. Finally it boarded a troop ship bound for Marseilles. It was a cheerless voyage on a British P&O liner, on the decks of which the sleeping soldiers wrapped in their blankets reminded Sassoon of the dead. After two days and nights in another transit camp outside Marseilles, the battalion was loaded into a train for three days and nights, then unloaded in the French countryside with the familiar rumble of heavy guns firing in the distance.

Because Sassoon's battalion had been in the Middle East since 1915, the men would have to be retrained for trench warfare. He himself would have to relearn much of what he knew after so many months away from the front. The one bright spot was that despite the reluctance of Heinemann to include some of the more biting war poems, Sassoon's second volume, *Counter-Attack*, had just been published, adding to the controversy that had surrounded him ever since his declaration. Heinemann feared that the book would be prosecuted under DORA, the Defense of the Realm Act, but typical of the muddled British view of censorship, no attempt was made to suppress it. Edward Marsh was certain that none of the more provocative poems should be removed from it, while at the same time he was concerned that it might give comfort to the enemy. The collection of thirty-nine poems was widely reviewed—Sassoon's name was in print even more often than when he had staged his protest—and the reactions ranged from shocked outrage to the rather odd suggestion that he be made a Knight of the Garter.

More than a month after he sailed from Alexandria, he was back at the front, only a few miles from where he had been wounded in April 1917. In temporary command of a company, and recently promoted to acting captain, Sassoon drove himself hard to look after his men. His company was his family, his children, "the smartest turn-out you ever saw," he wrote proudly to Graves, adding tellingly, "(and they *did it all for me* and no one else)." His pride in them was fierce and touching. His platoon commanders, NCOs, and men seem to have genuinely admired him. Despite the nagging guilt that he was going to lead many of them to their deaths, he was happy.

The stretch of front line that his battalion was taking over from the First East Lancashires was dismaying. The rapid German advance had uprooted the British from the elaborate, carefully dug, in-depth trench systems of 1916 and 1917 into something more approaching open warfare. It had proved impossible to dig a deep trench in the marshy ground around Saint-Venant in the Pas-de-Calais near the Belgian border, so the line was hardly more than a wet furrow dug in the mud of a field. "Breastworks" of mud-filled sandbags linked one shell hole to the next. His company's field-of-fire was obscured by a healthy crop of corn, and nothing more than a thin, hastily planted band of barbed wire was in place to slow down a German attack—and the German trench line lay only one hundred yards away. Despite his exhilaration at being back in action, it did not fill Sassoon with confidence.

He placed his company headquarters in a shallow dugout hollowed into the side of a shell hole. On the first night, he decided to make a personal reconnaissance of no-man's-land, taking one junior officer and a few NCOs with him. Armed with his pistol, several grenades in his pockets, and a stout knobkerrie, he led them on a long crawl through the corn without incident. Then having taken them back to the headquarters dugout, he went out again on his own and actually reached the German front line undetected. He crawled back, having taken a German stick grenade from their front trench. This was clearly against orders, since company commanders were not supposed to be waging their own private war, but it was also a sign of heady overconfidence.

Siegfried had acquired a reputation for personal bravery in 1916 and 1917, which he was eager to maintain. It had won him a Military Cross, but it was also a form of inebriation: a soldier can get as drunk on bravery as he can on liquor. To use a modern expression, he was high on excitement. He saw with heightened, almost surreal clarity of vision the stern, impassive faces of two of his best men, a lance-corporal aiming his Lewis light machine gun, and Sergeant "Wickham," an older man who had won both the Distinguished Combat Medal and the Military Medal, and who represented for Siegfried all that was best about British regular NCOs.* Wickham was almost unnaturally keen and ambitious, as well as full of wisdom about the army, from a career that went back to the Boer War.

For several nights Siegfried was prevented from patrolling by constant German shelling, possibly provoked by his own patrol in no-man's-land—the First East Lancashires had left well enough alone there. He received a direct hit on top of his dugout, which fortunately for him failed to explode. But on the night of July 12, infuriated by a burst of shellfire that had killed the pack animals bringing up the company's rations, he decided to go out again. He was in an exhausted, or perhaps overexcited state, but he was determined to locate the exact position of a German machine gun and eliminate it if possible. His patrol found it slow going, crawling in

---

* He named the sergeant "Wickham" in *Sherston's Progress,* the third volume of his autobiographical novel. In a regiment like the RWF, a high standard for bravery was taken for granted. It was rare for a sergeant there to be awarded both a Distinguished Combat Medal (second only to the Victoria Cross) *and* a Military Medal.

the pitch dark, and by the time they got back to their own line, dawn was breaking.

Siegfried had been crawling on his belly for hours. As he approached his own front line, he stood up to stretch and removed his steel helmet. The corn-covered swales, at this point, hid him from the sight of the Germans. He was, however, plainly visible from his own front line, silhouetted against the breaking dawn, and had taken off his helmet, the shape of which would have shown that he was British. This was the moment when sentries were at their most alert, or most nervous, since attacks usually started at first light. Mistaken for a German, Siegfried was hit by a bullet fired from his own front line.

"A second later I was down again, half stunned by a terrible blow on the head," is how he described it. "It seemed to me that there was a very large hole in the right side of my skull." Blood poured into his eyes (head wounds are notoriously bloody), blinding him. He assumed he was dying, but luckily for him, his cool-headed corporal examined the wound and wiped it clean. The bullet had hit Siegfried a glancing blow, opening a terrible gash, but it had not penetrated the skull.

Ever since that morning, there has been intense speculation on the subject of who shot Siegfried Sassoon. He himself claimed it was the overzealous Sergeant Wickham, hoping to add a bar to his Military Medal, but that seems unlikely. Wickham was a cool customer and a good shot; at such a close range, he would have been unlikely to miss killing Sassoon. Others have suggested, more plausibly, that Sergeant Wickham noticed a nervous young sentry aiming for Sassoon and knocked his rifle sideways with his elbow, thus saving Sassoon's life. Still others believed that the whole incident was a failed attempt by the government or the War Office to assassinate Sassoon, but this too seems unlikely. Nothing suggests that anyone in the British government wanted Sassoon dead. After all, his poetry was not affecting British morale—indeed Winston Churchill, the minister of munitions, would soon offer Siegfried a job at the ministry, which he would hardly have done had the government been plotting to eliminate him or been worried about his poetry.

Siegfried managed to regain his feet and walk back to battalion headquarters, followed by the corporal carrying his helmet. He was chatty and determined to return to his company shortly, but as he was moved by ambulance from one level of medical care to the next, it became increasingly obvious that the wound had caused more damage than he had assumed. He was irrationally loquacious and unable to sleep. He could not decide whether to go back to his company or allow the medical system to return him to England. At the casualty clearing station, he was badly shaken by the presence of several officers more badly wounded than himself, including one whose jaw had been blown off by a grenade and whose tongue had been tied forward so as to prevent him from choking on it. "The war had gagged him—smashed him—and other people looked at him and tried to forget what they'd seen," Siegfried wrote.

The sight and sound of the disfigured man seems to have created in Siegfried's mind an unbearable ambivalence between shame at having suffered less than the man had and at abandoning his men and wild desire to put the war behind him at last and get on with his life. He had, as it were, given the war one last chance to kill him, and it had failed. The decision about what to do was taken out of his hands in Boulogne, when an infection set in, causing him to be evacuated to a hospital in London. There he was visited by Churchill's mother, Lady Randolph Churchill, and by two members of the royal family. But the visit that buoyed him the most was from Captain Rivers, his doctor at Craiglockhart. Rivers seems to have persuaded Siegfried that he had already done his best for his men, that going back to die for them would be pointless, and that it was now his duty to get on with his life and put his talents to good use.

Now that he was back in England, Siegfried had the leisure to look through the reviews of *Counter-Attack*. Seldom has any short collection of poems been so extensively reviewed. Heinemann had already been through three printings and made its author into a celebrity even among people who did not normally read poetry. The title poem of the collection was a searing picture of the war, in all its cruelty, futility, and violence. "He has told the truth about the war," one reviewer stated bluntly and accurately.

We'd gained our first objective hours before
While dawn broke like a face with blinking eyes,
Pallid, unshaved and thirsty, blind with smoke.
Things seemed all right at first. We held their line,
With bombers posted, Lewis guns well-placed,
And clink of shovels deepening the shallow trench.
The place was rotten with dead; green clumsy legs
High-booted, sprawled and grovelled along the saps
And trunks, face downward in the sucking mud,
Wallowed like trodden sand-bags, loosely filled;
And naked sodden buttocks, mats of hair,
Bulged, clotted heads, sleeping in the plastering slime.
And then the rain began,—the jolly old rain!

A yawning soldier knelt against the bank,
Staring across the morning, blear with fog;
He wondered when the Allemands would get busy;
And then, of course, they started with five-nines
Traversing, sure as fate, and never a dud. . . .

He crouched and flinched, dizzy with galloping fear,
Sick for escape,—loathing the strangled horror
And butchered, frantic gestures of the dead. . . .
Then the haze lifted. Bombing on the right
Down the old sap: machine-guns on the left;
And stumbling figures looming out in front.
"O Christ, they're coming at us!" Bullets spat,
And he remembered his rifle . . . rapid fire . . .
And started blazing wildly . . . then a bang
Crumpled and spun him sideways, knocked him out
To grunt and wiggle—none heeded him; he choked
And fought the flapping wings of smothering gloom,
Lost in a blurred confusion of yells and groans . . .

Down, and down, and down, he sank and drowned,
Bleeding to death. The counter-attack had failed.

"The jolly old rain!" is a perfect Sassoon touch, a sudden intrusion of English cheerfulness, dropped into a mounting description of horrors, reaching a climax with a blunt last sentence that epitomizes the futility of the battlefield.

The floodgates had indeed opened, and Siegfried was deluged with visitors, including Lady Ottoline Morrell, still in pursuit of him, much to his annoyance. He diagnosed his own state as "a combination of sex-repression, war-weariness, vanity and pride—with a little 'decent feeling,' and a touch of nerves thrown in." This was all true enough, but the army wanted something a little more definite, so once he was released from hospital, he would be obliged to revisit Craiglockhart so Rivers could have him examined by a medical board again. Fortunately, there was little danger at this point that he would be returned to the front.

PERHAPS MOST IMPORTANT, Siegfried saw Wilfred Owen one last time. He had urged Wilfred to find a job somewhere at home, rather than go back to the front, but one after the other, the jobs had fallen through. Wilfred did not have Siegfried's network of important friends, and perhaps too he *needed* to go back again, to prove to himself and to others that he had never been a coward. They met at a lavish tea party and harpsichord concert given in London by Osbert Sitwell, surely the best-connected and wealthiest of poets, who had served in the trenches at Ypres. They cannot have had much opportunity to talk, Wilfred was in any case entranced by the music, but he walked Siegfried back to the hospital afterward, and it may have been on this occasion that Siegfried promised to stab him in the leg if he went back to the front. There was by then no possibility of Wilfred's *not* being sent into action, as he must have known, but may not have wanted to tell Siegfried.

Waiting at Folkstone to board a troop ship bound for Boulogne, Wilfred took a swim in the Channel with a boy from Harrow School, "of superb intellect & refinement," he wrote with undisguised admiration; "intellect because he detests the war more than Germans, and refinement because of the way he spoke of my going away. . . . And now I go among cattle to be a cattle-driver." The next day he wrote Siegfried from Boulogne that he was "in hasty retreat towards the Front" and advised him not to go to the trouble of buying a dagger with which to stab him in the leg.

A week later he was on his way to the Second Battalion of the Manchester Regiment, pausing for a few days in the ruins of Amiens, where he was billeted in a gutted house without windows and spent a good deal of time writing letters in the Australian YMCA hut. He did not have to make the journey up to the Second Battalion, for it came back to Amiens for a "rest" before going back to the front—a rest that consisted of endless, training for open warfare. Wilfred was pleased that many of the men remembered him, and he made the acquaintance of the battalion officers. He liked his company commander, something of a hero, a former honors student of English literature with a Military Cross and bar,* as well as the adjutant and the colonel, an agreeable "non-ferocious" gentleman. He was wary of the second-in-command, a particularly ferocious major seconded from the Irish Guards who had been wounded ten times and was "the most arrant utterly soldierly soldier," he had ever come across. Wilfred described him without admiration as "bold, robust, dashing, unscrupulous, cruel, jovial, immoral, vast-chested, handsome-headed, of free, coarse speech."

Wilfred was given command of a platoon and due to his seniority was made second-in-command of the company, a position of considerable responsibility. Nobody seemed to remember or to have heard of his "loss of nerve" in April 1917, or perhaps they simply overlooked it. To men in action, anything that had happened over a year ago was already in the distant past. Wilfred himself was a little contemptuous of his fellow second lieutenants, describing them to his mother as "quite temporary gentlemen." For as the supply of public school graduates ran out, the army was indeed combing through Other Ranks for NCOs to select for a commission.

Although Wilfred could not have known it, the Second Manches-

---

* A bar indicates the award of the same medal twice.

ters were about to become a part of the bloody, final battle of the war. Field Marshal Haig had often promised a big push, to drive the Germans out of their trench system and resume open warfare, but this time it was actually going to happen. Behind the scenes, great events were unfolding. In the Middle East General Allenby, with the help of T. E. Lawrence's Arab desert army, had at last taken Damascus, the Ottoman Empire was crumbling fast, and negotiations for its surrender were beginning. The Austro-Hungarian Empire was breaking apart, and the Austrian government was seeking from President Woodrow Wilson the terms for an armistice. Only Germany among the three Central Powers was still fighting, despite the determination of the new German chancellor, Prince Max von Baden, to seek an armistice before widespread social unrest brought an end to the monarchy.

A great offensive by the Allies, Great Britain, France, and the United States was intended to drive the Germans out of the Hindenburg Line and end the war. On September 28 Wilfred's battalion moved forward to play its part. Wilfred urged his mother to read the newspapers carefully over the next few days if she wanted to know what he was doing. It was as much of a warning as he could give her that he was going into battle.

The area in front of the Second Manchesters was challenging, despite one of the biggest artillery and gas bombardments of the war. The trenches of the Hindenburg Line were deep and cunningly situated. Belts of wire and broad, concrete blockhouses protected German machine guns from anything except a direct hit, while deep canals were exposed to German rifle and machine-gun fire. For the first couple of days, the Second Manchesters were in the rear and took minimal casualties, but on October 1 they moved to the front, and Wilfred led his platoon into action at close quarters. His soldier-servant Jones was badly wounded in the head and lay for a time with his head against Wilfred's shoulder as they both took shelter under heavy fire. The young man was bleeding profusely but was still alive.

"Can you photograph the crimson-hot iron as it cools from the smelting?" Wilfred asked Sassoon a few days later, describing the boy's blood as it soaked his shoulder. The incident seems to have sparked off a rage in Wilfred—he may have been fond of the boy—

and transformed him into a hero. In Wilfred's own words, he "lost all [his] earthly faculties and fought like an angel," immune to fear and danger.

The company commander had been hit, so Wilfred took over, leaving the wounded behind to be picked up by stretcher-bearers. The company's sergeant-major was hit too, so Wilfred appointed a "seraphic" young lance-corporal as his acting sergeant-major, and led what remained of the company up the hill in front of them with such determination that the German machine-gunners facing him surrendered or ran. He took "scores" of prisoners and, demonstrating cool-headed, skilled marksmanship, stopped to shoot and kill a German with his revolver from a distance of thirty yards, a remarkable shot. He then fought off a German counterattack, and when the next one came, he turned one of the machine guns he had captured on them. With his "seraphic" acting sergeant-major acting as his loader, he kept on firing from a completely exposed position in full view of the enemy and his own battalion, to the amazement of both sides.

Wilfred would afterward be praised for his "great coolness throughout" and be awarded an immediate Military Cross,* for "conspicuous gallantry and devotion to duty." He had been mildly envious of his friend Siegfried's Military Cross and felt that being awarded one himself would not only validate his anti-war poems but finally refute the allegation of his nervous breakdown under fire. Now he had his own decoration. He had not only behaved gallantly, but demonstrated a high standard of leadership, as well as resourcefulness under difficult circumstances. "The War is nearing an end," he wrote his mother, but if anything the fighting went on, fiercer than ever.

He did not have time to write again until October 4 or 5, he wasn't sure which. On October 8, he was able to write to his mother more coherently about the battle. "All one day we could not move from a small trench, though hour by hour the wounded were groaning just outside. Three stretcher-bearers who got up

---

* Most decorations are recommended but not confirmed until reviewed by a higher authority at a later date. But a commanding officer has the right to make an *immediate* award in cases of singular bravery that are beyond dispute.

were hit, one after one. I had to order no one to show himself after that, but remembering my own duty. . . . I scrambled out myself & felt an exhilaration in baffling the Machine Guns by quick bounds from cover to cover." To Siegfried, he wrote more frankly, noting humorously that he desired "no more exposed flanks of any sort for a long time," which may or may not imply that he and Siegfried had had sex together.

By now, rumors of peace talks were rife on both sides. Even General Ludendorff, the bristling first quartermaster-general of the Great German General Staff, had lost confidence in the prospects for victory. He and his chief, Field Marshal von Hindenburg, were already advising the incredulous kaiser to seek an armistice. Wilfred was obliged to read, to what remained of his company, an order that "peace talk in any form is to cease in the Fourth Army," but it was impossible to stop talk about what every soldier could see for himself—that the Hindenburg Line had been breached and German soldiers were surrendering in large numbers.

The war was continuing automatically, waiting for someone to end it. Nobody on the British side was aware of the kaiser's wavering indecision, the German Army's reluctance to demand his abdication as the price of peace, or the simmering tide of mutiny that was about to engulf the German High Seas Fleet and plunge Germany into revolution. The Second Manchesters were now pursuing the Germans, who took the opportunity to dig in and defend themselves. To the east, the sound of big guns continued ceaselessly, as did the Allied reply. The countryside, sacked, mined, and destroyed by the Germans, was slowing down the advance as much as continued German resistance. It was a nightmare landscape of impoverished villagers, ruined houses, and dead horses, bisected by flooded canals.

The arrival of a more senior lieutenant brought to an end Wilfred's brief stint as a company commander. It saddened him, but he was momentarily cheered by a false rumor that Germany had accepted American peace terms. Shelling went on, as well as occasional bombing. Wilfred reported to his mother that he was making longer marches every day as the Germans fell back. He was spending the nights in the most primitive conditions, where very often he had no food except the Cadbury's Fruit and Nut bars that she had sent him. "It's a great life," he wrote to her, apparently without irony, from the smoky cellar of a forester's house, to thank her for sending cigarettes and new socks. "There is no danger here," he wrote her, "or if any, it will be well over before you read these lines."

Less than a thousand yards away, down a gentle slope strewn with the stumps of felled trees, was the straight line of the Sambre-Oise Canal in northeastern France, close to the Belgian frontier. The canal is about fifty feet wide and eight feet deep, with gently rising farmland on the far side—high ground on which the Germans had placed camouflaged machine-gun posts and infantry. The Germans had blocked the ditches that drained into the canal, so the approach to it was marshy, which would slow down the British troops as they neared it. The bridges over the canal had been destroyed, and the British would have to place temporary ones, under fire, before the canal could be crossed. The one for the Second Manchesters and the 16th Lancashire Fusiliers was to be assembled out of cork floats. The commanding officer of the 16th Lancashire Fusiliers, Lieutenant-Colonel J. N. Marshall, an experienced and courageous officer sent out to reconnoiter the ground, thought that the whole plan was impossible and the chances of surprising the enemy negligible, but his opinion was ignored. Several days had been spent bringing up the bridging material and training the pioneers who would build it, which virtually eliminated any chance of surprise.

Before first light on November 4, a five-minute artillery barrage intended to soften up the Germans began, after which the pioneers approached the canal at first light. They teetered under the weight of the cork floats as they crossed the drainage ditches on improvised plank bridges, followed by the heavily laden infantry. The Germans responded with artillery, mortars, machine-gun and rifle fire, whipping the surface of the canal into a bloodied froth. Nevertheless, the pioneers pushed the cork floats across the canal using long poles and somehow fixed them in place. Three-quarters of the pioneers were killed or wounded. In half an hour the bridge was usable. Two platoons scrambled across, only to find themselves stranded on the far side when a British shell hit the bridge and left it with a wide gap. The remaining pioneers and the infantry struggled hard to repair it under withering fire, and at some point on November 4, 1918, Wilfred took several of his men and tried to paddle a cork raft across to help fill the gap.

He was killed instantly.

WILFRED WAS PROMOTED TO LIEUTENANT on the very next day. His second pip, which he had wanted almost as much as the Military Cross, was included in the list of promotions in the *London Gazette*. Only four days later a reluctant General Wilhelm Groener, who had replaced Ludendorff as first quartermaster-general, was obliged to tell the kaiser what nobody else had the courage to say: the war was lost, the fleet had mutinied and was marching on Berlin, and the army would march back in good order, but not with the kaiser at its head. "But what about the oath to the colors?" the kaiser asked, ashen and thunderstruck. "The oath to the colors is now only words," Groener replied. The kaiser would have to abdicate. A day later, on November 10, six days after Wilfred Owen's death, the kaiser and his entourage took refuge in neutral Holland, "And now for a nice cup of tea," the kaiser said (he never forgot that he was a grandson of Queen Victoria) as he settled into his place of exile. The following day Germany signed the armistice, ending what was, until then, the greatest and surely the most avoidable of wars.

On that day, at eleven o'clock in the morning, the eleventh day of the eleventh month, as church bells rang all over Britain, by a cruel and supreme irony, Wilfred Owen's mother received the telegram informing her of his death.

SIEGFRIED SASSOON never altogether forgave himself for not having prevented Wilfred Owen from going back to the front.

Just as poets had mirrored every aspect of the war, from its delusive foretaste of glory, described perfectly by Rupert Brooke, to its protracted horror, it would fall to a poet, Siegfried Sassoon, to write of its end, in one of the best-remembered of all poems to emerge from the war.

> Everyone suddenly burst out singing
> And I was filled with such delight
> As prisoned birds must find in freedom
> Winging wildly across the white
> Orchards and dark green fields; on; on, and out of sight.
>
> Everyone's voice was suddenly lifted,
> And beauty came like the setting sun.
> My heart was shaken with tears and horror
> Drifted away. . . . O but every one
> Was a bird and the song was wordless;
> the singing will never be done.

# EPILOGUE

H ISTORY MOVES ON. IT IS 105 YEARS SINCE WIL-
fred Owen's death and the end of what was known until
1939 as the Great War, the war that President Woodrow
Wilson optimistically supposed would end war. Yet we still live
among its ruins, groping with the problems that the war created and
that the peace that followed it failed to resolve, or that it solved in
ways that only guaranteed more fighting. One might have supposed
that the First and Second World Wars, which between them were
responsible for some 120 million deaths, ought at least to have cre-
ated a peaceful and well-ordered Europe, but as I write this, fighting
is raging in Eastern Europe; troops are digging trenches and dying
in them. It is not even a futuristic war such as H. G. Wells might
have imagined, but mostly the same old story of mud, artillery bar-
rages, barbed wire, high explosives, machine guns, and tanks. Wil-
fred Owen and his fellow poets would have been quite at home in
the outskirts of Kyiv, and no doubt just as angry at the waste and at
death on a large scale as a substitute for diplomacy, negotiation, and
the rarest of human values, common sense.

History is a chronicle not of new events but of old ones remerging
in a different form. The war that killed Rupert Brooke, Alan Seeger,
Isaac Rosenberg, and Wilfred Owen also destroyed three empires
and created a large number of new nations in Eastern Europe and
the Middle East, many with borders that are still being fought over.
Iraq's frontiers, for example, far from being carefully thought out
after the defeat of the Ottoman Empire, were drawn in one after-
noon in 1921, in a hotel suite at the Mena House in Cairo, by Ger-

trude Bell, T. E. Lawrence, and Winston Churchill. Countless other nations and states were improvised just as casually. Whether they can or should all survive in their present shape and form remains to be seen. Judging by events in Ukraine as I write this, neither the peace settlement that followed the First World War nor that which followed the Second has produced in Eastern Europe, the Balkans, or the Middle East anything resembling peaceful stability.

Hence the First World War continues to engage the attention of historians. The documents of the major combatants attempting to explain how that war broke out, intended for the most part to direct the blame elsewhere, were still being edited and published in many languages when the second one began. The consequences of that war continue to haunt us. Reading about how a succession of relatively small misjudgments and poor decisions can lead, with surprising speed, to human catastrophe on an unimaginable scale should, if nothing else, make us wonder how much progress we have made in diplomacy and statecraft, if any, since June 1914.

I have been interested in World War I since childhood partly because I see it not as an isolated event but as the first step into an ever more threatening and dangerous world—a first step into the abyss. Telling the story of that war through the lives of some of the major poets who fought in it is to look at it through their eyes, perhaps to see it in a new way.

Seldom do poets play a significant role in history, or have a serious effect on politics or on public opinion. In the Second World War, which followed the First only twenty-one years later—thus demonstrating the truth of Marshal Foch's shrewd condemnation of the Versailles Treaty as "an armistice of twenty years"—poets and poetry played little or no part. Only in the Soviet Union did government take poetry seriously. Stalin not only *read* poetry, he had strong opinions on the subject, and he had no hesitation in sending poets whose work displeased him to the gulag. In the English-speaking world, however, poetry ceased to be a burning issue. The modernists, following in the wake of T. S. Eliot, no longer took their inspiration from current events, but turned inward instead. Indeed, for the most part, poetry that reflected the real world or current events was no longer taken seriously in literary circles. Poets wrote about their feelings, about relationships, and about nature, not about war, and poetry became largely irrelevant to people's lives.

The extraordinary thing is that through the chaos and the slaughter of World War I, poetry became, briefly, newsworthy. That is in part because Rupert Brooke was transformed almost overnight into a celebrity, and even, early in the war, a martyr, and partly because poetry was then still widely read, at least among the upper and middle classes. Kipling's poems sold like popular novels, and his productivity was phenomenal too. He knew what his readers liked, and he supplied it in enormous quantity. He and Brooke belied in different ways the whole idea of the poet as a cloistered figure scratching away at a few lines a day in a garret for meager pay. Kipling was like a one-man cottage industry, while Brooke, like Byron, had what we would now call rock star glamour.

The amount of attention the soldier poets received was also an unintended result of government censorship. The government vigorously censored letters and newspapers. Nor was it reluctant to use its powers under the Defence of the Realm Act to stifle doubts and criticism of the war. Even Bertrand Russell—a distinguished philosopher, mathematician, and heir to an earldom—served six months in prison and paid a substantial fine for expressing his opposition to the war. Somehow nobody had thought to subject poetry to serious censorship. It was left to magazine and book publishers to decide what to print, knowing the possibility of prosecution or being cut off from a supply of paper. What was more, the war poets were soldiers, not pacifists or conscientious objectors—"conchies," as they were then called—which made censoring them all the more difficult. They were not against *all* war, or against fighting, they simply thought that *this* war was being fought badly, wastefully, for the wrong reasons, and worse still was being prolonged when an end to it could have been negotiated.

Except for Brooke, their fame came after the war, as a general revulsion became widespread. The sharpness of much of their poetry was blunted as they were co-opted into the ritualization of solemn national grief, at one with the endless plaques bearing the names of the dead, the wearing of poppies on Armistice Day, the vast fields of white crosses stretching to the horizon in northern France and Flanders, tourist attractions now. The anger was drained out of the memory of the war, replaced by sadness and a certain jaunty nostalgia, as in films like *Oh! What a Lovely War*, a period piece rather than a tribute to four years of monumental pointless suffering.

Even the idea of grouping these poets together as "war poets" did not occur until long after the war. Not until 1985 was the memorial to them unveiled in Westminster Abbey. They did not think of themselves, nor did anyone else think of them, as a distinct, identifiable group, and their attitudes toward the war differed enormously, from Brooke's elation at the prospect of his own death to Sassoon's whiplash anger and sarcasm.

Most of those who survived tried to get beyond being defined as "war poets." Robert Graves branched out into historical novels,* learned if eccentric books about Greek mythology and much else, until he was made Oxford Professor of Poetry in 1961 (an honor of considerable renown, elected every four years). It was something of a consolation prize for missing out on the Nobel Prize, because one member of the academy had been unwilling to award Graves the Nobel Prize so long as Ezra Pound was still alive. Sassoon remained endlessly productive well into old age, and was awarded a rather modest Commander of the British Empire, also something of a consolation prize, which he considered turning down but was finally persuaded to accept. On the basis of their astonishing productivity alone, both men should have been awarded higher honors, but their war poetry, while it remained enormously popular, still seemed to carry a subversive hint.

In some cases, recognition came only after death. Only five of Wilfred Owen's poems were published while he was alive. It took the intense determination of Dame Edith Sitwell—Osbert's sister, an eccentric but influential poet and literary gadfly, whose poem "Still Falls the Rain"

---

* Two of his most successful works of fiction, *I, Claudius* (1935) and its sequel, *Claudius the God*, were to have been made into a film by my uncle Alexander Korda in 1937, starring Charles Laughton and my aunt Merle Oberon, with sets by my father Vincent Korda. Filming was brought to a halt, ostensibly because Merle's face was scarred in an automobile accident, but in fact because of differences between director Josef von Sternberg and Laughton. The twenty minutes of film that survive were acclaimed as being among the most brilliant in the history of British filmmaking and were the centerpiece of a BBC television documentary *The Epic That Never Was*, in 1965.

was set to music by Benjamin Britten—to get Owens's collected poems finally published in book form in 1931. Even then, it was not until the 1960s that the later war poets became widely admired and treated as a distinct school of poetry. During and after the Vietnam War, pity and compassion, combined with a generous dose of anger at the politicians and generals, made the war poets, except Brooke, relevant again, first among them Wilfred Owen, whose short life served as the basis for a hugely successful three-volume novel, a play, and two films.

Indeed, the entire war came to be encapsulated by the poetry that emerged from it. Even its end was best described by Siegfried Sassoon's poem "Everyone Sang," which together with John Lennon's "Imagine" two generations later, came to symbolize the futility and cruelty of warfare and the hope that humanity might pursue its destiny without it.

It is perhaps not in works of history, of which there is no shortage, that we can best understand the tragedy of the First World War and its continuing relevance, nor even in the thousands of volumes of letters, diaries and memoirs, but in the poems written by those who fought in the war. They described it in ways as different as a release from ordinary life into an adventure, or as a descent into inhuman, squalid, and miserable suffering for no purpose.

Whatever else it did, it did not end war—no war ever does.

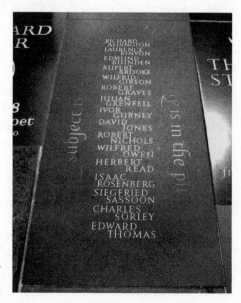

Plaque with the names of sixteen soldier poets, Poets' Corner, Westminster Abbey.

# ACKNOWLEDGMENTS

I AM DEEPLY GRATEFUL TO MY WISE AND PATIENT editor and friend, Robert Weil, at Liveright, for his enthusiasm and his careful reading of the manuscript, and for his inspired suggestions, and to his former assistant, Haley Bracken, for all her help.

The editorial advice and great enthusiasm of my dear friend and colleague Phyllis Grann was invaluable in shaping this book, as they have been many times before.

I am also grateful to Rebecca Karamehmedovic for her diligent and imaginative research for photographs and illustrations, and to Matthew Van Meter for his careful editing of the text and his meticulous source notes.

I would like to thank Bonnie Fulmer for her careful and far-reaching research into background materials for this book, and my assistant, Diana Lenz, for riding herd over every aspect of it.

I owe more than I can ever express to my friend and agent since 1978, Lynn Nesbit, who has guided my writing career over the years, and whose good advice I have always regretted ignoring on those rare occasions when I did not take it.

Most of all I want to thank my beloved wife, Maggie Simmons, for her wise comments, her editorial skill, her enthusiasm, and her love.

# NOTES

CHAPTER 1: HALCYON DAYS: RUPERT BROOKE AND THE LONG PEACE

1    **His companions:** Jones, *Rupert Brooke*, 234–36.

8    **"If I should die":** Brooke, "The Soldier," in *1914*, 15.

8    **"A young Apollo, golden-haired":** Cornford, "On Rupert Brooke," in *Poems*, 14.

9    **"I had been happier":** Brooke, *Collected Poems* (S&J ed.), xi–xii.

9    **"This is the word":** Sir Henry Newbolt, "Vitaï Lampada," reprinted in *Faber Reciter*, ed. Kingsley Amis (London: Faber & Faber, 1978).

10   **"My subconsciousness is angry":** Brooke, *Letters*, 611.

10   **his background:** Jones, *Rupert Brooke*, 2.

11   **Rupert Brooke's mother:** Jones, *Rupert Brooke*, 1–2.

13   **"Charm":** Waugh, *Brideshead Revisited*, 273.

14   **His mother:** Hassall, *Rupert Brooke*, 24.

15   **"And you, that loved":** Brooke, "Jealousy," in *Collected Poems* (Lane ed.), 80.

15   **"To die would be":** Brooke, *Letters*, 655.

15   **"throughout her life":** Hassall, *Rupert Brooke*, 21.

16   **"nervous breakdown":** Delaney, *Neo-Pagans*, 172.

16   **"It's the one thing":** Hassall, *Rupert Brooke*, 453.

16   **"I feel better for being":** Delaney, *Neo-Pagans*, 176.

16   **his sonnet "The Sea":** Hassall, *Rupert Brooke*, 74.

17   **"gyp":** Hassall, *Rupert Brooke*, 102.

18   **"in Greek the speeches":** Hassall, *Rupert Brooke*, 111.

20   **"the workers of the world":** Hassall, *Rupert Brooke*, 117.

20   **"his only Socialist":** Hassall, *Rupert Brooke*, 117n.

21   **"Some day I shall rise":** Brooke, "The Beginning," in *Collected Poems* (Lane ed.), 44.


CHAPTER 2: "THIS SIDE OF PARADISE!"

25   **A list of the people:** Hassall, *Rupert Brooke*, 154.

26   **"pink cheeks and bright":** Hassall, *Rupert Brooke*, 154.

27   **Noel, at fifteen:** Delaney, *Neo-Pagans*, 54.

27   **caused Virginia Woolf:** Delaney, *Neo-Pagans*, 175.

29   **"they wanted me to take":** Brooke, *Letters*, 130.

29   **"his short, spangled":** Hassall, *Rupert Brooke*, 165.

29   **"so short and tight":** Delaney, *Neo-Pagans*, 175.

29   **novelist Thomas Hardy:** Hassall, *Rupert Brooke*, 162–63.

30   **"dour and studious":** Jones, *Rupert Brooke*, 56.

31    **5 Raymond Buildings:** Jones, *Rupert Brooke*, 108.

32    **as being cocksure and conceited:** Hassall, *Rupert Brooke*, 168.

33    **"One last point":** Waugh, *Brideshead Revisited*, 26.

33    **"submit an essay":** Hassall, *Rupert Brooke*, 177.

33    **"Oh! Death will find me":** Brooke, "Oh! Death will find me, long before I tire," in *Collected Poems* (S&J ed.), 14.

35    **"I am John Rump":** Hassall, *Rupert Brooke*, 171.

36    **"But oh! Be tactful":** Hassall, *Rupert Brooke*, 179.

36    **the idea of wearing a disguise:** Hassall, *Rupert Brooke*, 179.

36    **"I was lost for four days":** Hassall, *Rupert Brooke*, 180.

36    **"And so I walked":** Hassall, *Rupert Brooke*, 181.

37    **"From being sad":** Hassall, *Rupert Brooke*, 180–81.

37    **"Your tidings make even":** Brooke, *Letters*, 170.

### CHAPTER 3: "UNDER AN ENGLISH HEAVEN"

40    ***The Duchess of Malfi*:** Hassall, *Rupert Brooke*, 135.

41    **visit to Bedales School:** Hassall, *Rupert Brooke*, 190.

42    **put Brooke into a simmering:** Hassall, *Rupert Brooke*, 199.

42    **"escape back into youth":** Brooke, *Letters*, 195.

43    **alarming signs of illness:** Hassall, *Rupert Brooke*, 213.

43    **unwelcome job:** Jones, *Rupert Brooke*, 149.

44    **"disgusting sonnet":** Jones, *Rupert Brooke*, 124; S. P. B. Mais, "Rupert Brooke," *Fortnightly Review* 98, no. 584 (August 2, 1915): 349.

44    **"The damned ship lurched":** Brooke, "A Channel Passage," in *Collected Poems* (Lane ed.), 94.

44    **"Suddenly he came":** Hassall, *Rupert Brooke*, 221.

45    **a repeat performance:** Hassall, *Rupert Brooke*, 248–52.

45    **wanted to marry her:** Jones, *Rupert Brooke*, 159.

45    **"they think two shots":** Brooke, *Letters*, 239.

46    **"I hate myself because":** Hassall, *Rupert Brooke*, 248–49.

46    **"H to H":** Jones, *Rupert Brooke*, 190.

47    **"Noel, Noel, Noel":** Jones, *Rupert Brooke*, 200.

48    **"The young lay around":** Hassall, *Rupert Brooke*, 256.

49    **Élisabeth van Rysselberghe:** Jones, *Rupert Brooke*, 250–55.

49    **"the whole sordid business":** Hale, *Correspondence*, 170–71; Jones, *Rupert Brooke*, 205–9.

50    **"a very rich and clever":** Brooke, *Letters,* 294.

50    **"It was a continual pleasure":** Hassall, *Rupert Brooke*, 277.

51    **"Come. We'll be wholly":** Jones, *Rupert Brooke*, 188.

51    **Ka was all the things:** Hassall, *Rupert Brooke*, 272.

52    **"the seasick lover":** Hassall, *Rupert Brooke*, 279.

52    **"How should I know?":** Brooke, "Libido," in *Collected Poems* (S&J ed.), 33.

53    **"a woman's smell":** Jones, *Rupert Brooke*, 198.

53    **"a secret fear":** Jones, *Rupert Brooke*, 208–9.

53    **invited Virginia Stephen:** Jones, *Rupert Brooke*, 224.

55    **"he could barely lift":** Hassall, *Rupert Brooke*, 289.

55    **"ostensibly to improve":** Jones, *Rupert Brooke*, 225.

59    **"an overfed puppy":** Hassall, *Rupert Brooke*, 299.

60   **"I'm so hampered"**: Jones, *Rupert Brooke*, 217.

60   **"But you, and only you"**: Hassall, *Rupert Brooke*, 299–304.

60   **"I can see the Ranee"**: Jones, *Rupert Brooke*, 223.

60   **"I thought I was mad"**: Hale, *Friends and Apostles,* 217.

61   **"a slough of despond"**: Brooke, *Letters*, 339.

61   coming to Cannes: Hassall, *Rupert Brooke*, 307.

61   **"I kiss every inch"**: Brooke, *Letters*, 356.

61   **"Your duty's so very"**: Hassall, *Rupert Brooke*, 319.

62   **"a broken blossom"**: Hale, *Friends and Apostles,* 220.

63   on the Starnbergersee: Jones, *Rupert Brooke*, 277.

63   results of this night: Delany, *Fatal Glamour*, 167–68.

64   **"The important thing"**: Delany, *Fatal Glamour*, 169.

64   **"Ka, you've once"**: Jones, *Rupert Brooke*, 284.

66   **"I think she suspects"**: Hassall, *Rupert Brooke*, 331.

66   First, his dissertation: Hassall, *Rupert Brooke*, 334.

67   **"Just now the lilac"**: Brooke, *Old Vicarage*, 7–13.

69   **"a silly quickly"**: Jones, *Rupert Brooke*, 310.

69   **"the impression of"**: Jones, *Rupert Brooke*, 310–11.

70   **"I remain dead"**: Hassall, *Rupert Brooke*, 344.

70   **"You see?"**: Hassall, *Rupert Brooke*, 349.

71   **"mop of silky"**: Jones, *Rupert Brooke*, 227.

72   **"a dark, tragic-looking"**: Beckett, *I Saw You*, 29.

73   **"the Romance of my Life"**: Brooke, *Letters*, 340.

73   **"The door opened"**: Beckett, *I Saw You*, 36.

73   **"with his wild golden hair"**: Beckett, *I Saw You*, 52.

74   **"He looked like"**: Beckett, *I Saw You*, 61–63.

74   **"If he should ever"**: Beckett, *I Saw You*, 66.

75   **"Oh, you gorgeous"**: Beckett, *I Saw You*, 75.

75   **"Has Rupert been"**: Beckett, *I Saw You*, 73.

75   **"Well, you are strange"**: Beckett, *I Saw You*, 71.

75   **"You're a fine"**: Beckett, *I Saw You*, 77.

76   **"O thou most"**: Beckett, *I Saw You*, 216.

76   **"would hardly do"**: Beckett, *I Saw You*, 114.

76   **"repelled"**: Delany, *Fatal Glamour*, 219–20.

77   **"I strove with Fate"**: Beckett, *I Saw You*, 187.

78   **"incredibly, devastatingly"**: Delany, *Fatal Glamour*, 218.

78   **"lovers"**: Delany, *Fatal Glamour*, 218–21.

CHAPTER 4: "SOME CORNER OF A FOREIGN FIELD
THAT IS FOR EVER ENGLAND"

80   travel pieces from him: Jones, *Rupert Brooke*, 389.

81   **"a silver boot"**: Brooke, *Letters*, 462.

81   **"If you were like"**: Brooke, *Collected Poems* (S&J ed.), 81.

82   **"America is no place"**: Brooke, *Letters*, 469.

82   **"Once, we came round"**: Brooke, *Letters*, 399.

82   **"A young man more"**: Hassall, *Rupert Brooke*, 399.

83   **"Would to God"**: Hassall, *Rupert Brooke*, 406.

83   Duncan Campbell Scott: Hassall, *Rupert Brooke*, 405.

84    **"the veritable picture"**: Hassall, *Rupert Brooke*, 405–06.

84    **"the most beautiful place"**: Hall and Martin, *Brooke in Canada*, 113.

84    **"daughter of a midwestern"**: Delany, *Fatal Glamour*, 230–31.

85    **"my little girl"**: Brooke, *Letters*, 504.

85    **"a woman who could speak"**: Brooke, *Letters*, 584.

86    **"I guess I shall be"**: Brooke, *Letters*, 511.

86    **"GOD BLESS YOU"**: Brooke, *Letters*, 515.

86    **"Clouds"**: Brooke, "Clouds," in *1914*, 37.

87    **"An empty tale"**: Brooke, "Waikiki," in *Collected Poems* (Lane ed.), 133.

87    **"One Day"**: Brooke, "One Day," in *Collected Poems* (Lane ed.), 129.

87    **"just a few feet away"**: Brooke, *Letters*, 518.

88    **"thrilling and tropical"**: Hassall, *Rupert Brooke*, 420.

88    **"a gaudy scarlet"**: Hassall, *Rupert Brooke*, 420.

88    **"Ho, but we shall"**: Hassall, *Rupert Brooke*, 424.

89    **"very English"**: Brooke, *Letters*, 554.

89    **"We bathe four times"**: Hassall, *Rupert Brooke*, 561.

90    **"The boat's ready"**: Brooke, *Letters*, 563.

90    **"slumberous South Sea"**: Hassall, *Rupert Brooke*, 563.

90    **"The water was four"**: Delany, *Fatal Glamour*, 239.

92    **"I wish you were here"**: Delany, *Fatal Glamour*, 244.

92    **"I have been nursed"**: Hassall, *Rupert Brooke*, 435.

92    **"I think life's"**: Brooke, *Letters*, 654.

93    **"Mamua, when our laughter"**: Brooke, "Tiare Tahiti," in *Collected Poems* (Lane ed.), 13–15.

94    **"The Game is Up"**: Brooke, *Letters*, 568.

94    **"Fish (fly-replete"**: Brooke, "Fish," in *Collected Poems* (Lane ed.), 21–22.

95    **"Mia cara"**: Brooke, *Letters*, 571.

95    sounds like a happy man: Brooke, *Letters*, 571.

95    **"Oh, God!"**: Brooke, *Letters*, 577.

95    **"Well, I'm going on"**: Delany, *Fatal Glamour*, 245.

96    **"I sail from New York"**: Brooke, *Letters*, 587.

96    back in the swing: Hassall, *Rupert Brooke*, 450.

97    **"radiant good looks"**: Hassall, *Rupert Brooke*, 450.

98    Brooke had every reason: Hassall, *Rupert Brooke*, 452.

98    **"It seems such"**: Brooke, *Letters*, 597.

99    **"& then thought about"**: Jones, *Rupert Brooke*, 9.

100   **"But this damn war"**: Brooke, *Letters*, 601.

100   **"Everything's just"**: Brooke, *Letters*, 603.

102   **"Territorial Bodies"**: Brooke, *Letters*, 608–9.

102   **"a neuralgic earache"**: Brooke, *Letters*, 616.

104   **"drilling like Hell"**: Brooke, *Letters*, 620–21.

104   **"Now, God be thanked"**: Brooke, "Peace," in *Collected Poems* (Lane ed.), 5.

105   **"people cheered wildly"**: Tuchman, *Guns of August*, 74.

106   **"Blow out, you bugles"**: Brooke, "The Dead," in *Collected Poems* (Lane ed.), 7.

106   **"Time [may] hold some"**: Brooke, "Safety," in *Collected Poems* (Lane ed.), 6.

108   **"After dark"**: Edward Marsh, "A Memoir," in Brooke, *Collected Poems* (Lane ed.), 151.

108   **"rivers and seas"**: Marsh, "Memoir," 154.

109   **"(1) A little mirror"**: Brooke, *Letters*, 626.

110   **"relapsed into a friendly"**: Brooke, *Letters*, 636.

110   **"Oc [Asquith] is about"**: Brooke, *Letters*, 641.

110 **"SEND MINCE PIES"**: Brooke, *Letters*, 642.

112 **"Come and die"**: Brooke, *Letters*, 655.

112 **"irritable, depressed"**: Brooke, *Letters*, 658.

112 **"It's wonderful"**: Brooke, *Letters*, 660–61.

113 **"If I should die"**: Brooke, "The Soldier," *Collected Poems* (Lane ed.), 9.

113 **"What follows"**: Brooke, *Letters*, 661–62.

113 **"Oh, Violet, it's too"**: Marsh, "Memoir," 162–63.

115 **"Briefly, we're"**: Brooke, *Letters*, 664.

115 **"We've had rather"**: Brooke, *Letters*, 665.

115 **"I suppose you're"**: Brooke, *Letters*, 669.

115 **see the gods**: Brooke, *Letters*, 670.

117 **"It began with"**: Brooke, *Letters*, 675.

117 **"We are encamped"**: Brooke, *Letters*, 676.

117 **"he ventured to think"**: Hassall, *Rupert Brooke*, 507.

117 **"as if to reach"**: Hassall, *Rupert Brooke*, 502–3.

119 **"seedy"**: Brooke, *Letters*, 683.

120 **"I sat with Rupert"**: Marsh, "Memoir," 180–82.

120 **"We buried him"**: Marsh, "Memoir," 182–83.

121 **"War will smash"**: Jones, *Rupert Brooke*, 423.

121 **"valiant spirit"**: "Death of Mr. Rupert Brooke: Sunstroke at Lemnos," *Times*, April 26, 1915. The first part of the obituary is signed "W.S.C."


### CHAPTER *5:* ALAN SEEGER'S "RENDEZVOUS WITH DEATH"

123 **"a spacious Victorian"**: Hill, *War Poet*, 2–3.

123 **"The family was enormously"**: Dunaway, *Keep from Singing*, 17.

124 **"wrapped up in"**: Werstein, *Sound No Trumpet*, 16–17.

125 **"long-haired"**: Werstein, *Sound No Trumpet*, 20.

125 **"Be they remembered"**: Seeger, "Ode in Memory of the American Volunteers Fallen for France," in *Poems*, 171.

127 **"I know a village"**: Seeger, "The Deserted Garden," in *Poems*, 10–11.

128 **"Watch the white"**: Seeger, "Deserted Garden," 12.

128 **"Seeger was serious"**: T. S. Eliot, Review of *Poems* by Alan Seeger, *The Egoist* 4, no. 11 (December 1917): 172.

128 **Eliot by then**: Hill, *War Poet*, 23.

129 **"truth and beauty"**: Werstein, *Sound No Trumpet*, 21.

129 **"the handsomest man"**: Hill, *War Poet*, 32.

130 **"no ambition other"**: Hill, *War Poet*, 36.

131 **"sometimes made"**: Hill, *War Poet*, 43.

132 **"What bright bazars"**: Seeger, "An Ode to Antares," in *Poems*, 114.

132 **"He always had"**: Werstein, *Sound No Trumpet*, 45.

133 **"Happiness engulfed him"**: Hill, *War Poet*, 53.

133 **"But, having drunk"**: Seeger, "Paris," in *Poems*, 45–48.

134 **The headlines**: Hill, *War Poet*, 56.

134 **"We passed three days"**: Hill, *War Poet*, 58.

135 **finding a place**: Hanna, *Rendezvous*, 42–44.

137 **sixty-eight out**: Hanna, *Rendezvous*, 38–48.

138 **rude awakening**: Hanna, *Rendezvous*, 55.

139 **"We rise at 5"**: Seeger, *Poems*, xxviii.

140    "But imagine how": Seeger, *Poems*, xxix.

140    "anything but romantic": Seeger, *Letters*, 29.

141    "The sentinel has": Seeger, *Poems*, xxxiii.

141    "We first saw fire": Seeger, "The Aisne," in *Poems*, 131–33.

142    "that chance to live": Seeger, "Ode in Memory of the American Volunteers Fallen for France," in *Poems*, 171.

142    "to face the barbed": Seeger, *Letters*, 30.

143    "the matter of eating": Seeger, *Letters*, 31–33.

143    "The army of deliverance": Seeger, *Letters*, 41.

144    "Purged with the life": Seeger, "The Hosts," in *Poems*, 139.

144    "I was shot": Seeger, *Letters*, 72.

145    "Presentez—armes!": Seeger, *Letters*, 81.

146    "But that night": Hemingway, "The Snows of Kilimanjaro," in *Stories*, 53.

146    "A shell surprised": Seeger, "Maktoob," in *Poems*, 141.

147    "Now turn we": Seeger, "Sonnet XI: On Returning to the Front after Leave," in *Poems*, 155.

147    "Amid the clash": Seeger, "Sonnet X," in *Poems*, 154.

148    "It is an altogether": Seeger, *Letters*, 83–84.

148    "If it must be": Seeger, *Letters*, 109.

150    "Meanwhile [at dawn]": Seeger, *Letters*, 65.

151    Moroccan Division: Werstein, *Sound No Trumpet*, 115–17.

151    "a regiment made up": Seeger, *Letters*, 153.

152    "marched away": Seeger, *Letters*, 155.

152    "in good spirits": Seeger, *Letters*, 156–57.

153    "The German positions": Seeger, *Letters*, 160.

153    "About twenty heavy": Seeger, *Letters*, 160.

153    "[I] expect to march": Seeger, *Letters*, 163.

154    "a magnificent spectacle": Seeger, *Letters*, 166–67.

154    "filled with": Seeger, *Letters*, 167–68.

155    "many splendid moments": Seeger, *Letters*, 170.

155    "the monotony of": Seeger, *Letters*, 175.

156    "a very good": Seeger, *Letters*, 176.

156    "We probably shall": Seeger, *Letters*, 177.

156    "two boxes": Seeger, *Letters*, 177–78.

157    "A storm": Horne, *Death of a Generation*, 61.

157    "The pounding was": Horne, *Death of a Generation*, 71.

158    "the only thing": Seeger, *Letters*, 188.

158    "I lay this votive": Seeger, "Sonnet IV: To . . . in Church," in *Poems*, 148.

158    "During the 'off-duty' time": Hill, *War Poet*, 121.

158    "Well, seeing": Seeger, "Sonnet IX," in *Poems*, 153.

159    "I don't believe": Hill, *War Poet*, 189.

159    "I took my fill": Seeger, *Letters*, 192.

159    "We are in": Seeger, *Letters*, 182–83.

160    "a terrific *rafale*": Seeger, *Letters*, 196–97.

160    "Lines of grey": Sassoon, "Attack," in *War Poems*, 40.

161    "It would have been": Seeger, *Letters*, 202.

162    "The prospects": Seeger, *Letters*, 209.

162    "in the heat": Seeger, *Letters*, 210.

162    "In the first hour": Hill, *War Poet*, 134.

163    **"beaming with joy"**: "The Point of View: Alan Seeger Killed in France—The Poet of the Foreign Legion," *Scribner's Magazine* 61, no. 1 (January 1917): 125.

163    **he was hit**: Werstein, *Sound No Trumpet*, 129.


### CHAPTER 6: ISAAC ROSENBERG: PAINTER AND POET

165    **"land of ruin"**: Rosenberg, "Home-Thoughts from France," in *Poems*, 96.

165    **"I never joined"**: Rosenberg, *Collected Works*, 227.

165    **His parents**: Cohen, *Journey to the Trenches*, 11.

167    **Hannah followed him**: Cohen, *Journey to the Trenches*, 17.

168    **"The gates of morning"**: Rosenberg, *Poems*, 140.

168    **"the attendance officer"**: Liddiard, *Isaac Rosenberg*, 37.

170    **"You mustn't forget"**: Liddiard, *Isaac Rosenberg*, 40.

171    **"art metal work"**: Liddiard, *Isaac Rosenberg*, 37.

171    **His meager earnings**: Cohen, *Journey to the Trenches*, 21–22.

172    **Rabbi Asher Amshewitz**: Cohen, *Journey to the Trenches*, 24–27

172    **"I really would like"**: Liddiard, *Isaac Rosenberg*, 54–55.

173    **Birkbeck College**: Cohen, *Journey to the Trenches*, 28–29.

173    **"You were there"**: Liddiard, *Isaac Rosenberg*, 56.

174    **"rosy and buoyant"**: Rosenberg, *Collected Works*, 277.

176    **"a painter who"**: Liddiard, *Isaac Rosenberg*, 75.

176    **"afford a halfpenny"**: Liddiard, *Isaac Rosenberg*, 77.

176    **"the difficult relationship"**: Liddiard, *Isaac Rosenberg*, 87.

176    **"You can call me"**: Liddiard, *Isaac Rosenberg*, 89.

176    **two pounds**: Cohen, *Journey to the Trenches*, 87.

177    **Israel Narodiczky**: Cohen, *Journey to the Trenches*, 79.

177    **"If the poems"**: Noakes, *Isaac Rosenberg*, 234–35.

178    **"Thanks for your"**: Noakes, *Isaac Rosenberg*, 353.

179    **"I know little"**: Rosenberg, *Collected Works*, 199.

180    **Distant as it was**: Liddiard, *Isaac Rosenberg*, 141–44.

181    **"solemn, preoccupied"**: Cohen, *Journey to the Trenches*, 84.

181    **Annetta Raphaël**: Cohen, *Journey to the Trenches*, 92.

181    **"I am not going"**: Rosenberg, *Collected Works*, 202–3.

185    **"a woman's magazine"**: Liddiard, *Isaac Rosenberg*, 149.

185    **"[Augustus] John, Cézanne"**: Liddiard, *Isaac Rosenberg*, 147.

185    **"Theirs is the terrible"**: Liddiard, *Isaac Rosenberg*, 148.

185    **"There's a lot"**: Liddiard, *Isaac Rosenberg*, 145.

185    **"gold dust"**: Liddiard, *Isaac Rosenberg*, 146.

186    **"I despise war"**: Rosenberg, *Collected Works*, 205.

186    **"I'm here in Rodensbosch"**: Cohen, *Journey to the Trenches*, 111.

187    **"a perfect nuisance"**: Rosenberg, *Collected Works*, 206.

187    **"a creature of the"**: Wilson, *Isaac Rosenberg*, 243.

188    **"Estrangement and hostility"**: Cohen, *Journey to the Trenches*, 113.

188    **"If you do find"**: Noakes, *Isaac Rosenberg*, 264.

188    **"That we can cheat"**: Rosenberg, *Collected Works*, 210.

189    **"I love poetry"**: Noakes, *Isaac Rosenberg*, 264.

190    **two pounds ten shillings**: Cohen, *Journey to the Trenches*, 117.

190    ***Colours*, a glossy**: Cohen, *Journey to the Trenches*, 114–15.

190    **"an aesthete with"**: Hassall, *Ambrosia and Small Beer*, xi.
191    **"begloried sonnets"**: Cohen, *Journey to the Trenches*, 153.
191    **"Kaiser William will"**: Cohen, *Journey to the Trenches*, 107.
192    **"I can only give"**: Rosenberg, *Collected Works*, 218.
192    **but with no result**: Cohen, *Journey to the Trenches*, 119.
193    **"raged and sobbed"**: Cohen, *Journey to the Trenches*, 125.
193    **"I have just joined"**: Cohen, *Journey to the Trenches*, 125–26.
194    **"Moses, from whose loins"**: Cohen, *Journey to the Trenches*, 127–28.
195    **"While the new lips"**: Rosenberg, "Moses," in *Poems*, 62.
195    **"in terrible agony"**: Cohen, *Journey to the Trenches*, 130.
196    **"The doctor here"**: Rosenberg, *Collected Works*, 222, 224.
198    **the second-in-command**: Cohen, *Journey to the Trenches*, 132.
198    **"My eyes catch"**: Rosenberg, "Marching (As Seen from the Left File)," in *Poems*, 88.
198    **struggling with**: Cohen, *Journey to the Trenches*, 133.
199    **"The plot is droll"**: Noakes, *Isaac Rosenberg*, 294.
200    **"a piece of his mind"**: Liddiard, *Isaac Rosenberg*, 198–99.
200    **"be ready for"**: Cohen, *Journey to the Trenches*, 131.
200    **"confined to barracks"**: Cohen, *Journey to the Trenches*, 134.
201    **"off at last"**: Rosenberg, *Collected Works*, 234.
201    **"I stood there"**: Cohen, *Journey to the Trenches*, 136.

CHAPTER 7: ISAAC ROSENBERG'S LIFE AND DEATH IN THE TRENCHES

203    **"could not be"**: Cohen, *Journey to the Trenches*, 156.
203    **"We made straight"**: Noakes, *Isaac Rosenberg*, 299.
203    **"Grotesque and quietly"**: Rosenberg, "The Troop Ship," in *Poems*, 87.
204    **"sucking, stinking"**: Cohen, *Journey to the Trenches*, 147.
205    **"The darkness crumbles"**: Rosenberg, "Break of Day in the Trenches," in *Poems*, 89–90.
206    **"We had an exciting"**: Cohen, *Journey to the Trenches*, 155.
206    **Letters back and forth**: Alan Johnson, "World War One: How Did 12 Million Letters a Week Reach Soldiers?," BBC News, January 31, 2014.
206    **Isaac wrote mostly**: Liddiard, *Isaac Rosenberg*, 209.
206    **"I am sorry"**: Cohen, *Journey to the Trenches*, 158.
207    **"The continued transfers"**: Liddiard, *Isaac Rosenberg*, 215.
207    **"Six miles from earth"**: Randall Jarrell, "The Death of the Ball Turret Gunner," in Ellmann and O'Clair, *Norton Modern Poetry*, 902.
208    **"The wheels lurched"**: Rosenberg, *Poems*, 107–8.
210    **"The other night"**: Noakes, *Isaac Rosenberg*, 332.
210    **"minutely carping"**: Hassall, *Ambrosia and Small Beer*, 53.
210    **"we [the soldiers] manage"**: Rosenberg, *Collected Works*, 258.
210    **two weeks leave**: Cohen, *Journey to the Trenches*, 170.
210    **On the termination**: Cohen, *Journey to the Trenches*, 171.
211    **"I see my sister"**: Liddiard, *Isaac Rosenberg*, 244.
212    **"We are very busy"**: Noakes, *Isaac Rosenberg*, 364.
212    **"Through these pale"**: Noakes, *Isaac Rosenberg*, 123.
213    **"Dragging these anguished"**: Rosenberg, "Returning, We Hear the Larks," in *Poems*, 92.

214    **press for its publication:** Cohen, *Journey to the Trenches*, 174–87.

214    **"a frail little":** Cohen, *Journey to the Trenches*, 187.


CHAPTER 8: ROBERT GRAVES: "THE NECESSARY SUPPLY OF HEROES
MUST BE MAINTAINED AT ALL COSTS"

216    **"If I were fierce":** Sassoon, "Base Details," in *War Poems*, 48.

219    **"unsoldierlike and":** Graves, *Goodbye to All That*, 74.

221    **"entertaining, likeable":** Tolkien, *Letters*, 353.

224    **"About half-way up":** Graves, *Goodbye to All That*, 67.

224    **"tough and rough":** Graves, *Goodbye to All That*, 92.

226    **"A German flare":** Graves, *Goodbye to All That*, 105.

226    **"had taken off":** Graves, *Goodbye to All That*, 106.

226    **"Sights at four":** Graves, *Goodbye to All That*, 107–8.

227    **"for your sake especially":** Graves, *In Broken Images*, 31–32.

227    **"I swear to you":** Graves, *Goodbye to All That*, 32.

227    **"Or you'll be dozing":** Graves, *In Broken Images*, 33.

227    **"Tomorrow we go":** Robert Graves to E. M. Marsh, May 22, 1915, letter ID 21703, https://robertgravesletters.org. This and all of Robert Graves's letters can be found at the online database at the URL.

228    **"Everything here is wet":** Graves, *Goodbye to All That*, 116.

228    **"Bloody lot of use":** Graves, *Goodbye to All That*, 118.

229    **"Wriggling flat":** Graves, *Goodbye to All That*, 133.

229    **"placed his hand":** Graves, *Goodbye to All That*, 138.

230    **"we'll get killed":** Graves, *Goodbye to All That*, 145.

233    **"We're sure to bungle":** Graves, *Goodbye to All That*, 151.

234    **"It's going to be":** Graves, *Goodbye to All That*, 153.

234    **"cold, tired and sick":** Graves, *Goodbye to All That*, 155.

234    **"All we heard":** Graves, *Goodbye to All That*, 158.

235    **"gas-blood-lyddite-latrine":** Graves, *Goodbye to All That*, 164.

236    **"continued to swell":** Graves, *Goodbye to All That*, 170.

237    **It was the first book:** Graves, *Goodbye to All That*, 181.

239    **"He is a strange":** Wilson, *Siegfried Sassoon*, 183.

240    **"realistic":** Wilson, *Siegfried Sassoon*, 210.

240    **"and we go":** Graves, "Limbo," in *Over the Brazier*, 23.

240    **"To-day I found":** Graves, "A Dead Boche," in *Fairies and Fusiliers*, 35.

241    **"'Fall in!' A stir":** Graves, "Night March," in *Complete Poems*, 811.

241    **"But the boys who":** Graves, "Armistice Day, 1918," in *Complete Poems*, 633.

242    **"Mad Jack":** Wilson, *Siegfried Sassoon*, 207.

245    **"physical discomfort":** Wilson, *Siegfried Sassoon*, 93.

246    **At Marlborough he never:** Wilson, *Siegfried Sassoon*, 89.

246    **"Try to be more":** Wilson, *Siegfried Sassoon*, 105–6.

248    **"richness of fancy":** Wilson, *Siegfried Sassoon*, 144.

249    **"entirely unspotted":** Wilson, *Siegfried Sassoon*, 132.

251    **enlisting in the ranks:** Wilson, *Siegfried Sassoon*, 154–56.

252    **"You can't have them":** Sassoon, *Fox-Hunting Man*, 260–61.

252    **"a soldier manufactory":** Sassoon, *Fox-Hunting Man*, 261–64.

253    **"cell-like":** Sassoon, *Fox-Hunting Man*, 262.

253    **"had the obvious good looks":** Sassoon, *Fox-Hunting Man*, 268.

254    **"was like perpetual":** Sassoon, *Fox-Hunting Man*, 269–70.

254    **The relationship:** Wilson, *Siegfried Sassoon*, 197.


## CHAPTER 9: SIEGFRIED SASSOON: "BROTHER LEAD AND SISTER STEEL"

256    **"Went on a working":** Sassoon, *Fox-Hunting Man*, 275–76.

256    **"I see them":** Sassoon, "Dreamers," in *War Poems*, 13.

256    **"He pushed another":** Sassoon, "A Working Party," in *War Poems*, 23.

257    **"Already we were":** Sassoon, *Fox-Hunting Man*, 277.

257    **"He faced me":** Sassoon, "The Redeemer," in *War Poems*, 15.

258    **"And here you":** Sassoon, "Atrocities," in *War Poems*, 54.

258    **"To these I turn":** Sassoon, "The Kiss," in *War Poems*, 64.

259    **"The star turn in":** Sassoon, *Infantry Officer*, 11–12.

259    **rejoin David Thomas:** Wilson, *Siegfried Sassoon*, 239.

260    **"he distinguished himself":** Graves, *Goodbye to All That*, 219.

261    **"The battle winks":** Sassoon, "The Dream," in *War Poems*, 31.

261    **"At dawn the ridge":** Sassoon, "Attack," in *War Poems*, 40.

262    **"I thought I had":** Wilson, *Siegfried Sassoon*, 276.

262    **"'Good-morning'":** Sassoon, "The General," in *War Poems*, 50.

263    **"You smug-faced crowds":** Sassoon, "Suicide in the Trenches," in *War Poems*, 39.

264    **"You can't believe":** Sassoon, "Glory of Women," in *War Poems*, 57.

265    **"The third winter":** Sassoon, *Infantry Officer*, 103.

265    **"The man's been":** Sassoon, *Infantry Officer*, 119.

266    **He was relieved:** Wilson, *Siegfried Sassoon*, 328.

267    **"a murderous":** Sassoon, *Infantry Officer*, 157.

268    **"somebody half hidden":** Sassoon, *Infantry Officer*, 159.

268    **"a tremendous blow":** Wilson, *Siegfried Sassoon*, 350.

274    **"a man of great":** Wilson, *Siegfried Sassoon*, 382.

274    **"the poor little thing":** Sassoon, *Infantry Officer*, 231.

274    **"to become a martyr":** Graves, *Goodbye to All That*, 272; Wilson, *Siegfried Sassoon*, 383.

275    **"shell-shock":** Wilson, *Siegfried Sassoon*, 284.

276    **"Where men are crushed":** Sassoon, "Break of Day," in *War Poems*, 18.

276    **"out of themselves":** Wilson, *Siegfried Sassoon*, 391.

278    **"peace in the pools":** Quinn, *Missing Muse*, 277.

278    **His friend Edward Marsh:** Egremont, *Siegfried Sassoon*, 157–58.

278    **"very unexciting":** Egremont, *Siegfried Sassoon*, 164.

279    **Rivers had secured:** Wilson, *Siegfried Sassoon*, 441.


## CHAPTER 10: WILFRID OWEN: "MY SUBJECT IS WAR, AND THE PITY OF WAR"

282    screw up his courage: Hibberd, *Wilfred Owen*, 264–67.

282    **"to sweat your guts":** Wilfred Owen to Leslie Gunston, August 22, 1917, First World War Poetry Digital Archive, http://ww1lit.nsms.ox.ac.uk/ww1lit/education/tutorials/intro/owen/letters.

283    **Wilfred Owen's family:** Hibberd, *Wilfred Owen*, 1.

284  Salter's young widow: Hibberd, *Wilfred Owen*, 3–10.

285  Tom Owens was: Hibberd, *Wilfred Owen*, 26–27.

286  "Sir Wilfred Edward Salter-Owen": Hibberd, *Wilfred Owen*, 1.

287  "the intense purposefulness": Harold Owen, *Journey from Obscurity*, 84–85.

287  "mutual respect": Harold Owen, *Journey from Obscurity*, 88.

288  Shrewsbury Borough Technical College: Hibberd, *Wilfred Owen*, 38–52.

288  "his quiet gentleness": Harold Owen, *Journey from Obscurity*, 354.

289  Wilfred's position: Hibberd, *Wilfred Owen*, 56.

291  "I see that justly": Wilfred Owen, *Collected Letters*, 205–6.

291  "obstinately c-nst-p-t-ed": Wilfred Owen, *Collected Letters*, 209.

291  "Your headaches seem": Wilfred Owen, *Collected Letters*, 239.

292  "elegant rather than": Wilfred Owen, *Collected Letters*, 271.

292  "unimpeachable": Wilfred Owen, *Collected Letters*, 271.

293  "All women, without": Wilfred Owen, *Collected Letters*, 234.

293  "receives glances from": Wilfred Owen, *Collected Letters*, 275.

294  "immensely happy": Wilfred Owen, *Collected Letters*, 276.

294  "amiable hostess": Wilfred Owen, *Collected Letters*, 276.

295  "He received me": Wilfred Owen, *Collected Letters*, 282.

296  "Affair Léger": Wilfred Owen, *Collected Letters*, 286.

296  "the Léger episodes": Wilfred Owen, *Collected Letters*, 288.

297  "I begin to suffer": Wilfred Owen, *Collected Letters*, 295.

297  Mlle. de la Touche's house: Hibberd, *Wilfred Owen*, 148–50.

298  "tea-party examination": Wilfred Owen, *Collected Letters*, 316.

298  "present life was not": Wilfred Owen, *Collected Letters*, 325.

299  British Industries Fair: Hibberd, *Wilfred Owen*, 154–56.

300  "will be sent": Wilfred Owen, *Collected Letters*, 335–40.

302  "Thereby she set": Wilfred Owen, "The Little Mermaid," in Stallworthy, *Poems and Fragments*, 39.

303  "marooned on a Crag": Wilfred Owen, *Collected Letters*, 395.

303  "the Slough of Despond": Wilfred Owen, *Collected Letters*, 429.

304  "let down gently": Wilfred Owen, *Collected Letters*, 422.

304  "We eat and drink": Wilfred Owen, *Collected Letters*, 423.

304  "the face of the moon": Wilfred Owen, *Collected Letters*, 429.

305  "transformed": Wilfred Owen, *Collected Letters*, 426.

305  "Those fifty hours": Wilfred Owen, *Collected Letters*, 431.

305  "We'd found an old": Wilfred Owen, "The Sentry," in *War Poems*, 103–4.

306  "marooned on a frozen": Wilfred Owen, *Collected Letters*, 430.

306  "Hideous landscapes": Wilfred Owen, *Collected Letters*, 430.

306  He hit his head: Hibberd, *Wilfred Owen*, 226.

307  "long rest has shaken": Wilfred Owen, *Collected Letters*, 448.

307  "without relief": Wilfred Owen, *Collected Letters*, 450.

308  "horribly disinterred": Hibberd, *Wilfred Owen*, 240.

308  "to be shaky": Hibberd, *Wilfred Owen*, 241–42.

309  "Do not for a": Wilfred Owen, *Collected Letters*, 453.

309  "shaky": Wilfred Owen, *Collected Letters*, 456.

309  "a kind of wizard": Wilfred Owen, *Selected Letters*, 456.

310  "a decayed Hydro": Wilfred Owen, *Collected Letters*, 472.

311  "make the patient face": A. M. Crossman, "*The Hydra*, Captain A. J. Brock, and the Treatment of Shell-Shock in Edinburgh," *Journal of the Royal College of Physicians Edinburgh* 33, no. 2 (2003): 119–23.

311 **"I feel a kind"**: Wilfred Owen, *Collected Letters*, 475.

311 **"an outstanding figure"**: Wilfred Owen, *Collected Letters*, 492.


CHAPTER 11: APOTHEOSIS

313 **"The Dead-Beat"**: Wilfred Owen, "The Dead-Beat," in *War Poems*, 73.

314 **"a piece of perfect"**: Wilfred Owen, *Collected Letters*, 489.

314 **"He drowsed and was"**: Sassoon, "The Death-Bed," in *War Poems*, 90.

314 **"Siegfried called me in"**: Wilfred Owen, *Collected Letters*, 449.

315 **"a severe fleshly trial"**: Wilfred Owen, *Selected Letters*, 315.

315 **"Sassoon I like"**: Wilfred Owen, *Selected Letters*, 316–17.

316 **"What passing-bells"**: The revision process for "Anthem for Doomed Youth," which began its life as "Anthem for Dead Youth," is laid out carefully by Dominic Hibberd in his edition of Owen's *War Poems and Others*, 147–55.

318 **"He [Graves] is"**: Wilfred Owen, *Collected Letters*, 499.

319 **"Bent double"**: Wilfred Owen, "Dulce et Decorum Est," in *War Poems*, 79.

320 **"Out there, we've"**: Wilfred Owen, "The Next War," in *War Poems*, 75.

320 **"over a private"**: Wilfred Owen, *Selected Letters*, 326–27.

321 **"Know that since"**: Wilfred Owen, *Collected Letters*, 505.

322 **"dozen batmen"**: Wilfred Owen, *Collected Letters*, 509.

323 **"Puff out your chest"**: Graves to Owen, December 1917, letter ID 87293, from https://robertgravesletters.org.

323 **"I go out"**: Wilfred Owen, *Collected Letters*, 521.

324 **"I suppose I may"**: Wilfred Owen, *Collected Letters*, 533.

325 **"An awful Camp"**: Wilfred Owen, *Collected Letters*, 535.

326 **"the first flickers"**: Wilfred Owen, *Collected Letters*, 553.

328 **"Why keep a jewish"**: Graves to Sassoon, July 27, 1918, letter ID 30178, from https://robertgravesletters.org.

329 **The collection of thirty-nine**: Egremont, *Siegfried Sassoon*, 207.

329 **"the smartest turn-out"**: Wilson, *Siegfried Sassoon*, 473.

329 **The stretch**: Wilson, *Siegfried Sassoon*, 483.

330 **Siegfried had acquired**: Wilson, *Siegfried Sassoon*, 485.

330 **For several nights**: Wilson, *Siegfried Sassoon*, 486.

331 **"A second later"**: Sassoon, *Sherston's Progress*, 163.

332 **"The war had gagged"**: Sassoon, *Sherston's Progress*, 168.

333 **"He has told the truth"**: Wilson, *Siegfried Sassoon*, 497.

333 **"We'd gained our first"**: Sassoon, "Counter-Attack," in *War Poems*, 41–42.

334 **"a combination of"**: Egremont, *Siegfried Sassoon*, 210.

334 **"of superb intellect"**: Wilfred Owen, *Collected Letters*, 570–71.

335 **"in hasty retreat"**: Wilfred Owen, *Collected Letters*, 572.

335 **"non-ferocious"**: Wilfred Owen, *Collected Letters*, 579.

336 **The area in front**: Hibberd, *Wilfred Owen*, 348.

336 **"Can you photograph"**: Wilfred Owen, *Collected Letters*, 581.

337 **"lost all [his] earthly"**: Wilfred Owen, *Collected Letters*, 580.

337 **"seraphic"**: Wilfred Owen, *Collected Letters*, 580.

337 **"All one day"**: Wilfred Owen, *Collected Letters*, 581.

338 **"no more exposed flanks"**: Wilfred Owen, *Collected Letters*, 581.

339 **"It's a great life"**: Wilfred Owen, *Collected Letters*, 586.

340 **"But what about"**: Wheeler-Bennet, *Nemesis of Power*, 3–5.

341 **"Everyone suddenly burst"**: Sassoon, "Everyone Sang," in *War Poems*, 95.

# BIBLIOGRAPHY

Beckett, Lorna. *The Second I Saw You: The True Love Story of Rupert Brooke and Phyllis Gardner.* London: British Library, 2015.

Brooke, Rupert. *1914 and Other Poems.* London: Sedgwick & Jackson, 1915.

———. *The Collected Poems of Rupert Brooke, with an Introduction by George Edward Woodberry.* New York: John Lane, 1918.

———. *The Collected Poems of Rupert Brooke, with a Memoir by Edward Marsh.* London: Sidgwick & Jackson, 1918.

———. *The Letters of Rupert Brooke,* ed. Geoffrey Keynes. New York: Harcourt, Brace & World, 1968.

———. *The Old Vicarage, Grantchester.* London: Sidgwick & Jackson, 1916.

Cohen, Joseph. *Journey to the Trenches: The Life of Isaac Rosenberg, 1890–1918.* New York: Basic Books, 1975.

Cornford, Frances. *Poems.* Hampstead, UK: Priory Press, 1910.

Delany, Paul. *Fatal Glamour: The Life of Rupert Brooke.* Montreal: McGill–Queen's University Press, 2015.

———. *The Neo-Pagans: Rupert Brooke and the Ordeal of Youth.* London: Macmillan, 1987.

Dunaway, David. *How Can I Keep from Singing.* New York: Random House, 1981.

Egremont, Max. *Siegfried Sassoon: A Life.* New York: Farrar, Straus & Giroux, 2005.

Ellmann, Richard, and Robert O'Clair, eds. *Norton Anthology of Modern Poetry,* 2nd ed. New York: Norton, 1988.

Graves, Robert. *Goodbye to All That.* 1929; reprint New York: Everyman's Library, 2018.

———. *In Broken Images: Selected Correspondence.* Edited by Paul O'Prey. 1982; reprint Mt. Kisco, N.Y.: Moyer Bell, 1988.

Hale, Keith, ed. *Friends and Apostles: The Correspondence of Rupert Brooke and James Strachey, 1905–1914.* New Haven, Conn.: Yale University Press, 1998.

Hall, Roger, and Sandra Martin. *Rupert Brooke in Canada.* Toronto, Ont.: Peter Martin Associates, 1978.

Hanna, David. *Rendezvous with Death: The Americans Who Joined the Foreign Legion in 1914 to Fight for France and Civilization.* Washington, D.C.: Regnery History, 2016.

Hassall, Christopher. *Ambrosia and Small Beer: The Record of a Correspondence between Edward Marsh and Christopher Hassall.* London: Longmans, Green, 1964.

———. *Rupert Brooke: A Biography.* New York: Harcourt, Brace & World, 1964.

Hemingway, Ernest. *The Complete Stories of Ernest Hemingway.* New York: Scribner, 1987.

Hibberd, Dominic. *Wilfred Owen: A New Biography.* London: Weidenfeld & Nicolson, 2002.

Hill, Michael. *War Poet: The Life of Alan Seeger and His Rendezvous with Death.* Charleston, S.C.: CreateSpace, 2017.

Horne, Alistair. *Death of a Generation: From Neuve Chappelle to Verdun and the Somme.* New York: American Heritage Press, 1970.

Jones, Nigel. *Rupert Brooke: Life, Death and Myth.* 1999; reprint with revisions London: Head of Zeus, 2014.

Liddiard, Jean. *Isaac Rosenberg: The Half Used Life.* London: Gollancz, 1975.

Noakes, Vivian, ed. *Isaac Rosenberg.* Oxford: Oxford University Press, 2008.

Owen, Harold. *Journey from Obscurity: Childhood.* Vol. 1 of *Memoirs of the Owen Family.* London: Oxford University Press, 1963.

Owen, Wilfred. *Collected Letters.* Edited by John Bell. London: Oxford University Press, 1967.

———. *Selected Letters of Wilfred Owen.* Edited by Jane Potter. London: Oxford University Press, 2023.

———. *War Poems and Others.* Edited by Dominic Hibberd. London: Chatto & Windus, 1973.

Quinn, Patrick. *The Great War and the Missing Muse: The Early Writings of Robert Graves and Siegfried Sassoon.* Selinsgrove, Penn.: Susquehanna University Press, 1994.

Rosenberg, Isaac. *The Collected Works of Isaac Rosenberg: Poetry, Prose, Letters, Paintings and Drawings.* Edited by Ian Parsons. New York: Oxford University Press, 1979.

———. *Poems by Isaac Rosenberg.* London: Heinemann, 1922.

Seeger, Alan. *Letters and Diary.* New York: Scribner, 1917.

———. *Poems of Alan Seeger.* New York: Scribner, 1915.

Sassoon, Siegfried. *Memoirs of a Fox-Hunting Man.* 1928; reprint London: Faber & Faber, 1960.

———. *Memoirs of an Infantry Officer.* 1930; reprint London: Faber & Faber, 1965.

———. *Sherston's Progress.* 1936; reprint New York: Penguin Classics, 2013.

———. *The War Poems of Siegfried Sassoon.* London: Heinemann, 1919.

Stallworthy, Jon, ed. *The Manuscripts of the Poems and Fragments.* Vol. 2 of *Wilfred Owen: The Complete Poems and Fragments.* London: Chatto & Windus, 1983.

Waugh, Evelyn. *Brideshead Revisited.* Boston: Little, Brown, 1945.

Werstein, Irving. *Sound No Trumpet: The Life and Death of Alan Seeger.* New York: Crowell, 1967.

Wheeler-Bennett, John. *The Nemesis of Power: The German Army in Politics, 1918–1945.* New York: Macmillan, 1953.

Wilson, Jean Moorcroft. *Isaac Rosenberg: The Making of a Great War Poet: A New Life.* Evanston, Ill.: Northwestern University Press, 2009.

# ILLUSTRATION CREDITS

19. SBS Eclectic Images / Alamy Stock Photo

20. © 2023 Delaware Art Museum / Artists Rights Society (ARS), New York

21. History and Art Collection / Alamy Stock Photo

22. With permission from Bernard Wynick

23. © National Portrait Gallery, London / Art Resource, NY

24. Isaac Rosenberg, Courtesy University of South Carolina. Rare Books and Special Collections

25. © Jörgens.Mi / Wikipedia, Licence: CC-BY-SA 3.0

26. Bill Brandt / Picture Post / Hulton Archive / Getty Images

27. GL Archive / Alamy Stock Photo

28. FLHC 20219 / Alamy Stock Photo

29. GL Archive / Alamy Stock Photo

30. IanDagnall Computing / Alamy Stock Photo

31. Artepics / Alamy Stock Photo

32. Iain Sharp / Alamy Stock Photo

33. Reproduced by kind permission of the Syndics of Cambridge University Library, Copyright Siegfried Sassoon by kind permission of the Estate of George Sassoon

34. Courtesy OEF

35. Fotosearch/Getty Images

36. Courtesy OEF

37. © Hulton-Deutsch Collection/CORBIS/Corbis via Getty Images

# INDEX

Page numbers in *italics* refer to illustrations.